THE CAPITALIST PHILOSOPHERS

Also by Andrea Gabor

The Man Who Discovered Quality
Einstein's Wife

THE
CAPITALIST
PHILOSOPHERS

The Geniuses of Modern Business—Their Lives, Times, and Ideas

ANDREA GABOR

JOHN WILEY & SONS, LTD
Chichester • New York • Weinheim • Brisbane • Singapore • Toronto

Published 2000 by   John Wiley & Sons Ltd,
                             Baffins Lane, Chichester,
                             West Sussex PO19 1UD, England

                             National   01243 779777
                             International (+44) 1243 779777
                             e-mail (for orders and customer service enquiries):
                             cs-books@wiley.co.uk
                             Visit our Home Page on http://www.wiley.co.uk
                                           or http://www.wiley.com

Other Wiley Editorial Offices

John Wiley & Sons, Inc., 605 Third Avenue,
New York, NY 10158-0012, USA

WILEY-VCH GmbH, Pappelallee 3,
D-69469 Weinheim, Germany

Jacaranda Wiley Ltd, 33 Park Road, Milton,
Queensland 4064, Australia

John Wiley & Sons (Asia) Pte Ltd, 2 Clementi Loop #02-01,
Jin Xing Distripark, Singapore 129809

John Wiley & Sons (Canada) Ltd, 22 Worcester Road,
Rexdale, Ontario M9W 1L1, Canada

British Library Cataloguing in Publication Data

A catalogue record for this book is available from the British Library

ISBN 0-471-49247-7

Book design by Janice Olson

Printed and bound in Great Britain by Biddles Ltd, Guildford and King's Lynn
This book is printed on acid-free paper responsibly manufactured from sustainable
forestry, in which at least two trees are planted for each one used for paper
production.

For Jose

Contents

Introduction

Contrary to common wisdom, it is possible for individuals to have a major impact on history. Albert Einstein, Franklin Roosevelt, and Margaret Sanger are just a few individuals who profoundly shaped the course of the twentieth century.

Another example of a visionary with historic reach was Frederick Winslow Taylor. Like other twentieth-century movers and shakers, Taylor was not the first, or the sole, originator of the idea with which his name has become inextricably linked: scientific management. But the unique combination of Taylor's vision of the factory as machine, his single-minded quest for the "One Best Way," and the social and political milieu in which he operated helped ensure that Taylorism became a national obsession. While Taylor's impact was arguably the greatest in the United States, the power of his ideas was such that they spread quickly around the world, to countries as diverse as Germany and the Soviet Union, India and China.

The longest-lasting measure of Taylor's influence is his contribution to modern prosperity itself, for his production methods helped create the highest standard of living the world has ever seen. Precision in manufacturing and improved production controls were also crucial to the success of the large-scale enterprises that became a hallmark of American industry.

Equally important was Taylor's ideology, especially his obsession with measurement and management control, and his hostility to organized labor—ideologies that have all woven themselves into the fabric of American management culture. The modern reader need look no further than the most recently reengineered corporation in her own backyard to see the reincarnation of the Taylorist mantra. Employees at Sunbeam Corporation, led by "Chainsaw" Al Dunlap, who, in his quest for shareholder value, slashed jobs, eviscerated morale, and booked sales long before goods were delivered to stores (prompting an SEC investigation of the company's accounting practices), were experiencing one legacy of Taylorism—albeit an extreme example. (Though, as you will see, there are few personalities as extreme as F. W. Taylor himself.) In case you missed reengineering, Six Sigma, a statistical measure of quality, is right around the corner.

Indeed, one sign of Taylor's impact has been the century-long backlash against scientific management within the business community itself, in the form of the human relations movement. While humanistic, as opposed to scientific, management has not been led by a single crusader of Taylor's fame and stature, it has been driven by a number of prominent thinkers, including Elton Mayo and Fritz Roethlisberger, who worked on the famous Hawthorne experiments; Abraham Maslow, the renowed humanist psychologist; Douglas McGregor, originator of Theory X and Theory Y; and most recently Peter Senge and W. Edwards Deming. (Unlike his predecessors, the latter has straddled the scientific and humanist movements; see Chapter 7.)

The trouble is that adherents of *both* motivational and quantitative methods often suffer from the same weakness: excessive devotion to their own "one best way." Beginning with Taylor, the capitalist philosophers have pursued a relentless search for the silver bullet of improved productivity, a search that continues to the present day. As a result, companies have submitted to a dizzying spiral of fads, lurching from the extremes of scientific engineering to humanistic, motivational remedies.

The fault isn't all with Taylorites and their scientific descendants. Many companies that espouse democratic values, for example, push motivational techniques that do little more than manipulate their employees, but they shy away from any changes that might fundamentally alter the system, breeding cynicism and apathy as a consequence. For years, Dilbert cartoons have shone a poignant spotlight on the petty humiliations that employees endure in the workplace—whether mind numbing Tayloresque micromanagement or the hypocrisy of well-meaning, if superficial, make-nice programs.

As a business writer who has covered management since the competitiveness crisis of the early 1980s, I was well aware of the management fads that have been embraced by American companies only to go the way of other fashionable relics such as bell-bottoms and platform shoes. But like the pendulums of fashion, seemingly obsolete management ideas have a way of resurfacing, evolving, and gaining a permanent place in management culture. Reengineering is scientific management designed for the information age. Similarly, consider the resurgence of interest in a cyberspace version of Abraham Maslow's 1960s management classic, *Eupsychian Management,* which Maslow wrote while observing the pioneering, humanistic management practices of Non-Linear Systems, a technology company in California. Interest in the cyberspace edition prompted the republication of Maslow's book in 1998 under the title *Maslow on Management;* (see Chapter 6).

As we approach the end of the American Century and a decade of reengineering and globalization, it seemed to me to be a good time to look at the roots of American management. I wanted to explore the ideas and personalities that not only have shaped twentieth-century business but have helped make the corporation a pivotal institution of American society. In so doing, I wanted to create a "cool" historical lens through which to analyze the "hot" new ideas with which managers are bombarded almost daily.

I set out to tell the story of American management through the ideas, lives, and times of more than a dozen "philosophers" who defined the art and science of management as we know it today. Almost from the beginning, I was struck by the power of the two seemingly irreconcilable visions of management—the scientific and humanistic—that have battled for hegemony both in the corporate workplace and in American society itself.

At the root of the conflict between the humanistic and the scientific are two warring images of the business organization and its purpose in American society: One sees the corporation as a pivotal institution of democracy with complex responsibilities to a host of constituencies, including its employees, its customers, and the community. The other, much more utilitarian, view recognizes one primary corporate constituent—the shareholder—and a single purpose—profit making.

The tension has been evident almost from the beginning of the century: in disagreements between Taylor and a few maverick followers, who challenged his strong antiunion stance; in the humanistic writings of Kurt Lewin and Mary Parker Follett, which date back to the early 1920s; and in the historic Hawthorne experiments, which took place in the late 1920s and 1930s. Thus, this book traces the development of both the scientific and humanistic traditions from the beginning of the century and follows the battle of ideologies up to the present.

It is a curious—and important—fact that the most influential capitalist philosophers worked outside the corporate mainstream and were corporate "outsiders." Indeed, they were important precisely because as outsiders they often saw what those closer to the action couldn't make out. F. W. Taylor, Mary Parker Follett, Peter Drucker, and W. Edwards Deming were primarily consultants. Elton Mayo and Fritz Roethlisberger; Herbert Simon, a Nobel laureate in economics; Alfred Chandler, the apostle of corporate strategy; and Abraham Maslow and Douglas McGregor were first, and foremost, academics. Thus, the individuals portrayed in this book provide at least anecdotal evidence for the old adage that meaningful change almost always comes from the outside.

At the same time, American management is also the story of some of the country's most influential institutions, and the tendrils that link them to one another. Through the life and work of Elton Mayo and Fritz Roethlisberger, for example, *The Capitalist Philosophers* explores not only the evolution of the human relations movement, which they helped spawn, but also the rise of the Rockefeller Foundation, which funded much social science research in the 1920s and 1930s, and the Harvard Business School, where they worked during its formative years.

Like the home of a savvy Washington political hostess, the Harvard Business School has been a destination—and a meeting point—for most of the philosophers portrayed in this book. Taylor and Chester Barnard both lectured at HBS. Alfred D. Chandler (see Chapters 6, 7, and 9) taught there. Robert McNamara was a young accounting professor when he was recruited to work for the Air Force's Statistical Control office during World War II and then brought his "Stat Control Whiz Kids" back to HBS for training. And Peter Drucker once tried to get a job there.

Finally, *The Capitalist Philosophers* explores the life and work of a handful of men who were both philosophers and practitioners—Alfred Sloan, Pierre du Pont, Robert McNamara, and lesser-known Chester Barnard—and the institutions they helped build. These practitioners are singled out here not necessarily because they were brilliant businessmen—indeed, neither Barnard nor McNamara possessed exceptional leadership skills—but because they created new corporate forms or in some other way changed the way executives as a group think and practice the art and discipline of management. Thus, this book shows how Alfred Sloan and Pierre du Pont pioneered the multidivisional corporation during the 1920s. Chester Barnard made his mark with his seminal book, *The Functions of the Executive,* a comprehensive theory of cooperative behavior in organizations that broke new ground in looking at companies as social systems rather than as elaborate engineering constructs. And McNamara is included because of his pioneering work in the use of quantitative methods to control the finances at Ford Motor Company, techniques that for better and for worse had a great influence on American management following World War II.

By omitting all but a few brief references to great entrepreneurs, such as Bill Gates, I do not mean to minimize their sizable contributions to the American economy. The visions of men such as Gates have inexorably changed American technology, entire industries, and our way of life. Microsoft has provided the infrastructure for the "virtual corporation." But neither Gates nor his company has pioneered the management ideas that will ultimately determine whether—and how—a virtual corporation or any other organization will work.

One key premise of this book is that management is fundamentally about *people*, not technology. It is the story of how management has harnessed, alternately, technology, force, persuasion, and inspiration to get *people* to accomplish the goals of an organization.

The Capitalist Philosophers also trains its lens on large organizations, not small ones, for it was the problem of how to manage large organizations that gave rise to the field of management in the first place. Then too, the complexity of big organizations often magnifies the problems and challenges that companies face, whether improving worker productivity or mastering rapid discontinuous change, and complicates their solution.

At the end of the day, almost every single one of the capitalist philosophers portrayed in this book had a significant impact on several major corporations with which they personally came in contact. Thus, the chapter on Peter Drucker traces his influence at General Electric as it planned a historic restructuring in the years following World War II, as well as later, when he advised Jack Welch, the company's current CEO. Similarly, Chapter 9 focuses on how Alfred Chandler, the foremost student of big corporations, revealed and explained the historic changes that were taking place at such companies as DuPont in the 1920s, General Motors in the 1950s, and IBM in the 1960s; in so doing, his books, especially *Strategy and Structure*, helped provide the impetus for the field of corporate strategy and influenced changes at scores of companies. And the story of Robert McNamara traces his influence at both Ford and the Department of Defense and the ripple effect of the changes at those organizations on numerous other corporations. Finally, Chapter 7, explores how W. Edwards Deming and the pioneers of the learning organization tried to undo the excesses of the legacy left by McNamara and other latter-day Taylorites at companies such as Ford and Xerox.

For all the ideological rivalries that have defined the two main camps of management thinking during the twentieth century, *The Capitalist Philosophers* is a history of ideas and the rich cross-fertilization that occurs between people and disciplines often in seemingly unrelated fields. Through the capitalist philosophers, breakthroughs in sociology, psychology, and economics have mingled and shaped the practice and theory of management. As such, the portraits in this book provide a taxonomy of management's rich multidisciplinary heritage.

The best companies, it turns out, have learned from more than one school of thought. As the stories of Ford, GM, GE, and the SAS Institute show, success rarely comes from applying ideological prescriptions blindly. Nor does success accrue to the faint of heart or for dabblers in superficial remedies. Rather, it belongs to companies that strive to employ both the scientific and humanistic state of the art, that are committed to genuine learning, and that are not afraid of radical change. By going back to the sources and examining the ideas of the most influential capitalist philosophers, I hope to give readers insights that can help them make judgments about the next "new" revolutionary idea that comes along.

THE CAPITALIST
PHILOSOPHERS

He couldn't stand to see an idle lathe or an idle man. Production went to his head and thrilled his sleepless nerves like liquor or women on a Saturday night.

—John Dos Passos[1]

Frederick Winslow Taylor

The Father of Scientific Management

The year 1899 marked the dawn of the American Century. Across the vast continent, the railroad barons were laying track that would weave distant towns together into the world's largest consumer market. On both coasts, immigrants came ashore, bringing with them a hunger for opportunity and the energy to fuel a young nation's growth. And at Bethlehem, Pennsylvania, Frederick Winslow Taylor was at work on what is remembered as his most famous industrial experiment—one that would define both the struggle and terms of industrial productivity for the coming century.

The focus of Taylor's experiment was the immigrant laborers themselves—Hungarians and Germans, most of them—whose job it was to haul bars of pig iron weighing ninety-two pounds each onto railroad cars. For two days, Taylor and two deputies observed ten men as they lugged bars of pig iron from the Bethlehem Steel yard to the railcars. Laboring at a backbreaking pace, Taylor's ten "Hungarians" each loaded an average of seventy-five tons of pig iron per day, nearly six times the previous rate.[2]

On the basis of those observations, Taylor established a production quota. To complete a fair day's work, he determined, each worker would have to haul forty-five tons per day—an output level still about *three times as high* as the average output before Taylor appeared on the scene. To be sure, Taylor offered to pay men who met the quota a higher wage. But to the Bethlehem laborers, Taylor was simply asking too much. In the ensuing weeks it became clear that some of the men were physically incapable of meeting the quota. Others simply refused to try. Either way, the Bethlehem workers lost their jobs by the dozen. By some accounts, Taylor was so deeply hated by the men that he had to walk home under armed guard for fear of an attack on his life. Years later, Taylor, referring to his unhappy relationships with his workers, said, "It's a horrid life for any man to live, not being able to look any workman in the face without seeing hostility."[3]

Into this tinderbox stepped "Schmidt," a German immigrant of "sluggish" intelligence but possessing the power and stamina of a forklift truck. Schmidt, according to Taylor, had just the "ox-like" mentality needed to do the brutish physical labor that Taylor demanded of his workers. Uncomplaining and apparently indefatigable, Schmidt met Taylor's quota, happy to collect a few cents of extra pay at the end of each day.[4]

The story of Schmidt would become the defining allegory of scientific management, even though Taylor scholars point out that the story is misleading in almost every respect. The name Schmidt itself was a pseudonym, and most of the character traits imputed to the fictional Schmidt were invented by Taylor for dramatic effect. Moreover, according to Daniel Nelson, a leading Taylor scholar, the story was inaccurate in its description of "the nature of Taylor's contributions and the character of scientific management."[5] For one thing, the Schmidt story failed to convey the power of Taylor's thinking: his rigorous analysis of processes and his maniacal efforts to systematize work, his pioneering studies of manufacturing processes, his penchant for invention, and his very real contributions to the science of steel fabrication.

The Schmidt story did, however, capture two important aspects of Taylorism: First, it conveyed "the essence" of Taylor's combative personality, including both his considerable class prejudices and his autocratic management style.[6] Second, it revealed his utter inability to understand human nature, a shortcoming that became embedded in his ideas and carried into twentieth-century management practice. Yet for his time, Taylor was every bit as much of a maverick as Bill Gates and Thomas J. Watson. At a time when the work practices of individual laborers were more art than science, he raised fundamental questions about work processes and control. Achieving high productivity, he realized, would require standardizing tools and production techniques and imposing a level of control over labor that had never been attempted before.

Although he is best known for his attempts to make labor more productive, his work on tool steel, which revolutionized the use and fabrication of steel, were in many respects more successful. With the birth of large-scale manufacturing at the beginning of the century, his work on tool steel was every bit as important as the development of user-friendly software would be to the information age at the end of the twentieth century. Because his innovations with tool steel made it possible to dramatically speed up production, they helped to create the manufacturing conditions that demanded greater precision and control over labor. And it was his work on tool steel that won him legitimacy in the factory and explained why manufacturers backed his divisive attempts to increase labor productivity and overlooked his eccentric and difficult personality. "If Taylor preferred to see high-speed steel as a footnote to the larger cause he championed, out in the real world the influence often went the other way," writes Robert Kanigel, Taylor's biographer. High-speed steel provided the "opening into which the earth-moving wedge of the Taylor system could be slipped."[7]

Taylor's life and Weltanschauung (of which the Schmidt story was a representative theme) were, in fact, emblematic of the rationalist spirit of the turn of the century and proved pivotal to defining modern industry as we know it today. Taylor's greatest contribution was in recognizing that scientific method was key to the success of industrialization, especially in running the new enterprises that were of a scale and scope heretofore unimaginable—factories so large they used small railroads to transport men around them, factories peopled by thousands of workers operating enormous, power-driven machines. The new manufacturing behemoths could not be managed with the casual methods and supervision of the relatively small plants of the so-called first factory period.

Taylor's effort to develop a science of management had a profound impact on American industry. Decades later, the key ideas and trends in management have sped along the tracks that Taylor laid. Henry Ford's assembly line was a logical extension of Taylor's efforts to break up and speed up individual production tasks. The detailed measurement of processes and systems of Robert McNamara's Whiz Kids, at both Ford and the Pentagon, represented a sophisticated, high-technology spin on scientific management. Similarly, the decades-long search for the Holy Grail of employee productivity—and the quest for the perfect incentive pay formula—can be traced back to Taylor's attempt to develop the first scientifically based formula for determining a labor rate that would produce the greatest output. Most recently, the reengineering craze of the 1980s, in which so-called turnaround experts gutted company payrolls in an employee-be-damned frenzy, echoed the excesses of Taylorism.

Indeed, Taylor was perfectly at home with the technology of industrialization and its logistical challenges. Where he was often completely out of his element was in his relations with people, especially those outside his class and immediate social circle. Thus, his most troublesome legacy involved his solutions to the "labor problem," which for a long time threatened to swamp the advances made by industrialization.

For the enterprising and the fortunate, the turn of the century represented a world of opportunity. But for the vast majority, the workplace was filled with peril. In Taylor's day, the average worker possessed little more than his capacity to work and his tools. Yet setting foot into a factory was fraught with risks that could end his livelihood any day. In heat-treating plants, such as steel foundries, the rate of serious and fatal injuries was well over *1 percent* of the workforce each year. On the railroads, it was higher. Those who escaped with their lives intact worked in brick mausoleums with little natural light or ventilation and breathed the smoke and foul odors of hundreds of candles and kerosene lanterns. Toilets and water fountains were a rarity.[8]

For their trouble, most industrial workers were paid barely enough to survive while they were working. Few laborers owned their own homes. And there was no safety net for those who were injured or those who were laid off during inevitable slowdowns. (While a few craft unions flourished in trades such as printing, mass production reduced the dependence of U.S. firms on skilled labor.)

Such conditions gave rise to the Socialist Party in 1901 and to the American labor movement. Although many European businessmen saw unions as an antidote to labor unrest, in the United States the mantra of individualism and free enterprise made unions anathema to most American companies.[9] In fact, U.S. industrialists sometimes met the threat of labor unions with guns. And shoot-outs between factory owners and union organizers became another frequent cause of death, injury, and unemployment.

Like many of his peers, Taylor was an ardent opponent of unions. He understood, however, that workers at the turn of the century were not being paid fairly and that companies would have to pay higher wages to improve productivity. "The fundamental principle upon which industry seems now to be run in this country," he wrote, "is that the employer shall pay just as low wages as he can and that the workman shall retaliate by doing just as little work as he can. Industry is thus a warfare, in which both sides, instead of giving out the best that is in them, seem determined to give out the worst."[10]

Taylor sensed the destructive force of labor-management antagonism, and sought to bring peace to the industrial battlefield. However, while he walked among the workers, his vantage point was wholly that of a Philadelphia Brahmin. His unquestioning allegiance to the aristocratic values with which he had been raised hampered his judgment when it came to finding solutions to the "labor problem." In the end, his methods and pronouncements about the human side of enterprise only served to increase the distrust and divisiveness between labor and management.

The scion of a prominent Quaker family, Taylor carried the rigid rationalist values of his class into the messy working-class milieu of the nineteenth-century factory. In the spirit of Adam Smith, he believed in the proposition that men are motivated largely by financial gain; thus, he could justify almost any productivity-enhancing measure as long as it improved wages. He was wrong, however, in assuming that men would willingly sacrifice their souls for a bigger paycheck. He pressured workers into producing quantum leaps in efficiency in exchange for incremental increases in pay. In the process, he may have contributed more to labor unrest than AFL founder Samuel Gompers and Socialist Party founder Eugene V. Debs combined.

More than perhaps any other thinker of the early twentieth century, Taylor's work embodied both the progress and the pain that define periods of torrid economic development. An energetic and creative innovator, his production methods helped create the highest standard of living the world had ever seen. His ideas were embraced by such leaders of the Progressive movement as Walter Lippmann and Louis Brandeis, who was known as "the people's lawyer" before he became a Supreme Court justice. For better or worse, wrote Robert Kanigel in *The One Best Way*, a biography of Taylor, "it's not just industry that bears his imprint today but all of modern life."[11]

To Taylor's detractors, Taylorism was the essence of the mechanistic, alienating character of modern industrialism. Under Taylor, standardization and managerial control, professionalism and scientific method were championed as never before. A new cadre of slide rule– and stopwatch-wielding experts commandeered the factory floor.

Along the way, scientific management changed the way of life of the expanding ranks of industrial workers. The most skilled among them saw the Taylorites break their work down into its component parts so that men with little skill or training could master it. Bit by bit the factory worker lost control of his tools, the process of production, even the way he moved his body as he worked.

Half a century later, a new generation of management experts, including industrial psychologists and quality experts, would see wisdom in capturing the knowledge and know-how of the workers on an ongoing basis (see Chapters 6 and 7). But Taylor, a man whose personality and innovations provoked legendary battles on the factory floor, saw workers as particularly noisome cogs in a much larger machine.

While he respected many of the skilled workers he encountered in the factory, especially during his apprenticeship, Taylor never broke with the elite attitudes of the society into which he had been born. Indeed, in his commitment to "dumbing down" labor and creating elaborate shop-floor hierarchies, he far surpassed the antilabor sentiments of many of the industrialists of his day. For instance, he was incapable of empathizing with the men who worked for him, which helps explain his use of what now seem like shockingly crude stereotypes to describe the Schmidts of his world. An aficionado of amateur theatricals ever since he was a boy, he undoubtedly embellished Schmidt's personality for effect. Yet it is clear from his ideas and teachings that for him, workers were to a large extent all "Schmidts" of his own creation, crude creatures to be made productive or discarded; they were not real men of brain and brawn who would have to be grappled with.

Whatever the source of Taylor's social limitations, they had a profound impact on the shape not only of Taylorism but of the entire management legacy that he passed on to modern industry. As he developed it, scientific management became technology-centered, hierarchical, and highly bureaucratic—a legacy that industry has only recently sought to shake off. It is interesting to speculate how differently the character of management and especially of industrial work might have evolved if someone with a more democratic conception of the workplace, or one more in tune with the new psychological theories of work and motivation that were coming to the fore, especially after World War I, had written the gospel of scientific management.

◼

Taylor's fondness for establishing rules and exercising authority was evident from an early age. His boyhood friends recalled that "even a game of croquet was a source of study and careful analysis for Fred, who worked out carefully the angles of the various strokes, the force of impact and the advantages and disadvantages of the understroke." Not surprisingly, the officious streak in a prepubescent Fred Taylor grated on his playmates. "We were inclined to rebel sometimes from the strict rules and exact formulas to which he insisted that all of our games must be subjected," recalled Birge Harrison. "It did not seem absolutely necessary that the rectangle of our rounders court should be scientifically accurate, and that the whole of a fine sunny morning should be wasted in measuring it off by feet and by inches."[12]

By his thirteenth birthday, Taylor began to focus his penchant for rules and details not on games but on how the world worked. In 1868, he and his family—his parents, Emily Winslow Taylor and Franklin Taylor; his older brother, Win; and his younger sister, Mary—embarked on a three-and-a-half-year-long grand tour of Europe. During the trip, Fred began to keep a diary of his travels. In Germany, he filled his notebooks with details of the methods of extracting salt from underwater lakes, 1,200 feet below the surface. In Antwerp, his entries noted the prices of black silk sold by different vendors. In Sweden, he detailed the specific arrival and departure times of the carriages in which the family traveled and which were required to change horses every seven miles.[13]

Years later, Fred Taylor dismissed the European expedition as an undertaking he "disapprove[d] of for a young boy." It was, indeed, a luxury that only the most affluent, leisured class of American families could afford. Fred's father, a Main Line Philadelphian, didn't have to work to support his family. Franklin held a law degree and, at least through the Civil War, maintained an office on Walnut Street in Philadelphia. Most of his time, however, was spent in such gentlemanly pursuits as studying foreign languages and history, doing charitable work, and managing his properties.[14]

Although, as an adult, Taylor would reject his father's leisurely way of life, he absorbed the values and the sense of entitlement that were a part of his upbringing. Although he certainly had the drive and ambition to find employment on his own, most of his jobs were won with the help of family connections. He never moved far from Germantown. And when he was ready to build a house, he located Boxly in the same affluent Philadelphia neighborhood where his parents had settled after their European tour. It was from Boxly, which served as both private residence and Mecca of scientific management, that he would preach his gospel during the last decade of his life.

Upon returning from Europe, Fred enrolled at Phillips Exeter Academy in New Hampshire. From there, he prepared for the inevitable rite of passage for a young man of his upbringing: a college education at Harvard.

Fred never did reach Harvard, however. As early as his first year at Exeter, he began contemplating becoming an engineer. It was an extraordinary idea for a young man of his background. For one thing, while the rise of scientific management would eventually create a boom in the engineering profession, in 1872 there were fewer than 7,000 engineers in the entire country. (That number would jump to 135,000 by 1920.) Then too, in the late nineteenth century engineering was still firmly "rooted in the shop floor." In addition to learning mathematics and chemistry, engineering students studied drafting and the rudiments of regulating boilers and machine tools.[15]

Hastening Fred's unusual choice was an ailment of seemingly mysterious origin. For years he had periodically suffered from severe headaches. At Exeter, his headaches began to worsen. And by the fall of 1873, his parents had reason to worry that his eyesight might be at risk. Later in life, he would be diagnosed with severe astigmatism. Left untreated, the condition, which causes blurred vision, can cause severe eyestrain, especially if the sufferer spends a great deal of time reading and writing. But in the 1870s, the condition was still largely unknown. Thus, in a letter to Fred and Win, who was now also at Exeter, Franklin wrote, "My own feeling is that it would be more prudent for Fred to give up Latin and Greek and apply himself to mathematics and the exact sciences, in the study of which he would not be obliged to overstrain his eyes."[16]

In the winter of 1873, toward the end of his first term, Fred left Exeter and returned to Germantown. Sometime during the next year, he took his first job, as an apprentice patternmaker, at Philadelphia's Enterprise Hydraulic Works, which made steam pumps and other hydraulic equipment. Although the city, a major industrial center, was reeling from the economic crisis that had started the year before, his father had probably used his connections to help find his son a job.[17]

Though this was a far cry from Harvard, it was not unheard of for even an upper-class young man to hold an apprenticeship in nineteenth-century Philadelphia. In those days, apprenticeships were still as common a way to enter industry as graduation from one of the handful of universities that offered engineering degrees. Of course, at least initially, Fred was torn about his choice, and in the spring of 1874 he took the Harvard entrance exams. Although he passed with honors, he would not go on to the family alma mater.[18]

If Fred's course seemed out of character for a scion of the Taylor family, it was not so for a descendant of his maternal grandfather, Isaac Winslow. Indeed, Fred's mother, Emily, may have recognized in her son's newfound interest the adventurousness and hard-driving nature of her father.

Like her husband, Emily was a Quaker from a prominent East Coast family. In contrast to the Taylors, however, the Winslows were activists in every sense of the term. Emily's father had been an entrepreneur and an adventurer. At one time, he had commanded a fleet of whaling vessels at sea. He was also an abolitionist.

Fred unquestionably inherited a good measure of his grandfather Winslow's drive. As his career progressed, there was even something of a maniacal, all-or-nothing compulsiveness in the way in which he pursued his vocation. Remarked Charles Harrah, an industrialist and one-time owner of the Midvale Steel Company where Taylor worked for several years and pioneered many of his management ideas and experiments with tool steel, "Do you know what I am going to do when I have made a few more millions? I am going to build the finest insane asylum this world has ever known, and you, Taylor, are going to have there an entire floor."[19]

While Fred was hardly a political or social firebrand, the apprenticeship opened up a whole new world to him, one that he was determined to master on his own terms. At Enterprise Hydraulic Works—more commonly known as Ferrell & Jones, after the company's owners—Fred was taken on as an apprentice patternmaker. "If any trade was apt to subvert a rich boy's stereotypes about men who worked with their hands, that of the patternmaker was it," wrote Kanigel.[20]

Few trades required greater skill than patternmaking, which entailed the creation of an ingeniously designed wooden pattern, crafted with perfectly smooth contours, that would serve as a facsimile of the metal part that was to be fabricated. The pattern was placed into a wooden box with sand packed in around it and was later carefully removed in such a way as to leave behind a perfect imprint in the sand. (One of the biggest challenges lay in designing a pattern of such perfect dimensions and smoothness that sand particles wouldn't come away with the pattern when it was removed from the sand, thereby ruining the mold.) To create the part itself, molten metal would be poured into the sand cavity that was left by the pattern after its removal. Because metal contracts as it cools, the patternmaker had to factor in shrinkage and the tolerances required by the process for which the parts ultimately would be used, as well as the complexities of hollowed-out shapes.[21]

At Ferrell & Jones, Fred came under the tutelage of John R. Griffith, the head patternmaker and master craftsman, with whom Taylor would maintain contact sporadically for years to come. It was under Griffith, as well as the other patternmakers and machinists, that Taylor developed an appreciation of, and respect for, the individual artistry each skilled workman brought to his craft. "The influence and teaching of John Griffith . . . made a permanent impression on Fred and laid the foundation for his life work," wrote Ernest Wright, a friend from Germantown who also served an apprenticeship and would go on to become an engineer. Concurred Taylor, "I look back upon the first six months of my apprenticeship as a patternmaker as, on the whole, the most valuable part of my education."[22]

But Taylor's was not a typical apprenticeship, one that he would have to work at for years. Less than two years after becoming an apprentice patternmaker, he took on another apprenticeship, as a machinist.

Much of his later work in scientific management was an effort to capture and standardize the skill and artistry he had first seen at Ferrell & Jones. Ironically, in the process, he would play a huge role in marginalizing the role of the craftsmen he credited for his education.

Indeed, Taylor's stint as an ordinary workman must have seemed like just another opportunity at playacting. During his European travels, he had learned to speak fluent French and German and had developed a keen ear for languages and dialects. (He was known for telling Uncle Remus stories in Negro dialect and mimicking a "dhick eggzent" of a German professor.) He frequently played in amateur theatricals. Now, on the shop floor, he picked up the hard-cussing speech of a working-man, a fondness for profanity that never left him. The pioneer of scientific management played his new role so convincingly—and kept his life so compartmentalized—that it took two and a half years, according to Taylor, for his coworkers at Ferrell & Jones to figure out that he was "a gentleman's son."[23]

In 1878, when Taylor was twenty-three, family connections helped to secure him a new job at Philadelphia's Midvale Steel Company. The Taylors were friends with Edward W. Clark, one of Midvale's chief investors. And it was this job that planted the seeds both for Taylor's pioneering work in scientific management and for a "twenty-six-year search for the laws that governed the cutting of metal."[24]

Midvale was a propitious place from which to start his career. The company was a pioneering manufacturer of steel, the temperamental "miracle" material that was harder, stronger, and more malleable than iron. Although steel had been discovered during the Iron Age, fabricating it was so tricky that for centuries it could be made only in relatively small quantities and at great expense. It wasn't until the nineteenth century that new techniques—the Bessemer and open-hearth processes, in particular—made it possible to produce large quantities of steel relatively cheaply.

For its day, Midvale was a high-tech pioneer of steel production, manufacturing everything from cutting tools to the beams and channel sections that were used to build the Brooklyn Bridge. Midvale's success was due in no small part to William Sellers, Clark's partner and the man who ran Midvale. Sellers was known as "the greatest mechanical engineer in the world" and would become one of Taylor's chief mentors.[25]

In 1875, Midvale became the first U.S. manufacturer to win a Navy contract for steel cannons. (Until that time, the U.S. military contracted with foreign suppliers, the Germans in particular.) Throughout the 1880s, as government ordinance expenditures grew, so did Midvale's role as a government contractor. By the 1890s, the company had become one of the largest defense contractors in the country.

The combination of the technical complexity of Midvale's military contracts and the surge in demand that followed the depression of the mid-1870s furnished much of the impetus for Taylor's most innovative work at the company. At Midvale, he began a series of groundbreaking experiments with "tool steel" that would revolutionize the use of machine tools. It was also at Midvale that he began experimenting with the key elements of what would become the hallmarks of scientific management: time study, the dissection of each job into its component parts, the codification of each process, and the "Faustian bargain" by which management would impose ever-greater demands and control over workers in exchange for increased pay.[26]

When Taylor went to work for Midvale as a "common, unskilled laborer," American industry was still suffering from the crash of 1873. Taylor implies that his lowly position, working a lathe in the Midvale machine shop, was due to the depression. Given his close ties to the owners of Midvale, however, he almost certainly could have gotten a white-collar job had he wanted one. Instead, he climbed the shop-floor ladder and eventually became a gang boss, an ascent that would have repercussions far beyond Midvale.[27]

Since his days at Ferrell & Jones, Taylor had prided himself on fitting in with the other workers. As a laborer on Midvale's shop floor, for example, Taylor worked under the byzantine piece-rate system that was widely in use at the time. Under the system, workers ostensibly were paid not on the basis of hours worked but on the number of parts, or pieces, produced. In theory, the more one worked, the more one earned. But as a routine practice, management carefully monitored the payroll. As soon as workers began earning "too much," management cut the piece rate and employees found themselves earning no more than they had before, even though they were more productive.[28]

In reaction, workers developed their own system for averting rate cuts and the need to work harder to earn the same amount of pay. In a widespread practice known as "soldiering," they scaled back their output, in effect creating their own unofficial quota. To make sure that no enterprising laborer showed up the group and wrecked the rate by working harder and producing more, peer pressure kept everyone working at the same lackadaisical pace. Said Taylor, "Hardly a competent workman can be found in a large establishment who does not devote a considerable part of his time to *studying* [author's emphasis] just how slowly he can work and still convince his employer that he is going at a good pace."[29]

As a Philadelphian, Taylor could not have been oblivious to the growing labor unrest that was spawned by the nation's rapid expansion and industrialization. In 1835, the City of Brotherly Love had been home to the nation's first general strike, when workers, both skilled and unskilled, had gone on a daylong walkout. In 1892, hundreds of Pinkerton guards would do battle with striking workers at Carnegie Steel in Homestead, Pennsylvania. Ten men died and dozens were wounded as guns and a cannon were fired during the melee that ended only when the state militia was called in to quell the violence. (In 1910, Philadelphia would see a second general strike, which began another wave of labor unrest that would sweep the country.)[30]

As an ordinary lathesman at Midvale, Taylor had soldiered along with the rest of his coworkers, "never [breaking] a rate." However, as soon as he was promoted, he became determined to break the shop floor of its habits and to wring an honest day's work out of each and every laborer. Thus began a dramatic new phase in the war between capital and labor.[31]

In his role as Midvale gang boss, Taylor revealed his startling lack of what today would be called people skills. Boyish-looking and "wiry as a steel spring," he possessed an air of determination that belied his years.[32] Donning with ease the authoritarian style that became his trademark, he took the first steps in attempting to determine the maximum level of output that could be expected of each job and process on the shop floor. At first his approach wasn't very scientific. Sometimes sitting down at a lathe himself, he would show a worker "how to work fast and right." When a worker refused to follow his example—which is what often happened—he simply fired him.

Finally, out of sheer exasperation, Taylor announced that unless the shop floor produced what he considered a fair day's work, he would cut the piece rate in half. Gradually, a few of the men fell into line with his plan. When disgruntled workers disabled machinery by, for example, literally throwing monkey wrenches into the works, he imposed a series of heavy fines, as much as two dollars per infraction—a full day's pay—for a broken machine part. His hardball tactics produced a measure of compliance, but not without creating a venomous atmosphere on Midvale's shop floor.[33]

For all of Taylor's clumsiness in dealing with workers, his own experience in straddling two worlds—that of the factory floor and the executive suite—gave him important insights into the nature of industry. It gave him a close-up look at the unsystematic, decentralized managerial methods of the first factory system. He saw clearly the contrast between the scientific, rationalist approach with which Midvale engineers tackled technical problems and the haphazard and often destructive way in which foreman and workers handled tools, parts, machinery, and often one another. Just as Taylor understood that the piece-rate system was rigged against the worker, he came to realize that capricious management tactics and disorderly factories made it impossible to get a fair day's work out of laborers.

While Taylor's system began as an attempt to develop the perfect pay-for-performance formula, it quickly came to encompass broader issues of "work" and "control." Achieving true productivity, he soon realized, would mean standardizing work, tools, and maintenance techniques. Standardization, in turn, demanded a level of control over work that had never been attempted before.

Taylor's first challenge was to determine how quickly he could work men and machines without breaking them. Taylor lamented the fact that in most factories such details as the care of belting and the shape of cutting tools, including the methods used to temper, grind, and store them, were determined by foremen and even individual workers. The speed, feed, and depth of cut determined both how quickly a worker could cut away metal and the cost and efficiency of completing a job. Up to a point, the faster a worker cut away steel, the lower the cost would be. But if he cut too quickly, he risked wearing out his tool in no time. The balance between cutting efficiency and tool maintenance was a matter of hunch and habit, not a scientifically determined process.[34]

Taylor would change all that. Even as he was exhorting his men to work harder, he sought Sellers's permission to begin a series of metal-cutting experiments. These experiments were a direct outgrowth of Taylor's determination to deconstruct and systematize every phase of production. Over the course of the next twenty-six years, he recorded between 30,000 and 40,000 metal-cutting experiments, as well as scores of others for which he kept no records. That Sellers permitted the metal-cutting experiments was partly a function of the "spirit of rational inquiry" that hung in the air at Midvale. Then, too, a boom in business, especially for technology-intensive military contracts, demanded more reliable production methods and an expansion in Midvale's manufacturing facilities.[35]

In 1883, when Midvale began to build a new machine shop, management put Taylor in charge of both design and construction. He turned the machine shop into something of a laboratory for his inventions. These included one of his first metal-cutting innovations: the discovery that a stream of water directed at a cutting tool would cool the blade and thereby raise the speed of the tool by one third. He also devised a colossal, six-ton steam hammer used for pounding enormous slabs of steel into cannons. His innovation was to incorporate a kind of spring mechanism that prevented the giant hammers from literally "batter[ing] themselves to death."[36]

Other innovations followed. Taylor tackled the problem of troublesome leather belts, which were looped over pulleys and delivered power to the machine tools. Frequently measuring more than thirty feet in length, the belts were prone to stretching and breaking, bringing the machine shop—or at least a section of it—to a halt. Thus, for more than a decade, he studied the failure rate—and the costs associated with failures—of belts and experimented with a new system of fatter belts and bigger pulleys. In 1893, he published "Notes on Belting," the culmination of his work.[37]

Taylor's own life during this period was a monument of almost maniacal dedication to work and study. Even as he was climbing the ladder at Midvale, working ten hours a day, six days a week, he enrolled at the Stevens Institute of Technology in Hoboken, New Jersey. Although he almost never attended classes, he maintained an obsessive schedule both on and off the job, frequently studying through the night and then taking a half-hour jog through the quiet Germantown streets before setting off for the two-mile walk to work.

Taylor's days at Midvale are a saga of dedication almost bizarre in its intensity. On one occasion, for example, when workers failed to clear a clogged drainage pipe, he vetoed a suggestion that would have entailed digging twenty to thirty feet below the foundations of the building to clean out the drain, a plan that would have shut down the mill for several days. Instead, the father of scientific management "put on overalls, tied shoes on his elbows, shoes on his knees and leather pads on to his hips to keep from getting cut in the drain, and then crawled in through the black slime and muck of the drain" for a hundred yards, until he reached the obstruction. After clearing the blockage, he backed out the same way he had come in.[38]

Such antics were undoubtedly meant to prove to the workers that Taylor wasn't above getting his hands dirty, that it wasn't only the workers of whom he demanded sacrifices to the job. For even as he was beginning his metal-cutting experiments, he began a series of inquiries into the nature of work and the limits of human endurance. The purpose of his investigations was to determine scientifically "that elusive quantum of work which each worker should turn out daily."[39]

Taylor began by examining not just how long a particular task took to complete but how long it *should* take. Having received permission from Sellers to conduct productivity experiments with workers, he studied men at work on such unmechanized manual tasks as shoveling, bricklaying, and loading and emptying wheelbarrow loads of loose dirt. Plucking two good workers off the shop floor, he promised them double pay if they would put their whole effort into a series of arduous tasks. He then calculated the performance of his workers by the number of "horsepower" expended to complete each task. The initial results of these experiments were highly inconsistent and not particularly useful since they showed wide discrepancies in the amount of time needed to complete each task. However, to conduct his tests, Taylor used a stopwatch and recorded his observations in a notebook in what may have been the first attempt to conduct second-by-second examinations of work. It was the first time he broke each job and work process down into discrete parts, studying and timing the movements of men and machines.[40]

Time study became a crucial element of the Taylor system. He described its steps as follows:

a) Divide the work of a man performing any job into simple elementary movements.

b) Pick out all useless movements and discard them.

c) Study, one after another, just how each of several skilled workmen makes each elementary movement, and with the aid of a stop watch select the quickest and best method. . . .

d) Describe, record, and index each elementary movement, with its proper time, so that it can be quickly found. . . .

e) Study and record the percentage which must be added to the actual working time of a good workman to cover unavoidable delays, interruptions, and minor accidents, etc.

f) Study and record the percentage which must be added to cover the newness for a good workman to a job, the first few times he does it.

g) Study and record the percentage of time that must be allowed for rest, and the intervals at which the rest must be taken, in order to offset physical fatigue."[41]

A few years later, Sanford Thompson, one of Taylor's principal followers and collaborators, would study the Midvale data in what turned out to be an unsuccessful attempt to determine the optimum output for a day's manual labor. Thompson perfected time-study techniques, including a notebook—a so-called watch book—that concealed a stopwatch and enabled the time-study expert, at least in theory, to time workers unobserved. Thompson concluded that most of the time-study data taken at Midvale were inaccurate or contained crucial omissions and were therefore largely useless.[42]

One of Thompson's most insightful observations went largely unheeded by Taylor. "One of the greatest difficulties I have found in arriving at averages is due to the fact . . . that the 'personal equations' of different men vary greatly," Thompson reported. Years later, James Mapes Dodge, the chairman of Link-Belt, one of the companies Taylor came to hold up as a model of scientific management, made the same point shortly before Taylor's death: "I believe that we are making a mistake in saying that Scientific Management is based on exact science when, as a matter of fact, the base rates and the percentages we add to our time studies are matters of human judgment and cannot, in my judgment, be arrived at sufficiently well to be called 'Scientific' determinations."[43]

Taylor, however, never could bring himself to consider seriously the maddening unpredictability of the human dimension in industry and its impact on productivity. He continued for years to attempt to develop a scientific standard for the optimal output of manual labor. Wrote Daniel Nelson, "It is unlikely that he ever fully reconciled himself to the notion that men could be as complicated as machines."[44]

It's worth noting that over time Taylor and Thompson parted company dramatically on the subject of labor unions. Even before Taylor's death in 1915, a number of his followers had become receptive to unionism and had become convinced that "enlightened management" and "industrial democracy [were] the key[s] to industrial efficiency."[45] This was a viewpoint Taylor was never willing to concede.

It was technology, not people, that interested Taylor. Harnessing his knowledge of metal-cutting technology and his time-study observations of workers while still at Midvale, Taylor began to reengineer the Midvale metal-cutting jobs themselves. He began by carefully studying the work practices of skilled laborers in an attempt to break metalworking jobs down into "elementary" tasks, such as adjusting a machine for each cut, cutting the metal, removing bolts and stops, lifting a finished piece from the table, and returning it to the floor. While two machinists might be working on entirely different products, such as a railroad tire and an engine part, the "elementary" steps in the job might be the same. The secret of improving productivity, he decided, was to improve and standardize the elementary steps and apply them to a wide range of tasks—the labor equivalent of designing a family of products with a relatively small number of standardized parts. By breaking each job down into its component parts, he could study each element to determine, say, how production machinery could be modified and individual operations improved or eliminated.[46]

Eventually, Taylor devised a series of instruction cards that specified, in great detail, each step in the process of machining, say, a locomotive tire. They included everything the worker needed to know about how, and in what order, to do a job, including machine settings and the length of time each step in the process was supposed to take. Now when a machinist sat down to his lathe, he no longer performed the job his own way; rather, he was handed an instruction card with strict specifications for the order in which each step of the process should be completed:

Set tire on machine ready to turn. . . .
Rough face front edge. . . .
Finish face front edge. . . .
Rough bore front. . . .
Finish bore front. . . .[47]

The instruction card was to the men in Taylor's planning department what the blueprint is to a draftsman. Eventually he also broke up the job of the foreman, creating functional foremen with circumscribed specialties such as tool maintenance or inspection, and created factory planning departments. While not all of his innovations survived, taken together, the instruction cards and the planning departments and functional foremen were forerunners of the factory management systems that would be developed at Ford and part of the inexorable process of de-skilling labor.[48]

In the process of breaking down each job into its individual components, Taylor inevitably identified process improvements that saved both time and costs. Working on an elaborate instruction card for boiler maintenance, for example, he discovered that the cramped positions in which maintenance crews were forced to work slowed them down. To mitigate the discomfort of the workers, he designed knee and elbow pads and special tools for the job. His innovations slashed the cost of boiler maintenance from $62 per boiler to just $11.

Scientific management could actually make an onerous job easier. Much of the work done by the Gilbreths, whose innovations were in many ways as outlandish and obsessive as Taylor's, was essentially ergonomic. The couple's innovations included Frank's famous brick pallets, which were designed to end the bricklayers' eternal bending and lifting, and the fitting of shock absorbers onto the workstations of handkerchief stitchers to stop the vibration of their sewing machines and chairs.[49]

But in Taylor's mechanistically oriented imagination, the common laborer wasn't a potential source of ongoing ideas and process improvements but rather a particularly problem-prone piece of the machinery. While he was eager to learn from the best of the skilled workmen, especially machinists, and was prepared to promote them to foreman positions, those who were left to operate on the factory floor were stripped of the individual artistry each worker brought to his job.

Before the onset of scientific management, a skilled worker had an "almost emotional relationship" with his tools. A machinist, for example, cared for his own tools, including the equipment that was assigned to him on the job. He was responsible for grinding and oiling them. He owned his own monkey wrenches, calipers, and scribers. Under scientific management neither tool maintenance nor "the cutting speed of a machine, the feed and depth of the cut," nor even the decision as to which tool was called for in a given situation, could be left to the "subjective judgment and discretion of the individual machinist."[50]

Taylor's answer was to strip the worker of responsibility for his tools and the entire work process itself. Nearly a century later, the total quality movement, under the impetus of W. Edwards Deming, would imbue Taylor's systematic approach to process improvement with a more advanced understanding of human motivation (see Chapter 7). To come up with a better method of loading pig iron, for example, Deming would have advised Taylor that when pig-iron handlers and railway workers put their heads together, they would come up with a far better solution than any stopwatch-wielding efficiency engineer. But such collaborative approaches to work would take decades to develop.

Thus, even as champions of Taylorism hailed the dawning of a new age, workers came to view scientific management as a disenfranchising, even dehumanizing, influence that reduced the average worker to little more than an appendage of the machine at which he labored. To union organizers, such as Samuel Gompers, who headed the American Federation of Labor (AFL), Taylorism had to be fought at all costs. "[The Taylor system makes] every man merely a cog or a nut or a pin in a big machine, fixed in the position of a hundredth or a thousandth part of the machine, with no need to employ more than a few mechanical motions nor any brain power except the little required in making those motions," wrote Gompers.[51]

No one, however, articulated so well the concerns of labor as A. J. Portenar, a mild-mannered printer and organizer in the typographical union, whose book *The Problems of Organized Labor* had been brought to Taylor's attention by Louis Brandeis. Portenar's thoughtfulness and articulate writing style initially led Taylor to believe that Portenar was "free of the pernicious influence of Gompers and [John] Mitchell," the general organizer for the AFL. He thought Portenar could be won over to "our side."[52]

Taylor, however, was to be disappointed. After several weeks of correspondence between the management scientist and the union organizer, Portenar wrote Taylor:

> I have read another third of one of your books. It depresses me
> horribly. The whole thing looms up vaguely before me as an un-
> human, inexorable machine, gliding smoothly on its way, but
> crushing not only all in its way, but sapping the vitality of all

connected with it. A machine geared to its highest specs, and
. . . calculating flesh and blood, as it calculates the tools and
materials it works with. . . .

I have tried to read and think about it without prejudice. I
have tried to be impersonal. . . . But sitting at my machine, and
noting the variations in my own hourly output, I have felt that it
would be terrible to know that I am in the grip of a remorseless,
unfeeling, unknowing system, that has set me a task that taxes
my powers *at their best,* while I realize that I am *not always able
to do my best.* There are days when I can with ease do much
more than on other days I can do with effort. But nervous energy
is sure to be burned more rapidly than it can be replaced under
the artificial stimulus of your task and bonus.[53]

In Portenar's measured, seven-page handwritten letter, the printer
went on to explain how variation not only in human abilities but in the
very conditions of work makes it virtually impossible to establish a single production quota that can reliably be met *every day.* Portenar intuitively understood the havoc that can be wreaked by variability in a
complex process. But the laws of statistical variation were still virtually
unknown in manufacturing. Decades later, W. Edwards Deming would
hear Portenar's lament and champion the importance of understanding
and controlling variation in production processes as a first step to improving both quality and productivity (see Chapter 7).

Taylor, however, turned a deaf ear not only to Portenar's plea for
greater understanding of the human dimension of work but also to the
intimation that there might be a flaw in his scientific calculations. After
receiving Portenar's letter, Taylor wrote to Morris L. Cooke, a leading
disciple, "I am inclined to think that Portenar is so strongly prejudiced
against the essential Principles of Scientific Management that there is
no use fooling with him."[54]

In Taylor's view, the manufacturing world was inexorably bifurcated
between the interests of labor and management. For all his rhetoric
about cooperation, he was a staunch advocate of the prerogatives of
management and capital. To him, cooperation meant giving the
Portenars of the world an opportunity to agree with him. If they disagreed, they could go work elsewhere.

■

To put a stop to soldiering and bring peace to the factory, Taylor
wanted to end the practice of rate cutting. "I think that scientific management can be justly and truthfully characterized as management in

which harmony is the rule instead of discord," he said years later. Certainly at the beginning, he was driven by a determination to develop a "just system" to deal with the entire problem of soldiering.[55]

From the beginning, however, Taylor's conception of justice was a highly limited one. In keeping with his own laissez-faire sense of fair play, he was determined to get every bit of horsepower that he could out of his men; but he was equally determined to pay them for their efforts.

Taylor almost certainly knew nothing about the work of another contemporary, Émile Durkheim, a French sociologist who was among the first theorists to write about the importance of the social satisfactions of work (see Chapter 4 on Elton Mayo and Fritz Roethlisberger). Even if he had, it is unlikely that Taylor, the consummate engineer, would have had much real sympathy for the new psychological theories of motivation that began to gain currency during the early twentieth century. As it was, in the pre-Freudian world of the late nineteenth century, Taylor's formula was a straightforward commercial exchange: the total submission of labor in return for a "fair" day's wage.

Taylor wasn't the first person to divine the self-defeating nature of the so-called bogey, or piece-rate, system. For instance, Henry R. Towne, president of the lock maker Yale and Towne, had been one of the first manufacturers to advocate a "systematic application . . . of efficient management methods" and devised the first "gain-sharing" system, which divided any savings accrued from a reduction in production costs with the workers who had been responsible for the saving. However, since there was "no direct relationship between an individual's effort and his reward," the system soon failed to produce the desired results and Towne scrapped it in favor of an executive profit-sharing plan. Indeed, Towne's and Taylor's efforts can be seen as the first in a century-long pursuit of the ultimate management panacea: pay for performance (see Chapter 7).[56]

The new pay plan that Taylor began to devise in 1884, which came to be known as the "differential rate," became wildly popular among managers of Taylor's day. For one thing, the differential rate seemed to offer an answer to the twin problems of rate cutting and soldiering. And unlike the incentive plans introduced by a few other pioneers of the day, such as Towne, Taylor's differential rate didn't rely on historical precedent to determine rates of pay and output. Rather, time study would determine *scientifically* what the correct output level of a "first-class" worker should be. Workers who produced less than the predetermined rate would earn about 50 percent less than those who produced more than the scientifically determined amount.

Part of what made the differential rate so appealing to Taylor's clients was that the production quotas established by Taylor's scientific methods were far higher than anything that had been demanded of workers before. Thus, while Midvale's cutting-edge production system had turned out three to five axles per day, Taylor demanded double the output. By 1887, one Midvale machinist estimated that workmen were earning double the going rate of $1.50 per day and producing two to three times the quantities of just a few years earlier.[57]

Taylor detailed the differential rate in "A Piece Rate System, A Step Toward Partial Solution of the Labor Problem," which he published in the late 1890s. Appearing just a few years after the bloody Homestead strike of 1892, the differential piece rate combined with time study was put forward, in Taylor's paper, as the answer to the "permanent antagonism" that existed "between employers and men." It was meant by Taylor to be a socially progressive treatise and was received as such by many who heard it.[58]

By establishing a scientifically determined "fair rate" for each job, as well as the procedures for performing each task, the differential rate was expected to resolve the bitter disputes between management and labor. The system was intended to serve as "a means of affording substantial justice to the employee, while requiring him to conform to the best interests of his employer," wrote H. L. Gantt, one of Taylor's engineers at Bethlehem. Because the rates were to be determined "scientifically," there would be no grounds for rate cutting. Wrote Gantt, "The employee was not told in a general way 'to do better,' but had a definite standard set for him, and was shown how to reach that standard, for which he was awarded compensation in addition to his usual day's pay."[59] What's more, built into the pay system itself were both a guarantee against soldiering and an incentive to exceed the standard rate.

The trouble, as both critics and a few of Taylor's followers came to realize, was that the rate-setting process wasn't scientific at all. Among other shortcomings, it did not take into account the tremendous variability in the production process. In the absence of a truly scientific way to determine optimum output, some of Taylor's colleagues suggested including workers in the standard-setting process—a suggestion Taylor was never willing to entertain.

In the absence of input from labor, the pseudoscience of the rate-setting process often led to an arbitrary ratcheting up of the pace of work. Indeed, part of the challenge, as Taylor saw it, was to determine how quickly he could work men and machines without breaking them.

Another challenge was to figure out the *minimum* payoff that "human nature" demanded for the extraordinary new demands placed on the worker. Taylor advocated a premium for the most productive workers, but never more than 30 percent of the savings produced by their greater efforts; the dim-witted laborer of Taylor's conception couldn't handle more money. Paying the Schmidts of the world "too much" would lead them to become "shiftless, extravagant and dissipated," he wrote. "For their own best interest it does not do for most men to get rich too fast." Never mind that Henry Noll, the real Schmidt, was in many respects the model of an enterprising new immigrant.[60]

Taylor himself acknowledged the onerousness of his demands. You couldn't expect men to go "busting themselves all day long," without adequate recompense, he would say. Indeed, his standards were "purposely made so severe that not more than one out of five laborers (perhaps even a smaller percentage) could keep up."[61]

Significantly, in advocating even a 30 percent wage increase for productivity improvements, Taylor was more generous than his 1990s reengineering offspring, Michael Hammer and James Champy.

Ironically, Taylor himself considered the differential rate to be "one of the comparatively unimportant elements" of scientific management. Yet, presaging management's decades-long romance with pay-for-performance schemes, the differential rate was quickly embraced by managers—so much so that Taylor came to view the publication of "A Piece Rate System" as "a very great blunder" because it distracted management from more important elements of his system. During the congressional investigations of scientific management in 1912, Taylor testified, "The idea of setting a measured standard of work for each man to do each day—was the most prominent feature" of his system, not the differential rate itself.[62]

Indeed, at the Bethlehem Steel Works, where Taylor completed his metal-cutting experiments, met "Schmidt," and conducted his most famous pig-iron experiments, he hardly used the differential rate at all. It is likely that mounting labor unrest may have prevented him from introducing the differential rate on a widespread basis. Daniel Nelson notes that in nearly one third of the factories where Taylor and his protégés worked, the Taylorites "evoked such opposition that their services were terminated before they had an opportunity to introduce the incentive wage." However, at Bethlehem at the turn of the century, as at most companies today, management clamored for nothing so much as that elusive placebo: incentive pay.[63]

■

In 1899, in the wake of a government contracting scandal, Taylor was recruited to Bethlehem. The scandal involved several U.S. companies that were accused of charging the U.S. government higher prices for weaponry than those paid by their European customers. The scandal spread to Bethlehem, one of the nation's largest military contractors, when the government charged the company with price gouging on armor plate. The government insisted on a 50 percent price reduction, from $600 per ton to $300 per ton. Taylor was brought in to lower costs as a way of cushioning the pain of the price cut.[64] At Bethlehem, his first job was to reorganize the large, complex machine shop. Because he couldn't risk creating production delays, he didn't, at first, introduce time-study experiments. However, he had given up neither his interest in time study nor his determination to establish a scientific correlation between physical exertion and output.

Thus, he initially confined his time-study experiments to the yard workers whose job it was to load pig iron onto railcars. The pig-iron workers were a particularly primitive crew, according to Taylor, doing a job "so crude and elementary" that an "intelligent gorilla" would do it as well as Bethlehem's immigrant laborers. Because of his machine-shop duties, the time studies, at least initially, were a low priority. However, in the winter of 1899, the Spanish-American War created a surge in the demand for pig iron. Prices climbed from below $10 per ton to $12.50, prompting Bethlehem to sell off ten thousand tons of the gray iron bars. "This gave us a good opportunity to show the workmen, as well as the owner and managers of the works, on a fairly large scale the advantages of task work over the old-fashioned day work and piece work," said Taylor.[65]

Thus began the now-famous pig-iron experiment.

For a man of Taylor's maniacal devotion to precision, the entire pig-iron episode was astonishingly haphazard. Not only did the new production quota represent an enormous increase over the previous output level, it had been arrived at after *less than two days* of study. The quota itself was based on little more than guesswork. Taylor and his assistants arrived at the forty-five-ton quota by taking the seventy-five tons that the men hauled at a breakneck pace as their baseline and making a rough estimate of the time needed for rest periods and other delays.

Men who failed to meet the new quota would suffer a substantial penalty. The maximum piece rate of 3.75 cents per ton, or $1.68 per day, would be paid *only* to the pig-iron handler who filled his full forty-five-ton quota. In fact, what at first blush seemed like a wage increase actually turned out to be a pay cut unless the pig-iron handler *more than tripled* his previous output. A man who merely doubled his former output, for example, hauling twenty-six tons per day instead of thirteen tons, would earn only 91 cents per day, a pay cut of more than 20 percent from the going rate of $1.15.[66]

The particularly onerous nature of the quota soon became evident. For one thing, Taylor continued to have trouble in finding what were, by his definition, "first-rate men" who could "make a fair day's wages." Most of the Bethlehem workers, Taylor acknowledged, would "break down after two or three days," an indication of how physically debilitating his standards were.[67]

Only a virtual revolt by the Bethlehem workers prompted Taylor to ease up on his requirements. His beasts of burden soon figured out that unless they worked at a killing pace, they would be worse off than before. When he assigned the "ten best men" who had been his subjects to work under the new piece-rate plan, they refused. He responded by firing them en masse. His attempts to impose the piece-rate system continued to attract protests from the rest of the laborers, who won some backing from supervisors who were themselves at odds with Taylor. Only when Taylor and his men agreed to some concessions, including giving men who were tired or injured "work of a higher description," did resistance to the piece-rate system begin to subside.[68]

One of the only pig-iron handlers who seemed to be able to meet Taylor's exacting standards was Henry Noll. In Taylor's rendition of the man, in which he imitates Noll's Dutch accent—perhaps even embellishing it for effect—he depicts a workhorse of doltlike docility who responds with abject submissiveness to every command and financial incentive: "Vell—Did I got $1.85 for loading dot pig iron on dot car tomorrow?" asks "Schmidt."

"Yes, of course you do," responds Taylor.

"Vell, dot's all right. I could load dot pig iron on the car tomorrow for $1.85, and I get it every day, don't I."

"Certainly you do—certainly you do."

"Vell, den, I vas a high-priced man."

"Well, if you are a high-priced man, you will do exactly as this man [the supervisor] tells you tomorrow, from morning till night. When he tells you to pick up a pig, and walk, you pick it up and you walk, and when he tells you to sit down and rest, you sit down.... And what's more, no back talk....

"This seems to be rather rough talk. And indeed it would be if applied to an educated mechanic or even intelligent laborer. With a man of the mentally sluggish type of Schmidt it is appropriate and not unkind, since it is effective in fixing his attention on the high wages which he wants and away from what, if it were called to his attention, he probably would consider impossibly hard work."[69]

Thus did Taylor himself immortalize the pig-iron episode. Despite its narrative effect, the Schmidt story was hardly representative of the full spectrum of Taylorite innovations that would come to be known as scientific management. There are, however, two aspects of the Schmidt story that are particularly puzzling: First, given the time and care Taylor devoted to his work, especially the metal-cutting experiments, how could he tolerate the cavalier arbitrariness of the rate-setting process in the Bethlehem yard? The day or two during which his assistants observed two men loading pig iron hardly constituted a systematic study.[70]

Second, it raises the question, as Sudhir Kakar, the author of a psychoanalytic analysis of Taylor, puts it, "How can Taylor's avowal of cooperation as the basic tenet of scientific management be reconciled with the authoritarian streak that dominates the story?"[71]

The answer, according to Kakar, is that Taylor never meant to eliminate authority—or even authoritarianism—from the factory, only the *arbitrary nature* of authority. Scientific management established rules and procedures, which would supplant whim and rules of thumb. Yet Taylor's depiction of Schmidt, even more than his assumption that only management—engineers or supervisors—could design the work process and establish rules, betrayed the full extent of his class prejudices.[72]

Though relatively little is known about Henry Noll, he fared considerably better than most of his coworkers—but not because he was the brainless drudge that Taylor had described. Though he was an immigrant at the lowest end of the labor scale, to be sure, he could read and write. Although he was known to be a womanizer and a heavy drinker, he jogged to keep fit. He also saved his earnings, and in 1899, even as Taylor used him in the pig-iron experiments, he bought a parcel of land and began to build a house during the few off-hours his job at Bethlehem afforded him. A small one-and-half-story clapboard structure, the house survived until 1960.[73]

More than a decade after the pig-iron experiments, when Congress had mounted an investigation of scientific management, Taylor's detractors spread rumors that Noll had died of overwork as a direct consequence of the experiments. To refute his critics, Taylor launched a search for Noll. The pig-iron handler was found in 1914, healthy and, according to A. B. Wadleigh, the man hired to find Noll, "able to do, and doing, a hard day's work, erect and active, looking as well as any man of his age (44 years)." In fact, Noll survived Taylor by several years.[74]

It is telling that in his congressional testimony, Taylor entirely reinvented the pig-iron episode, conveniently erasing the anger and acrimony that preceded "Schmidt's" convenient arrival on the scene. "[O]ne of the first requirements of scientific management is that no man shall ever be given a job which he cannot do and thrive under through a long term of years," he testified. "Of course certain men are permanent grouches and when we run across that kind we all know what to expect. But, in the main, they [the Bethlehem workers] were the most satisfied and contented set of laborers I have ever seen anywhere." Gone from his narrative was the revolt of the pig-iron handlers and the mass firings.[75]

Indeed, in Taylor's own mind the pig-iron experiments were a huge success. The number of yard laborers had been slashed from 600 to 140. Those who remained "constituted the finest body of picked laborers that [he had] ever seen together," according to Taylor. Those who didn't have the physical stamina, or who were simply unwilling to work at the breakneck pace prescribed by Taylor, had either quit or been fired.[76]

■

For all the attention the Schmidt story attracted, the differential piece rate was not Taylor's only, or even his main, innovation. His work at Bethlehem encompassed the full spectrum—and potential—of scientific management.

Not long after he had established new quotas for the pig-iron loaders, Taylor laid out his plans for simplifying foremen's jobs. At the time, highly skilled foremen were in short supply. Taylor's answer to this manpower shortage was to circumscribe the work of each foreman so that one man might have responsibility for large lathes, say, while another one was responsible for tool maintenance. In Taylor's new plant-floor bureaucracy, there would be speed bosses, gang bosses, quality bosses (or inspectors), and sometimes even repair bosses. By "de-skilling" the foremen's jobs, no single foreman needed to understand the entire range of supervisory work. Less experienced men could take on individual pieces of the work. One man might then be responsible for teaching workers how to run the machines, while another made sure the work was done in the proper sequence. Yet another foreman would be responsible for tool maintenance.[77]

Taylor also introduced an elaborate planning department that was responsible for coordinating the work of the foreman. The planning department helped to design work flow and conducted cost-accounting reviews. No materials in the plant could be moved without a written order from a recording clerk in the planning department. Nor could the work itself begin without a drawing and instruction card, which described the standardized tools, speed, and method with which a job had to be done; these were issued by the planning department's route clerk.[78]

Taylor had started by speeding up the work of particular workers and machines. He was now systematizing and standardizing entire factories. Large maps laid out the entire production flow in the Bethlehem machine shop. Standards even covered the penmanship and type of paper that were to be used for time cards and reports: block letters and brown and green forms, which ocular research showed were easiest on the eyes. Although functional foremanship would not survive, Taylor's efforts to systematize every facet of the manufacturing workplace have very much endured.

In 1903, two years after leaving Bethlehem, Taylor presented a paper called "Shop Management" at a gathering of the American Society of Mechanical Engineers that became the bible of the new philosophy. Its theme was the complete separation of thinking from doing. Its goal was to institute management control over the planning and execution of every facet of production.

The human cost of the new system was both clear to Taylor and worth the sacrifice. Testifying before Congress a decade after presenting "Shop Management," Taylor made a big show of the "intimate, close personal cooperation" that scientific management had created between management and labor, the "friendly, brotherly" helping hand extended by the supervisor to his worker.[79]

The reality he described in his famous paper was something quite different, however. Some men, Taylor acknowledged, would have "no place" in the factory of the future because they were either unable or unwilling to submit to the new "rigid" and "inflexible standards." He proposed using a combination of "force and persuasion" to achieve his aims.[80]

Nor was the unskilled laborer Taylor's chief target. "The potential of functional foremanship will not have been realized until almost all of the machines in the shop are run by men who are of smaller caliber and attainments, and who are therefore cheaper than those required under the old system," he wrote.[81]

To lull the more astute among the workers into submission, Taylor recommended that "[t]he first changes . . . should be such as to allay the suspicions of the men and convince them . . . that the reforms are after all rather harmless. . . . Such improvements, then, as directly affect the workmen least should be started first." For the best results, he recommended that routine work should be assigned to men whose "abilities are barely equal to the task."[82]

This, then, was a deliberate dumbing-down of work. "You are not supposed to think," he told his workers. "There are other men paid for thinking around here." What Taylor proposed was nothing less than what A. J. Portenar referred to as a "recindescence of feudalism" featuring a "generous, but arrogant overlord and his loyal and well-treated

but subservient vassals." The professional expert became the unassail-
able lord serving the whims of the kings of capital.[83]

Ironically, it was Taylor's own maverick nature, his unwillingness always to follow orders, and his need to pursue his creative instincts that
led to a collision with Bethlehem's management. The creative venture
to which he kept returning was high-speed tool steel, which turned out
to be one of his greatest innovations. "My head was full of wonderful
and great projects to simplify the processes, to design new machines, to
revolutionize the methods of the whole establishment," he wrote. "I was
devoting every minute of my spare time at home and on Sunday and entirely too much of my time at the works, to developing these wonderful
and great projects."[84]

At Bethlehem, Taylor had picked up where he had left off at Midvale.
Throughout 1899, even as the battles over the pig-iron experiments
raged, Taylor worked with Maunsel White, a Bethlehem metallurgist, on
the development of a superdurable tool steel. The Taylor-White process,
as it came to be known, would be hailed as "the most important advance" in the metallurgy of steel "since the invention of the Bessemer"
process. The cutting speed and durability that the process made possible even led some experts to contend that it "contribut[ed] to the
American victory in the First World War," since more durable tools
made it possible to produce as much as five times the quantity of mu-
nitions that could have been manufactured using conventional tools.[85]

The cutting speed made possible by the Taylor-White process fit perfectly with Taylor's interest in scientific management. With faster cutting
speeds, the time workers spent setting up their machine tools accounted
for a larger portion of the job—and offered the next clear opportunity for
improving efficiency. Then, too, Taylor needed a quicker way to calcu-
late the optimum cutting speed and feed for each job using the new
high-speed cutting tools. The solution came from Carl Barth, a mathe-
matician who, like Taylor, was a brilliant, stubborn individualist. Barth
developed a slide rule that could make Taylor's complex speed and feed
calculations in mere minutes. His innovation placed him among
Taylor's closest associates.

Barth's slide rule was one of the arsenal of tools and techniques that
became indispensable in Taylor's factory of the future and that further
separated the thinking of Taylor's foremen and planners from the doing
of the workers. With faster speeds made possible by the new tool steel
came a demand for greater electrification, bigger and stronger belts, and
more resilient machine parts. Faster machines left less room for error.[86]

Ironically, at Bethlehem the success of high-speed steel eventually
worked against Taylor. U.S. firms were beating a path to Bethlehem's

door, both to buy the rights to use the Taylor-White process and to witness the new Mecca of machine-shop practice. By 1901, foreign rights for the new technique had also been sold in more than half a dozen countries. Though Taylor retained a portion of the foreign rights, for several years it was Bethlehem that reaped the lion's share of the earnings from high-speed tool steel, which Taylor and White had patented in 1899.

Yet to Taylor's bosses at Bethlehem, work on high-speed steel was just another of his distractions from the day-to-day business of running the machine shop. His superiors were particularly irritated that he had been slow to introduce the differential piece rate outside the Bethlehem yard.[87]

Taylor's failure to introduce the differential rate was part of a larger problem. Despite the success of high-speed steel, the new slide rules that were wielded by a new cadre of planners, the functional foremen, and countless other innovations he introduced, which altogether had cost the company more than $1 million, the machines at Bethlehem frequently stood idle. "Do not see where the $1,100,000 went to in the last two years," wrote Robert Sayre, one of Bethlehem's owners. "Think the bringing of Taylor here . . . was and is a failure."[88]

In just two years, Taylor had succeeded in antagonizing both the workers and a large segment of the management at Bethlehem. The failure of his innovations to bear abundant fruit in the Bethlehem plants may well have been caused, at least in part, by deliberate sabotage on the part of workers. But workers weren't the only ones he succeeded in antagonizing.

The man who became known at Bethlehem as "Speedy" Taylor had a "genius for making enemies." Throughout his career, he was reviled by workers and had repeated fallings-out with his clients. In his confrontations at work, Taylor proved himself to be stubborn, vindictive, and confrontational. Even his wife, Louise, who suffered from numerous ailments during her marriage, experienced a seemingly miraculous recovery after his death. (Their children, whom he and Louise adopted relatively late in their marriage, were apparently the only ones with whom he seemed to enjoy a warm relationship.) Archibald Johnston, one of the few Bethlehem executives whom Taylor did not succeed in antagonizing, said of Taylor, "[M]any of the schemes proposed by Fred Taylor had a great deal of merit, [but] he personally did not seem to have the ability to carry them out in a reasonable time. This was due principally to the antagonistic methods used by him in handling men."[89]

For a man who demanded the unquestioning obedience of his workers, Taylor continuously chafed under the scrutiny of his own superiors.

On one occasion he showed up at an appointment with Robert Linderman, the president of Bethlehem, half an hour late, swinging a golf club and regaling the fuming executive with the details of his game. In the spring of 1901, just two years after Taylor came to Bethlehem, Linderman fired him.[90]

It is worth noting that Taylor's admirers were always able to make the distinction between the brilliance of his ideas and the tremendous problems with their implementation—problems that often were exacerbated by his difficult personality.

Bethlehem would be Taylor's last permanent job. In subsequent years, he worked primarily as a consultant and lecturer. In the decade after his departure from Bethlehem, two key events propelled him to national prominence.

First, in 1901, Taylor began to build an exquisite estate known as Boxly. He lavished all of his inventiveness on Boxly, experimenting with new types of grass and replanting the large boxwood hedges that filled the property and after which the estate had been named. On the recommendation of a trusted adviser, Taylor turned Boxly into a temple of scientific management from which he preached the gospel of Taylorism to a growing flock of followers.

The second event took place a decade later, when Taylor came to the attention of Louis Brandeis. At the time, the future Supreme Court justice was a liberal lawyer and consumer advocate fighting a famous case before the International Commerce Commission to prevent a rate hike by the railroad barons. Brandeis got his break when the preliminary hearings showed that the railroad executives didn't understand the cost structure of the railroads. He seized on this fact, together with the advances known to have been made by scientific management, to show that a rate hike wasn't justified. The railroads, he argued, couldn't demonstrate the need for higher rates because they had not done everything in their power—that is, used the new scientific management methods—to improve the efficiency of their operations.

There is considerable irony in the alliance between Brandeis, the "people's lawyer," as he was known, and Taylor, the blue-blooded father of scientific management. To be sure, Taylor's experience in the early 1890s running pulp mills for Manufacturing Investment Corp., an ambitious but ultimately unsuccessful paper-making venture that was financed by a consortium headed by William Collins Whitney, had made him a foe of big capital. In fundamental respects, however, Brandeis and Taylor were at opposite ends of the political and social spectrum.

Brandeis, the son of Jewish immigrants, was an ardent advocate of the workers' right to organize. At a time of heightened labor unrest and the violent suppression of union activity by big business, he came to play a pivotal role in domestic policy, especially labor reform, during the Wilson administration. Without industrial democracy, he maintained, political democracy was "a mockery." Industrial democracy demanded that employees have "the opportunity of participating in the decisions as to what shall be their conditions and how the business shall be run," he said. "What is the use of having industry if we die in producing it?"[91]

Brandeis's view of scientific management was shaped very much by Taylor himself, who took over Brandeis's education in the new science of management. Taylor helped to track down "Schmidt," proving that he was alive and kicking and had not, as rumor had it, been felled by overwork. Most significantly, perhaps, before the start of the ICC hearings, he arranged for Brandeis to tour Link-Belt, one of two small Philadelphia companies that had become showcases of scientific management, in part because they had avoided the labor unrest that had dogged Taylor elsewhere. Link-Belt, in particular, was decades ahead of most companies in applying what would later be called "humanistic management methods"—no thanks, however, to Taylor, who openly disagreed with the company's most labor-friendly measures!

Indeed, at no time is the disingenuousness of Taylor's attitude toward labor clearer than in his calculated cultivation of Brandeis. While Taylor worked assiduously to improve the image of scientific management and to downplay what, from labor's perspective, were the harsher elements of his system, he never went beyond appearances. At no time did he acknowledge any of labor's grievances.

Thus, Taylor touted Link-Belt not because he agreed with the company's labor policies, which were so different from Bethlehem's, but because they served his public relations purposes. He regaled Brandeis with lengthy correspondence on the benefits of scientific management, showing that "under scientific management the employees of our companies are happy and contented, and on the most friendly terms with their employers." He even compiled statistics to show "how few of the employees of one or two of our companies leave their employment."[92]

One letter, in particular, a seven-page paean to the benefits of scientific management, cites a self-serving list of the salutary "effects" of scientific management, including "Orderliness, Neatness, Cleanliness . . . Temperance, Comfort, Happiness . . . Faithfulness . . . Democratization . . . Honesty . . . Morality . . . Loyalty to and confidence in the management."[93]

By tapping Taylor and the scientific management movement in his fight against the railroads, Brandeis succeeded both in winning the ICC case and in bringing fame to both Taylor and scientific management. Even before the ICC turned down the request for a rate increase—though not explicitly because of the scientific methods Brandeis advocated—scientific management had made big news. "The testimony of the 'efficiency' witnesses opened the whole matter of American effectiveness in the use of capital, of labor, of materials, and of time," declared *The American Machinist* in an editorial at the time. Wrote Ray Stannard Baker, a leading "muckraker," before the hearings, "Few of those present . . . had ever even heard of scientific management or of Mr. Taylor, its originator. . . . The effect of the insertion of the scientific management argument into the rate hearings contest was felt almost instantaneously by the whole country."[94]

In the ensuing months, journalists flocked to Boxly. When Taylor was ready to publish his famous treatise *The Principles of Scientific Management*, it was serialized in *American Magazine*, a leading organ of the Progressive movement, the journalistic home of such muckrakers as Baker and Ida Tarbell.[95]

Even as Brandeis and the *American Magazine* series bathed Taylor in the luminous glow of progressivism, opponents cast him in a harsher light. Upton Sinclair, author of *The Jungle*, a fictional exposé of the meatpacking industry, wrote this response to the first installment of the *American Magazine* series on Taylor: "I shall not forget the picture which he gave us . . . of the poor old laborer who was trying to build his pitiful little home after hours, and who was induced to give 362 per cent more service for 61 per cent more pay."[96]

Organized labor also took up the Taylor challenge. Protesting the use of Taylorism in government installations, including arsenals and shipyards, labor leaders charged that Taylor's "insidious system . . . reduced men to virtual slavery and low wages." To protest the introduction of scientific management, in August 1911 workers at the Watertown, Massachusetts, government arsenal went out on strike. The arsenal, which both stored and manufactured weapons, was considered one of the most inefficient facilities of its kind.[97]

The Watertown Arsenal strike prompted a full-blown congressional investigation by the "House Committee on the Taylor and Other Systems of Management" that began on October 4, 1911. It was, as its title implies, an investigation of Taylorism itself.

Once again, Taylor mustered all the ammunition he could in defense of scientific management. He urged Representative William Redfield, who was one of the most sympathetic members of the congressional committee investigating scientific management, to come to Philadelphia. He was "very anxious to go through both the Tabor Co.

and the Link-Belt works," he told Redfield, and to introduce him "to a number of the workmen."[98]

Taylor also pressed manufacturers, including Henry Towne and executives at Bethlehem and Midvale, to testify. When they balked, not wanting to antagonize labor by testifying on Taylor's behalf, the father of scientific management would not take no for an answer. "We are at peace now with our employees and with organized labor, and do not wish to be drawn into any controversy with either," pleaded Towne. "May I have your assurance that you will not call on us in this way." Taylor responded by bringing the investigators to Towne's doorstep in Stamford, Connecticut.[99]

Throughout Taylor's testimony, Taylor demonstrated his own disingenuousness. While making a compelling case that increased productivity could, by lowering the cost of goods, create greater demand and employment, he shed an entirely false light on the role he envisioned for the workingman in the modern factory. In the rosy picture he painted of factory life under Taylorism, he testified, "Perhaps the greatest gain . . . accrued to the workmen who have been working under scientific management." It was "not the increase in wages received by the workmen" that represented the greatest benefit of scientific management, he said, "but the fact that those who are working under scientific management have come to look upon their employers as their *best friends*" [author's emphasis].[100]

Taylor quickly compounded the hubris of this assertion with a flight of pure fancy. To underscore the happy state of workers under scientific management, he asserted that "during the 30 years that scientific management has been gradually developed . . . there has never been a single strike of employees working under scientific management—never one in all the 30 years in which it has been used." The revolt and firing of the pig-iron handlers was conveniently forgotten, as was the Bethlehem Steel machinists' strike of 1910. A year before his death, Taylor boasted to Ida Tarbell that scientific management was still alive and well at the company; indeed, the iron and steelmaker continued to purchase more stopwatches for time study than any company but Link-Belt.[101]

William B. Wilson, congressman from Pennsylvania and the chairman of the commission, didn't buy Taylor's arguments: "The fact that no strikes have occurred does not prove anything as to the private relationship between employer and employee. . . . Isn't it also true," he asked, "that peaceful relations almost invariably exist between master and slave, that no strikes occur?"[102]

Rather than acknowledge that at least some labor problems remained unresolved, Taylor evaded every attempt to pin him down. In response to a question about how scientific management proposed to take care of displaced workers, such as the pig-iron handlers who had been fired, he embarked on an elaborate evasion of the issue. On the subject of dislocation, Taylor replied, "[I]n those establishments in which scientific management has been introduced there is not a single case that I can recall in which, after scientific management was introduced, there were less men employed than before. . . . Sometimes many of the men who under the old system of management were workmen have been transferred from the working side to the management side, you understand, and in that case there may have been fewer workmen employed. . . . But in this case the men who formerly did the work with their hands have been transferred to the management side, they have become teachers, guiders, and helpers. However, I do not think I can mention a single case in which there have been fewer men employed. . . .

"[I]n nine hundred and ninety-nine cases out of a thousand it has been our practice to have the workman cooperate with us in the most friendly manner." (In fact, while some of the most skilled workmen were promoted from the laboring ranks to management, the number of recalcitrant workers fired by Taylor himself numbered in the hundreds, if not thousands.)[103]

Taylor was especially evasive on the fate of workers he did not deem to be "first-class." Said Wilson, "You said a 'first-class' workman can be taken care of under normal conditions. That is what you have already said. Now, the other class that is in your mind, other than 'first class,' how does your system propose to take care of them?"

"I cannot answer that question," Taylor replied, not until "you know my definition of that term."

"My question has nothing whatever to do with the definition of the words 'first class.' It has to do with the other class than 'first-class,' not with 'first class.' "[104]

And so the debate raged, until finally Taylor, digging in his heels, was allowed to give his definition of a "first-class" worker. Resorting to his favorite metaphor—a telling one, at that—he compared choosing first-class workers to picking a good workhorse: "We will all agree that a good, big dray horse is a 'first-class' horse to haul a coal wagon. . . . I mean that there are big powerful men suited to heavy work, just as dray horses are suited to the coal wagon, and I would not use a man who would be 'first-class' for this heavy work to do light work for which he would be second-class, and which could be just as well done by a boy who is first-class for this work, and vice versa. . . . For each man some line can be found in which he is first-class. There is work for each type of man, just, as for instance, there is work for the dray horse and work for the trotting horse."[105]

Of course, he acknowledged, there was a particularly pernicious sort of " 'second-class' horse." Among the " 'first-class' big dray horses that are hauling coal wagons you will find a few of them that will balk, a few of them that can haul, but won't haul. You will find a few of these dray horses that are absolutely lazy . . .

"Scientific management," he continued, mixing his metaphors, had "no place for a bird that can sing and won't sing."[106]

Wilson, pointing out that there were as many as 4 million unemployed workers in the United States at any given time, making it one of the biggest social problems of the day, remained unconvinced. "We are not in this particular investigation dealing with horses nor singing birds, but we are dealing with men who are a part of society and for whose benefit society is organized."[107]

Three years later, A. J. Portenar voiced similar objections to the "first-class" men of Taylor's conception: "Always you speak of first-class men. More than once you say, let others go elsewhere. But if your system were general, where else could they go?

"For men in the mass are not first class. If they were they would all be in one class and there could be no such distinction. There *is* such a thing as an average man, and an average day's work for that man."[108]

The hearings, however, produced little more than a "toothless" condemnation of Taylorism. While the report declared that "[n]either the Taylor system nor any other should be imposed from above on an unwilling work force . . . [a]ny system of shop management ought to be the result of . . . mutual consent," it also reaffirmed key aspects of scientific management, including standardization and motion study. While the committee concluded that time study should not be done without the consent of workmen, it stopped short of explicit condemnation or of advocating legislation to ban stopwatches, for example.[109]

■

Indeed, no amount of criticism or congressional scrutiny could slow the engine of scientific management. Since 1904, pilgrims had been flocking to Boxly, where they listened to an hours-long lecture by Taylor. The culmination of the Boxly experience was a visit to two small companies, Tabor Manufacturing and Link-Belt, which were not only ardent converts to scientific management but also showcases of success. It was to Tabor and Link-Belt that Taylor took not only Louis Brandeis but journalists, congressmen, university professors, and any union leaders he thought he could win over to his cause.

Taylor made it clear that he insisted on exercising as much authority over his clients as he did over foremen and factory workers: "[F]or many years past, I never undertook to systematize a company unless I was absolutely sure that the owners of the company *wanted* scientific management, and *wanted it very badly.* . . .

"I invariably made a clear-cut bargain with them that whenever there was a conflict of opinion between themselves and myself as to what details should or should not be used in introducing the new system of management, *my* decision must be final."[110]

In retrospect, it is telling that Taylorism's two poster children were among the companies where Taylor had the least personal contact with the rank and file. As a result, while in important respects they were models of scientific management, both avoided the harshest elements of Taylorism.

Taylor's connection to Tabor began in 1903, when Tabor found itself in financial trouble and Taylor agreed to invest $20,000 to shore up the company. As a condition of his investment, he demanded that Tabor's owner, Wilfred Lewis, introduce scientific management. Busy with Boxly and enjoying the affluence that came from his inheritance and the investments he had made over the years, Taylor was free from having to work on the factory floor. Instead, he recommended that Tabor hire Carl Barth, who would have primary responsibility for introducing scientific management at the company. (Indeed, though he continued to teach and to lecture until the end of his life, after 1901 he refused to accept any remuneration from his clients.)

The innovations introduced by Barth and Horace K. Hathaway, another Taylor disciple, were in many respects a textbook recipe of the best practices of scientific management. The Taylorites systematized tool and machine maintenance, organized a planning department, trained functional foremen and speed and gang bosses, and introduced time study and incentive pay.

With the help of scientific management, Tabor recovered from its financial troubles. The company broke even by 1906, thanks in large part to cost reductions. For several more decades, the systems introduced by the Taylorites helped Tabor stave off growing competition by larger firms with more modern facilities.[111]

Tabor enjoyed another key benefit that, despite the labor unrest that followed Taylor everywhere, like a cloud of dust, seemed to correlate with the introduction of scientific management. Although Tabor had had a history of labor problems before the introduction of Taylorism, the company experienced none of the resistance that Taylor had encountered at Bethlehem. When a citywide machinists' strike rocked Philadelphia in 1910, only one Tabor employee walked off the job.[112]

To understand the unusually long hiatus in labor unrest at Tabor, it helps to know what was happening at Link-Belt at the same time. The experiences at Link-Belt and Tabor were identical in several respects. Barth served as principal consultant to both companies. The innovations he introduced were similar. And the work began at both companies almost simultaneously, in 1903. It is safe to assume that what Barth learned while he consulted with one company, he applied to the other.

As Barth set about attempting to turn around the operations at Tabor, he would certainly have been aware of the one key characteristic that set Link-Belt apart from not only Tabor but also most manufacturing operations at the time: at Link-Belt, scientific management was introduced *after* James Mapes Dodge, the company's president and an early proponent of welfare capitalism, had made a host of what were, for the time, groundbreaking efforts at improving labor-management relations.

Dodge, who had gotten to know Taylor through the Unitarian Society and had first been attracted to his metal-cutting innovations, had a reputation as "a benevolent employer whose men were well paid and contented." Long before Barth arrived on the scene, Dodge had guaranteed piece-rate workers against rate cutting. He had also established procedures by which workers had "unheard-of opportunities" for "venting personal grievances and discussing the affairs of the company with the higher officers."[113] L. P. Alford, an official with the American Society of Mechanical Engineers, wrote that the Link-Belt management had made "a deliberate attempt to arrange shop conditions [so] that the men would find their work not only profitable but pleasant."[114]

Although Dodge was against unionization, he resorted to none of the suppressive tactics that were common among businesses at the time. When his workers finally decided to organize in the 1890s, he insisted that they go on strike if ordered to do so by the union. "If you would break faith with the union, can you be trusted to keep it with me?" he said. This attitude "so disarmed the union militants," according to Daniel Nelson, that efforts to organize at Link-Belt collapsed. Then, in 1915, over Taylor's objections, Link-Belt launched a company union, which was meant to encourage the workers "to take an interest in the determination of base rates and piece rates."[115]

Dodge even went so far as to attempt to temper Taylor's fervent antiunionism. In a letter to Taylor written in January 1915, shortly before Taylor's death, Dodge wrote, "I think our side of the question could be stated much more concisely and that there is a lot of irritating matter in our statements that could be left out to very good advantage. I refer, among other things, to the three or four references to 'Soldiering.' You know I have never been in sympathy with making a feature of this, and I think it is especially unfortunate that we should try to make any use of it in the present crisis. It is looked upon by all the Unionists as a general insult to all American workingmen and it makes them mad every time they run across it, and whether it be true or not it will give us no possible benefit."

He continued, "[U]ntil the two sides to this controversy can decide on the human unit we are talking about all other questions can be left unanswered [sic] there is no use of the tons of testimony being taken when the fundamental questions are not touched upon. . . .

"I believe that it would be perfectly possible to harmonize Scientific Management with Trade Unionism if an earnest effort were made by *both parties* [author's emphasis]."[116]

Dodge acknowledged that many aspects of scientific management, including the rate-setting process, were matters of "human judgment" and not particularly scientific. By 1915, he decided to allow a shop committee to help establish the rate-setting process, a proposal that Taylor advised against strongly. "I think you are making a great mistake in doing this," Taylor wrote. "[H]aving these shop committees would only have the effect of stimulating your men in the direction of trades [sic] unionism."[117]

Thus, when Barth arrived at Link-Belt in 1903, he encountered little of the distrust of and antipathy to new ideas he had met at Bethlehem. What is clear is that Barth's innovations, which included improvements in the maintenance and handling of machinery and the introduction of functional foremen, were introduced slowly, over a two-year period. At Link-Belt, there was none of the slapdash upheaval there had been at the Bethlehem yard. Perhaps guided by Dodge's conciliatory influence, Barth went to unusual lengths to prepare the Link-Belt workers for the changes ahead. The men who would work under the functional foremen were "taken into the superintendent's office and talked to by me personally in the presence of three functional foremen," he reported. "I set forth the whole principle on which we proposed to treat them in the future." The men cooperated and were given bonuses.[118]

As at Tabor, the results at Link-Belt were impressive. By 1910, costs plunged by 20 percent, output per worker doubled, and workers' average pay increased 25 to 30 percent.[119]

In subsequent years, Taylor's defenders often cited Link-Belt and

Tabor to refute the dehumanizing image of scientific management. Significantly, Louis Brandeis gleaned his eyewitness view of scientific management from a visit to Link-Belt just before the ICC hearings.[120] What few recognized, however, was that the success of scientific management at Link-Belt—and to a lesser degree at Tabor—was due in large measure to the groundwork that had been laid by management in winning the trust of the rank and file. This groundwork was utterly lacking at most companies that embraced Taylorism.

Among the visitors to Boxly—and hence one of the early recipients of the Tabor and Link-Belt success stories—were two emissaries from Harvard. Wallace C. Sabine, dean of Harvard's Graduate School of Applied Science, and Edwin Gay, the first dean of the fledgling Harvard Business School, sought out Taylor before launching HBS in 1908. The academics were initially reticent about Taylorism, in large part because of Taylor's hostility even to the need for an undergraduate education. Before the visit from Harvard's emissaries, Taylor had told the Harvard Engineering Society that he had "ceased to hire any young college graduates until they [had] been 'dehorned' by some other employer."[121]

Indeed, long after he had developed a close working relationship with HBS, Taylor, in several letters to Edwin Gay, insisted that demanding a college degree as a prerequisite for business school made as much sense as stipulating that M.B.A. students "should have taken a course in medicine or law." As he put it, "[T]he man who has spent too many years in getting a college education and has been removed for too great a length of time from actual practical every-day hard work, is highly unlikely to make good in this profession. . . . If any one entrance requirement is demanded," he insisted, it should be experience working as "heads of departments or as business managers of some sort."[122]

However, the Harvard men soon became enthusiastic Taylorites. "Beginning with . . . a very vague idea of your work, I found myself more and more persuaded of the very real problem that you are solving and the fact that it is a problem capable of surprisingly exact solution," wrote Sabine after his visit to Boxly. "[W]hile listening to you . . . I am persuaded that you are on the track of the only reasonable solution of a great sociological problem. The systematization and standardization of work has a bearing far beyond the organization of a particular business or industry." Taylor, Sabine believed, was about to uncover the "solution of a problem on which socialistic and cooperative movements have time after time been wrecked."[123]

Shortly after HBS opened its doors in September 1908, Dean Gay organized a course on industrial management that featured luminaries of the systematic management movement, a precursor of scientific management, which applied cost-accounting principles to every facet of production. Chief among the speakers was Taylor. The lectures on scientific management were the "capstone" of the course. While there were those at Harvard who were skeptical of a management system "whose advocates . . . made such extravagant claims as to their efficiency," Gay backed Taylor wholeheartedly. In 1911, the school launched a second-year laboratory course at the Rindge Manual Training School, a technical school in Cambridge, where six hundred students would be furnished with "proper instruction" under the direction of three Taylor disciples, Barth, Hathaway, and Cooke. About this time, another Taylorite, Sanford Thompson, was also hired to teach a course in industrial organization at HBS. Gay also petitioned Taylor to join the Harvard faculty. "Could you by any possibility . . . come here next year and join our staff in the Business School, taking charge of the advanced course in scientific management?" he wrote. Taylor declined.[124]

That may have been a good thing. The college-educated Harvard men were not as easily won over to Taylor's assertions as other audiences were. For one thing, several of the Harvard students took issue with the questionable production quotas of the pig-iron experiments, protesting that "it was impossible to handle pig iron at the rate of 47 tons per day." Taylor responded by adamantly defending his figures, invariably concluding his arguments with a specious anecdote about the 80- to 125-pound loads he had carried during camping trips through the Adirondacks as a young man.[125]

Nor did the students take well to Taylor's monologues, which typically lasted 2.5 hours. At the beginning of 1912, Taylor asked his nephew Franklin Taylor Clark, who was a Harvard student at the time, what the students thought about his uncle's lectures. "Several of them say that they did not get much from your lectures due to the fact that they were a repetition of what you say in your book," Clark responded, noting that the students wanted more time to ask questions and, presumably, to debate his ideas and conclusions. "You must remember, Uncle Fred, that the Universities of the country play an important part in forwarding all progressive movements. . . . [I]t is through them that progressive ideas . . . are to a considerable extent imparted to the people at large."[126]

In 1914, HBS dropped its first-year course on scientific management, a move that reflected both student disinterest and the mounting public backlash against Taylorism. "[T]he reaction against efficiency and the 'scientific' ideas is already setting in," wrote Archibald W. Shaw to Dean Gay. Shaw was the founder of *System*, one of the country's first business magazines, which later became *Business Week*.[127]

■

Whatever backlash Taylor experienced, it was temporary. Taylorism was one of those rare phenomena that recognized neither geographic borders nor ideologies. From the United States and France to India and eastern Europe, scientific management came to be universally embraced throughout the world. That Germans, with their ingrained respect for efficiency and order, should have embraced Taylorism is not surprising. But even Lenin, shortly after Taylor's death, came under the spell of scientific management, embracing the new system as the great hope for modernizing Russian industry.

If American management became a global standard, it was due in large part to the foundations laid by Taylor. The Ford assembly line was a logical extension of Taylor's efforts at breaking down and systematizing individual factory jobs and work processes. His greatest contribution to management was that he brought a scientific outlook and systematic analysis to industry. Without Taylorism, large-scale mass production would have been impossible.

Taylorism also hardened the battle lines between management and labor. Ironically, it also catalyzed a reaction to scientific management in the form of the motivational techniques and democratic, collaborative philosophies that began to be developed soon after Taylor's death by Elton Mayo at Harvard and Mary Parker Follett, respectively. It would take decades to chip away at the distrust and hierarchy that characterize the modern corporation and that continue to bedevil management to this day.

Indeed, well into the twentieth century, as new approaches to scientific management have continued to be developed, they have almost all precluded a more inclusive, collaborative relationship with the rank and file. The analytical techniques that Robert McNamara and the Whiz Kids borrowed from the Air Force helped save Ford Motor Company but also aggravated the divisions within the company, with devastating results in the 1970s and 1980s. Reengineering is the most recent divisive legacy of Taylorism.

The tragedy of Taylorism and its influence on American life and the workplace is that neither Taylor nor many of his followers recognized his most serious shortcoming: he failed to see that a factory—like a corporation—is as much a social system as an agglomeration of machines. The secret ingredient in the success of scientific management at companies such as Tabor and Link-Belt—the cooperation of labor—was never fully acknowledged by either Taylor or his heirs.

Only so far as business leaders and administrators can identify themselves with the underlying social impulses of their time can they hope to plan and build great organizations. They must be in accord not only with the interests of their stockholders, the desires of their consumers and the temper of their workers, but also with the deep flowing currents of opinion which are shaping the society of the future. It is because Mary Follett's philosophy of organization opens up the possibility of such an identification that it is the most important contribution to the business literature of our time.

—Colonel Lyndall Urwick, "The Problem of Organization: A Study of the Work of Mary Parker Follett"[1]

Mary Parker Follett

The Mother of Postscientific Management

Mary Parker Follett may be the most obscure of the capitalist philosophers. Yet in her day she was a friend of and adviser to the leading pioneers of so-called welfare capitalism, among them the retailer William Filene and the noted East Coast manufacturer Henry Dennison. She was one of the earliest and strongest advocates of collaborative, participative approaches to management and cross-functional problem solving. She also argued that true authority and leadership are a function of an individual's knowledge and experience, not his rank in a corporate hierarchy.

In U.S. corporate circles, Follett's name receded after World War II, though it never completely disappeared. Meanwhile, the Japanese, those indefatigable excavators of American management treasures, rediscovered her during their efforts to rebuild war-torn Japan. Most remarkably, perhaps, her name appeared in General Electric's four-volume management bible among those of a small cadre of apostles, including Frederick Winslow Taylor and Peter Drucker, who helped influence the company's historic restructuring in the mid-1950s. Her work remained an important touchstone for Douglas McGregor (see Chapter 6) throughout his life. It continues to be read by industrial psychologists and sociologists.

In 1995, when her essays were republished in *Mary Parker Follett: The Prophet of Management,* she was embraced as a long-lost soul mate by such management experts as Peter Drucker, Rosabeth Moss Kanter, and Warren Bennis, who calls her "a swashbuckling advance scout of management thinking." Outside the boundaries of the corporation, new ideas in "democratic experimentalism" that draw on the work of Follett and are designed to revive a more participative form of government at the local level are finding new advocates among legislative reformers.[2]

■

It is significant that Mary Parker Follett came to the study of organizations as an expert in democratic government. Follett rose to prominence, first as a political scientist and later as an oracle of modern management, in the years immediately following the death of Frederick Winslow Taylor. At a time when a brawny, mindless "Schmidt" still represented management's idea of a model worker and violent battles between labor and management still raged, she brought a passion for democracy and citizenship, as well as twenty years of experience in grassroots organizing, to the practice of management.

A tall, thin reed of a woman, Follett emerged on the American management scene in the 1920s and came to be embraced by the most forward-looking management thinkers of her time, many of them admirers of scientific management. Yet two more different thinkers than Taylor and Follett cannot be imagined. If Taylor was the father of scientific management, Follett was the mother of a more behavioral, postscientific approach to managing human organizations. During the decade before her death, she would pioneer ideas such as constructive conflict resolution, participative management, and flatter organizations. "Follett was, no doubt, the first modern management thinker to propose a mode of organization that could serve as an alternative to the traditional bureaucratic hierarchy," notes Nitin Nohria, an associate professor of organizational behavior at Harvard Business School. Wrote Eduard C. Lindeman shortly after her death, "[S]he went straight toward the most perplexing problem, the persistent conflict between a willful individualism and a compulsive, although uncreative, collectivism."[3]

An intellectual Renaissance woman, Follett's studies both at Harvard and in Cambridge, England, took her on an unlikely journey from the ivory tower to the mean streets of east Boston and finally gained her an advisory role in the executive suite. Although her academic credentials were in political science, she had also discovered the work of the Utopian philosophers and the pioneers of psychology and had become an early advocate of group dynamics.

But Follett was not merely an ivory-tower theorist. What lent her work and ideas particular power was that they emerged as a direct result of her career as a social activist and her deep-rooted commitment to democratic values. She had "tested over and over again in the rough-and-tumble of American cities this belief of hers that everyone has something to contribute to the national life," eulogized a former Cambridge classmate on the occasion of her death in 1933. During a period closer in time and sentiment to the Civil War than the civil rights era, Follett argued that diversity of ideas and of people held the key to creativity, that "real democracy has as much to do with the representation of minorities as majorities." A 1912 committee report of the Women's Municipal League of Boston, which under Follett's leadership had just won the right to use public school facilities for after-school recreation and evening classes to serve teenage laborers, foreshadowed Follett's philosophy: "The test of any civilization is where to put its centre of consciousness. . . . The glory of our day is that we are learning to put it not in the individual, or in a group of the strong or of the clever, or even in the majority, but in the Whole."[4]

The greatest testament to the power of Follett's personality and her ideas is that despite her gender and her dedication to social reform, she had a profound impact on several of the era's leading management thinkers. These included Lyndall Urwick, the pioneering British management consultant; Henry Dennison, who was, ironically, also a disciple of Taylor—albeit one who parted company with Taylor on the subject of organized labor, and Chester Barnard, whose *Functions of the Executive* was for decades the bible of executive leadership. "I cannot explain that strange charm of hers. It worked with everybody—Haldane of Cloan, Professor Harold Laski . . . the tram conductor, the girl behind the counter," recalled Urwick. "I think it was her absolute intellectual sincerity and her vivid interest in how other people worked and thought." It was that "charm" that enabled Follett to "influence the influencers," as Pauline Graham put it in her introduction to *Mary Parker Follett: The Prophet of Management.*[5]

■

By any standard, Follett was an uncommon woman for her time. Though she was always secretive about her family and her past, the roots of her zeal for civic life can be traced back to her childhood in Quincy, Massachusetts, just outside Boston. The descendant of pilgrims who had come over on the *Mayflower,* Follett grew up in the stately white Georgian house that belonged to her maternal grandfather, Daniel Baxter. A self-made man with interests in whaling, banking, and retailing and vast local real estate holdings, Baxter made a home for his daughter and her children after Mary's father died prematurely, when she was just a teenager.

Charles Allen Follett played a pivotal role in fostering his daughter's personality and ambitions. Mary and her father adored each other, according to Harriet Mixter, a girlhood friend who was enrolled with Mary at the Thayer Academy, a prestigious prep school in nearby South Braintree, and who frequently visited the Follett household. Charles took great pride in his daughter's intelligence, boasting to his friends about her ability to do mental arithmetic.[6] As a child, Mary shared her father's religious devotion; Charles Follett was so devout that one of Mary's childhood friends assumed he was a minister. Follett's actual profession isn't known; he is referred to by some as a skilled tradesman and by others as a mechanic.[7] Religion remained important to Follett throughout her life, though she revealed her spiritual leanings only to those she thought would understand them. Father and daughter also looked alike: tall and gaunt, with blue eyes and brown hair tinged with red.

Charles Follett's death left his daughter isolated both within the family and from her peers. Mary's mother, Elizabeth Curtis Baxter Follett, was, by some accounts, interested more in clothes and society than in either religion or her children. Mary's brother, George, extolled his mother for her "brilliant mind," business acumen, and wide-ranging interests; "under different circumstances or, say, in a different age, [she] would have been known for her mind," he said of her.[8]

Whatever Elizabeth Follett's frustrated ambitions may have been, of her two children, she almost certainly favored her son. "[T]here was little sympathy between her and Mary," recalled Mixter. On one occasion when two girlfriends visited Mary and they spent the afternoon reading *Tess of the d'Urbervilles* aloud to one another, Elizabeth Follett came into the room, looking "tall, pallid, peevish and artificial." She seemed "very alien to all our interest," recalled one of Mary's friends.[9]

Soon after Charles's death, Elizabeth Follett became a "nervous invalid," and many of the burdens of caring for her and the household fell on Mary. For a time, Mary even assumed responsibility for her mother's investments.[10] "She used to watch her school companions going off swimming or skating while she had to hurry home to take care of her mother and her younger brother," wrote Dame Katherine Furse, Follett's close friend and companion. One of the few people whom Follett became close to as a teenager, was Anne Boynton Thompson, a teacher at the Thayer Academy, who kindled in Follett an interest in philosophy and scientific method.[11]

Of the threesome that was left after Charles's death, Mary clearly came to feel like the interloper. While George remembers his sister fondly as always having been "very kind," even after she left home, brother and sister were "no more alike than peanuts and peas," according to George's son, Stephen. "My father was one of those who dreamed of home and children, while Mary cut her ties here and led a scholarly life."[12]

Mary's departure for college represented almost literally an escape from Quincy—both from her mother and from the lifestyle her hometown represented. For one thing, she did not begin her undergraduate studies until she was twenty years old, several years after having graduated from the Thayer Academy. The intervening years were almost certainly spent in the service of her mother. After she did finally leave home, Stephen Follett remembers, his aunt visited Quincy no more than a dozen times in his lifetime. Although she corresponded with her nephew until the end of her life, her contacts with her mother were, as often as not, through go-betweens.[13]

Even with her closest friends, Follett almost never spoke of her past or of her family. After her death, Katherine Furse and Henry Dennison corresponded about the difficulty involved in making contact with Follett's relatives. "You cannot imagine what relief it was to get your letter of October 11th, giving me Mr. Stephen Follett's address," Furse wrote to Dennison. "[Mary] spoke of him once or twice, but never in a way to make me realize that she was in close touch with him. . . . Mary always inferred [sic] that she did not want her brother brought into anything."[14]

Follett's unconventional life undoubtedly played a role in her estrangement from her family. Had her father lived, he might have endorsed the ambitions of his intellectual daughter. It isn't clear what Follett's mother and brother thought of her plans for attending college, her subsequent career as an intellectual and social worker, and her failure to marry. However, it is hardly likely that a woman of Mrs. Follett's social ambitions would have approved of her daughter's life.

In Boston, Follett joined a group of maverick young women at the Society for the Collegiate Instruction of Women by Professors and Other Instructors at Harvard, what was then still known as "The Annexe." Though it was not yet formally affiliated with Harvard, the Annexe became Radcliffe College before she graduated. In 1890, she took a year off to attend Newnham College in Cambridge, England. And sometime before graduating summa cum laude in 1898, she also studied in Paris.[15]

At the Annexe, Follett came under the influence of Professor Albert Bushnell Hart, with whom she took the equivalent of ten semesters of history. Her first book, *The Speaker of the House*, on the functions of the Speaker in the U.S. House of Representatives, started out as a required thesis for a two-semester history course taught by Bushnell.[16]

Follett's thesis foreshadowed the pragmatism and care that she would bring to her intellectual interests and endeavors. Her book was meticulously researched. Although she was still a college student and a woman to boot, she even sought out and interviewed several former congressmen and congressional speakers for her study. After its publication, *The Speaker* won the praises of, among others, Teddy Roosevelt, who said that she "understood the operation of Congress a great deal better than Woodrow Wilson." This was high praise, indeed, since Wilson's *Congressional Government* was considered a classic that continued to be read for decades after he wrote it in 1883.[17]

However, it was Follett's year of study in England that nurtured her interests in philosophy and psychology, as well as politics and literature, and gave her intellectual ambitions distinct form. It was at the Historical Society at Newnham that she presented her first paper on the research that eventually became her thesis. Throughout her life, the friendships she made during her year abroad kept drawing her back to England.

Also at Cambridge, Follett, who was fluent in both German and French, became enamored with German idealism, a philosophy that, during the nineteenth century, had a strong influence on many American intellectuals, including Woodrow Wilson. However, not long after her stay in Cambridge, German idealism, with its veneration of the cameralist state, which advocated a centralized economy and a strong public administration, would begin to lose its appeal for many Americans. In Germany, philosophical idealism became the ideological foundation of totalitarianism. In turn-of-the-century America, meanwhile, it was superseded by a more pragmatic ideology encompassed by the Progressives.[18]

Follett's belief in the importance of organizations in a modern democracy was, in fact, perfectly in tune with the World War I era. Woodrow Wilson's own administration was characterized by the search for a way to "graft efficient . . . cameralist-style administration" onto an American political system that prized individualism. One solution backed by Wilson and other reformers was the cultivation of a new cadre of administrators, who were expected to replace the corrupt influences of political bosses and the robber barons. (Although these administrative "aristocrats" often came from humble beginnings, they hardly represented the working-class values that Follett would have encountered among the young people she was organizing in east Boston.) America's victory during World War I owed everything to the unprecedented levels of collaboration between business and government, a level of administrative coordination without which the massive military mobilization of World War I would not have been possible. Throughout the 1920s, professional administrators in government, universities, philanthropies, and research centers were seen as the guardians of the nation's social and economic agenda. And during the crisis of the Depression, even as big business was discredited in many respects, its principles were adapted and applied "to the structure of government itself," most notably in the creation of regulatory agencies such as the Securities and Exchange Commission (see Chapter 3).[19]

Long after leaving England, Follett remained in many respects a romantic and a utopian—albeit one grounded in the practicalities of commerce and politics. Back in Boston, however, she gradually parted company with the Wilsonians. Instead, she came under the influence of Walter Lippmann and John Dewey, who stressed the importance of political participation at the community level and the inclusion of as broad and diverse a constituency as possible in decision making. Dewey's mantra, which would be adopted by Follett and other like-minded progressives, was that "humankind must perpetually act in an experimental fashion in order to survive and flourish."[20] For these thinkers, modern industry created the opportunity for "a vast experiment in cooperation."

Follett took to heart the dicta of experimentalism and participative democracy. No nineteenth-century individualist, she believed that true freedom came through the participation of each individual in civic life and civic institutions. "Follett's ideas presaged the approach to welfare capitalism taken by progressive employers in the 1920s," wrote Sanford M. Jacoby, author of *Modern Manors: Welfare Capitalism Since the New Deal.* "The notion was to develop an industrial community, a Gemeinschaft, that would be an alternative to Taylorized bureaucracy and to market contractualism."[21] Decades before Elton Mayo wrote *Human Problems of an Industrial Civilization,* Follett was concerned with the social costs of industrialization (see Chapter 4).

Unlike Mayo and other intellectuals (including Dewey), Follett stepped out of the academy and into the streets to see what she could do. Many of her friends expected her to pursue an academic career. Instead, she became an activist. Perhaps she knew that as a woman she would have difficulty making her way in an elite academic institution, the only sort of university position that would have interested her. Or perhaps she simply wanted to put her ideas to work.

Whatever her reasons, no sooner had she graduated from Radcliffe than she became involved with "social work" in Roxbury, a neighborhood that was then part of Boston's notorious Seventeenth Ward. At the time, Roxbury teemed with teenage laborers, many of them fresh from the countryside, who had no place to go after work. Recognizing that the young people she encountered in Roxbury were "not prepared for life . . . for their industrial life, their home life, their social life, [or] their civic life," Follett founded first the Roxbury Debating Club for Boys and later the Highland Union, a social, athletic, and educational club for young men living in the area. The clubhouse was open in the afternoons and evenings and on Sundays for young men and boys, many of whom had left high school by the age of fourteen to look for work.[22]

Follett had more in mind than providing after-hours recreational activities to keep young workers off the streets. She also offered classes in debating and public speaking, insisting that these were important skills for anyone who wanted to "participate in the deliberations of men in civic life." During the course of the next few years, she could be found walking through the district, talking to shopkeepers and factory superintendents and studying the social and educational needs of the area.[23]

She soon found a way to institutionalize her youth clubs. In about 1902, she founded the Roxbury Industrial League for Boys, a club she located in a public school on Yeoman Street, where the school furnished light and heat and Follett paid for the janitor and other expenses. That program became the model for a citywide effort led by Follett—one that eventually was copied nationwide—for putting public schools to wider community use. As head of the Committee on Extended Use of School Buildings of the Women's Municipal League of Boston, she campaigned for the extended use of school buildings. In 1912, her committee successfully lobbied the Massachusetts legislature for an annual appropriation for the extended use of public schools.

Follett's work with the Boston Evening Centres, as they became known, eventually led her to develop job-counseling services in the neighborhood. In 1902, a visit to Edinburgh and London, where she saw some pioneering efforts in vocational guidance, inspired her to create a job placement bureau in east Boston. For a time, she recruited students from Harvard and Radcliffe to search out job opportunities for unemployed teenagers. The leads were then passed on to guidance counselors at the evening centers. In 1912, when the Boston School System set up a Placement Bureau in connection with several schools and the Girls' Trade Union League, she became a member of the first Placement Bureau Committee. This Placement Bureau eventually became the city's Department of Vocational Guidance.[24]

Over the years, Follett's civic work expanded. She came to represent the public on arbitration boards and to serve on the first Minimum Wage Board of Massachusetts.[25]

If the Roxbury experience gave Follett a firsthand laboratory for her ideas on citizenship and democracy, her work on job placement and the Minimum Wage Board gave her an insight into the relations between employers and employees. "With each new phase of activity she was being brought more and more closely into contact with industry and industrial problems," wrote Urwick.[26]

At the turn of the century, when Follett began working in the Roxbury neighborhood, it would not have been surprising if the work she pursued had occurred only on the margins of political life. But she used her intellectual commitment, her private income, and her ties to Boston's establishment to make her own mark on city life.

Ever since leaving home, Follett had poured her energies into both her work and a wide-ranging network of friendships that helped fill the void that she had left behind in Quincy. "[H]er soul emerged like the sun in finding college studies and social work and Isobel Briggs," wrote Ella Lyman Cabot, a Boston Brahmin and close friend, referring to the woman with whom Follett lived for close to thirty years in what was then known as a "Boston marriage."[27]

Follett met Briggs while she was still at Radcliffe. At the time, Follett was teaching political science part-time at a secondary school where Briggs, an Englishwoman some twenty years her senior, was the head-mistress.[28] Despite the vast reservoirs of energy and commitment Follett brought to her work and writing, her emotional and physical health were fragile. For close to thirty years, Briggs provided much of the emotional support and stability that she needed to work. Briggs, who "moved in the most distinguished circles," also introduced her to Boston's elite. A close friend of Follett recalled the home on Otis Place that provided, for Follett, much more than just a room of her own:

> [A]lways there was the house . . . to come to, with its rather big room, the large windows, a pretty glimpse of the river, the bright rug on the floor . . . the deep comfortable couch and easy chairs, the green masses of Miss Briggs' ivy plants . . . and the walls hung close with paintings and photographs. To me, it seemed one of the most delightful rooms I knew. It was a room you could settle down with and live in. There Mary worked from very early morning all day long in fierce absorption. Around her lay piles and piles of yellow paper, some with but a word or two scribbled on them, for that was her method of work, to jot down a thought, a quotation, a reference. . . . Sometimes the whole floor was covered with yellow sheets when she began to write, and her mind was so absorbed, so utterly concentrated on the creative chapter that was shaping and formulating itself out of what looked like a mere scattering of papers that ordinary living and intercourse was for the time being suspended. Everything was burned up in a fierce white creative glow which left her exhausted physically, nervously and mentally. . . . Miss Briggs was utterly devoted to Mary; "no one who did not share it will ever know what Isobel's

> contribution was ... her entire subordination of herself to
> Mary's interests and work."[29]

Follett was so busy with her social work in Boston that it was nearly twenty years after the publication of *The Speaker* before her thoughts and experiences coalesced into another book. When they did, the appearance of *The New State: Group Organization, the Solution of Popular Government*, immediately following World War I, "put her in the front rank of contemporary political scientists." In the book, she explored the nature of authority in a complex modern democracy and the problem of winning the consent of the governed—two strands that became important themes in her management philosophy.[30]

The New State, written during the course of World War I, was one of a number of books that attempted to "clarify the role of the state in an era when its fusion with nationalism and its vulnerability to revolution seemed painfully apparent and poorly understood." The book centered on the tension between nineteenth-century liberal individualism and the growing need for organization in the modern world, where, as Follett put it, "the majority is too big to handle itself." Much of her analysis focused on the psychological aspects of consent and the conditions under which it could be made "spontaneous and effective." One solution she put forward was the need to restructure government, to allow for the emergence of small grassroots groups. Such grassroots organizations would help a natural "aristocracy" of experts and leaders come to the fore. Wrote Follett, "The group organization movement ... rests on the solid assumption that this is a man-made not a machine-made world, that men and women are capable of constructing their own life.... The potentialities of the individual remain potentialities until they are released by group life."[31] These themes, which represent a radical departure from Taylor's approach to scientific management, would play a major role in her management writings in the years to come.

Follett's ideas also found practical expression in the so-called social center movement, an attempt to put participative democracy to work at the grassroots level in cities such as Cincinnati and government agencies such as the Forest Service. (In Cincinnati, for example, in the Mohawk-Brighton district, the effort involved creating a collaborative network of elected community representatives, public health officials, and doctors to coordinate health care initiatives designed to combat milkborne tuberculosis and high infant mortality.)[32]

To Follett, the state—indeed, any large-scale human organization—was much like a tree: "Its branches will widen as its roots spread." She conceived of the state, and later the business organization, as "an organic, ever-changing entity that requires individual involvement, action and experimentation to achieve organizational goals."[33]

Some critics have seen an internal contradiction in Follett's work. To be sure, her voice was a rare one in her day, arguing for the acceptance of diverse views and greater understanding among disparate segments of society (see Chapter 3). Yet she was also an early advocate of welfare capitalism, and her ideas were embraced by such pioneering welfare capitalists as William Filene and Henry Dennison in the United States and B. Seebohm Rowntree in the United Kingdom.

Indeed, *The New State* widened her circle of admirers, who also came to include Felix Frankfurter; Bernard Bosanquet, a British neo-Hegelian philosopher; and Lord Haldane, a British statesman and philosopher. Haldane, in response to *The New State*, wrote to Follett, "I am much impressed by the idealism and knowledge which the book breathes, and not less by the hopeful possibilities of the group or neighbourhood method of bringing the State into reality in the individual which you are pressing on public attention."[34]

In 1918, *The New State* was followed by a largely psychological book, *Creative Experience*, which examined politics in the light of Gestalt psychology, which was being developed in Germany at the time and Follett's own considerable experience serving on numerous public boards and committees in Boston. In this book, she expanded on her interest in basic human emotions, the psychological foundations of all human activity, "and the emotional reactions that come into play in the working of human groups." The Gestalt school's focus on "wholes," as opposed to a more atomized approach to human associations, would, she correctly predicted, "have more influence on all our thinking than any single concept has for long exercised." She was interested in the dynamic forces that shape human organizations, noting that, as in physics, the act of observation changes the thing observed. "Behavior is not a function of environment but a function of the relating of behavior and environment," she wrote. "My response is not to a rigid, static environment, but to a changing environment ... an environment which is changing because of the activity between it and me."[35]

In her own life and work, Follett epitomized the spirit of voluntarism and experimentation that characterized the Progressive era. Her role as "welfare entrepreneur" had given her a unique insight into the challenges of coordinating long-term projects in a situation where neither coercion or remuneration was an option. The focus of her writings on both government and industry was always on the psychological forces that motivate men and women and their participation in groups. Thus, not only was she one of the earliest and most astute thinkers on the problem of leadership and human motivation, she brought to the problem a variegated perspective that both promoted participation and explored the prerequisites for achieving collaboration. "Intensely conscious of man's group life, she saw that his association with his fellow men gives rise to powerful emotions which colour his every action as a member of a group. . . . A human group, Mary Follett thought, thus has a life that is something more than the sum of the individual lives composing it."[36]

By the 1920s, Follett's books, her explorations of the latest ideas in politics and psychology, and her forays into east Boston had brought her to a crossroads. As Urwick put it, "[T]his brilliant, cultured, eminent woman, steeped in academic tradition and with no practical experience of business, stepped quietly over this yawning chasm as if it were the most natural thing in the world. And the interesting point is that, given her strong sense of reality, her undeviating interest in social order, and her scientific mind, it was not only natural; it was inevitable."[37]

In 1924, Follett gave the first of a series of papers on industrial organization at the Bureau of Personnel Administration in New York. The bureau, which held annual conferences for executives who came to listen to the most prestigious thinkers in industry, gave her the imprimatur of "a front-rank management thinker." Following her first bureau presentations, Follett found herself in great demand as a speaker and consultant. Though she couldn't have been more different from the conventional slide rule–toting Taylorite, she was regularly sought out for advice by the businessmen who attended the bureau conferences. While she did occasionally visit manufacturing facilities, such as those of Henry Dennison and the Rowntree chocolate works, which were run by the British management pioneer B. Seebohm Rowntree, much of her advice was dispensed over the luncheon table. "I never had such interesting meals," she would say of her meetings with businessmen.[38]

Follett continued as a regular conference leader at the Bureau of Personnel Administration for four years. Many of her lectures at the bureau were published posthumously by Metcalf and Urwick in *Dynamic Administration*. These papers elaborated the following principal themes, which would become a hallmark of her management thinking:

• ***Authority and the "law of the situation."***   Follett's law of the situation set traditional notions of authority on its head. Authority, she argued, grew out of an individual's knowledge and function in an organization, *not* his or her place in its hierarchy. She understood that the exercise of power by one individual over another can only breed resentment. By contrast, most men and women will "accept the logic of a situation and the demands of facts.... Orders and authority must be depersonalized."[39]

The law of the situation was a revolutionary concept. It exploded notions of hierarchy and traditional command-and-control authority. In Follett's organization, knowledge and competence created natural authority. Employees must have command of the facts to enable them to do their jobs, she said, and their competence gives them authority and responsibility in their respective domains. The chief executive, explained Urwick in one elaboration of Follett's work, "should be less of an autocrat and more of a co-ordinator."[40]

"Arbitrary authority," by contrast, was riddled with pitfalls, according to Follett. These included "the loss of possible contributions from those directed" and the fact that arbitrary directives are "apt to cause friction between workers and foremen." A third problem, she noted, is that "no one has a greater asset for his business than a man's pride in his work," which arbitrary orders can undermine. And finally, arbitrary commands "decrease [an individual's] sense of responsibility."[41]

Follett's idea that authority grew out of the law of the situation was in many ways inimical to the hierarchical approach that governed most large U.S. organizations at the time. It was, however, embraced by Chester Barnard as a key premise of *The Functions of the Executive.*

"It is because Mary Follett's philosophy of organization opens up the possibility of such an identification that it is the most important contribution to the business literature of our time," wrote Urwick.[42]

• ***Power-with.*** "Whereas power usually means power-over, the power of some person or group over some other person or group, it is possible to develop the conception of power-with, a jointly developed power, a co-active, not a coercive power," wrote Follett. When power is depersonalized, she argued, "[t]he personal sense of power over others and subordination to others disappears. In its place there develops a spirit of true cooperation in carrying out 'what the law of the situation demands.' "[43]

• ***Leadership and decision making as a "continuous process."*** "An executive decision is a moment in a process," Follett told a rapt audience of the Taylor Society in a paper she presented in 1926. "The *growth* of a decision, the *accumulation* of authority, not the final step, is what we need most to study.... [W]e should guard against thinking this [final] step is a larger part of the whole process than it really is." To Follett, leadership and decision making were part of a "continuing process" of coordination—one that, to be effective, had to involve as many constituencies as possible.[44]

Follett's ideas about leadership grew directly out of her assumptions about the source of true authority. In Follett's view, explained Rosabeth Moss Kanter, "a leader is one who sees the whole situation, organizes the experience of the group, offers a vision of the future, and trains followers to be leaders." Thus, adds Nitin Nohria, Follett gives "one of the clearest statements of what the current buzzword 'empowerment' really means."[45]

While Follett's ideas are rarely prescriptive, they are usually grounded in practical examples that she encountered in her own work and consulting engagements during the 1920s. To illustrate how contemporary her views on pluralistic authority and cross-functional decision making are, consider her example of a typical problem in materials purchasing: the authority for purchasing materials, she explained, "should be assumed by the purchasing agent and by the department which gives its specifications to the purchasing agent. If the purchasing agent thinks that some of these specifications could be changed and cost thereby reduced without decreasing quality, he should discuss this with the department in question. While I realize that much can be accomplished by friendly relations between individuals, I think that organization should have for one of its chief aims to provide for a joint authority in those cases where combined knowledge is necessary for the best judgment."[46]

Cross-functional teams eventually became the heart of Japanese quality management. In the 1980s, they were a chief focus of U.S. manufacturers trying to improve their showing in the face of Japanese efficiency. Nohria points out that Follett's ideas "define the behavioral principles that are at the heart of contemporary wisdom on high-performance teams."[47]

• *Constructive conflict.*   The proper response to conflict is neither victory nor even compromise but the "integration" of both points of view, according to Follett. "Although Follett idealized the solidarity of groups and organizations, she nevertheless was a trenchant critic of power balancing," wrote Jacoby. "Follett argued that a fundamental problem with trade and company unions was their insistence on drawing an absolutely sharp line between management and labor." In so doing, Follett argued, management and labor emphasized "grievances instead of problems" and focused on bargaining instead of "integrative unity."[48]

Follett was, in fact, an early advocate of organizational learning—though she never used those words explicitly. Her assumption was that when there is conflict, both sides are correct and the solution must reflect multiple viewpoints. "When two people arrive at a common decision, that decision is only really satisfactory if it represents an integration," she wrote.[49]

Follett believed in the diversity of opinions and actually made the connection between constructive conflict and creativity. "[I]t is to be hoped . . . that we shall always have conflict, the kind which leads to invention, to the emergence of new values."

She was, however, concerned that the adversarial nature of conflict in most industrial settings served to entrench differences rather than to achieve progress. "I do not like the 'trouble specialists' of the Ford plant," she said, for example. "I wish it were not so often stated that shop or department committees were formed to 'settle disputes.' If you will get lists of these so-called 'disputes,' you will find that often they have not so much of the fight element in them as this word implies."[50]

• *A role for labor.* Follett's work in Roxbury gave her an empathy for the workingman that was rare among contemporary management philosophers. Her ideas on empowerment stemmed from the "law of the situation"; collaboration and cooperation with labor, she argued, were the only rational ways to run a business.

While Follett's writings on conflict resolution have been among her most enduring legacies, her views on organized labor were, for her time, just as noteworthy. It is in her perspective on and attitudes toward labor that she differed most markedly from other pioneers of human relations, especially the Harvard Circle. While Mayo and Company thought it was important to make workers *feel* important, Follett was one of the first theorists who thought they *were* important. "The main problem of the workers is by no means how much control they can wrest from capital or management," she argued. "Their problem is how much power they can themselves grow. . . . Take, for instance, what is called 'the instinct for workmanship.' Formerly, in the time of individual production, this 'instinct' was expressed in the individual's own work. Now that individual production has given way to group production, this 'instinct' cannot be expressed unless the individual workman has something to say about group organization and the technique of group production. This seems to me a natural development of genuine power."[51]

At a time when most Americans saw little difference between organized labor and communism, even the most progressive of the early-twentieth-century management theorists were opposed to labor organizing and collective bargaining. Follett was an exception. Again, she was motivated not so much by her sympathies for labor per se but by a sophisticated understanding of the source of much labor-management conflict and the high costs of such antagonism. "Employees do not respond only to their employers, but to the relation between themselves and their employers," she said. "Trade unionism is responding, not only to capitalism, but to the relation between itself and capitalism."[52]

Follett also believed in the potential benefits that would accrue to an organization that included all of its constituents in the decision-making process. "[M]y very strong advocacy of employee association is not chiefly to bring about equal power, but because this helps us to approach functional unity. . . . If I were a manufacturer I should want to consolidate my workers, not in order to give them greater strength in a fight but in order that they should, by conscious unity, be a stronger part of my plant and thus strengthen my whole organization."[53]

■

A year after her first lectures at the Bureau of Personnel Administration, Follett was invited by B. Seebohm Rowntree, the pioneering head of S. I. Rowntree & Company, to address the weeklong biannual Oxford Management Conference he had started at Balliol College.

Rowntree, one of the most forward-thinking executives of his time and one of Follett's most ardent promoters in England, also became a great influence on her. Although he was said to have "never for a moment compromised on questions of efficiency," he believed ardently in industrial democracy and welfare capitalism. "He appreciated more clearly than most of his contemporaries the importance to the workers of their status in industry," wrote Urwick, who was working for Rowntree during the 1920s, when he met Follett. Rowntree, he recalled, took what most of his contemporaries considered "great risks in applying democratic principles in all matters directly affecting the employee."[54]

Many of Rowntree's initiatives were designed to remove the fear and uncertainty that characterized the lives of industrial workers at the time. As early as 1906, Rowntree established a pension fund for workers at the company and company-funded unemployment compensation to supplement state insurance for married workers.[55]

Rowntree was no mere paternalist, however. For Rowntree, a pioneer marketer who also adopted a variety of scientific management methods, industrial democracy was just one more innovation in the course of a lifelong quest to develop a state-of-the-art company. At his York Cocoa Works, for example, all work rules—new ones as well as amendments to old ones—had to be approved jointly by a committee made up of both management and workers. Workers could appeal disciplinary actions and company policies to an Appeal Committee that included workers' representatives. What impressed Follett the most, according to Urwick, was the annual briefings, where the year's business results were presented and discussed and to which workers were invited. "[T]hat the employees of the concern should be taken into confidence by the management, as they were, left on her a deeper impression than anything else."[56]

Follett's work in the management field was relatively short-lived, however. Around the time she accepted Rowntree's invitation to lecture at Balliol, Isobel Briggs died after a long, painful bout with cancer. Follett was devastated. With the loss of her "anchor," many of her friends wondered if she would have the strength to continue her work. A year later, Ella and Richard Cabot took Follett to Geneva on holiday. There she met Dame Katherine Furse, a beautiful and accomplished woman who had been a director of the Women's Royal Naval Service and the World Association of Girl Guides and Girl Scouts. "Just like Lyndall Urwick and like everyone else who met Follett, [Furse] fell for her," wrote Graham. A year later, Follett decided to set up housekeeping with Furse in London, where she would occupy the top floor of Furse's home in Chelsea.[57]

But Furse wasn't the ballast Briggs had been. Having numerous interests of her own, she was not prepared to mold her life around Follett's the way Briggs had done. Follett's years in London were not her happiest. Her health began to deteriorate, and she was frequently in pain. Away from her network of friends in Boston, she was often lonely and even occasionally envious of Furse's other friendships.[58]

Yet she continued to work. In 1932, for example, when the London School of Economics launched the Department of Business Administration—now known as the Department of Industrial Relations— she was invited to give the inaugural lectures.[59]

A year later, however, worried about the impact the Depression was having on her financial investments, Follett rushed home to Boston, where she also decided to undergo an operation on her thyroid. During the operation, the doctors discovered that her body was riddled with cancer. She died soon after surgery, on December 19, 1933.[60]

■

To a twenty-first-century reader, Follett's turn-of-the-twentieth-century views on democracy and citizenship seem almost naively idealistic. Yet her insights into organizational relationships and behavior are among the most insightful and contemporary of those of any of the twentieth-century management philosophers. To this day her ideas echo in the work of Peter Senge, Warren Bennis, Tom Peters, and Rosabeth Moss Kanter, to name only a few.

Yet in her own day her star was exceedingly short-lived. For one thing, during the turbulent and divisive period of the 1930s and 1940s, the idealistic, conciliatory nature of her philosophy, with its focus on small-group collaboration, was seen as quaintly impractical and even "subversive." The Red scare that swept the United States in the aftermath of World War I and the Bolshevik Revolution in Russia also cast suspicion on her efforts at grassroots organizing. Indeed, the Cincinnati health care experiment, which drew many of its ideas from Follett, soon came to be perceived as a threat to local authority. Part of the problem was that, by its very nature, this sort of "democratic experimentalism" challenged official authority. Thus, although a referendum in the Mohawk-Brighton district, where the project was located, produced a vote in favor of it, the mayor of Cincinnati charged the plan and its organizers with creating "a government within a government, a step away from Bolshevism" and soon put an end to the project.[61]

Indeed, in the face of a depression and another world war, America faced problems that seemed to call for the muscle of big government and large institutions. This may explain why Kanter says of Follett that she was not only ahead of but also "wrong for her time."[62]

Similarly, Follett's ideas on conflict resolution would have been "unintelligible" during this period. "*Politically* those decades were dominated by men and creed that knew the proper use of conflict was to conquer," says Drucker. "They did not believe in conflict resolution, they believed in unconditional surrender. . . . [S]ociety was dominated—permeated, in fact—by a profound belief in class war, in which the very attempt to understand what was important to the other side was a sell-out."[63]

While Follett might have been out of step with the early-twentieth-century zeitgeist, Rosabeth Kanter also believes that her gender got in the way of her acceptance. While acknowledging her influence in Japan and the United Kingdom following World War II, Kanter notes, "It is hard to found or build a discipline without disciples." In fact, there were few disciples more loyal and respected than Urwick and Dennison were. But it didn't help that Follett's work was inherently philosophical, with little in the way of practical prescriptions.[64]

Ultimately, it was the philosophical and practical disturbances of the Depression and World War II that combined to drown out Follett's voice. Lyndall Urwick, who posthumously edited Follett's work on management, wanted to publish an anthology of her papers soon after her death (this despite the fact that Follett had instructed Furse to burn her papers). However, a dispute between Urwick and H. C. Metcalf at the Bureau of Personnel Management, where many of Follett's management papers had been presented, delayed publication of *Dynamic Administration* until 1942, nine years after her death. By then, management philosophizing and experimentation had given way to the expediencies of war. (Follett's books were even out of print for a time after her publisher was bombed during the Blitz.)

After World War II, Follett's ideas enjoyed a revival in the United Kingdom, where Urwick continued to promote her work. Along with other management innovators, including W. Edwards Deming, she was also embraced by the Japanese. In America, however, the pressure to increase consumer production, as well as renewed labor strife and a resurgent fear of communism, combined to revive Taylorism and marginalize what were perceived as "softer," humanistic approaches to management. Peter Drucker, an admirer of Follett's, recalls that by the time the next generation of management experts "resumed serious work on management—under the impetus of World War II, the Marshall Plan, and the productivity teams—people such as Herbert Simon, Frederick Herzberg, and I worked without any knowledge of Follett."[65]

In considering Follett's long-forgotten legacy, it is important to note that many of her ideas, especially her conciliatory approach to labor, which are still heresy in some circles today, would have been exceedingly hard to swallow in the 1920s. Urwick took the occasion of Lillian Gilbreth's death, in 1971, to defend Taylor against his rivals and detractors. Against substantial evidence to the contrary, which Urwick was in an ideal position to see, he defended Taylor's definition of scientific management as one entailing "a mental revolution" for both employers and employees that involved the "substitution of co-operation for conflict." In a sanitized version of the events that led up to the pig-iron experiments, Urwick wrote admiringly of "Taylor's method of *persuading* one or two workers to try a new method without making a lot of publicity about it, and *only extending it to others when the first two or three have found out that it is to their advantage* [author's emphasis]."[66]

What Follett would have thought of Taylor's strong-arm tactics (which involved firing scores of workers until two men finally capitulated and then ratcheting up the pace of work by as much as 300 percent) seems clear. Lillian Gilbreth, in what Urwick says is one of the few times that he found her to "fall short of Abraham Lincoln's 'With Charity for all,' " told him, "He was not a nice person. You wouldn't have liked him."[67]

It is not surprising, perhaps, that Urwick, a "classical theorist" who believed that management had a great deal to learn from the discipline and hierarchy of the military, would have sympathized with scientific management and soft-pedaled Taylor's antidemocratic views. As a protégé of Rowntree and admirer of Follett, Urwick, in his defense of Taylorism, shows that industrial democracy has been a hard sell, indeed. While Urwick admired many of Follett's views, he almost certainly would have been uncomfortable with the practical consequence of those ideas—that labor might actually help shape the direction of management.

Ultimately, World War II wiped out most traces of Follett's work in the United States. Douglas McGregor was one of the few prominent management thinkers who continued to advocate Follett's ideas. And although the "law of the situation," as well as many of her ideas about authority and leadership, endured in Barnard's *The Functions of the Executive*, Barnard never credits Follett directly.

Pauline Graham's *Mary Parker Follett: The Prophet of Management*, a 1995 anthology of Follett's management writings, brought her to the attention of such eminences as Drucker and Kanter. Today Follett's work has been rediscovered and applied to a wide range of fields, including management and dispute resolution.

Most provocatively, perhaps, the ideas of "democratic experimentalism" with which she was so closely associated are being revived in legal circles as a way of decentralizing decision making and promoting self-government. The idea put forward by, among others, Michael Dorf and Charles Sabel of Columbia University, is to allow citizens to "utilize their local knowledge to fit solutions to their individual circumstances"; the role of regulators and regional governments, in this context, is to encourage the pooling and dissemination of knowledge and the development of "best-practice performance standards based on information that regulated entities provide in return for the freedom to experiment with the solutions they prefer."[68]

This modern form of democratic experimentalism is "informed by the example of novel kinds of coordination within and among private firms." It also emphasizes the inclusion of a broad cross section of constituents in the decision-making and standard-setting process. While still in its infancy, this approach is already beginning to emerge in such areas as the regulation of nuclear power plants, community policing, and weapons procurement. It is, in fact, a foundation of the most forward-looking practices of modern management, including the quality movement, as conceived by W. Edwards Deming.[69]

Any good military man will tell his officers "Your job is to get this done" by persuasion. . . . Anytime you have to court-martial too many people, there is something wrong with your management.

—Chester Barnard[1]

Chester Barnard

The Philosopher King of American Management

By the beginning of World War II, few American companies served as a better model of professionalism in management and its role in fostering social stability and economic prosperity than did American Telephone and Telegraph (AT&T). Bell Laboratories was on its way to becoming a powerhouse of scientific research. AT&T operations pioneered scientific production methods. And in the early 1920s, AT&T collaborated with the National Academy of Sciences on the famous Hawthorne experiments; though the surprising results of the experiment would revolutionize personnel management, they were designed—with their focus on how lighting changes affect productivity—as an ergonomic exercise (see Chapter 4).[2]

For AT&T, a pioneer of so-called welfare capitalism, responsible management was a strategic priority. Beginning nearly a century ago, as AT&T consolidated its acquisitions of once-independent telephone and telegraph firms, the company saw good governance as its chief means of winning public acceptance of a telecommunications monopoly. In the process, AT&T trained a cadre of professional managers to run the company as a public trust.

It is fitting, then, that what may be the century's seminal book on corporate leadership was written by Chester Barnard, the president of New Jersey Bell Telephone (NJBT) who, beginning in the 1920s, built his career at AT&T over the course of several decades. Considering that Barnard wrote his groundbreaking book, *The Functions of the Executive*, in the 1930s, his range of ideas is remarkably broad. In one of the first books written on modern management and leadership, he anticipated almost every important tenet of modern management. In particular, he emphasized the psychological and behavioral aspects of leadership, rather than the militaristic, command-and-control model that prevailed at the time. Management's authority, he realized, rested in its ability to persuade, rather than to command. Its challenge was to reconcile—and balance—the inherent tension between the needs of individual employees with the goals of an organization. He also recognized that much of the creative potential of an organization rests in informal networks, not in the formal hierarchy; drawing on Follett, he understood the role of constructive conflict. And he warned against a simplistic pay-for-performance approach to compensation, anticipating much of the debate about pay and motivation that would occupy management for decades to come.

While the leadership gurus of our day, Tom Peters and Robert Waterman, to cite but two, have learned from the writings of thinkers such as Barnard, Barnard himself had few managerial antecedents to draw on. Instead, he pieced his theory together practically from scratch, mining an eclectic array of writings in such fields as sociology, psychology, philosophy, and economics, as well as his own experience as a practicing executive.

As one of the foremost intellectuals of his day, Barnard was an atypical executive. Yet the way he approached his own role as an executive made him an exemplar of the new professional management class that came to prominence in the 1920s and 1930s and established the organization—the public corporation, in particular—as the "representative" institution of twentieth-century American democracy. It was of companies such as AT&T and managers such as Barnard that Herbert Hoover wrote in 1934, "The manager's restless pillow has done more to advance the practical arts than all the legislation upon the statute books."[3]

The power of professional management first emerged during World War I. It was during the Great War that the country, for the first time, achieved military mobilization through an unprecedented level of collaboration between business and government. At the same time, "[t]he combined pressure of labor unrest and labor shortages, produced a rapid expansion of workplace reforms," including the development of personnel departments and employee benefits. And AT&T was at the vanguard of industrial reform.[4]

As early as 1911, during the ICC rate hearings, the leaders of the Progressive movement had seized on scientific management as the answer to rationalizing business and bringing social benefits, in the form of lower freight rates, to the public (see Chapter 1). After World War I, the reformers promoted professional management and welfare capitalism—not just engineering efficiencies—as an antidote to both the greed and corruption of the robber barons and simmering social unrest. Corporations, run by professional managers in collaboration with a professional cadre of administrators in government, universities, philanthropies, and research centers, argued the reformers, were ideally placed to establish a national social and economic agenda. Though Hoover was no statist, he envisioned "an era in which interdependent private organizations voluntarily forge cooperative arrangements among themselves, with the federal government lending a helping hand to encourage those efforts."[5]

Postwar optimism was not the only factor driving the new "managerial state." The labor unrest that had periodically erupted before the war, revealing the tarnished underbelly of the Gilded Age, broke out again at the end of World War I. In 1919, some 4 million American workers went out on strike. In the backyard of the Harvard Business School, which was about to complete its transformation into the "West Point of capitalism," a walkout by the entire Boston police force resulted in three days of looting. Many Americans feared that the "ill winds" of Bolshevism and fascism that already had hit Europe would soon blow through the United States.

To leading intellectuals, among them Barnard and Wallace B. Donham, the dean of HBS, the problem was that science and technology had far outpaced society's ability to cope with change. "A technological civilization seems to me to be incompatible either with absolute governments . . . or [with] democratic systems so far as they have as yet evolved," wrote Barnard to Lawrence J. Henderson, Harvard's legendary biologist, sociologist, and philosopher, on the eve of World War II. There is an "almost complete absence of appreciation in this country of the difficulty and the long time to train and select the immense numbers of leaders required" to cope with a rapidly changing technological world.[6]

While Barnard lamented the inability of civilization and formal organizations to cope with technological change, Donham, in an address to Harvard students in 1926, placed the blame squarely on the scientific community. Science, Donham charged, had "let loose on the world powerful and revolutionary forces which were the start and are now and always will be outside the control of the scientific group."[7]

Both Donham and Barnard were advocates of private corporatism—of which AT&T was a prime exemplar—as a stabilizing influence. "For the corporatists, modern industry was viewed as a vast experiment in cooperation," writes Sanford M. Jacoby in *Modern Manors*. "These corporatists were liberals, but they were wary of what they perceived as Luddite tendencies within the labor movement. They also were skeptical of legislative responses to social problems, preferring instead to rely on private solutions—especially programs associated with welfare capitalism."[8]

Donham's mission for the business school, in which he largely succeeded, was to train a cadre of management leaders who, because they would control the great corporate engines of finance, distribution, and production, would be entrusted with the mantle of "national stewardship." In an effort to "socialize the results of science," Donham believed it would be necessary for the school's faculty to collaborate with business leaders.[9]

Chief among those leaders was Chester Barnard. Although Barnard never received a formal appointment at Harvard, Donham encouraged Barnard's long association with the business school. He was a regular guest lecturer at Henderson's sociology classes. It was also due to the prodding of his friends at Harvard that Barnard published *The Functions of the Executive*.

From his first days at AT&T, where he worked in the statistics department, Barnard had an ideal vantage point from which to view not only the brilliant leadership of Theodore Vail, AT&T's legendary president, but also the cutting edge of American managerial practice. He absorbed the lessons of management in what was then arguably one of the best-run corporations in the world, as well as one that saw its role as being a guardian and steward of the public trust. Barnard's own career at AT&T, which was interspersed with periodic assignments running government agencies and programs, also exemplified the ideal of management as a form of public service.

Significantly, Barnard was not a Brahmin, no more than Donham had been, or for that matter Elton Mayo or Fritz Roethlisberger, the pioneers of human relations at HBS (see Chapter 4). He was born poor, the son of a mechanic; his mother died giving birth to his third sibling when he was just five years old. Yet the Barnards were not a typical working-class family. Most of the family were "intellectuals." And several of Barnard's relatives were Freemasons.

A tall, serious youth, Barnard learned to fend for himself at an early age. Upon graduating from grammar school, in Cliftondale, Massachusetts, at the age of fifteen, he worked as a piano tuner. But he had ambitions. After two years on the job, he enrolled at the Mount Hermon school, a prep school in Northfield, Massachusetts, and later at Harvard, where he became a member of the legendary class of 1910 that included T. S. Eliot and Walter Lippmann. Even after getting into Harvard, he continued to work at odd jobs, running a dance orchestra, typing student papers, frequently "working all night." Although Barnard finished most of the requirements for a bachelor's degree in just three years, a lack of funds forced him to drop out of college before he completed a final science requirement.[10]

Thus, Barnard had the number one pedigree for joining the new managerial class, which held professional expertise and merit as its principle membership requirements: he had worked his way up from the bottom. William G. Scott, in *Chester Barnard: Guardians of the Managerial State*, wrote that the legitimacy of the new management class was based not on "property ownership, inherited wealth, [or] election to popular office but on the control of property, professional credentials, merit-based appraisal methods, and the widely held belief among Americans in the efficacy of managerial expertise for creating higher standards of living."[11]

Barnard the man was as complex as his ideas. His personality reflected the contradictions of a poor boy who had grown up in a working-class household where "endless hours of arguments" centered not on the perpetual lack of money but on books and philosophy. He lacked the coordination to play sports. But he developed a commanding physical presence that combined the savoir faire of "a successful banker" with the edge of a "journeyman machinist." Gripped by the impatience typical of self-made men, he was known for an explosive temper. Yet he was cherished by friends and subordinates as a compassionate humanist. Those who knew him described him as both "a warm and thoughtful person, a man with a twinkle in his eye and a keen sense of humor" and, alternately a "bull in a china shop" who, once he set himself on a given course of action, had "the subtlety of a pile-driver."[12]

Barnard joined AT&T straight after leaving Harvard. Barnard's mentor at AT&T was Walter S. Gifford, who ran the statistics department when Barnard was hired and who would become the company's longest-reigning CEO. Gifford and Barnard had grown up in neighboring towns. Gifford was also a Harvard man, though he had preceded Barnard by about five years. Coincidentally, Gifford and Grace F. Noera, whom Barnard would marry a few years after he had joined AT&T, had been childhood friends.[13]

Gifford's role in fostering Barnard's career is a curious one. For while he was almost certainly behind Barnard's promotion to the presidency of NJBT, he also kept Barnard away from the "Valhalla" of AT&T corporate headquarters in New York. There is probably some truth to Peter Drucker's contention that Gifford considered Barnard's strength as a philosopher king superior to his performance as a hands-on executive.[14]

Barnard's first job at AT&T was in the statistics department, one of the first of its kind in a U.S. corporation. Vail had set up the department as a "broadly defined information-gathering enterprise" that collected data about everything from the cost and quality of AT&T services to comparative data on how AT&T performed relative to its rivals—both those in the United States and the government-controlled systems in Europe. Indeed, this was a period when Vail had undertaken a "massive campaign" to acquire numerous independent telephone companies and consolidate them under the AT&T umbrella. In doing so, Vail not only had to fight the U.S. Post Office, which wanted to nationalize the telephone and telegraph services under its own auspices, but also had to woo a skeptical public. Vail was determined that AT&T would fight nationalization by delivering superior service. The statistics department was set up as a sort of propaganda department to collect data that would demonstrate the superiority of AT&T's performance.[15]

Barnard, for one, didn't need to be convinced of AT&T's managerial prowess. Because he had a facility for languages, he was put in charge of surveying the rates and services of telephone companies in Europe. "He concluded from this research that state ownership resulted in higher rates, poorer quality equipment, and restricted distribution of telephone facilities," wrote Scott.[16]

Barnard would spend close to thirty years at AT&T, most of that time at New Jersey Bell Telephone. While he worked in the statistics department, his reports on telephone rates caught the attention of the company's leadership. His success in winning a rate increase for some regional operating companies won him his first promotion to a line job, as vice president and general manager of Pennsylvania Bell Telephone Company. In 1925, Gifford was named president of AT&T. Two years later, he promoted Barnard to the presidency of the newly formed NJBT.

NJBT came into existence during the boom years of the late 1920s, out of the merger of two regional operating companies. Barnard's first job involved the integration of the two companies and expansion of telephone service in the rapidly growing state. NJBT prospered, earning an 8 percent return on investment in both 1928 and 1929.[17]

Barnard's second major challenge was to convert NJBT to dial service. In this he was less successful. A fundamentally conservative executive, he put the brakes on dial conversion during the Depression. Thus, while NJBT nearly quadrupled its conversion rate to 32 percent in 1933, up from just 8 percent in 1928, it lagged behind the Bell System average for years to come. By 1937, it had converted only 35 percent of the state's phones, while the rest of the Bell System had converted half. NJBT's slow conversion rate proved to be a problem during World War II, when the company struggled to provide adequate telephone service both for wartime production in the state and for business and private use.[18]

While Barnard might have lacked technological vision, he excelled at organization-building skills—and a commitment to corporate welfare policies. His tenure at NJBT was marked by a sense of public service and personal integrity that are almost unimaginable to many today. For example, in 1933, at the height of the Depression, Barnard announced a no-layoff policy—a major accomplishment even within the Bell System—choosing to reduce employees' working hours instead. Such policies, combined with his penchant for rolling up his sleeves and personally negotiating labor disputes, inspired an unusual level of employee loyalty. Barnard's files are also full of detailed personal responses to specific customer complaints, which ran the gambit from complaints about a twenty-five-cent charge for a handset to a one-dollar charge for reconnecting telephone service.[19]

Today it is easy to view Barnard's managerial style as an anachronism. But his focus on the psychological and behavioral aspects of management was remarkable for an executive of his generation. More clearly than almost any other management philosopher before or since, he sensed that the central challenge of management was balancing both the technological and human dimensions of organization. Moreover, he understood that this was a dynamic process, constantly in need of attention and fine-tuning. As he put it, "There should be a certain degree of friction in the organization. . . . [W]ith every decision you make you have to be aware that there are alternatives that you've rejected and you can never find out because you can never repeat the situation."[20]

Though never an ardent opponent of unions, Barnard believed that unions were useful only in competitive businesses where "bad treatment" of employees is forced on companies by "chiseling" competitors. By contrast, he believed that AT&T was in a position to "persuad[e] and propagandiz[e] employees to prefer cooperation to confrontation."[21]

Beginning in World War I, Barnard held a series of government posts. His experiences in government and academia reinforced his belief in the power of voluntary cooperation and coordination between the private sector and government. Again following in the footsteps of Gifford, who had become deputy chief of the War Industries Board (WIB), which involved business leaders in the planning of wartime production, Barnard served as an adviser to the same agency during the war. At the beginning of the Depression, Herbert Hoover recruited Gifford to head the National Unemployment Commission; Barnard, in turn, was tapped to run the New Jersey Emergency Relief Administration.[22]

Throughout his career, Barnard juggled government work with his duties as president of NJBT. During World War II, he distinguished himself as the president of the United Service Organizations (USO), which provided recreational and welfare services for the armed forces and for which service he received the Medal of Merit from Harry S. Truman. In 1942, he was approached about the possibility of replacing Henry Morgenthau, Jr., as secretary of the Treasury; he ducked the offer, noting that he was not a New Dealer and hinting that he had no taste for political maneuvering. Three years after the war, he won the "plum" of nonprofit assignments, when he became head of the Rockefeller Foundation and finally left NJBT. From there he would go on to head the National Science Foundation and to serve with a number of philanthropies and government commissions, including the United Nations Atomic Energy Committee.[23]

Years later, Barnard claimed that it was his years at USO that helped confirm his philosophy of management—especially his view of authority. To get an organization that, at any given moment, relied on literally hundreds of thousands of volunteers to work required the *voluntary* consent of the governed. Authority had to be "accepted"; it could not be dictated. As he explained, "I can say, 'I now hold you responsible for this,' but if you don't accept that then there's nothing I can do about it. . . . You can dissemble, you can give me the runaround; but if you don't accept it, it just doesn't work. . . . [N]early everything depends upon the moral commitment," as opposed to a formal requirement.[24]

Like Hoover, Barnard and Gifford believed in *voluntary* coordination and cooperation between industry and government, based on the model they had established at the WIB during World War I. Both men, however, strongly disagreed with the massive government intervention of the New Deal and what Barnard referred to as its "make-work" schemes.[25]

Barnard's exposure to the so-called Harvard Circle also reinforced his belief in the importance of professional management and honed his interest in the psychological and sociological aspects of management. Throughout his years in industry and government service, he read voraciously, including the works of Karl Marx, Max Weber, and Kurt Lewin. In fact, he developed a grounding in everything from sociology and psychology to philosophy and physics that was rare even among academics, let alone executives.

Beginning in the 1920s, Barnard became involved with several of the leading intellectuals in the social sciences at Harvard. This group of like-minded, powerful personalities included Mayo, Henderson, and Dean Donham, who shared with Barnard the dubious distinction of having nearly been forced to drop out of Harvard College for lack of funds. (Donham was saved by a loan from A. Lawrence Lowell, a government professor who became the president of Harvard; see Chapter 4.)

The Harvard man who probably influenced Barnard the most was Henderson. Barnard was particularly intrigued by Henderson's interpretations of the work of the Italian sociologist Vilfredo Pareto, who emphasized both the dynamic nature of organizations and the impact of emotions on human behavior. Barnard also shared Mayo's view that the "deterioration of human collaboration was the most pressing issue of the day."[26]

The Harvard Circle saw the social sciences as the key to learning more about "what makes people tick" and to blunting the "radicalism" (i.e., Marxism) that "fester[ed] beneath the surface of prosperity." During the course of the 1920s, HBS had built a new campus fit to foster Donham's vision of a new managerial elite. Indeed, by the 1930s Donham's earlier vision of HBS as the "West Point of capitalism" would be transformed. Wrote Donham, "Effective responsibility has passed rapidly from capital to a *new managing class*, the executive heads of great corporations and firms."[27]

The 1920s marked a period of consolidation and the creation of oligopolies. As the new management elite gained in power, their motives and willingness to serve as stewards of the public interest were increasingly called into question. One cause of the distrust was that consumer prices never fell as much as the costs of production.[28] With the beginning of the Depression, the very legitimacy of managerial capitalism came under attack.

The economic crisis and a wave of business closures buoyed the critics of big business. In 1933, Adolf A. Berle and Gardiner C. Means published *The Modern Corporation and Private Property*, in which they argued that the interests of managers were divorced from those of owners and concluded that the nation would best be served if business were guided by public policy. They called for government to impose more effective regulation of industry to safeguard the interests of the public. Otherwise, they warned, the "public interest would be held hostage to the private cupidity of managers."[29]

In the 1930s, such attacks were not merely theoretical. For one thing, Adolf Berle, an economist at Columbia University, joined other opponents of big business as an adviser to Franklin D. Roosevelt. The economic crisis of the 1930s brought about a shift in both moral and actual authority from the private (corporate) to the public (government) sector. Antibusiness rhetoric escalated, and big business came to fear for its existence as never before. In the end, the power of the corporations was never seriously threatened. For while the Roosevelt administration launched an antitrust movement in the late 1930s, many of the initiatives and controls launched during the early part of the New Deal, including the National Recovery Act and the National Industrial Recovery Act were initiated and led by businessmen.[30]

To answer their critics, the defenders of managerial capitalism sought to regain the moral authority they lost during the 1930s and to rekindle the spirit of voluntarism that had been sparked during World War I and continued during the Hoover administration. Corporations, they argued, had to meet new quasi-public responsibilities toward a wide constituency of customers, employees, and community.

It was Barnard, writing during the 1930s, who articulated the principal defense of managerial capitalism. He argued that management possessed the "moral authority" to both run and modernize the nation and to harness the forces of technological change for the public good. "[A]n expanding technological civilization depends so much on very large markets, i.e., upon large scale production, and very wide . . . sources of supply," wrote Barnard to his friend and fellow member of the Harvard Circle, Lawrence B. Henderson. "Moreover, a technological civilization . . . requires decisions based upon *special technical experience and knowledge,* neither of which are effectively taken into account in general systems of government as yet developed." Wrote Scott, "Barnard's work must be understood as an ideological attempt to restate the Progressive case for the consistency of the American dream with the managerial order." Barnard argued that the "professional managers of the largest and most powerful American corporations had to be as dedicated, energetic, and committed to reform as their administrative counterparts in government. Only then could they hope to reassert their rightful leadership."[31]

The book itself grew out of a series of extemporaneous lectures given by Barnard at Boston's Lowell Institute, which had been founded by Dr. A. Lawrence Lowell, the former president of Harvard. At the urging of Donham and Mayo, Barnard reworked his lectures and published them in 1938.

The Functions of the Executive was written at "a high level of discourse," as Barnard put it.[32] It is an abstract and theoretical book and would strike contemporary readers as frustrating in many respects. To give his ideas greater precision, Barnard invented terminology that, rather than clarifying matters, made the book an especially difficult read. Yet the hands-on experience of the working executive emerges between the lines.

The book also demonstrates Barnard's unique ability to traverse back and forth between the empirical and theoretical realms and to weave together the latest developments in everything from psychology to sociology. "I can think of no one who excels him in the simultaneous exercise of the twin capabilities of reason and competence or in the exploitation of their combined power," wrote Kenneth R. Andrews in his 1968 introduction to *The Functions of the Executive*. "For these reasons *The Functions of the Executive* remains today, as it has been since its publication, the most thought-provoking book on organization and management ever written by a practicing executive."[33]

Indeed, in almost every respect *The Functions of the Executive* was decades ahead of its time. For one thing, in sharp contrast to the mechanistic conceptions of Taylor and even Fayol, Barnard viewed the organization as a complex social system. He concentrated on the complexities of the human element in organization, on the "psychological forces of human behavior," and on behavioral approaches to managing the complexities of human behavior and coping with its limitations.[34]

Management's paramount challenge, according to Barnard, is achieving cooperation among the groups and individuals within this social system, in the interests of achieving organizational goals. The magnitude of the cooperative challenge, he felt, is such that "successful cooperation in or by formal organizations is the abnormal, not the normal, condition."[35]

At the heart of Barnard's argument is the tension between achieving organizational goals, which he called "effectiveness," and the need for individuals to achieve personal goals, a process he called "efficiency." Organizational goals, he argued, can't be accomplished unless the leadership of the organization acknowledges a host of complex individual aspirations and devises a means of helping employees achieve them. Cooperative systems work best, he argued, if there is a balance between the two.

Barnard also recognized the link between authority and legitimacy and argued that authority derives from those who are being led, not from the leaders. Noting that most employees "keep their fists clenched in their pockets," he argued that they consent to authority in varying degrees. Thus, he devised the concept of "zones of indifference, neutrality and unacceptability" to describe the boundaries within which people evaluate the orders given to them. (The "zone of indifference," paradoxically, refers to the highest level of acceptance.) He believed that management's job was to widen the zone of acceptable orders, "because the positive employee behaviors forthcoming from it would establish management legitimacy." While there would always be a tension between personal and organizational goals, management's challenge was finding a way to make them complimentary.[36]

In navigating between effectiveness and efficiency, Barnard, like Pareto, argued that one of management's biggest challenges involved grappling with the irrational, emotional side of human behavior.

Nonlogical decision making, he believed, predominated, and posed a special challenge for management—though not necessarily a negative one. For instance, Barnard once chided the director of the Batelle Laboratories for "exaggerating" the role of rational discovery in scientific invention, and underestimating the role of "inventive [i.e., intuitive] genius."[37]

Indeed, Barnard was a strong believer in the power of intuition and cautioned against the rationalist's excessive reliance on reason. As he wrote, "[T]he institutions of society from ancient to modern times are based upon non-logical motives.... Much of the error of historians, economists and of all of us in daily affairs arises from imputing logical reason to men who could not or cannot base their actions on reason....

"The harm...lies in the consequent deprecation of non-logical mental processes more than in the misuse of reason."[38]

Barnard was also the first theorist to elaborate on the nature and importance of the informal organization. Moreover, he recognized the importance of what we now call corporate culture and the role played by the informal organization in developing a company's values and rituals.[39]

Although Barnard knew both Roethlisberger and Mayo, he later claimed to have known little about the Hawthorne studies, which were completed before he wrote *Functions of the Executive;* he said it was the teachings of Pareto, via Henderson, that influenced his thinking on informal organization. Indeed, while *Management and the Worker,* which was published a year after Barnard's book, had viewed the informal organization of workers in a bank-wiring room as frequently undermining the goals of management, Barnard viewed the informal organization in a more positive light. Informal networks, he believed, were a natural and necessary corollary to the formal management hierarchy: "[A] very large part of the organized activities of today are carried on by temporary limited combinations under contracts without a general coordinating 'authority.' "[40]

"Whatever their origins, the fact of such contacts, interactions, or groupings changes the experience, knowledge, attitudes, and emotions of the individuals affected," he wrote. Informal organization, he added, is a "condition which necessarily precedes formal organization.... [F]ormal organizations are vitalized and conditioned by informal organizations."[41]

It is interesting to note that one of the "newest" management initiatives in high-tech industries, at companies such as Xerox and National Semiconductor, is an attempt to tap the knowledge of the "informal organization" by developing so-called communities of practice. This effort grew out of the need to find better ways of piggybacking on existing technology to develop new, more complex products and to do so at an ever-quickening pace of new-product development. Communities of practice involve informal groups of software designers who are encouraged to get together to brainstorm ideas *without* a managerial agenda. One idea implicit in communities of practice is that formal teams organized by management aren't as effective at achieving results as are software engineers who troubleshoot at the grassroots level. Solutions often emerge from freewheeling, around-the-water-fountain conversations, unstructured by agendas and deadlines, where the members of an informal group know where to find other individuals (often hidden in seemingly minor or tangential jobs) who might have the expertise to help solve a problem. Meanwhile, in fly-on-the-wall fashion, representatives of the "formal organization" (i.e., management) try to extract helpful ideas from the freewheeling exchanges without inhibiting the process of informal dialogue. For the members of the informal group, the communities of practice serve as the ultimate meritocracy—a diehard techie's dream—wherein an employee becomes part of the group because his or her peers recognize his or her ability to help solve a challenging problem. Barnard's ghost would be perfectly at home in such a setting.[42]

Although Barnard did not refer explicitly to the notion of corporate culture, he recognized that the values of an organization reside in the informal organization. He saw that informal organizations generate "customs, mores, folklore, institutions, social norms and ideals"—in short, culture. They are also a key to communication, which Barnard identified as one of the most important functions of the executive.[43] Wrote Scott, "Barnard's insights on organizational culture were the wedge that opened up the possibility for control of the group. Culture, a system of shared symbols woven into elaborate tapestries of images and metaphors, imparted meaning to employees' work roles. More importantly ... [they] placed individuals in the larger mythic context of the organization. By doing so, they enriched an individual's understanding of self." Decades later, Peters and Waterman would popularize the focus on corporate culture. It was Barnard, however, who established the groundwork.[44]

Barnard also introduced the concept of management by objective—although, of course, his terminology was not nearly as catchy as that of Peter Drucker, who popularized and elaborated on the subject. One of management's greatest tasks is to communicate and sell the idea of co-operation to its employees, as well as a specific organizational purpose. As he wrote, "The inculcation of belief in the real existence of a com-

mon purpose is an essential executive function. . . . This willingness requires the belief that the purpose can be carried out, a faith that di-
minishes to the vanishing point as it appears that it is not in fact in
process of being attained." Always returning to the problem of cooperation, he argued that the continued willingness of employees to work toward organizational goals depends "upon the satisfactions that are
secured by individual contributors in the process of carrying out the
purpose."[45]

Significantly, he understood better than most other executives the
importance and difficulties of conventional "incentive" schemes.
People, he believed, "are moved by different incentives, at different
times, and in different combinations." He anticipated the sophisticated
psychological arguments of Herzberg and Maslow's hierarchy of needs.
(Herzberg called money "a hygiene factor," and argued that not enough
of it will cause dissatisfaction; but money alone does not serve as a mo-
tivator.) "At the bare subsistence level . . . material inducements are on
the whole, powerful incentives," he wrote. The problem, he argued, is
that inadequate financial incentives are often used when nonfinancial
ones would be more appropriate. "Under favorable circumstances," he
wrote, "to a limited degree, and for a limited time, this substitution may
be effective"—but not in the long haul. He lamented a state of affairs in
which organizations "creat[e] sentiments in individuals that they *ought*
to want material things."[46]

Indeed, Barnard perceived that the logic of conventional incentive
schemes was, in essence, a self-fulfilling prophecy. Presaging Maslow by
close to a decade, Barnard argued that beyond a certain level of equitable compensation, employees are not necessarily driven by financial
incentives. Rather, the elaborate rituals of bonuses and incentives devised by management create a culture of avarice in which money becomes the prevailing symbol of success. Commenting on the
"ephemeral" nature of incentives, Barnard once said, "I remember
when we were young and first married, I'd come home and tell my wife,
'Well, we got a raise today!' She'd say, 'When are you going to get the
next one?' People are elated at an improvement in condition; but after
they get used to it they take it for granted, and they're still looking for
the stimulus of another improvement of condition. Of course, that can't
go on indefinitely."[47]

Barnard understood the magnitude of the challenge involved in balancing organizational and individual needs: "To establish conditions
under which individual pride of craft and of accomplishment can be secured without destroying the material economy of standardized production in cooperative operation is a problem in real efficiency. To maintain

a character of personnel that is an attractive condition of employment involves a delicate art and much insight in the selection (and rejection) of personal services offered.... To have an organization that lends prestige and secures the loyalty of desirable persons is a complex and difficult task in efficiency—in all-round efficiency, not one-sided efficiency."[48]

Barnard was correct in pinpointing the conundrum of corporate incentives. No problem continues to confound management more than the search for the optimum incentive formula![49]

A corollary point, Barnard recognized, was that individual effort is only as meaningful as the system within which employees work: "It is ... evident that ability is not something that is possessed by an individual independently of his environment." He believed it is necessary to "diagnose" and improve the environment in which employees work to achieve maximum productivity. The "development" and "training" of employees are, according to Barnard, of paramount importance.[50]

In tackling the question of establishing a "common purpose" and subsidiary goals that help organizations achieve that purpose, Barnard focused on the problem of decision making. He recognized that human choice and action are constrained by a range of "physical, biological, and social factors.... At every turn ... the executive is confronted ... with requirements, prohibitions, limitations, disabilities, inertia, obstruction, recalcitrance, disintegrating influences....

"Thus back and forth purpose and environment react in successive steps through successive decision in greater and greater detail" and complexity. Borrowing a concept from the noted economist John R. Commons, Barnard argued that because of human limitations, management has to select from the myriad variables affecting any given situation and focus on the "strategic" few that would offer "the greatest leverage over the outcomes of a particular decision" and in the interest of accomplishing a "common purpose."[51]

Herbert Simon would build his theory of bounded rationality on two important elements of Barnard's work: first, a view of organizations as entities of tremendous complexity, made up of diverse individuals and interests that are held together by web of "deals" and understanding—what Barnard called inducements and contributions[52]—and second, the significance of limited human knowledge and choices. Simon explicitly argues a point to which Barnard only alludes: that severe constraints on people's decision-making capability result in "satisfactory," as opposed to "optimal," decisions (see Chapter 8).[53]

Finally, Barnard suggested that deciding what decisions *not to make* is almost as important as the decisions management does tackle. "The fine art of executive decision consists in not deciding questions that are not now pertinent, in not deciding prematurely, in not making decisions that cannot be made effective, and in not making decisions that others should make."[54]

To modern readers, the most provocative—and controversial—aspect of Barnard's philosophy may be his belief in the moral imperative of management. "Organizations endure . . . in proportion to the breadth of morality by which they are governed," he insisted. In dealing with the "multifarious activities" of essentially autonomous groups—the informal organization that makes up the blood and guts of a company—"moral authority," according to Barnard, is the only effective authority.[55]

For Barnard, moral integrity was a key to the organization's role in a civilized society. In an organizational context, "morality" refers to the "good of the organization," the "interests of society," and the "prescriptions of law." As he put it, "[M]odern Western Civilization is morally complex, far beyond other civilizations. This view seemed to me to be confirmed by the marvelous orderliness and stability of our society."[56]

Indeed, what would strike modern readers as heretical today was Barnard's view that moral integrity—that is managerial integrity—requires individual sacrifices in the interest of the greater good. Wrote Barnard in a speech he delivered in 1932 when he was awarded a medal for distinguished service to the city of Newark, New Jersey: "The protection of the economic rights of the individual requires limitations of the economic privileges of the individual, just as the protection of the political rights of the individual requires limitation of his personal privileges." Cooperation, he added, "means genuine restraint of self . . . [and] actual service for no reward, it means the courage to fight for principles rather than for things, it means genuine subjection of destructive personal interest to social interest."[57]

From the perspective of a managerial class that has enjoyed the unprecedented affluence of the 1990s, no suggestion could seem more out of date. However, seen in the context of an uncertain global economy on the cusp of a new millennium, Barnard's philosophy seems eerily prophetic.

We have an economics that postulates a disorganized rabble of individuals competing for scarce goods; and a politics that postulates a "community of individuals" ruled by a Sovereign State. Both these theories foreclose on and discourage any investigation of the facts of social organization.

—Elton Mayo, *The Social Problems of an Industrial Civilization*[1]

Fritz Roethlisberger and Elton Mayo

Two Creative Misfits Who Invented "Human Relations"
(and Put the Harvard Business School on the Map)

They were two sides of the same coin—opposites, yet racked by similar insecurities, consumed by their own distinctive neuroses, and perpetual outsiders in the world around them. Fritz Roethlisberger, a small, timid man with deep-set eyes and a habit of peering out from under his eyebrows, was easily overlooked.[2] Just Fritz, as he was called by both colleagues and students, stumbled on his chosen profession after nearly ten years that were tormented by anxiety, false starts, and metaphysical doubts about the purpose of his life.

Elton Mayo, on the other hand, was a towering, flamboyant figure, an Ivy League celebrity whose outward demeanor of assertiveness and self-assurance concealed his self-doubts—most significantly, a nagging suspicion that he was destined to fail.

Roethlisberger and Mayo were part of a new immigrant intelligentsia who would challenge the parochialism and sense of entitlement that characterized America's elite at the turn of the century—the very community that had produced Frederick W. Taylor. As relative newcomers, they felt for the plight of the workingman. They were representative of an FDR-era democracy; internationalists who believed in the possibility of global cooperation and champions of enlightened bureaucracy and paternalistic corporate governance.

Most important, Roethlisberger and Mayo were, if not true Freudians, then enthusiastic proponents of the new psychological interpretations of human motivation. They saw the factory as a complex social system—not, as did the Taylorites, as a gigantic, impersonal machine. To Mayo and Roethlisberger, psychological techniques and social interaction, including collaboration and teamwork, were the key to managing the relationships within these social systems and to achieving improved morale and productivity. Together they conducted and interpreted one of the most famous and controversial studies in employee motivation, the famous Hawthorne experiments. Their methods would be hotly contested for many years—and, for a time, discredited.

Yet today it is the objections to the Hawthorne studies that seem naive and their conclusions that beg for a second look. Today the struggle to foster organizational creativity and to develop collaborative management forms and "flatter" organizations, as well as the decline in the role of labor unions and the radical downsizing of industry—with their negative impact on morale—make the questions asked at Hawthorne, as well as some of the lessons learned, seem surprisingly fresh.[3]

Nor is it only the duo's emphasis on collaboration and on treating ordinary workers as complex individuals that resonates today. Roethlisberger and Mayo challenged the notion of economic man as a purely rational being; they insisted that employees' behavior is influenced as much by their role in a work group and their relationship to their colleagues as by the promise of economic gain. The "Mayoite" perspective—and its challenge to some long-held assumptions of economic liberalism—is at the heart of the continuing debate on motivation and reward systems in industry. Finally, Roethlisberger and Mayo, who, together with Chester Barnard, were part of the so-called Harvard Circle, were among the first observers of modern industry to notice, and comment upon, the power of the informal organization (see Chapter 3).

Mayo, who had a genius for self-promotion, understood the importance of the work that the human relations pioneers were doing, especially at AT&T's Hawthorne works. On the eve of the Great Depression, Mayo wrote to G. A. Pennock, the assistant works manager at AT&T's Western Electric Division, where the Hawthorne studies were conducted:

> You are in a fair way to effect a change in industrial method that will have all the characteristics of a major revolution. By this I mean that its effect, immediate and remote, will be as revolutionary—industrially and socially considered—as the Industrial Revolution of the late 18th century. This last ushered in the machine age, precision in manufacturing, production and enormous growth in human capital of material resources. The change which you and your associates are working to effect will not be mechanical but humane.[4]

Of course, in predicting that Western Electric would change the tide of management, Mayo cast himself as midwife to that revolution. The sea change Mayo predicted has occurred fitfully over many decades. Yet few today would question the correlation between employee well-being and worker productivity. Enhancing the quality of human capital and, ultimately, productivity is arguably the greatest challenge industry has wrestled with since the time of the Hawthorne studies.

Together Roethlisberger, the philosopher scholar, and Mayo, the salesman psychologist, legitimized and humanized the then-embryonic "science" of management. Almost single-handedly, this odd couple of American management created the human relations movement. They influenced a Who's Who of policy makers and management thinkers, including Peter Drucker (see Chapter 10), Chester Barnard, the president of New Jersey Bell Telephone (see Chapter 3), and Justice William O. Douglas, who praised Mayo's *Social Problems of an Industrial Civilization* as "one of the most significant publications of this generation."[5]

Finally, Roethlisberger and Mayo were instrumental in elevating the Harvard Business School, and with it a new class of M.B.A. programs, from backwater trade schools to academic institutions of international prestige.

Fritz Roethlisberger

It was Fritz Roethlisberger's long and agonizing search for purpose and certainty in his own life that eventually led him to plumb the sources of motivation and meaning in the lives of industrial workers. The picture Roethlisberger painted of his own background is one of a fractured identity built on rocky immigrant beginnings. Roethlisberger was the son of a French mother and a Swiss father who had settled in Staten Island, New York, at the turn of the century. From the earliest age, young Fritz was conscious of the tensions between his French relatives, who claimed some royal ancestry, and the Roethlisberger clan, which had supplied a pungent, eponymous cheese to the royal families of Europe for three hundred years. Yet the senior Roethlisberger's purpose in the United States—to introduce the Roethlisberger cheese to the New World—was aborted when he died before reaching the age of thirty, a victim of pneumonia and alcoholism. (It is telling that in Roethlisberger's autobiography, *The Elusive Phenomenon*, he identified all his relatives except his parents by their first names.)[6]

The untimely death of his father would turn young Fritz into an outsider within his own family—a position he would occupy in society as well. The alienation Fritz felt from his mother is summed up in his description of the circumstances of his birth and that of a sister, Isa, fourteen months his senior: "My mother was not emotionally ready either for marriage or for the arrival of Isa, and even less for me. . . . I doubt very much that she wanted to be saddled with two brawling brats at the age of 19." Roethlisberger's feelings toward his sister seem to be dominated by resentment over the fact that he was forced to be in the same grade at school with Isa; despite the fact that he was more than a year younger, he felt superior to her academically. The distance he felt from his mother was exacerbated after her second marriage and the birth of three other children, the first of whom, Carl, was born eleven years after Fritz, making him an unlikely companion. His relations with his mother may actually have grown worse following the death of his youngest brother, Max, who died in childhood—a blow from which, he says, his mother never recovered. Although Roethlisberger showed no animosity toward his stepfather, Max Thaten, a German immigrant, he expressed no interest in him either.[7]

Whatever psychological scars were left by a childhood experienced in an emotional vacuum, young Fritz developed a penetrating, peripatetic intellect that was marked by a somewhat dour reclusiveness. "I was fascinated with the number patterns found in arithmetic, algebra, geometry, and the sciences of physics and chemistry," he recalled. "These subjects were to me neat, orderly, true, certain, and real. They contrasted sharply with the higgledy-piggledyness of my personal and family life, where it seemed to me we were always getting into heated arguments involving the definition of words or matters I then called superstitions, or ideas about taste, manners and modes of life derived from the old country."[8]

Roethlisberger had little patience for the petit bourgeois thinking and lifestyle of his family. In the Roethlisberger and Thalen households, meals were frequently eaten in silence, the menus set predictably according to the day of the week. Conversations, when they did occur, were "in both quality and quantity . . . not very high."

"At age 14 I was running away from all this like mad," he later recalled.[9]

Nor did he socialize much with his peers. At the Staten Island Academy, the private school he attended, Roethlisberger had few friends. He joined the Boy Scouts but never earned any merit badges. In his free time he read voraciously—but since there were no books at home and few at school, he devoured all the Horatio Alger stories he could lay his hands on at the local library.

In high school, two illnesses served to further cut Roethlisberger from his classmates and to reinforce his sense of isolation. "Both these illnesses . . . turned me inward toward my own reflections as a source of satisfaction," he recalled. "This private world of hopes and fears I shared with no one, and in an important sense I was not in touch with it myself. It was leading me more by the nose than I was directing it. But I was not aware of this at the time: I discovered it only later." It wasn't until the late 1960s that Roethlisberger, by his own admission, "realized how closely my search for my subject matter and my search for my identity had been related."[10]

Upon graduating in 1917, Roethlisberger enrolled at Columbia University, the first stop in a long and often frustrating quest to discover his professional destiny. Roethlisberger fit in no better at Columbia than he had on Staten Island. While he joined a fraternity, Beta Theta Pi, he soon got into a dispute with his fraternity brothers over a point of fraternal ritual. "I excommunicated myself from Beta Theta Pi, just as I had already disinherited myself from my family."[11]

Roethlisberger left Columbia in 1921 with an A.B. degree in engineering, still uncommitted to a professional goal and uncertain as to where life would lead him. He enrolled at MIT in a new bachelor's degree program that combined economics and engineering in what soon appeared to be another academic dead end.

Roethlisberger detested the MIT program almost from the start. He reserved special contempt for MIT's Course XV, which combined economics and engineering in the then avant-garde study of scientific management and efficiency engineering and which reflected all the antilabor biases of Taylorism. Indeed, Course XV was launched by Erwin Schell, a disciple of Taylor. Thus, Course XV embodied everything Roethlisberger would reject in his pioneering work in human relations. Even then, Roethlisberger "took great delight in collecting [and recounting] 'horror stories' " from Course XV, such as the one about a professor who advocated keeping employees' restrooms hot in the summer and cold in the winter, so that employees would not congregate there.[12]

Course XV helped convert a high-strung, nervous Fritz Roethlisberger into an ardent socialist and cast more doubt on his choice of engineering as a profession. "My introduction to the economic and social world through Course XV was so disillusioning that I began to question seriously whether I had chosen the right field for my career. One thing was clear, it was not scientific management." Always a voracious reader, he discovered Karl Marx, Thorstein Veblen, and Upton Sinclair.[13]

Roethlisberger was then twenty-four years old. Disillusioned with his academic experience, he decided to put his engineering degree to work. In 1922, he took a position as a chemist with the American Smelting and Refining Company in El Paso, Texas. His job was to act as a kind of referee between the mines and the smelters about the amount of metal contained in the ores that were shipped from the mine to the smelters. Roethlisberger found the analytical component of the job, which entailed greater engineering expertise than he possessed, overwhelming and the organizational disputes trivial. So before he could be fired, he quit and went to visit a friend across the border in Aguascalientes, Mexico, where he spent three months drinking and picking up girls.

Roethlisberger had "dropped out." After leaving Mexico, he moved to Greenwich Village and threw himself into the life of a bohemian socialist. Having read the classics, Roethlisberger immersed himself in the literature of the so-called lost generation, with whom he thoroughly identified. He read Sinclair Lewis, Theodore Dreiser, John Dos Passos, and the members of the so-called Algonquin Group. At last he found intellectual soul mates who shared his angst: "These writers put in words things about which I felt strongly, but which I had not been able to articulate. Although they reinforced my pessimism and tarnished my Horatio Alger picture of the American dream, this disenchantment fitted well into my continuing interest with socialism as a cure for the ills of the modern world. Man's human condition and his social condition were for me at the time unseparated."[14]

Yet his new milieu did little to satisfy his yearning for certainty and his craving for a place for himself in the world. As intellectually adrift as ever, in the autumn of 1924 he entered the Department of Philosophy in the Graduate School of Arts and Sciences at Harvard University. At that time, the department was dominated by Alfred North Whitehead, who had just arrived from Cambridge, England, and who, together with Bertrand Russell, had written *Principia Mathematica*, which sought to restore the crumbling foundations of arithmetic.

Whitehead became Roethlisberger's first mentor at Harvard. Finally, Roethlisberger felt as though he had found an intellectual home. "I learned to speak the language of mathematics, where 'you never know what you are talking about or whether what you are talking about is true,' " he recalled. "This logical austerity was like a breath of fresh air; I was enthralled even though I also was chilled to the bone. At the time more than the foundations of mathematics were crumbling for me. I . . . needed something firm upon which to stand—something a bit more tangible than I felt 'and,' 'or,' and 'not' to be."[15]

Eventually, however, as he worked to complete his degree in philosophy, Roethlisberger was forced to venture outside the comforting embrace of Whitehead's seminars. As he did so, he once again found himself in crisis. "I could not see how the study of ancient history or how becoming a philosopher's philosopher was going to help my plight. It seemed to me that 90 percent of philosophy was unmitigated nonsense, though I did not dare say so even to myself. The consequences of such an admission would have been too terrifying."[16]

Once again, he found himself adrift and beset by mounting anxiety. Inexplicably, despite his attachment to Whitehead, he had chosen to do his Ph.D. dissertation (on Descartes) with Étienne Gilson, a visiting professor from the University of Louvain in Belgium. Without the nurturance of a true mentor and faced with the task of slogging through vast and dusty volumes of Descartes in the original French, he abandoned his latest course of study. Once again, he had reduced his life to "dust and ashes."[17]

Yet just when Roethlisberger seemed sure that he was destined to remain adrift, his failure in philosophy proved to be the turning point of his career. Someone—probably Whitehead—had suggested he talk to Elton Mayo, who had just joined the Harvard Business School faculty to conduct some research on workers' motivation. Though Roethlisberger concedes that he "did not see the connection" between his philosophical studies and Mayo's research, his backers in the philosophy department probably thought highly of his intellect.[18] Then, too, philosophy, in those days, was considered a foundation for the study of psychology; Mayo himself had studied philosophy in Australia. So, in the spring of 1927, Roethlisberger walked across the verdant Harvard Business School campus to the basement offices of Morgan Hall. (The location, according to L. B. Barnes, a former Harvard professor and protégé of Roethlisberger, was "symbolically indicative" of the attitude of the hard-nosed, scientifically oriented faction at Harvard, which disapproved of the human relations group and Dean Wallace B. Donham's newfound interest in it.)[19]

It was the beginning of one of the most fruitful collaborations in American management history. Together Roethlisberger and Mayo would be instrumental in the creation of the human relations movement in management. Together they analyzed one of the most famous and controversial studies in employee motivation, the Hawthorne experiments. Their work at Hawthorne also provided a unique window on the evolution of corporate paternalism, especially at AT&T, in the years preceding and during the Depression. And, in large part through the work of Mayo, Roethlisberger, and their closest associates, Harvard became the cauldron in which many of the most exciting new ideas about the workplace and human capital would take shape.

The collaboration between Roethlisberger and Mayo, which lasted for more than a decade, also brought together two troubled, eccentric souls who seemed unlikely characters to play a pivotal role in the development of the Harvard Business School. By his own admission, Roethlisberger spent his first two years at the business school sitting "at Mayo's feet, spellbound by his knowledgeability, creative imagination and clinical insights." Shy and reticent as he was, Roethlisberger must have been in awe of Mayo, a towering, flamboyant figure—a "strange giraffe of a man," as someone once described him—who wore white gloves and chain-smoked cigarettes from a long, elegant cigarette holder.[20]

What Roethlisberger almost certainly didn't know was that Mayo was racked by his own sense of failure. Roethlisberger would have had no reason to suspect that the tall, gangly Australian, whom no one would ever think of addressing as anything but *Dr.* Mayo, was no doctor at all. While Mayo was descended from a long line of medical men and women, he had repeatedly flunked his medical courses—a failure that had sent him into a years-long period of self-doubt and soul-searching. Although it is unclear whether Mayo's backers at Harvard knew that Mayo lacked an M.D., the letters sent by Dean Donham to Harvard's president, A. Lawrence Lowell, refer to his new recruit as "Dr. Mayo." Even Mayo's master's degree was hastily arranged by Sir William Mitchell, Mayo's mentor at the University of Adelaide, *after* his appointment at Harvard.[21]

Elton Mayo

Elton Mayo grew up in a less-than-conventional household in Adelaide, Australia, the second of seven siblings. Although his father was an unambitious businessman who built a small real estate practice, Elton's grandfather, George Elton Mayo, was a prominent physician. And when Elton's sister, Helen, decided to buck convention and go into medicine, her parents were delighted. A brother, John, followed Helen to medical school.

Elton had inherited something of his father's lackadaisical nature—George Mayo believed that "heavy effort was . . . more comical than virtuous."[22] Yet at the same time, he struggled to win his mother's approval and to meet her exacting standards. As a result, he didn't find his calling quite as easily as had Helen and John. Pressured by his parents to follow Helen into medical school, Elton became a student of medicine at the University of Adelaide in 1899. He passed his first year's exams with flying colors but failed the examinations his second year.

Mayo may have lost interest in medicine, but his parents had not. In 1901, they enrolled him at the University of Edinburgh. While he matriculated the following September, he did so largely by avoiding medical courses. Still not giving up, his parents enrolled him in a small medical program run by St. George's Hospital in London. In December 1903, however, he dropped out of medicine for the third time.

No one knows precisely why Mayo failed at the study of medicine. According to his sister Helen, he had simply lost interest in medicine and been distracted by his friends. His brother Herbert wrote Mayo's failure off to womanizing and horseracing. Whatever the reasons, "Hetty and George were deeply disappointed." In 1938, Mayo wrote his sister, Helen, about his "phantasy": "I should like to meet my father and grandfather in the happy hunting grounds (on terms of complete equality) and to compare and discuss experiences with them." Years later, when Mayo had already built a name for himself as the world's leading industrial psychologist, Helen, perhaps still sensing her brother's lingering doubts about himself, sought to reassure him: "I can't help thinking how proud and happy Father and Mother would have been at you achieving the destiny which they had full confidence that you would."[23]

Like Roethlisberger, Mayo set off on what was to be a long and frustrating journey in search of his life's vocation. After a brief detour working for a diamond mine in West Africa, Mayo returned to England in 1904 and decided to take up a career as a writer.[24] Staying at the home of his uncle Colonel Charles Mayo, the younger Mayo dabbled at journalism, writing occasionally for the *Pall Mall Gazette* and working as a proofreader for a Bible publisher.

Mayo had an unmistakable flair for writing. However, the contrast between his sister's accomplishments—Helen was hard at work at the School of Tropical Medicine in London—and what seemed like his own flailings exacerbated Mayo's loss of self-esteem. Mayo took to staying up half the night, and getting up after 11 A.M. He became such a nuisance that he alienated most of his British relatives and was forced to move out of his uncle's home. Mayo moved to rooms in Great Ormond Street, not far from where his sister, Helen, now lived, where he "talked to no one" and ate many of his meals on his own, feeling utterly useless and alone. Despite—or perhaps because of—the fact that his father was supporting him, he had "no energy and little inclination for work." Ashamed and depressed, he alternated between blaming himself and blaming his parents for not understanding him, and he stopped writing home altogether.[25]

It wasn't until the fall of 1904, when he happened to pass by a three-story house on Great Ormond Street that housed the Working Men's College, that he finally broke the vicious cycle of loneliness and self-denigration. The Working Men's College, which had been founded to "provide working men with organized human studies in a self-governing and self-supporting institution," gave Mayo, then twenty-four, an unexpected new purpose in life. The spirit of Christian fellowship and self-improvement set the tone for human relations in the college. "Freedom and order were the prominent values; working men were to be unshackled from their forced ignorance and shown the right order of their social and political world."[26]

Mayo began teaching an advanced course in English grammar at the college. He soon became a favorite among the students, both for his considerate manners and for his oratorical ability. Perhaps the best indication of Mayo's popularity at the college was the fact that despite the school's liberal environment, Mayo led the Debating Society in an argument entitled "This house welcomes the recent downfall of the Labour Ministry in Australia" and won his argument by a vote of 10 to 5. Of Mayo's six-month tenure at the school, the college journal wrote, "It is remarkable to what extent he entered into the College life during the six months. . . . He carries many friendships and pleasant memories . . . with him."[27]

For the first time, Mayo had tasted success and won the respect of his peers. His experience at the Working Men's College would explain much about his eventual affinity, however paternalistic it may have been, for industrial workers. Years later he wrote to his wife, Dorothea, "As a youngster I walked into the Working Men's College and was immediately taken into the confidence of the workers themselves," who were his students.

Yet it would be a number of years before he settled down to his chosen vocation. In the beginning of 1905, he was ready for a new adventure and made plans to travel to Canada, expecting to borrow his fare from Helen. Although Helen had always been supportive of her younger brother's efforts at finding himself, this time she refused to underwrite another quixotic journey and urged him to return home. Mayo finally acquiesced. Upon returning to Adelaide, he went to work for several years at a printing company. Although his parents greeted him warmly, he still felt insecure, later recalling, "When I came back to Australia from England . . . everyone [was] pointing the finger of scorn or else disregarding me." He was considered a pariah not only for failing medicine—which was bad enough—but for going into business.[28]

By 1907, however, he realized that he wasn't suited for the world of commerce either. For one thing, an unregenerate bohemian, he could not get used to normal working hours and routines. (Years later, he would outrage many of his colleagues at Harvard by arriving at his office after 11 A.M. and for taking long lunches.) Then, too, he maintained an unbusinesslike interest in writing. In 1905, he had gained a reputation as a great wit and showman who could keep an audience entertained with impromptu performances. He took great pleasure in poking fun at the petit bourgeois hypocracies of Adelaide society, even as he danced at its edges. At one party, for example, he asked his fellow guests what they thought of a new book entitled *Perdition*. Some said they liked it; others said they didn't. In fact, no such book existed, a joke he shared with no one but his brother Herbert.

Mayo also wrote flippant dialogue and verses, in which he cast himself as the "Ostracized Agnostic." In one of these, he wrote, tellingly, "To be in the world, fortuitously as it were . . . is a far happier condition than to be of it socially. To be content with ephemeral pleasure is, no doubt, a crime; but it is more easily justifiable than to exist for the single purpose of snubbing one's next door neighbor. . . . Nothing annoys me more intensely than the complete self-satisfaction of those 'society leaders.' "[29]

He began to take courses at the University of Adelaide and decided to get an undergraduate degree in philosophy. In addition, he studied economics and psychology, a course for which he won the highest prize at the university.

While Mayo was beginning to distinguish himself academically for the first time, he hadn't changed his peripatetic instincts. He became a star of the Pickwick Club, a debating society, where he argued topics ranging from art to politics. In his honors thesis, "Criteria for Social Progress," he took up a favorite subject: social progress and, as a subtext, socialism. At one time, he had been vehemently antisocialist. Now, however, he had modified his views. "Socialism could not be justified if its aims were achieved through extreme action," he wrote. "One important basis on which socialism could be justified was . . . 'skill in administration.' " Thus, he favored government by "aristocrats of intellect," who were, in his view, preferable to aristocrats of wealth—a viewpoint that put him in perfect sync with the managerial meritocracy that would gain ascendance in the United States after World War I (see Chapter 3).[30]

Mayo's honors thesis contained the initial formation of a worldview that would come to inform his work at the Harvard Business School years later. His position on socialism, in particular, betrayed two key features of his Weltanschauung: he was both an elitist and a fervent moderate. For all his flailings against society, he could never bring himself to work against the status quo—a fact that no doubt helped him to gain acceptance in business circles but also proved a weakness in his management theories. In England, during his brief foray into journal-

ism, he had railed against socialism because it flourished on mob ignorance and preferred "a high ethical Socialism" that developed from the
"voluntary sacrifice of certain advantages by a more cultured class in
order to raise the moral and intellectual level of their less enlightened
brethren." Mayo also remained resistant to the need for unions, asserting that enlightened employers, by anticipating unionization, would
make it obsolete.[31]

With the successful completion of his thesis, for which he won both
a prize and an honors degree upon his graduation in 1911, Mayo was
set on an academic course—though one that was not yet clearly defined.
He received a glowing recommendation from Sir William Mitchell, who
had been both his thesis adviser and his mentor and who said of Mayo
that he was "the best student" he had had in fifteen years. Soon after
graduating, Mayo took up his first academic position in Brisbane, at the
newly established University of Queensland, teaching courses in logic,
psychology, and ethics.[32]

Mayo was ready to make up for lost time. During the next few years,
he held a number of academic posts, gradually making a name for himself primarily in psychology—though he maintained his interests in a variety of other subjects as well. He was known to be a memorable
lecturer. While most professors spoke standing behind a lectern, Mayo
began his talks sitting cross-legged on a table, occasionally pacing back
and forth, frequently punctuating his remarks with humorous asides.
His students marveled at the way he moved effortlessly, and without the
aid of notes, from one topic to another, weaving together the classics
with observations about, say, psychology and anthropology.[33]

Mayo's activities extended far beyond the classroom. He took on
public speaking engagements and published articles on everything from
religion and psychology to philosophy and adult education. He coached
the dramatic society and came to be so beloved by the students that he
was elected president of the Student Union. He even became involved
with settling disputes over worker education and the role the university
should play in educating laborers.

Mayo would remain in Australia for another decade before moving to
the United States. During the remainder of his Australian period, three
events occurred that would have a significant effect on his later life and
work.

First, in 1913, he married Dorothea McConnel, the daughter of one
of Queensland's most prominent families and a young woman who
"gave the appearance of a natural aristocrat," according to Richard
Trahair, Mayo's biographer. In his own mind, Mayo had married "up,"
a fact that was important to his evolving perception of himself. But if

his academic triumphs served to bolster his sense of self-worth, his choice of a bride served subtly to undermine it. For one thing, the salary of a university lecturer was hardly enough to support Dorothea in the style to which she was accustomed—especially since she never learned to manage money. Then, too, she seemed perpetually dissatisfied.[34]

While Dorothea was attractive, intelligent, and kind, it is clear that Mayo was drawn equally to the needier side of her nature; indeed, she may have been the first in a long line of friends and relatives on whom he began to test his psychological theories. For Dorothea, who had endured a harsh, puritanical upbringing, was high-strung and neurotic. She was obsessed with cleanliness and neatness to the point that soon after arriving in the United States the Mayo family moved into the Colonial Inn in Bryn Mawr because Dorothea felt she couldn't maintain a house to her own high standards. Indeed, throughout their marriage, she was perpetually on the move, seemingly always dissatisfied with her living arrangements. Thus, the Mayos' marriage became a migratory one in which Dorothea frequently found a reason to live apart from her husband. During much of their marriage Mayo lived virtually alone; his years at Harvard, for example, were spent in a hotel room, while Dorothea lived alternately in Switzerland and England, an arrangement that put a "severe strain" on him.[35]

Like a frog prince who could never quite believe that he had won the heart of his princess, Mayo continued to idealize Dorothea and to long for her, even while accepting her absences with little rancor. During their long separations, he wrote to her almost daily. Their correspondence reveals not only an unusual marriage but also the insecurities with which he continued to wrestle. During Dorothea's first absence, in 1915, when Dorothea traveled to Tasmania following the birth of their eldest daughter, Patricia Elton Mayo, to escape the hot Brisbane summer, he confessed that he was "afflicted by fears and tremors—so dependent am I—and cannot understand how I can be cross with the dearest woman." (A second daughter, Gael, was born six years later.)[36]

Another important relationship of Mayo's during this period, especially in light of Dorothea's frequent absences, was with the anthropologist Bronislaw Malinowski, whom Mayo met in 1914. Mayo and Malinowski shared a common interest in the psychological and social factors involved in human behavior. Both men were convinced that people's behavior and experience were best understood when seen in the context of their social environment. Malinowski's approach to anthropology, in marked contrast to the theoretical bent of his colleagues, was to study the actual behavior and experience of exotic tribes. Mayo and Malinowski met as the anthropologist was beginning his groundbreaking studies of Australian Aborigines and the Mailu of Papua, New Guinea. During the 1920s they would meet again at Harvard, where the anthropologist's work would become a key building block of Mayo's human relations school.[37]

By the end of World War I, Mayo not only had been promoted to full professor, he had also developed a reputation as a successful clinical psychologist. In 1919, his work attracted the interest of a young doctor, Thomas R. H. Matthewson, who was working with soldiers who had returned from World War I and were suffering from shell shock. Mayo, who had read Freud, Jung, and Piaget, used a variety of techniques, including free association, hypnosis, and attempts at activating early childhood memories, to treat them. Mayo and Matthewson were pioneers, in Australia, in the use of psychoanalysis as a therapeutic treatment.

Although the Brisbane medical establishment was skeptical of Matthewson's practice, the doctor soon had more work than he could handle. By 1920, he had begun referring some of his most difficult "psychoneurotics" to Mayo.[38]

Increasingly, Mayo was torn between his obligations in the philosophy department and his interest in doing psychological research, including research in industrial psychology. Finally, in 1920, he resigned his position in the Brisbane philosophy department to take on a new, temporary research chair in psychology. It was at about this time that he began lecturing on the need for psychological research into the causes and consequences of industrial unrest and outlining the importance of the "human factor" in work.[39]

Yet despite his very obvious accomplishments, Mayo remained dissatisfied with his career. He disliked the bureaucratic aspects of his job, including the university board meetings he was expected to attend, and he detested the petty academic politics. Mayo's dissatisfaction crystallized when he was not offered a chair in philosophy that suddenly opened up at the University of Sydney. Even though he had not applied for the job, he felt angry at what he perceived as a snub. Once again, he overreacted and decided to take a leave of absence to do research in Britain.

Mayo's restlessness undoubtedly was fueled by a continuing sense of insecurity. Through his own position at the university and the connections he had made through Dorothea's family, he enjoyed a place among Australia's elite. Still, he continued to be plagued by his failures in medicine.

Throughout his published papers and debates, Mayo took issue with the medical profession. On one occasion, for example, he accused doctors of running a club designed to keep out new members. And in a debate at the University of Queensland, he joined the affirmative side of a debate on whether the medical profession should be nationalized. He was also quick to feel a snub, especially from a doctor; at a dinner attended by Brisbane's one hundred most notable citizens, for example, Mayo was convinced that Dr. Espie J. Dods, a long-standing friend of the Mayo family, had slighted him.[40]

Mayo was still searching for some final, elusive imprimatur of success. He heard that a position had come open at the University of Melbourne, a city he preferred to Brisbane and where he hoped Dorothea might finally feel at home. Worried that he didn't have sufficient international experience to clinch the job, he set off for a study leave in England. First, however, he decided to make a detour to the United States, where he would deliver a series of psychological lectures, partly because he needed the fees to finance his journey. With several letters of introduction, including one to the University of California at Berkeley, where he hoped to give a series of lectures, as well as one to Standard Oil, Mayo set sail alone for San Francisco on July 12, 1922.[41]

Mayo's U.S. trip began inauspiciously, however. His contacts failed to produce the lecture engagements he had been counting on. San Francisco, the first stop on his journey, proved to be far more expensive than he had expected, and his funds were soon depleted.

Once again, he was haunted by doubts, and he took to brooding and wandering aimlessly through the streets of San Francisco. Upon learning that his mother was gravely ill, he couldn't bring himself to write to her. He was convinced that the setbacks he had suffered would be interpreted by Hetty Mayo as signs of his failure and would impede her recovery.[42]

Just as he was about to give up on his prospects for clinching any lecture engagements in the United States and return to Australia, Mayo got an all-expenses-paid invitation from the National Research Council to go to Washington, D.C. The NRC, impressed with Mayo's understanding of industrial sociopsychology, gave him a recommendation to Beardsley Ruml and Raymond Fosdick at the Laura Spelman Rockefeller Memorial Foundation. "This is the best thing that ever happened to us," he wrote Dorothea.[43]

Mayo could not have known how right he was. From then on, "the breaks [were] with" him, as he liked to say. For Mayo's encounter with Ruml coincided with Ruml's own plans for the Rockefeller Foundation. At the helm of one of the country's richest foundations, Ruml set out on an ambitious plan to alter the organization's philanthropic mandate from supporting small traditional projects on current issues to disbursing its more than $75 million on long-range, large-scale studies covering everything from sociology and political science to psychology and anthropology. Eventually, his work would earn him a reputation as a founder of the modern social sciences. Mayo would be one of the first beneficiaries of Ruml's vision and largesse.

Ruml also became one of Mayo's closest friends in the United States and the man who helped pave Mayo's way in academia. Ruml and Mayo were natural soul mates. At twenty-seven, Ruml had just become the director of the Rockefeller Foundation. A brilliant and engaging young man, Ruml had earned his Ph.D. in psychology and education from the University of Chicago. Like Mayo, he was something of a bon vivant. Years later, Mayo wrote to Ruml, saying, "I do not know whether you remember our original talks in 1922, but you certainly were the person who started me off on the road we have traveled since."[44]

It was Ruml who introduced Mayo to Professor Joseph H. Willits, head of the Industrial Research Department at the University of Pennsylvania's Wharton School of Finance and Commerce. Wharton, established in 1881, was the first undergraduate school of commerce in the United States; its graduate program had been launched in 1908. A year before Mayo's arrival in the United States, Wharton had established the Department of Industrial Research, which was to deal with problems relating to employment, executive leadership, wages, and personnel practices, focusing on the Philadelphia area.[45]

Initially, Willits booked Mayo to deliver only a few weeks' worth of lectures. But Willits, who agreed with Mayo's assessment that modern society was undergoing something akin to a "nervous breakdown," soon extended his assignment.

Mayo became a valuable source of advice to Willits on the mission of the Industrial Research Department. "Somewhere in the industrial structure of society there is a defect, the effects of which have become increasingly manifest since the industrial revolution of the 18th century," Mayo wrote to Willits in 1923 in response to Willits's request for suggestions on extending the work of the Industrial Research Department. "The social unrest which began with the chartist riots has made itself felt more widely and more often in the ensuing century. . . .

"Industrial research should be guided by consideration of its social value, its industrial value and its educational value."[46]

At Wharton and elsewhere on the lecture circuit, Mayo was making a name for himself with his ideas on psychology, especially his interpretations of the work of Jung, Freud, and Pierre Janet, a prominent turn-of-the-century French psychologist, whom Mayo met in 1925. In particular, he had become a key proponent of what he termed "psychopathological revery"—in layman's terms, daydreaming. "Reveries were becoming central to his personal experiences, his professional pronouncements and his family life," notes Mayo's biographer Richard Trahair.[47] Indeed, as he readily admitted to Dorothea, during his first years in Philadelphia, he was often plagued by morose reveries: "If only this works out as it seems likely to—I'm so stupid, a foolish anxiety reverie makes me afraid to trust good fortune.... [W]hen I'm in action, I never question my capacity for fortune; it is only when I sit back 'to think.' "[48]

To Mayo, reveries could be either a positive or a negative psychological force; they were, however, central to every person's mental makeup. In a genius, for example, reveries could produce creative insight. In the neurotic, on the other hand, they provide a refuge from concentration. The problem of industrial workers' reveries was particularly acute, he believed. Faced with monotonous work, workers enter into hostile reveries that engender resentment against the society that sets the terms of employment and fosters rebellion and radicalism.[49]

In particular, Mayo believed that workers were affected by irritability and depression more than most people because these irrational emotions were exacerbated in an industrial setting by the lack of opportunity for personal expression. He believed that through industrial research, he could study and expose the irrationalities that interfered with productive work, help to assuage them, and thus achieve a better integration of revery and concentration.[50]

Mayo himself was amazed at how readily his ideas were received in the United States—the term "revery" even became something of a catchword. He also attracted a coterie of private patients. "Such a change from Australia," he wrote to Dorothea, "rather wonderful by comparison with the anxiety of Sydney." For the first time, he began thinking about making his break with Australia permanent.

Mayo's contacts at Wharton and the Rockefeller Foundation, together with his reputation as a lecturer and as a clinician, won him a position at Wharton, with funding from the Rockefeller Foundation. Willits also introduced Mayo to a host of prominent business leaders, frequently inviting twelve to fifteen businessmen to the university's Lenape Club. In this clubby atmosphere, Mayo would press his case for the need for industrial research, a pitch that eventually led to several important research projects. "There are many burning questions of the day that are crying out for specialized investigation and no such investigation is being done," wrote Mayo to Willits in 1923. "Instead we have the spectacle of various 'schools of social science' expounding the opinions of a particular group or class.... Questions that demand specialized work range from broad inquiries, such as the real significance of 'democracy'

to narrower issues such as the causes of seasonal and periodic unemployment."[51]

Mayo's first attempt at treating the industrial psyche took place in the
engine room of C. H. Masland & Sons, a textile manufacturer in north
Philadelphia. "My original idea was to treat a factory as if it were a
'shell-shock' hospital and to examine each individual in it with the ob-
ject of discovering: in what respect his attitude to life was abnormal . . .
and the effect of such abnormality upon the collaborative work in the
factory," he explained.

In fact, his efforts at treating individual employees at Masland for an
array of psychological problems, including paranoia, chronic
headaches, and sexual fears, turned out to be something of a fiasco. He
conducted his consultations in a noisy corner of the factory. While the
workers' response to Mayo was initially welcoming, few came to him for
help since they assumed, probably correctly, that he was there to promote management's interests, not their own. He was forced to conclude
that his approach "neglect[ed] unduly the part played by the departmental organization within the factory." It didn't help that the company,
which was conservative and fiercely antiunion, "discouraged all attempts to organize the social life of the factory."[52]

Mayo's most important experiment in industrial psychology during
this period took place at Continental Mills, not surprisingly a company
that had a much more labor-sensitive culture than Masland had. The
company, which made woolen fabrics, was a pioneer in personnel practices, offering its workers health benefits, bonus schemes, recreation activities, and savings plans. The company's negligible worker turnover
rate, which averaged about 5 percent annually in most departments,
mirrored its enlightened management practices. Yet, mysteriously,
turnover in the company's spinning department was 250 percent per
year—the conundrum that Mayo was brought in to solve. "My first case
in the industrial nervous breakdown field," he wrote to Dorothea.[53]

With the backing of Continental Mills's management, Mayo launched
a systematic investigation into working conditions at Continental Mills
and arrived at some of his most successful conclusions. When he examined the turnover rate in the spinning department, he discovered
that the spinners were much more irritable than those in other departments. The spinners complained of chronic fatigue and depression.
Alcoholism was also more prevalent in the department than elsewhere.
These problems existed even though management had tried to institute
"a number of bonus schemes" in the department, as well as "extensive
amusements and games," an "admirable personnel department," and a
generally high "spirit of cooperation."[54]

Mayo concluded that the problem had to do with the exceptionally monotonous nature of the work. (The theme of monotony and its effects on industrial workers would become a major focus of Mayo's later work.) The workers spent ten hours each day walking among the machines, looking for broken threads, and twisting them back together. To fix the threads, the spinners had to stretch awkwardly across their machines, which exacerbated their muscle fatigue.

To mitigate the effects of monotony and fatigue, Mayo suggested a regimen of rest pauses every few hours. Before long, Mayo was able to demonstrate that rest pauses had improved productivity by 30 percent in some departments at Continental Mills. As at Link-Belt, in Taylor's day (see Chapter 1), a labor-friendly atmosphere at Continental Mills—unlike the one that prevailed at C. H. Masland—helped produce improved results. Best of all, the results achieved at the company helped Mayo clinch three more years of funding from Rockefeller.[55]

Mayo's work in Philadelphia during this period revealed another important feature of his work, which helped account for his increasing success: he had an uncanny knack for getting his subjects—whether they were workers or executives—to open up to him. His greatest talent, perhaps, was as an analyst of the human condition. His work in Philadelphia, as in later years, was peppered with observations about the social and psychological makeup of the industrial world.

For example, Mayo discovered that one worker at Continental Mills, who was of Italian-American origin, had grown irritable because his working wife refused to have children. Without children, he was convinced, he would have an impoverished old age. (Both in his consulting engagements and as a teacher—in addition to his work at Wharton, Mayo taught at the Philadelphia Labor College—Mayo attempted to counteract the widespread ignorance about sex by offering his students advice and reading materials on gender and sexuality.) Years later, working on the Hawthorne studies, Mayo made the observation that while domestic problems can affect a worker and his work, a good supervisor can often compensate for them.[56]

With the success of his work in Philadelphia, Mayo cabled the University of Queensland to request an extension of his leave of absence. His request was denied. So in February 1923 he resigned his post at Brisbane. With additional funding from Rockefeller now secured, Mayo sent for Dorothea and his daughters.

By the time his family arrived in Philadelphia in June 1923, Mayo's reputation in both the local academic and business communities was shining. Most important for Mayo, he had also gained entrée into Philadelphia's prominent medical circles through his friendship with

S. DeWit Ludlum, a leading Philadelphia psychiatrist who became a mentor to him. Ludlum sent him patients, arranged for him to attend meetings at the Neuropsychiatric Clinic of Philadelphia General Hospital, and nominated him for membership in the University Club.[57]

Mayo's star had risen so fast in Philadelphia that he soon attracted the attention of the dean of Harvard University's fledgling School of Business Administration.[58] Mayo was lured to Harvard at a pivotal moment in the young life of the business school. What had started in 1908 as a tenuous academic experiment with limited funding suddenly gained a firmer financial footing and, under the leadership of Dean Wallace B. Donham, underwent a sea change in its philosophy and leadership. With a $5 million donation from George F. Baker, a New York banker, and his son, George Baker, Jr., Harvard had just added to its endowment and constructed a brand-new business school campus that had been designed by McKim, Mead & White, a prominent architecture firm, and Frederick Law Olmsted, a leading landscape architect. The once-controversial case method pioneered by HBS was gaining a following in schools around the country. And, fueled by the business boom of the Roaring Twenties, HBS graduates were in great demand.[59]

Most important, HBS's conception of itself as a school of applied economics was dissolving. "The facts of concrete situations refused to stay within the concepts of our economists," recalled Donham years later. "Non-economic facts persisted in coming into situations. By so doing, they forced us to recognize that problems faced by men of affairs—either public or private—can almost never be treated as problems in applied economics." Donham shared the apocalyptic view of prominent intellectuals and leaders of the new managerial elite that the scientific and industrial boom of the early twentieth century combined with the decline of religion was fomenting an economic, political, and spiritual crisis.[60]

In 1924, building on a series of Saturday-afternoon conversations with Alfred North Whitehead, who had joined the Harvard faculty, Donham concluded that science in the modern world had been "elevated to a position of false authority." Donham was convinced that the problems created by scientific materialism—the very ones that business leaders would have to resolve—were human ones. The challenge, he believed, was to "socialize the results of science."[61]

Donham embarked on a wholesale effort to change the focus of the business school from one of applied economics to the study of human relations in industry. Only a decade earlier, scientific management had been the core of HBS's manufacturing-based curriculum, and Donham's predecessor had lobbied hard to recruit Frederick W. Taylor to join HBS's faculty. (Taylor, who had never attended college and who said that he refused to hire any "young college graduates until they [had] been 'dehorned' by some other employer" refused the offer; he did, however, give annual lectures at HBS until his death in 1915; see Chapter 1.)[62]

Now Donham set out to assemble an interdisciplinary group of experts in everything from sociology and anthropology to medicine and philosophy who would develop research on human relations in industry. Mayo was the first and most important of Donham's recruits.

Mayo probably first came to Donham's attention as a result of several provocative articles he had published in *Harper's* magazine. The two men met for the first time at a dinner in New York City in 1925. They must have realized almost immediately that they shared the same concerns about the potentially disruptive social costs of industrialization. A year later, having secured funding from the Rockefeller Foundation, Donham was able to offer Mayo a position as HBS's first associate professor of industrial research on an "experimental" basis.[63]

From the beginning, Mayo occupied a position of privilege at Harvard. Although HBS's faculty was oriented toward teaching, Mayo was not expected to teach. Thanks largely to the Rockefeller Foundation, he commanded both a salary and research funds beyond those of most Harvard professors.[64]

Although many of his colleagues would come to resent him, Mayo had powerful allies at HBS. Donham proved to be a staunch supporter throughout Mayo's career in Cambridge. He found a supporter in Philip Cabot, a Boston Brahmin and founder of HBS's executive education program, whose own iconoclastic leanings were reinforced by a near brush with death in the 1920s. Equally important, he developed a close relationship with Lawrence J. Henderson, a brilliant and highly mercurial man who was, at once, one of the most respected and most feared figures at Harvard. Mayo, Henderson, and Donham made up the core of the Harvard Circle, a group of social scientists that also included Chester Barnard (see Chapter 3).[65]

Henderson, who was a biochemist and a faculty member at both the Harvard Medical School and the business school, occupied a position at Harvard that was almost as ill defined as Mayo's. Known for a "slightly malicious" sense of humor, Henderson was said to "treat everyone like an ass until he proved the contrary." George Homans, then a junior member of the budding human relations movement at Harvard noted that Henderson's "manner in conversation was feebly imitated by a piledriver."[66]

Henderson was, in fact, a highly respected blood chemist who had done pioneering work on acid-based equilibrium in the body.

(Henderson's work on the chemical equilibrium of blood led to the development of blood plasma.) He had become intrigued with the possibility that social equilibrium might follow laws similar to those of physiological equilibrium. In particular, he had become an ardent proponent of the Italian economist and sociologist Vilfredo Pareto, who argued for a sort of sociological homeostasis; according to Pareto, a social system could adapt to incremental change by restoring its natural state of equilibrium—provided that the change in variables was not too great. It could do so because of the interdependence of the variables that made up the system. Pareto's view of systems and the importance of how emotions affect human behavior provided the "theoretical hook upon which the Harvard Circle hung its interpretation of the Hawthorne studies," wrote William G. Scott. A driving force behind the human relations movement was the fear that industrialization had brought dislocations so great that it would be difficult for society to regain its equilibrium.[67]

In the early 1930s, Henderson also launched a series of seminars on Pareto that were a cross between an academic firing line and a soiree. For the seminars, which were held during the late afternoons in the junior Common Room of Winthrop House, Henderson rounded up the most illustrious intellectuals around Harvard, including Joseph Schumpeter, then a professor of economics at Harvard, Mayo, Roethlisberger, and Robert K. Merton, then a graduate student in sociology. Henderson lectured imperiously to the assembled crowd. "This seminar in time became famous, because it was attended by many distinguished professors from most of the disciplines in the University as well as by some distinguished men from outside," recalled Roethlisberger, noting that it looked to him as though "Henderson had organized the seminar to tell his colleagues and friends what's what."[68]

The Pareto seminars helped provide an intellectual framework for the human relations school. In addition to his theories on social equilibrium, Pareto had made a distinction between logical and nonlogical thinking, noting that many actions were based on nonlogical motives, such as superstitions. In effect, these nonlogical motives, particularly feelings and sentiments, were as important in understanding a social system as were facts and logic. Thus, Pareto, as interpreted by the Harvard Circle, offered a powerful counterpoint to rationalist explanations of the behavior and motivation of economic man. By interpreting and popularizing Pareto—even within a relatively sophisticated intellectual circle—Henderson's seminar helped disseminate Pareto's work among such disparate management thinkers as Chester Barnard, Peter Drucker, and Joseph Juran, the quality management theorist.[69]

Henderson also became one of Mayo's few close friends at Harvard. Mayo was one of the only people with whom Henderson, whose wife had been committed to a mental institution, could discuss his personal problems. Since both men lived alone, Mayo spent many evenings at Henderson's house on Willard Street, where their conversations ranged from discussions of the scientific method to the nature of human thought, meaning, and action. Given Henderson's stature as a medical man, the gift of his friendship undoubtedly helped salve Mayo's lingering doubts about his own medical failures. Henderson's sudden death in 1942 was a "heav[y] blow" to him. As he wrote at the time, "He was not directly involved in the industrial researches, but for 16 years I had the benefit, more or less every morning, of his comment on topics and events. Personal considerations apart, his disappearance from the scene leaves a void that cannot be filled."[70]

Whatever the personal undercurrents, the biochemist, the industrial researcher, and the dean (Donham) collaborated in an effort to apply new medical theories, both physiological and psychological, to the study of organizations. Their discussions led to the establishment, under Henderson, of the Harvard Fatigue Laboratory, which sought to identify correlations between physical well-being, especially fatigue, and working conditions and productivity. With its treadmills and unusual (by business standards) research projects in the physiology of exercise, the Fatigue Lab, in the basement of Morgan Hall, remained on the periphery of the business school. It did, however, help to buttress the Hawthorne studies by providing "a financially secure and academically respectable base for social science research," according to J. H. Smith, a professor of sociology at the Southampton University in England.[71]

By the time Mayo arrived at Harvard, he had wrapped himself in the mantle of a bona fide medical man—not that he would have lied outright about his qualifications. Still, there was no question that by academic standards he was something of a dilettante. While HBS adhered to strict working hours, with most professors arriving at work promptly by 9:00, Mayo made a great show of never getting to his office before 11:00 and taking long lunches. Nor did he have a taste for "the heavyweight treatise." His published output was lean by most academic measures; he published only one slim volume during his tenure at Harvard, *Human Problems of an Industrial Civilization*. Two others, *The Psychology of Pierre Janet* and *Social Problems of an Industrial Civilization*, were published after he left Harvard. A voracious reader, he stacked the tables in his office and hotel room with books on subjects ranging from human sexuality to anthropology.[72]

Yet it was the peripatetic nature of Mayo's personality and intellectual interests that also fed his unique creativity and insights. As Alan Gregg put it, Mayo had a unique ability to "reexamine facts and squeeze new juice out of fruit discarded by the generality."[73]

It was Mayo's ability to draw on the threads of many disciplines and to stimulate debate and ideas among his colleagues that laid the foundations of the Human Relations School. His journey from philosophy to psychology and ultimately to industrial sociology informed his humanistic approach to industrial problems. As Wallace B. Donham, in a foreword to *Social Problems of an Industrial Civilization,* wrote, "It was chiefly on the basis of Mayo's work that the case for the sociological study of industrial behaviour was advanced. It also paved the way for the introduction of sociology into business school courses and management education generally."[74]

Among his peers, Mayo's zest for discourse and his leadership skills made up for his meager published output. "His chief products were the people that he influenced and helped to develop," said Roethlisberger of his mentor. Mayo described his approach this way in a letter to Harold J. Ruttenberg, the research director of United Steel Workers of America, in March 1945: "As you know, I am not very fond of a research that begins in questions that seem too specific. I do not believe it works as well [as] when one walks out into the great world with the idea of finding out what is happening there. It is my experience that the most fruitful researches have begun either by asking the wrong question, or by asking a question that demanded constant restatement as work proceeded. Put in other words, one needs to be desperately quick upon one's feet in a mental sense, to realize the direction in which an investigation is leading. The Western Electric researches, which you know well, began with a whole series of comic errors in respect to the questions asked."[75]

Adaptability, the key to the research approach Mayo was describing, had become his mantra. "It [is] more interesting to live in a time of change," Mayo liked to say. Adaptability was also the key to the rapidly changing world of the 1920s and 1930s. "In recent years the whole character of group organization in this allegedly civilized world has changed," Mayo wrote to Ruttenberg. "We are no longer an established society, but an adaptive society. We can no longer expect that our trade will last through several generations of men; nor can we expect that our present associates will remain associates for our lifetime.[76]

The major problem, as Mayo saw it, was that while the United States had made huge advances in technology and commerce, social skills, especially cooperative skills, had been neglected. "When the tempo of technical change was accelerated, no one posed a question as to the consequence for individuals and society of a failure to maintain and develop social skill." The very success of American capitalism, Mayo believed, sowed the seeds of calamity. "The general effect is to concentrate attention on technical problems and to blind us to the importance of the problems of human co-operation."[77] The human problems, as Mayo saw it, had their roots in the shift from the skilled trades of the nineteenth century, with their strong community ties, to the rise of masses of unskilled, migrant laborers. Modern society had no replacement for the training, self-esteem, and sense of tradition that most skilled tradesmen had enjoyed. Similarly, Mayo believed that industry was ill equipped to deal with the alienation, disaffection, and neuroses of blue-collar workers, most of whom had been uprooted from their communities and in many cases their countries. "No longer does the supervisor work with a team of persons that he has known for many years or perhaps a lifetime; he is leader of a group of individuals that forms and disappears almost as he watches it. . . . [F]or the individual worker the problem is really much more serious. He has suffered a profound loss of security and certainty in his actual living."[78]

However brilliant Mayo's insights may have been, academics couldn't forgive him for his decidedly unscholarly approach and his tendency to shoot, sometimes extravagantly, from the hip. "Mayo was the sort to come up with the big idea, but not necessarily to follow up on it," says George Lombard, who became a student at HBS shortly before Mayo retired and went on to become a professor at Harvard and one of the last standard-bearers of the human relations school. "Mayo jumped around all over the place intellectually. He never could sit still long enough to write things out carefully."[79]

Mayo also often flouted his own advice to social scientists "to begin work by a thorough painstaking acquaintance with the whole subject matter of their studies." Mayo had a sometimes alarming ability to oversimplify and, in the process, undermine his own astute observations about society's ills. "If our social skills had advanced step by step with our technical skills there would not have been another European war," he wrote in reference to World War II.[80] The naïveté of this statement is surpassed only by his "analysis" of Hitler himself. In a letter to Neville Chamberlain dated November 1938, the same year Chamberlain had secured "peace in our time" by signing the infamous Munich pact with Hitler, Mayo analyzed Hitler and applauded Chamberlain's strategy of appeasement:

> In industry we have begun to learn how to deal with such persons [as Hitler]; how to utilize their high capacity, how to diminish their nuisance function. We are training special officers

of personnel who, utilizing a method very similar to that of Sir Horace Wilson, befriended such solitaries, listen to them endlessly, to their terrors and ambitions, their oft-told life story. It not only gives these solitaries their first experience of an approximately human friendship, it also, in some fashion that we cannot explain, tends to develop in them a greater capacity for teamwork and for ordinary human association. . . .

Now the situation seen from some distance suggests that Herr Hitler is an instance of this type of not-very-happy solitary. . . .

The method you employed, Sir at Berchtesgaden and at Munich seems to have been the method which, in a far humbler way, we have found useful in industry. Careful listening friendship at the ordinary human level, no criticism until the individual himself becomes critical of what he says. . . . We hope that foolish criticism will not be permitted to divert you from the pathway of appeasement you have chosen.[81]

No wonder the role of Roethlisberger, the rigorous scholar cum reflective philosopher, was so essential. Roethlisberger was the one who collected and analyzed every bit of data, and his insights, when they finally surfaced, were original and often brilliant. He buttressed the intellectual integrity of the human relations school, grounding it in carefully documented research and theory. "Fritz was the best academic mind the business school had at that time," says L. B. Barnes, who was part of a loose-knit group that Roethlisberger referred to as his "informal [human relations] soul group." Says Barnes, "Mayo would never have been as famous and well known without . . . Fritz Roethlisberger. In many ways, Fritz, so unassuming, was the more magnificent of the two."[82]

Mayo and Roethlisberger

A year after Mayo had joined Harvard, Roethlisberger, still in profound crisis after his decision to abandon philosophy, looked him up. Far from being put off by the nervous and insecure Roethlisberger, Mayo was "curious and amused" by him. He may even have seen, in the scholarly, "sad young philosopher," an intellectual anchor for his own ideas.[83] He took Roethlisberger under his wing, even helping him talk through his problems. "Mayo turned my attention to all those matters from which I wanted to escape: my Swiss heritage, my father, my mother, my childhood, the cheese business … my stepfather, the machine, scientific management. With this new look at the adult world of which I could make no sense and from whose nonsense I was desperately trying to run, a new Fritz was born. What had been something from which to escape became now a new source of intense curiosity," recalled Roethlisberger. Noted Abraham Zaleznik, a Harvard professor and former protégé of Roethlisberger's, "All the people close to Mayo were, in one form or another, his patients."[84]

Mayo also put Roethlisberger to work doing research and counseling unhappy students. Living at Hostess House, a kind of halfway house for neurotic students, Roethlisberger counseled his young soul mates.[85]

Almost immediately, it became clear that in his newfound role as amateur psychologist, Roethlisberger finally had found his calling. "Roethlisberger [*sic*] … is doing well," Mayo wrote to a colleague. "Having apparently mastered his own obsessions, he is proving himself very much able to capture the obsessions of others—all this in a week or two."[86]

Roethlisberger was indeed gaining a reputation as an expert listener. In addition to the industrial research work he would soon take on, Roethlisberger continued counseling students off and on until World War II. By 1928, Mayo was referring most of his patients to Roethlisberger. Two years later, Roethlisberger became an assistant professor at Harvard with a salary of $3,600.[87]

But an assistant professor of what?

Roethlisberger's existential angst still had not been resolved. At the very least, however, he was now determined to master it. "It looked to me as if life had played me a queer trick in landing me at the Business School, in a setting which seemed incongruous for the development of my interests," he recalled. "Nevertheless, this time I was going to accept and live with the incongruity and the anxieties it generated. I was going to follow my own interests in the job I was in. This was one of the most important personal decisions I reached, and it was one I constantly reaffirmed."[88]

In 1928, Roethlisberger and Mayo became involved in interpreting the Hawthorne studies. Mayo and the Hawthorne studies liberated Roethlisberger from the elusiveness of academic theory. "Here was no dry and dusty scholarship for its own sake. This was bringing knowledge to bear on practice or what practice in the social sciences could be." This was adventure. Far removed from the dusty tombs and groaning stacks of Widener Library, this was at once an intellectual and a real-life adventure.[89]

The Harvard team's involvement began soon after Mayo gave a series of lectures at a personnel conference around the beginning of 1927. After one of the lectures he was approached by several AT&T executives, including G. A. Pennock, the assistant works manager at AT&T's Hawthorne Works—part of the Western Electric plant in Cicero, Illinois—who invited Mayo "to visit an experiment they were beginning at Hawthorne." While Roethlisberger and Mayo were not involved in setting up the early experiments, which were conducted between 1924 and 1927, they did help to interpret them. Each brought his unique perspective and skills to the problem: Mayo, that of the "blithe" and "creative mind"; Roethlisberger, that of searching philosopher. (The early studies, which took place under the auspices of Dr. C. E. Turner, a professor of biology and public health at MIT, sought to measure the impact various levels of illumination have on workers' efficiency. Over the course of several years, the studies' focus expanded from worker productivity to employee satisfaction and motivation, including the role played by fatigue and the role and attitudes of supervisors.)[90]

It was Mayo's job to interact with the top executives at Hawthorne, to keep them interested and informed. Roethlisberger, on the other hand, worked with the lower-level supervisors, men such as Harold A. Wright and William J. Dickson, who would become his coauthors on *Management and the Worker*, the monumental study that made the Hawthorne experiments famous. Roethlisberger helped to implement certain phases of the experiments as well as to document and interpret them.[91]

Adding vibrancy to the Hawthorne experiments, Mayo and Company drew on the expertise of an eclectic sampling of Harvard's Human Relations school. W. Lloyd Warner, a social anthropologist who had conducted the Yankee City research, the first effort of its kind to apply the techniques used previously only for researching primitive communities to the study of an urban industrial setting. George Homans and T. North Whitehead, the son of the philosopher and a member of Mayo's group, also spent brief stints at Hawthorne.[92]

During the course of the Hawthorne experiments, which continued in fits and starts throughout much of the Depression, Mayo and Roethlisberger made a series of observations about the social system within the factory and its impact on morale and productivity. The Harvard group's analysis helped expose the problems behind a whole series of assumptions in industrial work that are being debated to this day—most especially, the rationalist view of human behavior. The experiments revealed the power of the informal organization, which exists within most institutions and has the power to unlock creativity or to stymie progress. They exposed the inadequacy of the piecework system and cast doubt on the assumption that there was a neat correlation between pay levels and productivity—what we would call pay for performance. Finally, the experiments exposed the complex way in which the relationships between supervisors and workers can affect output.

While the results of the early tests were in many respects inconclusive, they were highly surprising. For example, in the first set of tests, known as the "illumination experiments," workers were divided into two groups—a test group in which the workers were submitted to increasing amounts of light and a control group, which worked under a constant light intensity. Contrary to expectations, productivity increased in *both* groups. The workers seemed to be responding more to the attention they were receiving from management than to any physical change in their environment. This response of the workers was called "the Hawthorne effect."[93]

Realizing that the illumination experiments might have been affected by any of the large number of uncontrolled variables that are found in the typical workplace, the researchers subsequently subjected their work to far stricter controls. In 1927, Western Electric established the Relay Assembly Test Room, where five women were taken off the plant floor and segregated in a room where their work conditions could be carefully monitored, their output measured, and their behavior analyzed. Under these controlled conditions, the women, whose job it was to assemble telephone relays from about forty parts, submitted to thirteen different experimental periods, which varied in the number and duration of rest pauses and in the length of their working day and week. In keeping with the researcher's original hypothesis that fatigue was a major factor in limiting output, their productivity steadily increased during the first year and a half of the experiments as their rest pauses were increased and their working day was decreased.[94]

The Harvard team, which arrived at Hawthorne shortly after the Relay Assembly Test Room had been set up, made a number of other observations:

1. Work conditions have more effect on production than the number of workdays in the week.
2. Outside influences tend to create either a buoyant or depressed spirit, which is reflected in production. A distinct relationship was apparent between the emotional status of the girls and the consistency of their output.
3. The supervisor's method is the single most important outside influence. Home conditions may affect the worker and his work. However, a supervisor who can listen and not talk can

in many instances almost completely compensate for such depressing influences.

4. Pay incentives do not stimulate productivity if other working conditions are wrong. A second experimental group was given a pay increase only; its productivity improved somewhat, but not to an extent comparable with the original group.

5. The most surprising result came toward the end of the experiments, during period XII—an experiment thought to have been introduced, at the last minute, by Mayo—when the researchers returned to the original forty-eight-hour week without rest pauses. Once again, productivity rose! Yet again, it seemed that the workers were responding to the positive concern of the experiments rather than to the physical work conditions.[95]

After all, the Harvard team realized, the experimenters weren't behaving like typical supervisors. Although a man from Hawthorne's piece-rate department observed and supervised the experiment, he did not, according to Mayo, behave like a typical "gong boss." Perhaps the solution to increased productivity lay more in the methods of supervision than in the physical work conditions? "What actually happened was that six individuals became a team and the team gave itself wholeheartedly and spontaneously to co-operation in the experiment," observed Mayo. This interpretation led the Hawthorne researchers to embark on a counseling program for supervisors that began in 1936 and would last for almost twenty years.[96]

There was, however, one more set of experiments that remained to be done before the so-called Interviewing Program began. This last set of investigations, known as the Bank Wiring Observation Room experiments, produced one of Roethlisberger's most important observations about the workplace. The Bank Wiring Observation room was staffed with fourteen workmen from three occupational groups: soldermen, wiremen, and inspectors. These men were paid according to a group piecework system, according to which the more components they turned out, the more money they made. Therefore, it was assumed that the most efficient workers would bring pressure to bear on the slower workers to maintain a high level of output.[97]

This proved not to be the case. Instead, the group had established an unofficial output norm based on what the workers considered a "fair" production quota. Workers who violated the norm by producing either too much or too little were ostracized by their coworkers. The experimenters discovered that there existed an informal organization that dictated the output of each worker based on its own standards of fairness and the position each worker occupied within the work group.[98]

The discovery of this informal organization presented a whole new avenue of research for the Hawthorne team, and for Roethlisberger in particular. It also became an important element in Chester Barnard's theories on leadership (see Chapter 3). In the coming years, Roethlisberger devoted much of his attention to the positive and negative effects of the informal organization and the problems of creating a state of equilibrium between official bureaucracy and the informal group. Wrote Roethlisberger:

> In many smaller organizations I was impressed with how many of the rules remained implicit, not only the operating rules and standards of performance, but also the rules of communication, that is, to whom one was supposed to go for help. Persons in these organizations were bound together by a set of relations that had nothing to do with what they were supposed to be doing. These relations seemed to me important indeed, not only for attaining the purposes of the organization but also for obtaining the cooperation of the people for these purposes. In fact, without these relations I felt that each organization would go to pieces. Yet, at the time all the standard textbooks about what made management never mentioned them. . . .
>
> I began looking for these relationships in all organizations, large and small; although they were somewhat camouflaged in the larger organizations, I found them there also. The relations of interconnectedness which I am talking about had to do with matters such as *liking, trusting,* and *helping.* . . .
>
> These relations of interconnectedness among persons which resulted often (but not always) in structures that are nonheirarchical, I call the strong, close, and warm relationships. They make the cheese more binding. The hierarchical ones in contrast are weak, distant, and cold. . . .
>
> It seemed to me that in most organizations the employees found these informal relationships rewarding. Whenever and wherever it was possible, they generated them like crazy. In many cases they found them so satisfying that they often did all sorts of nonlogical things (i.e., things that went counter to their economic interests) in order to belong.[99]

To Roethlisberger, the tension between the formal organization and the informal organization created "an unconscious battle between the logic of management and the sentiments of workers." In searching for a "state of equilibrium" between the formal bureaucracy and informal networks, Roethlisberger discovered what he termed the "man-in-the-middle syndrome," which affected low- and middle-level supervisors. The supervisor (the foreman, most particularly), Roethlisberger found, was caught between his role as a manager and his responsibility to make sure that management's goals were achieved, on the one hand, and on the other, the realization that he had to work with the informal organization, which sometimes flouted management's rules, to get the work done.

In their work, Roethlisberger and Mayo strove to cultivate the informal organization within management. In fact, it could be argued that both men, being the antithesis of what William H. Whyte termed "organization men," thrived on informal networks themselves. Consequently, they were well suited to plumbing the unique character of the informal organization, its creative potential, and the conflicts it could engender. At Hawthorne, which had a strong informal organization not only among the workers but also within management, Mayo's ability to cultivate relationships with senior management was a key to the duration and quality of the experiments themselves.

Everything Mayo did was outside the official bureaucracy of the company. Instead of conducting formal meetings or even semiformal lunches at the country club where Western Electric executives regularly dined, Mayo would take the higher-ups to lunch at a dive on Cicero Avenue, where the workers ate. Over a bowl of his favorite onion soup, Mayo would conduct seminars, rather than meetings, and appeal to the executives' logic and understanding of human nature. Observed Roethlisberger:

> Mayo could take some simple employee situation from an interview—the case of Hank, for example—and before one was aware of what was happening, Hank no longer was only a direct cost, a set of motions, a seeker of security, a coffee-breaker, a rate-buster, a feather-bedder, a trouble-maker, an apathetic worker. . . . Instead, as Mayo wove his spell, Hank became a person with motivations which the executives could share and identify. Many of these executives who had risen from the ranks had lost contact with the concrete, because their heads or minds were now supposed to be in the clouds of economic abstractions. They welcomed this return back home and felt rejuvenated. . . .
>
> The executives became once again curious about human motivation, especially in relation to some of their oversimplified

> logics of control, wage incentive systems, for example. Mayo
> never advocated that the toilets be hot in the summer and cold
> in the winter to keep Hank from staying there so long. He was
> interested in why Hank went to the toilet so often and stayed
> there so long.[100]

Despite the dislocations of the Depression, which brought an end to some of the experiments, Mayo, the researchers, and even the workers, most of whom were laid off, continued to keep tabs on one another. The inner workings of AT&T during the Depression provide a stark view of the chaos that faced both organizations and individuals during America's worst economic crisis. The company's efforts to mitigate the effects of that crisis on its employees not only helped keep the Hawthorne experiments alive, they also offer a useful contrast to the sometimes mindless downsizing of today.

While most of the workers at Western Electric were furloughed for at least part of the Depression, the company resorted to layoffs only as a last resort. At first, AT&T instituted a time-off system by which most employees' working hours were cut back to varying degrees based on the length of each employee's tenure. For a time, the arrangement succeeded in forestalling massive cutbacks.

The time-off policy permitted the experiments to continue, though on a curtailed basis. "Under the present arrangement of 'time off' our two test rooms will be in operation on an average of fourteen hours per week," wrote Hal Wright to Mayo in April 1932. "This will be accomplished by working four days one week, three days the next and then two weeks off. This is the more or less general plan for our shop departments where employees have less than ten years' service."[101] With jobs in jeopardy, the company was anxious not to appear to be squandering money on the Harvard team. So when Emily P. Osborne, Mayo's research assistant, arrived in Chicago in 1932, expecting to do work at Hawthorne, the Western Electric executives found themselves in a quandary. Although Harvard was paying her expenses, Pennock worried that her arrival at Hawthorne in the midst of the Depression would be misunderstood by the rank and file. Mayo solved the problem by finding her a research position elsewhere in Chicago, although she visited Hawthorne frequently and helped keep tabs on the research.[102]

Layoffs were, however, inevitable. To prevent panic in its workforce, the company initially dismissed a few workers at a time, scattering the pink slips throughout various departments, so as not to make the dismissals "too obvious." At the same time, the company retrofitted its shops to produce everything from doll's houses to furniture—in short, anything "to keep men working and busy and bringing in some income."[103]

Frontline workers weren't the only ones affected. By the fall of 1932, more than a third of the company's employees had been furloughed. The following summer, that number would rise to almost 50 percent, and rumors were rife that the Western Electric Company would close down entirely.[104] "It was becoming increasingly obvious that the research organization at the Chicago end was cracking badly, due to drastic cuts throughout the firm," Whitehead wrote to Mayo in late 1932. One major problem was that Wright and Dickson, Roethlisberger's collaborators on *Management and the Worker,* were both relatively "short-service" men and so were "very near to being sacked." To save the nucleus of their work, Roethlisberger and Whitehead proposed that Wright and Dickson be stationed at Harvard, though their salaries would continue to be paid by Western Electric.[105]

Thus, Wright and Dickson came to Harvard. Wright would stay for only six months before returning to a new job at Hawthorne, while Dickson stayed on for three and a half years as Roethlisberger's coauthor on *Management and the Worker.* Although their book was completed in 1936, it would take the Harvard team three years to convince Western Electric to agree to its publication.[106]

Meanwhile, through Osborne and his remaining friends at Western Electric, Mayo maintained his contacts at the company and even kept up with the progress of the test room subjects, especially the women from the relay assembly group, most of whom had been laid off. "I wonder if it would be possible for you ... to find out what Mary, Jenny and the other girls formerly of the test room are doing," Mayo wrote to Osborne after her arrival in Chicago. "I am not suggesting that you should enter into any sort of direct relationship with them; this might arouse hopes which we could not justify, but I should rather like to know what sort of varying success has attended their efforts to find work elsewhere."[107]

The responses of the young women were a testament to the impression the test room experience had made on them. "I was surprised to receive your letter and needless to say glad to hear from you," wrote Jenny Sirchio upon receiving Osborne's invitation. "It was very nice of you to send a stamped envelope and this writing paper, but really it's not that bad. I will be very glad to accept that invitation for Saturday. It will be good to see you and talk things over. So I will close this letter soon, so as we will have more to talk about, instead of writing about everything. Until Saturday at One O'clock I remain your beloved pressure subject. Jenny Sirchio."[108]

To Osborne's surprise, there seemed to be "no bitterness"in Jenny or the other former test room subjects. Noted Osborne: "Jenny says the Western Electric Co. gave them all good breaks and kept them so long as possible and did much more for their employees than any company she has heard of. . . .

"She was thrilled to be remembered and got in touch with Mary who asked to come in with her. They are all so pleased that I have asked Jenny to get in touch with all of them and arrange a date to come in and have lunch with me. . . . I gave [Jenny] money to cover stamps, telephone car fare etc. She was reluctant to accept it but I assured her that it was a legitimate research expense. She did not miss a detail of my apartment etc., was well poised and had a very nice manner."[109]

Three years later the contacts with the test room "girls" were still continuing. "A few weeks ago . . . Theresa Layman Ajak (operator no. 3 of the Test Room) called me by phone," reported Osborne to Mayo in May 1936. Layman showed up with her husband on a Sunday afternoon for "a purely social visit." The couple stayed for several hours despite the arrival of several other visitors. "They were in no way embarrassed and seemed to enjoy themselves," recalled Osborne. "The girls still look back on their Test Room days as something quite apart from anything else in their lives. They have a great liking for . . . nearly [everyone] with whom they came in contact."[110]

The Hawthorne project had also welded the executives and managers into a cohesive group. "We've got a hot idea," wrote Hal Wright to Roethlisberger toward the beginning of World War II, more than a decade after Roethlisberger and Mayo had made their first trip to Chicago. "We guys here think you guys there ought to come here for a homecoming celebration. Logics: To attend the AMA Personnel Division Conference in Chicago. . . . Non-logics: To obey a strong urge to get together and chew the fat. No kidding. Why not plan to spend an extra week in Chicago."[111]

With the core Hawthorne team kept largely intact, Western Electric launched the final phase of the Harvard team's research project in 1936. After the completion of *Management and the Worker*, Dickson returned to Hawthorne and, in collaboration with Wright and Mark L. Putnam, another Hawthorne manager, developed a counseling program for employees that involved the first concrete effort to apply the results of the Hawthorne findings. For the next few years, Roethlisberger shuttled between Harvard and Hawthorne, training counselors and spreading the gospel to employee relations people throughout the Bell system. The counselors, most of them foremen and mid-level supervisors, took on the role of clinicians and sought to get the workers to discuss their

concerns relating to their work and private lives. "Not only did this attempt to listen sympathetically but intelligently to what the workers had
to say produce in many instances what was now coming to be recognized as the positive Hawthorne effect, it also revealed the difference
the behavior of their supervisors made to the workers," observed
Roethlisberger.[112]

■

After the publication of *Management and the Worker*, the human relations movement was widely embraced. The sudden popularity of
human relations, however, troubled Roethlisberger. Although the counseling program at Hawthorne continued well into the 1950s, he lost interest in it at the start of World War II, in part because he didn't believe
that the program could effect a sea change on the plant floor.

Roethlisberger may have sensed the Achilles heel of most such programs. For example, the counseling program, as practiced at AT&T at the
time, suffered from many of the problems Mayo had encountered in his
earliest research experiments in Philadelphia. For one thing, listening
alone couldn't produce long-term improvement in working conditions if
the listener didn't have the power to change the work conditions.
Second, it would have been virtually impossible to train sufficient numbers of supervisors to be effective counselors. More important, perhaps,
the interests of the supervisor cum listener, as a member of management
whose aim was to maintain the organizational status quo, often were intrinsically in conflict with those of the worker. "It looked as if the
Hawthorne researches were regressing slowly, step by step, to the obvious and were not discovering any new gimmicks to make the workers
more productive and contented," Roethlisberger conceded.[113]

Years later, such management pioneers as W. Edwards Deming would
realize that long-term improvement in morale and productivity depends
on the involvement of top management, the only power strong enough
to effect lasting change in the workplace. Roethlisberger and Dickson,
having seen the often futile role that personnel men play in industry,
sensed this too. "I have [come to feel] that the conceptual scheme
developed in *Management and the Worker* is much better suited to the
executive than it is to the personnel man," wrote Dickson to Roethlisberger in 1943.[114]

While spearheading the counseling program, Roethlisberger also wit-
nessed the lethargy of corporate bureaucracy and didn't like what he
saw: "This assignment was my first experience with a large staff organization and the kind of work its members did. They seemed to be involved in a great deal of paper work; the language on their papers for a

while had me stumped . . . the language of these staff executives seemed to stay at a dead level, devoid of any relation to the concrete or to any ideas which made the blood circulate. . . .[115]

"Their heads were neither in the clouds nor their feet on the ground; they seemed to be out of touch with both the tops and the bottoms of the organization. Many of them seemed to me to be unhappy and in a state of suspended animation indulging in a monotonic mumbo jumbo which I found neither informative nor inspiring."[116]

Roethlisberger was traveling back from one of his frequent trips to Chicago by train when he heard about Pearl Harbor. He felt a sudden gnawing apprehension in the pit of his stomach. By the end of 1941, he knew that "something [had] come to an end" for him; as it so often had in the past, this latest ending brought with it another profound personal crisis.[117]

War was only part of the story. The global conflagration coincided with the sudden deaths of both Henderson and Philip Cabot. Their deaths "had a crushing effect upon Roethlisberger who . . . retired to Vermont for an indefinite period," wrote Mayo in 1942. What Mayo didn't mention—or perhaps failed to acknowledge—was the role he, and the change in his relationship with his erstwhile protégé, played in Roethlisberger's crisis.

In his own long letter to Dean Donham, written in August 1942, while Roethlisberger was still recuperating from his most recent breakdown, Mayo recalled his own version of the Hawthorne events. Coming as it did on the heels of Roethlisberger's sudden success with *Management and the Worker*, Mayo's account seems to be nothing less than an attempt to set the record straight—at least the record of his own role at Hawthorne: "For many years I had to do all this work [at Hawthorne] alone: I still was without competent assistants although Roethlisberger had joined me. Roethlisberger was still surrounded by the mists of Harvard philosophy which had not mixed well with his previous chemical and engineering training." On trips back to Harvard, Mayo recalled, his time was "wholly occupied with coaching Fritz."[118]

Finally, Mayo concluded, though he would have liked to have passed the mantle of leadership on to Roethlisberger, he could not in good conscience do so. "I was concentrating upon Whitehead and Fritz—later George Homans—as my successors and endeavoring to give them every qualification possible," he wrote to Donham. But Roethlisberger "did not, as I had hoped, throw himself completely into the work—this was a disappointment but perhaps my expectations were unreasonable." The realization that protégé may have surpassed master seems suddenly to have rankled.[119]

Roethlisberger's view, though much more generously put, was far different. "Mayo was satisfied to remain a fringe member of the Business School Faculty and I was not," he wrote. "Yet his approval and support were important to me, in fact more important than that of my other colleagues; and so my old anxieties about my identity and subject matter, which had been submerged but never completely liquidated, reared their ugly head again."[120] Given the facts of Mayo's life during the war years, including his lackadaisical working hours and frequent absences from campus, Roethlisberger's version of events rings much truer. Indeed, during the early years of the war Mayo was preoccupied with getting his daughter Gael and her husband, the feckless Count Vsevolod Gebrovsky, out of war-torn Europe; the young couple had been caught, *Casablanca*-style, in Paris just as the Germans occupied the city.[121]

The rift with Mayo helped to unhinge Roethlisberger, who dropped out of sight for about six months in 1942. Roethlisberger's refuge was a farm in Vermont called Spring Lake Ranch, which was run by Wayne Sarcka, who believed in the health benefits, both mental and physical, of agrarian labor. Pitching hay, doing farm chores, and building a small cabin did, indeed, help restore Roethlisberger's equilibrium. For it was in Spring Lake that he began to shake off his attachments to his mentors and to rely more upon himself. As he put it:

> There is no question that Mayo, Henderson, Donham, and Cabot opened up new worlds for me. But as each of them died, retired, or was about to retire, I had to face this new world alone without his support. This was frightening to the small child who, metaphorically speaking, still lingered within me in my preoccupations and with whom . . . I had still not learned to cope successfully. This small child was still looking for the certainty and security which I had not found when I was chronologically younger. . . .
>
> It took some time to learn how to deal with this small child. At first I tried to eliminate him . . . [but] the more I tried to kill him off, the more he would taunt me with the thought "So you think you are emotionally mature. Stop kidding yourself."
>
> I finally decided to take another tack . . . instead of hating him, I decided to love him more. After all, he was the source of both my creativity and my anxiety. With a bit more love . . . he might learn to grow up (the Hawthorne effect?).[122]

Even after returning to Harvard, Roethlisberger would periodically retreat to the cabin he had built at Spring Lake Ranch and the solace of "a bunch of nuts at the top of a magic mountain in Vermont."[123] For with the end of his involvement at Hawthorne and the irrevocable change in his relationships with his mentors—Mayo in particular— Roethlisberger faced two challenges: he had to figure out what to do with the rest of his life, and he had to cope with the implications of un- expected fame and success.

The Mayoites had found themselves in great demand during World War II, even as Mayo was beginning to withdraw from active participa- tion in the school, leaving Roethlisberger to carry on the work of the human relations group. Morale became a major problem during World War II, as industry tried to scale up for wartime production. At one point the War Production Board approached Mayo to help solve turnover problems in defense industries.[124] Hawthorne executives also had held seminars on counseling and interviewing techniques at companies, such as Northrup, that were striving to increase productivity.[125] After the war, Mayo received a letter from the State Department noting that his book had been among seventy-nine titles chosen to be translated into German by German publishers under license from the Information Control Division of the U.S. Army; many of the translated titles were to be used in the "reeducation" program in Germany.[126]

The war years also coincided with the sudden success of *Manage- ment and the Worker*. At a time when improving wartime industrial pro- ductivity had become a major challenge, *Management and the Worker* provided fresh insights into the long-standing antagonisms between labor and management. Not only did the book become a best-seller, it was also a "status symbol" that no "personnel man" could afford to be without. The two heavy volumes that made up *Management and the Worker* stimulated a whole crop of research and a mini-industry in cri- tiques of the Hawthorne experiments themselves. *Management and the Worker* became a classic in the social sciences, albeit one that would be fiercely debated for decades after its publication. Indeed, to a great ex- tent, many of today's debates about productivity, teamwork, human mo- tivation, and performance and compensation, revisit the ground covered by Roethlisberger, Dickson, and their critics.[127]

With some exceptions, the book was extravagantly praised during the early years, with the most fault found by reviewers who took up the book years after its publication. By a generation of social scientists, the book was lauded for its insights into the behavior of small work groups and its observations of the social systems that govern factories, includ- ing the role of both the informal and the formal organization. *Management and the Worker* was praised for identifying the impor- tance of relationships and teamwork in morale and productivity. "From the time of the publication of the results of the Hawthorne Studies on-ward, no one interested in the behaviour of employees could consider them as isolated individuals. Rather, such factors and concepts as group influences, social status, informal communication, roles, norms, and the like were drawn upon to explain and interpret the voluminous data from these studies and other field investigations that followed them," wrote L. W. Porter, E. E. Lawler, and J. R. Hackman.

The criticisms covered a wide range of academic objections, some of which no longer seem as valid as they did in the 1940s and '50s. The book was faulted, for example, for using "soft data"—anecdotal material based on the research of a small work group rather than quantifiable "hard" data based on a scientific survey. Academics are still leery of what Roethlisberger referred to as the "elusive phenomenon." Counters Jeffrey A. Sonnenfeld, an expert on organizational behavior: "Haw-thorne critics have generally misunderstood or misrepresented the modest ideological and methodological presumptions of this pioneering research, which was intended to generate, not verify, hypotheses. . . . [*Management and the Worker*] is a model of frank reporting on the step by step stages of research."[128]

The popularity of *Management and the Worker* continued immedi-ately after the war, turning Roethlisberger into something of a celebrity and human relations into a management craze. With companies around the globe striving to rebuild after the war and to increase productivity, managers flocked to Harvard wanting to see Professor Roethlisberger and hear about the Hawthorne Effect. In response, Dean Donham is said to have exhorted Roethlisberger, "For goodness sake, Fritz, I don't know just what these people want, but you seem to have the magic med-icine. Please package it in words of one syllable."[129]

The publicity surrounding the Hawthorne experiments prompted a number of companies to visit Hawthorne. In an early attempt at bench-marking, companies as diverse as Eli Lilly and Swift & Company flocked to Hawthorne to observe its personnel counseling program.[130]

Then too, there were fan letters from Roethlisberger's former stu-dents, many of whom had participated in HBS's executive program. "Since my return I have had the opportunity in two cases to utilize the Roethlisberger techniques and to date found that they really work," ex-ulted J. B. Shimer, an executive at Corning Glass Works. "I am now busy trying to pass your techniques on to my key supervisors and found some difficulties in duplicating your smooth class room approach. . . . I am hopeful that I can instill in my key supervisors just a portion of the deep cords you hit [with me.]"[131]

While the human relations craze was destined eventually to burn itself out, Roethlisberger built a following both inside and outside HBS. He was instrumental in establishing what eventually became known as the Organizational Behavior area at HBS. And, until he retired in 1947, Harvard's periodic "Mayo Weekends," conferences on human relations and administration, attracted such leaders as Donald S. Bridgman, a prominent AT&T executive, and Edwin Booz, a founding partner of Booz Allen & Hamilton, as well as Peter Drucker.[132] The ideas and techniques propounded by Roethlisberger and Mayo were also taught in a range of required and elective courses on human relations, administrative practices, and even business policy.[133]

■

Despite the self-affirmation Roethlisberger felt in having finally found a subject—especially one that was so relevant to the concerns of the day—he remained deeply ambivalent about the popularity of human relations. For he was painfully aware of both the complexity of human relations and its susceptibility to fads and trivialization. "Too many people have entered the field and tried to develop it too fast," he complained. "Participative management has become a slogan, blown up as if it were a cure-all for whatever ails the organization."[134]

Roethlisberger respected the work of the "humanistic psychologists," such as Abraham Maslow, Alfred Adler, and Carl Rogers, whose work was a logical development of some aspects of the Hawthorne findings. Yet, he believed, they too failed to achieve the right balance between plumbing the individual psyche and conducting scientific research. For example, in 1953, Roethlisberger participated in a so-called T-group (training group), an outgrowth of Lewin's group dynamics that was popularized by the National Training Labs. Roethlisberger came away from the experience feeling that T-groups perpetuated many of Hawthorne's shortcomings (see Chapter 6 on Maslow and McGregor). As he said, "There's a world of difference between the intrinsic growth of individuals that the humanistic psychologists speak of and the extrinsic knowledge about human behavior that social scientists speak of. There seems to be a kind of antithesis between the two. I'd like to keep the intrinsic and extrinsic together."[135]

Roethlisberger was also troubled by what he saw as the growing faddishness of the human relations school. After World War II, companies such as Ford Motor Company's Aircraft Engine Division put all of its supervisors through a few weeks of human relations training and then patted themselves on the back for having improved their relationship with the rank and file. "Our conferences were extremely successful in as much as we had high attendance and considerable praise from the conferees," wrote Malcolm R. Lovell, Jr., manager of salaried personnel, to Roethlisberger. "I have some doubt, however, as to whether our supervisory group is now more skilled in the handling of human relations, which after all was the primary purpose of holding the conferences in the first place." Lovell's comment is especially ironic given that Robert McNamara and the Whiz Kids were, at that very moment, winning a quantitative revolution at Ford that was aimed at eviscerating the softer, not strictly rational approaches to management![136] (See Chapter 5.)

Indeed, by the mid-1950s a powerful backlash was building up against human relations, which, at Harvard and other institutions, would soon be rechristened "organizational behavior" to describe the way organizations *did* behave, as opposed to how they *ought to* behave. At Harvard, the charge was led by Malcolm P. McNair, a respected professor of marketing. McNair aired his contempt for the "pseudoscience" of human relations in 1957 in a *Harvard Business Review* article entitled "Thinking Ahead: What Price Human Relations?" Wrote McNair: "[T]he cult of human relations is but part and parcel of the sloppy sentimentalism characterizing the world today."[137]

McNair's attack was particularly painful because it hit so close to the mark. He accused human relations practitioners of practicing "amateur psychiatry" and of giving students a "false concept of the executive's job." With human relations, charged McNair, there is a "de-emphasis of analysis, judgment, and decision-making."[138]

Interestingly, in his critique of human relations, McNair put his finger on a major problem with the movement, one that troubled Roethlisberger himself. "Consciously trying to practice human relations is like consciously trying to be a gentleman," wrote McNair. "If you have to think about it, insincerity creeps in and personal integrity moves out. With some this leads by a short step to the somewhat cynical point of view which students in Administrative practices courses have described by coining the verb 'ad prac,' meaning 'to manipulate people for one's own ends.' "[139]

Finally, McNair predicted, quite presciently, the ultimate demise of the human relations fad: "[F]airly soon the human relations cult in business will begin to wane and operations research or something else will become fashion."[140]

■

Mayo missed out on much of the debate that swept up the human relations–cum–organizational behavior debate in the years following World War II. Mayo had intended to retire in the early 1940s and return to his beloved England but had stayed on at Harvard because of the war and because of his continuing financial difficulties. Finally, in 1947, he did return, as a number of opportunities suddenly presented themselves. His daughter Patricia, who had followed in her father's footsteps, was named to head the research department for the new government-backed British Institute of Management, and he himself was offered a number of lecturing engagements around the country. He was on his way to a dinner party in London, where he was to be offered what must have seemed as a final accolade, the chairmanship of a new parliamentary committee to deal with industrial relations, when he suffered a stroke. His health never recovered and he died less than two years later.[141]

Roethlisberger's own struggle with the "elusive phenomenon," his attempt to reconcile art and science in the study of human organizations, continued for three more decades, until his death in 1974. "This is what Mayo did for me; he set me free to chase these soft data like crazy," wrote Roethlisberger in his autobiography, *The Elusive Phenomenon*. "These were the phenomena for me, and I was in no hurry to wrap a hard covering around them.... I felt very strongly that in these soft, gooey data there existed uniformities about human behavior that had to be coaxed out by a point of view and method that were perhaps different from those used by my more hard-nosed, realistic, objective and scientific... colleagues. This was my method, the method of clinical observation and interviewing, which I was advocating for the administrator to use in relation to many of his problems. Although this method did not make soft data into hard data, it did make them more understandable."[142]

Roethlisberger lived long enough to see both the fads and real progress of the movement he had helped spawn. To his students and protégés, Roethlisberger was always "the most memorable teacher" they had had at the school, a man who was more like a "soft, gentle ... inquisitive child in class ... than the quintessential HBS professor." By the 1950s—to the dismay of his students—Roethlisberger had stopped teaching. But over the years a number of leading management thinkers joined Roethlisberger's "informal soul group." At Harvard, Chris Argyris became one of the most prominent thinkers to take on the human relations mantle. Other kindred spirits had come to include Kurt Lewin, the founder of Group Dynamics; Abraham Maslow, the father of humanistic psychology; and Douglas McGregor, exponent of Theory X and Theory Y (see Chapter 6); as well as Peter Drucker, one of the most vocal proponents of the idea that fostering human capital is management's most important job (see Chapter 10).

∎

The once-unassailable search for the one best way would henceforth be challenged by a more complex and variegated approach to managing organizations. Thanks to Mayo and Roethlisberger, the search for the elusive phenomenon would continue. But Taylorism was far from dead. Even before McNair's 1957 attack on human relations, a powerful new brand of scientific management was beginning to sweep across the American industrial landscape. Rising out of the Allied victory, a new cadre of experts were determined to bring the techniques they had used to win the war to rebuilding American industry. They brought with them a brand-new tool kit of techniques for measuring business processes and an evangelistic determination to impose a new rationalism on management.

Once upon a time there was a CEO of a pet food company who wanted to increase his profits from making dog food. So he consulted the wisest men in his company, who knew all about developing computer programs that would analyze the nutrition needs of dogs and the nutrition content of various grains and food supplements. Eager to please the CEO, the wise men programmed their computers to come up with the optimum combination of grains and supplements that would meet the nutrition needs of man's best friend at the lowest price.

But a strange thing happened. During the first six months of selling the optimum nutrition mix at the lowest price, profit margins at the company declined. The next quarter, profits dived once more. "What is going on?" the CEO demanded.

Since his wise men didn't have an answer, the CEO consulted the greatest expert in the land, who knew all about the mysterious science of systems analysis and who conducted an extensive study (at considerable expense.) When he was finished, the expert appeared before the CEO.

"Have you discovered why our profits are declining?" the CEO demanded.

"I have," said the expert, leaning on a thick report. "The dogs don't like it."

Robert S. McNamara

The "Bean Counters" Usher in a New Era of Scientific Management

The Allied victory of World War II was, in many respects, a triumph of American ingenuity: technology, logistics, and management training. Between 1939 and 1945, the United States built or retooled $25 billion worth of manufacturing facilities, including buildings and equipment. New factories required legions of newly trained workers (many of them women who had never seen the inside of a factory), supervisory personnel on the factory floor, and entirely new organizational structures.[1]

One of the greatest U.S. military challenges involved the mobilization of the Army Air Corps. Before the war, the Army Air Corps had boasted only 412 planes, fewer than half of which were first-line combat aircraft. In 1940, President Franklin D. Roosevelt called for the construction of *fifty thousand* military and naval planes. Within a year, the production of military aircraft had skyrocketed to 2,464 per month from 402 per month in April 1940. By the end of the war, the air force commanded 230,000 planes and the necessary spare parts to service them all.[2]

To build an organizational apparatus that could meet those military projections, shortly before World War II the Air Corps was incorporated into the Army and later became the Army Air Forces, one of the largest enterprises in the world. (In 1948, Congress created the U.S. Air Force as an independent service.) To control the new behemoth, the Army Air Forces needed new management systems and a new breed of manager. Modern logistics, cost accounting, and systems analysis owe much to the systems developed by the Army Air Forces during World War II. As managers and experts attached to the Army Air Forces moved back into civilian life after the war, they also came to have a pivotal impact on the challenges and crises of the post–World War II era. These men left their mark on everything from the revival of consumer production after the war to military and government policy during the Vietnam War era.

One of the first individuals to grasp the challenges and opportunities created by the Army Air Forces was a minor bureaucrat by the name of Charles "Tex" Thornton. A twenty-eight-year-old major with no college degree or real military training, Thornton would create a "back office" for the Army Air Forces from which he would measure and analyze U.S. military capabilities, helping orchestrate the U.S. offensive during World War II.

Years later, Thornton and his core group of Statistical Control officers would become known as the "Whiz Kids"; for better and for worse, they would have a profound influence on a number of major institutions during the postwar years. Thornton himself would go on to found Litton Industries, one of the first major conglomerates of the 1960s. Between them, the Whiz Kids and their protégés came to influence such giant corporations as Ford, Xerox, Firestone, and Zenith.

Chief among them was a young Harvard professor and accountant by the name of Robert Strange McNamara. During World War II and the decades that followed, McNamara became one of the leading architects and champions of a new approach to management that emphasized sophisticated quantitative skills and financial controls.

Two inescapable facts characterized McNamara's profound career and impact over the course of more than thirty years following the end of World War II: First, through his positions in the executive suite at Ford, as secretary of defense, and later as president of the World Bank, McNamara presided over the restructuring of three of the most important organizations in the modern global economy. As David Jardini writes in "Thinking Through the Cold War: Rand, National Security and Domestic Policy, 1945–1975," a Ph.D. dissertation to be published in 2000, "Robert S. McNamara is one of the more outstanding counterexamples to the argument that individuals matter little to historical development."[3]

Second, McNamara did more to proselytize a rationalist, quantitative approach to management than perhaps any single individual since Frederick Winslow Taylor. When it came to quantitative methods, especially new methodologies such as systems analysis, which was first developed during World War II, McNamara was utterly bewitched. Though his devotion to numbers was probably not as monolithic as many of his critics later claimed, "he loved" the new methodologies, recalls Gustave H. Shubert, a senior fellow at the RAND Corporation, which pioneered many of the quantitative techniques that McNamara embraced and conducted during his tenure as secretary of defense. "McNamara seemed to place much more faith [in]—and exercised much less skepticism about—quantitative methods" than even the scientists who developed them.[4]

In fact, McNamara had a complex management vision, one that encompassed both the need for financial discipline and a belief in the corporate social contract. Probably no other senior executive in Detroit, before or since, advocated safety, environmental responsibility, utility, function, cooperation with government, and accountability to labor as ardently as McNamara. (Moreover, for a short time that vision actually succeeded in selling cars!) At the Pentagon, McNamara was driven by a comparable determination to avoid the twin dangers of nuclear escalation and a war between the superpowers, a vision that helped defuse the Cuban missile crisis and strengthen the country's conventional defenses.

The tragedy for both America and McNamara was that his belief in corporate social imperative was soon lost, partly because he was an intellectual elitist and lacked the patience and the ability to communicate with the rank and file, partly because social ideals were out of sync with the times. The combination of postwar management chaos and euphoria over America's technological prowess led many managers to seize on the Whiz Kids' most obvious achievement: a control- and numbers-driven approach to management.

While McNamara craves debate with those he considers his intellectual equals, he is in many respects a captive of his own high IQ and intolerance for anyone who doesn't meet his high intellectual standards. There were "not more than five or ten college graduates in the top one thousand executives," he still laments about his early years at Ford, "Manufacturing, sales, engineering, purchasing, personnel didn't have the management" talent, he adds, dismissing in one fell swoop almost all the car men he would have encountered after the war.[5]

In the chaos that followed World War II, the wartime successes of the Whiz Kids and McNamara's commitment to restoring order and fiscal discipline at Ford helped update scientific management for the second half of the twentieth century. A new cadre of Ivy League graduates swarmed into industry, marginalizing less sophisticated men, who, however, understood the nuts and bolts of their businesses far better than the new organization men. Following the war, new quantitative methods, including systems and game theory, were vested with seemingly unlimited powers of analysis and prediction. Not since Taylor's day had the measurement dimension of management systems assumed such great importance. As John Byrne, author of *The Whiz Kids*, put it, McNamara and the Whiz Kids gave new impetus to the idea "that measurement, through numbers and facts, could make America a mighty power, a global empire built on the ability to hold a yardstick up to nature."[6]

For a time, they succeeded.

◾

The Whiz Kids' Statistical Control operation was the stuff of legend. The brainchild of Charles Thornton, Stat Control was, from the beginning, a product of entrepreneurial chutzpah. Thornton, a poor boy from Texas who arrived in Washington in the midst of the Depression hoping to build a career, started out as a minor bureaucrat in the Works Progress Administration. A college dropout, he eventually got a job in the War Department. At the beginning of World War II, he suggested to Robert A. Lovett, a fellow Texan who was then assistant secretary of war for air and an architect of mobilization, that the Army Air Forces needed a better handle on "friendly intelligence"—i.e., information about its own capabilities.[7]

Within the newly formed Army Air Forces, chaos reigned. When, for example, General Henry "Hap" Arnold, commanding general of the Army Air Forces, had trouble figuring out just how many personnel were under his command, four different sections offered four estimates. Typically, Arnold selected the two that came closest to agreement. "Lovett was almost at wits' end," recalled McNamara. "He had been a prominent investment banker in New York and understood how crucial the flow of information is to good management." Thornton was both appalled and thrilled at the opportunity he saw in the chaotic situation: "[N]ot even a single combat group can operate on that basis, much less a complete air force," he told one commander. With Lovett's help, Thornton began to write his own job description and to develop a "rudimentary control system" for the Air Forces.[8]

Lovett paved the way for Thornton's job at Statistical Control with an open-ended brief to assess the number of planes and parts, as well as pilots and mechanics, that the Army Air Forces had at their disposal. Stat Control clerks would monitor such information as the status of planes—whether they were ready for combat, repairable, or out of action. While everyone else might be satisfied with guesswork, Thornton was determined that Statistical Control would corner the market on "internal intelligence" and the power that went with it.[9]

After Pearl Harbor, Thornton's operation became the nerve center of the Army Air Forces. Statistical control might sound like little more than "counting bottle caps at the PX," but its influence owed much to the innocuousness of its moniker, which led many of the military brass to underestimate Thornton's ambitions. In fact, Thornton and Lovett were in the process of creating a shadow command structure that would use a vast network of highly trained officers "to collect, organize, and interpret facts and figures on personnel and equipment." Using this knowledge, the Whiz Kids would help decide everything from how to transport troops and material to which bombers should be used for specific battles. "They would serve the role of corporate controllers, their reports flowing up to Air Force headquarters through a parallel and largely independent command structure headed by Tex," wrote Byrne.[10]

The success of Thornton's operation owed much to his dedication to managerial professionalism. Although Thornton probably knew nothing about Chester Barnard and the Harvard Circle, he was attuned to the managerial zeitgeist of the times and determined to assemble a cadre of military controllers who possessed both the know-how and the prestige to challenge the assumptions of the military's top brass.

To do so, in April 1942 Thornton boarded the train for Boston and the Harvard Business School. With little more than a vague brief to establish a unit of Statistical Control, he set out to woo Wallace B. Donham, dean of the Harvard Business School. His agenda was to persuade Donham to train his Stat Control officers, in the process giving his organization the imprimatur of the "West Point of capitalism."

Unbeknownst to Thornton, HBS, in the wake of Pearl Harbor, was casting about for a mission that could sustain the school during World War II. Donham welcomed the chance to turn HBS into a boot camp for Thornton's Stat Control officers. Just four months after Pearl Harbor, twelve young Harvard professors, including Bob McNamara, followed Thornton to Washington to design a training program for the Stat Control students. At the core of the program was a course in business statistics, a course widely disliked at HBS for its "mundane calculations of averages and regressions." But as the job of a Stat Control officer required being able to extract facts gleaned from the reports and special studies conducted by other staff officers and to present them in a form that would highlight the meaning and significance of the data, Professor Edmund P. Learned redesigned the course to focus on how to use numbers in decision making. In addition to training in quantitative methods, the trainees were given a series of case studies in human relations techniques—to hone their interpersonal skills—and in actual problems gleaned from Army Air Forces data.[11]

To ensure that only the best officers made it into Stat Control, Thornton handpicked the best and the brightest from the Army Air Forces' Officer Candidate School in Miami. Since a posting at Harvard's ivy-covered Mellon Hall appealed to the businessmen and academics among the officers, Thornton had little trouble convincing his favored recruits—the top two of each OCS class—to join him. Within a year, Harvard had suspended all civilian instruction and was devoted to training military personnel, most of them Thornton's officers.[12]

The Harvard-trained Stat Control officers fulfilled Thornton and Lovett's most ambitious expectations of creating a "parallel and largely independent command structure" within the Army Air Forces. By the end of the war, Stat Control commanded 15,000 personnel, as well as 3,000 of the best Harvard-trained officers scattered throughout sixty-six units around the world. Stat Control also orchestrated the deployment of vast amounts of equipment, spare parts, and military personnel wherever they were needed. One of Stat Control's first jobs, for example, was to determine how many planes the Army Air Forces had at their disposal. The report, known as No. 101, comprised a daily inventory of the number and location of every aircraft down to type, model, and serial number. Report 101, one of thousands compiled by Stat Control, became the basis for allocating airplanes and crews, making up training schedules, and moving troops.[13]

In many respects, Stat Control officers demonstrated the power of managing a far-flung, mechanized war by the numbers. Many of Thornton's men had little if any military training. Yet by analyzing the number of bombing runs, bombs dropped, and damage to aircraft, in many cases Stat Control literally determined which bombers the Army Air Forces should use. For example, at a time when the Army Air Forces relied heavily on the B-24 bomber, Stat Control threw the weight of its analyses behind the B-17 bomber, arguing that the B-17 delivered more firepower more reliably, while sustaining less damage, than the rival B-24. Stat Control's analysis led the Army Air Forces to scale back production of the B-24 in favor of the B-17. Later in the war, by showing that the B-29 was far more efficient in terms of the number of bombs dropped per combat hour than either the B-17 or B-24 (thereby saving both lives and gasoline), Stat Control advocated the deployment of the B-29 in the Pacific and halted the transfer of B-17s and B-24s from Europe to the Pacific theater.[14]

The new quantitative methods were not, however, an unalloyed success. After World War II, the U.S. bombing survey, which attempted to measure the success of World War II bombing campaigns, showed that efforts to analyze which bombing targets would produce the biggest bang for the buck had proved to be an "overall disappointment." The analytical techniques developed during the war were good at intrinsically *quantitative* calculations: how much of a particular weapon was needed, where it was to be located, and how and when it was to be transported. They were not nearly as successful at solving more complex and intuitive problems, explains RAND's Shubert. For example, the Army Air Forces gravely miscalculated the strategic importance of wiping out a particular oil refinery in Romania. The bombing run, which was made at great cost of life and equipment, proved to have "nothing like the effect that it was intended to have" in crippling the enemy, largely because the refinery was not nearly as important as the analysts supposed and the Germans had alternative sources of oil.[15]

Indeed, as Alfred D. Chandler observed during his stint as an interpreter of aerial reconnaissance photographs near the end of World War II, strategic bombing often failed to achieve its goals of crippling the enemy's industrial capacity because it simply forced factories "underground." It turned out that production capability was destroyed only if supply lines were severed or sources of energy knocked out—a lesson that would have important implications for Chandler's later work on corporate strategy (see Chapter 9).[16]

Yet, flush with victory, the Whiz Kids seemed oblivious to the limitations of the methodologies that had, with some exceptions, been so successful during World War II. After the war, the Whiz Kids would apply the unique talents they had used to win the war to reviving U.S. industry and the production of such consumer products as automobiles. At the same time, to continue military research begun during World War II, including systems analysis work, General Arnold was instrumental in establishing the RAND Corporation in 1946. (RAND, which stands for Research and Development, was founded initially as a unit of McDonnell Douglas; it was spun off as an independent, not-for-profit research organization in 1948.) RAND, in turn, became a leading developer of systems analysis and general systems theory, and would have a far-reaching impact on government, academia, and industry.

■

After the war, Thornton's team packed up its methodological tool kit and launched a civilian offensive every bit as audacious as its shadow Army Air Forces command had been. Assembling a core team of "Whiz Kids," Thornton set about selling his team and the techniques for conducting research and analysis they had developed for the Army Air Forces to American industry. He even wrote up a marketing brochure to sell the merits of his team. After flirting with both Allegheny Corporation and A. C. Nielsen, the Whiz Kids finally zeroed in on the Ford Motor Company.[17]

After the war, Ford was ready for a dose of the professional management and quantitative analysis that Thornton was selling. The country's third largest defense contractor was in such a state of chaos that the Office of War Production had arranged for Henry Ford II to be issued an honorable discharge from the armed forces in 1943 to return to Detroit to run the company his grandfather had built. At one time, there was even talk of the government taking over Willow Run, a mile-long Ford plant that built the B-24 and Liberator bombers on a seventy-acre production site that was racked by mismanagement and low morale. In the last years of old man Ford's reign, day-to-day control had virtually been seceded to Harry Bennett, head of the Rouge Service Department, whose "private army" of spies and thugs routinely intimidated workers and resorted to violence to quell union organizing.[18]

Henry II succeeded his grandfather Henry Ford, the company founder, in 1945. One of Henry II's first acts as president was to bring in the Whiz Kids. Their brand of cold logic and management by fact (which were usually translated into numbers) were just what Ford seemed to need. McNamara ordered the first audit the company had had in decades. Under McNamara and his two most trusted colleagues, Arjay Miller and Ed Lundy, Ford's core finance staff at headquarters blossomed to no fewer than four hundred. Dozens more financial analysts toiled in the field. "Under McNamara, for the first time in more than twenty-five years, the company always knew where it was, how much it was spending and how much it was making, and it could project both costs and earnings."[19]

Even before becoming controller in 1949, McNamara developed a range of financial systems and measurements that were meant to identify the "facts" that would facilitate "financial control." McNamara's systems gradually shifted more and more power to the finance staff. While the controller's office had previously functioned as accountant and keeper of financial records, McNamara reconceived the job as one of quantitative analysis, including forecasting and planning for the future. Wrote Byrne, "Bob McNamara was behind the effort to install profit centers throughout the corporation so they could take the pulse of each operation. The men went beyond the traditional control of manufacturing costs to include control over everything, from marketing to purchasing. They would figure out what Ford 'ought to pay' for products, rather than simply taking the best price possible.

"Slowly but surely, Bob was evolving a new lingo and new rules for corporate America."[20]

But as with predicting the complex strategic questions during the war, the quants weren't as successful with the more elusive problem of managing human relationships and product. Almost immediately, the finance men ran up against the production people, who were in many ways an easy—and natural—target. The financial analysts, dubbed "bean counters" by the car men, usually won. To be sure, the manufacturing plants at Ford were dirty and inefficient and still reeling from the constant conflicts between union and management. Yet the war between

the bean counters and the car men reflected a more fundamental difference in views. Explained David Halberstam in *The Reckoning:* "For
the product men were arguing taste and instinct, and the finance people were arguing certitudes."[21]

McNamara counters that the car men in Detroit were hopelessly out
of touch with the new postwar era and the changing consumer market.
"The auto industry didn't notice that the market was segmenting, and
some [consumers] would be interested in economy," recalls McNamara,
who ordered an analysis of Volkswagen buyers that revealed, to the
shock of the Ford men, that they included young professionals, not just
poor people. The car executives, McNamara found, "were irresponsible
about social goals and social responsibility, they opposed safety, and environmental standards, utility and function, and cooperating with the
government, and they opposed taking account of labor.

"My point is these men had never taken a course in ethics, in philosophy or morals. There's [still] a difference today between the management of Silicon Valley and the management of GM." Ford, he
believes, has carried on the Whiz Kid legacy, which has made it a
stronger company today than GM.[22]

McNamara's vision was, in many respects, ahead of its time. At a time
when Detroit cars were all tail fins and chrome, McNamara developed
a low-cost compact car known as the Falcon that was a model of relia-
bility and fuel efficiency. Introduced in 1959, the Falcon sold very well.

However, the Whiz Kids never let the rest of the company forget who
was boss. McNamara slapped a $5,000 cap—small change in the auto
business—on what a plant manager could spend without authorization.
Worst of all, the bean counters demanded quality but rarely gave the
plants the means to produce it. For example, a major battle emerged
over the condition of the plants in 1949, setting the stage for a show-
down between Operations and Finance. When Lewis Crusoe, who was
then general manager of the Ford Division, one of the most important
jobs in the company, wanted to modernize the Louisville plant (which
was so hopelessly antiquated that the aisles were too narrow for a forklift to get through), McNamara balked. Instead of approving the improvements, he ordered a study of all the plants—a study that dragged
on for three years until Crusoe made a desperate plea to Henry Ford:
"We can't wait anymore. The quality is bad, the paint is bad. We can't
even get our cars dried out. We can't meet our own standards."[23]

Of course, McNamara wasn't oblivious to the importance of quality.
The trouble was, his detractors charged, McNamara "didn't know what
quality was."[24]

Indeed, McNamara's solution invariably was to try to quantify quality. For a time, he attempted to do just that by assigning points for things gone wrong. The plants quickly learned how to "rig the numbers" by having a few high-quality cars on hand for the quality inspectors. The plant men also learned other tricks for evading what they considered counterproductive edicts from headquarters: to avoid showing a parts inventory after the end of a model's life, they would dump thousands of parts into the nearby Delaware River. McNamara and his men "talked about quality, but they did not give the plant managers the means for quality; what they really wanted was production. So the plant managers were giving them what they wanted, numbers, while paying lip service to quality." Halberstam wrote that by the 1970s, Detroit had "contrived not to improve but in the most subtle way to weaken each car model, year by year. The company, its drive for greater profit, would take the essential auto structure of the year before and figure out ways to increase the profits by reducing the cost of some of the parts."[25]

Another legacy of such cost-benefit analyses was Ford's Pinto, an inexpensive subcompact that had a nasty habit of blowing up in rear-end collisions. Exploding Pintos caused at least fifty-nine deaths and, as a result, gave Ford the dubious distinction of becoming the first U.S. carmaker ever to be charged with reckless homicide.[26]

Although the car was introduced in the 1970s, the Pinto problem could be traced directly back to the system of cost-benefit analyses that had been established by the Whiz Kids: The Pinto's problem was due to the placement and configuration of the gas tank, a design flaw that could have been solved by, for example, sheathing the inside of the gas tank with a rubber lining. But the cost of the solution—the rubber liners would have cost Ford $137 million—couldn't be justified under Ford's cost-accounting system. By comparison, the total cost of burn-related injuries and deaths, as well as damage to the cars themselves, was, according to Ford estimates, a relative bargain: $49.5 million. (One human life was worth $200,725, according to Ford's estimates, which in turn were based on calculations made by the National Highway Traffic Safety Administration; these calculations took into account lost productivity, hospital costs, pain and suffering, and funeral costs.) Since the price of avoiding burn accidents ($137 million) was nearly triple the benefit of doing so ($49.5 million), the company never authorized the change.[27]

Like a slow leak on a large surface, erosion can take a long time to detect. Had McNamara sold his vision of social responsibility along with cost controls to Detroit's car men, the results might have been quite different. But demand for cars was so great after the war and competition so limited that Ford felt no great pressure to innovate. During the 1950s and 1960s, the demand seemed insatiable. By 1953, the middle class, families with incomes of $4,000 to $7,500 in 1952, had surged to 35 percent of the population, commanding 42 percent of consumer spending—a 44 percent increase since the end of the war. Devoid of a strategic vision or a product imperative, management by the numbers became a goal unto itself.[28]

During the fifteen years the Whiz Kids had been at Ford, the company had won back large chunks of market share from General Motors. Its stock price had also soared. Six of the original group had become senior executives.

In the fall of 1960, McNamara got his final reward when Henry II named him president of the company. A few days later, John F. Kennedy was elected president. And on December 8, seven weeks after McNamara's appointment, McNamara got a call from the White House: JFK had tapped him as his new secretary of defense.[29]

Over the course of the next eight years—under both Kennedy and Lyndon B. Johnson—McNamara would bring the same analytical, rationalistic perspective that had revived Ford to running the Pentagon. Within three weeks of his appointment, he had identified a hundred topics—known as the "Ninety-nine Trombones"—on which he wanted studies done and papers prepared. He also moved to install a new cadre of quantitative Whiz Kids, including a number of researchers from the RAND Corporation.[30]

What attracted McNamara to the Santa Monica–based think tank was that RAND, another post–World War II offshoot of the Army Air Forces, had refined a powerful new analytical tool known as systems analysis. As conceived by RAND researchers, systems analysis was "a 'rational,' mathematically rigorous means of choosing among alternatives," especially in complex environments riddled with uncertainty. According to RAND's Shubert, the methodology consisted of two main parts: first, the development of a set of alternative solutions to a problem, based on a thorough understanding of existing systems and their flaws; and second, a systematic analysis of each alternative, including a cost-benefit analysis and a rigorous comparison of each alternative based on its relative cost and effectiveness.[31] (Alain C. Enthoven, deputy assistant secretary for systems analysis at the Department of Defense, under McNamara, once likened systems analysis to sin and virtue: it "means different things to different people," he said. Generally, he added, systems analysis involves the dissection of complex problems and the "sort[ing] out [of] the tangle of significant factors" influencing them, so that "each can be studied by the method most appropriate to it."[32])

Systems analysis usually employs an arsenal of analytical methods, such as economic theory, mathematical statistics, and operations research. But, said Enthoven, "[M]ost of the systems analysis work in the Department of Defense between 1961 and 1969 used nothing more complex than simple arithmetic and a pragmatic approach to problems that emphasized certain fundamental ideas or 'working' premises."[33]

At the beginning of the Cold War, RAND hoped that systems analysis would provide the means of developing an ultimate science of war. Although it soon became clear that the complexity of war defied any sort of definitive scientific solution. RAND continued to work on improving systems analysis and providing information to military decision makers that "sharpen[ed] their judgment and provid[ed] the basis for more informed choices." At its best, systems analysis combined quantitative methods, especially mathematical modeling, and qualitative analyses involving such diverse disciplines as psychology and economics. Eventually it came to be applied to a range of complex public policy issues. In New York City, for example, RAND conducted such analyses in 1969 for the police and fire departments that led to dramatic reductions in false alarms and a new approach to dispatching fire crews.[34]

But in 1950, the failure to develop a science of war—the effort had fallen victim to faulty assumptions and an oversimplistic cost-benefit analysis—prompted RAND to publish a report with the following critique of the methodology: "The great dangers inherent in the systems analysis approach . . . are that factors which we aren't yet in a position to treat quantitatively tend to be omitted from serious consideration. Even some factors we can be quantitative about are omitted because of limits on the complexity of structure we have learned to handle. Finally a system analysis is fairly rigid, so that we have to decide six months in advance what the USAF problem is we are trying to answer—frequently the question has changed or disappeared by the time the analysis is finished."[35]

McNamara, eager to seize on the methodology, which seemed ideally suited to perfecting the analytically based science of management that he had championed at Ford, wasn't prepared to heed the warning label RAND had slapped on its own product. It is doubtful that he ever appreciated the limitations of systems analysis or the complex range of disciplines, including qualitative analyses, that the most sophisticated applications of the methodology required.

After Kennedy's election, one of his priorities was to reestablish civilian control of the Pentagon, which during the course of the Cold War had grown into a "behemoth" that included 4.5 million military and civilian personnel and a budget of $280 billion (in 1994 dollars). By 1960, the Pentagon was bigger than America's top twenty-five corporations combined and seemed to many observers to be an "ungovernable force." (McNamara's determination to gain control of the armed services hardened when he discovered, soon after his appointment, that the much trumpeted missile gap, which had been a major issue during the presidential election campaign, was a fiction.)[36]

McNamara "had no patience with the myth that the Defense Department could not be managed" and was bent on asserting his rule. "I made it clear that I was determined to subordinate the powerful institutional interest of the various armed services and the defense contractors to a broad conception of the national interest," he wrote. "I wanted to challenge the Pentagon's resistance to change, and I intended that the big decisions would be made on the basis of study and analysis and not simply by perpetuating the practice of allocating blocs of funds to the various services and letting them use the money as they saw fit."[37]

McNamara wanted to apply the same rational decision-making processes that he had used at Stat Control and Ford to control defense strategy and weapons procurement. To wrest control of decision making from experienced military men who, however, by virtue of their service affiliations had strong vested interests, he had to find a way to centralize control within the DOD. But he opted against a wholesale reorganization of the Pentagon and the armed forces themselves, which would have ignited a political battle he might well have lost. Instead, he used the so-called PPBS (Planning, Programming and Budgeting System), a RAND-developed budgeting system, and associated analytical techniques to assert control, much the way the controller's office at Ford had used financial procedures to impose its will on manufacturing. He thus placed decision-making power in the hands of policy makers in his office—some of them alumni from the RAND Corporation—who had the "necessary detachment from parochial interests." (In fact, Charles Hitch, who headed the effort, had been head of the Economics Division at RAND and was a leading authority on program budgeting and the application of economic analysis to defense problems.)[38]

Analysts from RAND began moving into the Pentagon shortly after McNamara's appointment and soon developed and applied management techniques that came to pervade top echelons of the civilian establishment within the Pentagon. "For McNamara, RAND was a source of energetic young men who shared his detached, analytical outlook and in whose ability and judgment he had immediate confidence," wrote Jardini. RAND alums included Hitch, who became the assistant secretary of defense—comptroller; Enthoven, another RAND alumnus, became Hitch's deputy assistant secretary for systems analysis. They were committed to applying economic principles to defense policy and to transforming what had heretofore been little more than a "book-keeping device" and a "blunt instrument for keeping a lid on defense spending" into a vital policy-making instrument. At the same time, RAND researchers set up shop in Bethesda, Maryland, to conduct programming and budgeting studies and training.[39]

A book published in 1960 by Hitch and another RAND researcher, Ronald M. McKean, became the bible of McNamara's DOD. *The Economics of Defense in the Nuclear Age* defined one of the key challenges of defense planning as one of managing with scarce resources. The policy-making challenge, as defined by the RAND researchers, involved the following cost-benefit calculus, according to Jardini: "combining limited quantities of missiles, crews, bases and maintenance facilities to 'produce' a strategic air force that will maximize deterrence of enemy attack." This, according to Hitch and McKean, was every bit as much of an economics problem as that of "combining limited quantities of coke, iron ore, scrap, blast furnaces, and mill facilities to produce steel in such a way as to maximize profits." The dilemma, according to the RAND researchers, was that "[t]here is within government neither [a] price mechanism which points the way to greater efficiency, nor competitive forces which induce government units to carry out each function at minimum cost."[40]

Planning and budgeting were almost completely divorced from each other, with military experts developing military strategy years in advance while the civilians in the DOD allocated funds on a year-by-year basis. Budgeting and policy making were "carried out by different people at different times, with different terms of reference, and without a method for integrating their activities," complained Enthoven. "This gap between strategy and forces, on the one hand, and budgets, on the other, posed a serious obstacle to rational defense planning."[41]

Worse, there was considerable rivalry and little coordination between the services. The three services (Navy, Air Force, and Army) "develop their forces more or less in isolation from each other, so that a force category such as the strategic retaliatory force, which consists of contributions of both the Navy and Air Force, is never viewed in the aggregate. Similarly it is impossible to tell exactly how much continental air defense is being obtained from the defense budget since this is another category to which several services contribute," complained General Maxwell D. Taylor, former Army chief of staff. One consequence of this approach, and the divorce between budgeting and strategy, was that the defense budget was divided between the services based on a relatively fixed percentage that changed little from year to year. Between 1954 and 1961, about 47 percent went to the Air Force, 29 percent to the Navy and Marine Corps, and 24 percent to the Army.[42]

RAND analysts saw defense policy as being dangerously fragmented. "[D]efense budgeting was, in effect, conceived as being largely unrelated to military strategy," wrote Enthoven and K. Wayne Smith in *How Much Is Enough?* Writes Jardini: "Under the extant system, each of the military services retained virtual autonomy over the use of its budget share and thus pursued force planning according to its own set of objectives and interests. This created a situation in which the several services were rarely working with any coordination and were frequently pursuing strategies that ran at cross-purposes." For example, Hitch charged that the Air Force focused its resources on the strategic bombers and missiles but "starved" the tactical air units needed to support Army ground operations and to airlift troops to distant trouble spots. According to him, each branch of the armed forces was guilty of similarly single-focused strategies. Moreover, "when the Secretary of Defense was forced to make a cut, he had no adequate way of relating individual Service priorities to the overall national strategy and force structure."[43]

Events seemed to confirm the RAND researchers' critique of the defense establishment. When the Soviet Union launched *Sputnik I* in 1957, many experts blamed interservice rivalries and lack of coordination for allowing the Soviets to seize the "technological initiative." Nor was RAND the DOD's only critic: in 1958, the Rockefeller Foundation published a blistering critique of the diffuse nature of national defense policy making.[44]

In *The Economics of Defense*, Hitch and McKean had advocated a more holistic approach to defense, one that would conceptualize national security as a "complex system of relations" based on "total systems costs" and overall defense priorities. Wrote Hitch and McKean, "Strategy, technology, and economy ... [are] interdependent elements of the same problem. Strategies are *ways of using* budgets or resources to achieve military objectives. Technology *defines* the possible strategies. The economic problem is to choose that strategy, including equipment and everything else necessary to implement it, which is most efficient (maximizes the attainment of the objective with the given resources) or economical (minimizes the cost of achieving the given objective)—the strategy which is most efficient also being the most economical."[45]

McNamara and Hitch moved quickly to improve what they saw as a fragmented and inefficient system. In his first year as secretary of defense, McNamara rushed to adopt RAND's Planning, Programming and Budgeting Systems (PPBS) and related analytical techniques as DOD's principal budgeting process and as a cornerstone of his "management revolution."

PPBS sought to increase efficiency and effectiveness by "building in rigorous systematic analysis of alternative allocation strategies." It facilitated this by focusing the budgeting process on overall end-product programs and strategies, rather than individual weapons and budget items. By doing so, PPBS allowed McNamara to shift control of planning and strategy from military leaders to the DOD.[46]

Thus, as applied by McNamara, systems analysis became the quintessential late-twentieth-century tool of scientific management. It was a methodology that was conceived largely by economists and other quantitatively trained analysts. It evolved out of operations analysis as a way to increase the effectiveness of current operations and as a way to plan future operations. And it was intended to provide "transparency" by making both the analysis and the assumptions and calculations behind it "available to all interested parties."[47] Yet, as applied by McNamara, it concentrated power in the hands of the analytical experts. While the efficiency engineer of Taylor's day had wrested control of production from the worker, McNamara's bean counters wrested control of planning from operating executives in both auto manufacturing and the armed services.

McNamara and his cadre of RAND analysts were correct in many of their criticisms of the Pentagon during the Cold War era. McNamara is credited with improving the Pentagon's planning and budgeting process and with challenging an inherently conservative defense establishment with strong vested interests to reconsider its assumptions about the nation's defense. In particular, McNamara's DOD was determined to develop a more rational link between military needs and military spending at a time—in the years immediately following *Sputnik*—when the "public mood in the U.S. was one of support for almost anything proposed in the name of national security."[48] Despite the controversies that surrounded the Pentagon Whiz Kids and their analytical methodologies, the Office of Program Analysis and Evaluation set up by McNamara survives to this day and was adopted by numerous other government organizations in the years that followed. It is still the Pentagon's systems analysts who often question the conventional wisdom and defense priorities.

When President Bill Clinton proposed the first Pentagon budget increase since 1991—$12 billion in new spending in 2000 and $110 billion over the next six years—it was a mid-grade analyst in the Pentagon's Office of Program Analysis and Evaluation who sounded the alarm. "This is a horrible thing that's going on. . . . All it's going to do is reward the pathological behavior that's creating the problem," said Franklin C. Spinney, who charges that political consensus has formed around an increased budget even though "there has been very little debate about the need for one." While the Pentagon spends big bucks on advanced jets and tanks, Spinney argues, today's enemies are fighting guerrilla wars with cheaper weapons such as mortars and mines. Spinney first gained notoriety in the 1980s, when he charged that President Ronald Reagan's defense buildup wouldn't make the military any stronger; worse, by consistently underestimating the costs of weapons, the Pentagon was saddling the country with ever-increasing defense budgets. To men such as Spinney, the new military challenges are strategic, not budgetary. (Both Vietnam and Kosovo bear out this view.) At a time when few opposed the most recent round of Pentagon spending, Spinney has "generate[d] some critical dialogue that would not otherwise occur," says Christopher Helman, senior analyst at the Center for Defense Information, another research group that opposes the administration's most recent spending increase.[49]

McNamara, who established the Office of Program Analysis and Evaluation, undoubtedly brought a much-needed analytical perspective to some of the most ideologically charged crises of the Kennedy administration.

Yet, McNamara's eagerness to subject most decisions to detailed quantitative analysis was viewed with concern even at RAND. "I can't think of anyone more eager to embrace these techniques and to seek answers from them than McNamara," recalls Gustave Shubert, a senior fellow at RAND who supervised several studies on the Vietnam War during the mid-1960s, some of which cast doubt on American policy. "Unfortunately, as Vietnam revealed, unambiguous answers are hard to attain by any method, especially this one."[50]

In fact, what is noteworthy about Vietnam is that the decision makers were overwhelmed by analysis. While noting that "consistently overoptimistic reporting from the field denied Washington's decision-makers an accurate picture of developments there," Harold P. Ford, a former CIA officer and author of *CIA and the Vietnam Policymakers*, notes that both the CIA and the Defense Department realized early on that the reports from the field were unreliable. While not always delivering a consistent message, the CIA began to produce negative assessments of the war in 1962. In December 1963, John A. McCone, the director of Central Intelligence, and McNamara agreed that there had been a "complete failure of reporting." One National Security Council officer summed up the problem as follows: "The more we learn about the situation today, the more obvious it becomes that the excessively mechanical system of statistical reporting which had been devised in Washington and applied in Saigon was giving us a grotesquely inaccurate picture. *Once again it is the old problem of having people who are responsible for operations also responsible for evaluating the results.*"[51]

Certainly by early 1964, McNamara had become so skeptical of the evaluations of the military—who, he felt, were "looking at [the situation] through rose-colored glasses"—that he set up a special section at the CIA to evaluate the bombing campaigns and to issue monthly reports on the effectiveness of the campaigns. Each month's report confirmed that the bombing was "not achieving the objectives."[52]

And in March 1964, in response to a plan initiated by Walt Rostow to attack the North, the State Department assembled a multidepartmental committee to assess Rostow's thesis. The group, which consisted of twelve members drawn from State, Defense, the Joint Chiefs, the USIA, and the CIA, produced a "searching study" that concluded, in the words of John McCone, the director of Central Intelligence: "We are not sanguine that the posited US actions would in fact cause Hanoi to call off the war in the South."[53]

With so much evidence marshaled against the U.S. government's course in Vietnam, why were the reports ignored? One reason put forward by McNamara: "We believed the dominos would fall. We believed the Chinese and the Soviets' intention was to utilize a unified Communist Vietnam as a stepping-stone to extend their control across Asia. We totally misjudged the threat."[54]

Yet the CIA already had begun to raise some doubts about the domino theory. Wrote Ford:

> It was the Board of National Estimates, CIA's permanent panel of "wise men," that the White House at length asked to pronounce the analytical judgment on the domino thesis. The loss of Vietnam would of course be a shock, replied the Board on 9 June, but with the possible exception of Cambodia, the rest of East Asia would probably not fall rapidly to Communist control, and there would be much the United States could do to shore up the area. It is noteworthy (1) that the Board called into question one of the primary theses on which US policy and military planning were being based and, by June, briskly executed; (2) that CIA had not been asked for its view of the domino thesis until 10 weeks after the NSC had already inscribed it as formal US policy; and (3) that the Board's conclusions had no apparent impact on existing or subsequent policy.[55]

The administration was clearly locked in its own "mental model" of the nature of the problem. The decision makers were overwhelmed by a flurry of conflicting reports and assessments, utterly overcome by "the fog of war."

As Vietnam would show, neither new management technologies, such as systems analysis, nor an avalanche of reports, nor centralization of power could make up for poor human judgment. What was missing, acknowledges McNamara, is debate. "I clearly erred by not forcing—then or later, in Saigon or in Washington—a knock-down-drag-out debate over the loose assumptions, unasked questions, and thin analyses underlying our military strategy in Vietnam. I had spent twenty years as a manager, forcing organizations to think deeply and realistically about alternative courses of action and their consequences. I doubt if I will ever fully understand why I did not do so here."[56]

Yet in the midst of the crisis, when everyone, including McNamara, feared being wrong, table pounding alone was unlikely to produce any meaningful insights or epiphanies. For meaningful debate to occur, the decision makers would have had to create an atmosphere in which alternative views could be openly debated. Instead, "senior officers of the Kennedy and Johnson administrations brushed aside and at times demeaned" those who "openly doubted the wisdom of U.S. actions in South Vietnam"—men such as George Ball, Mike Mansfield, and John Kenneth Galbraith, according to Harold P. Ford. At the DOD, in particular, critics charge that a kill-the-messenger atmosphere prevailed. "McNamara's personality created an environment in which subordinates didn't present dissenting views," argues Jardini.[57]

While McNamara disputes this charge, he did concede, "We failed to address fundamental issues, our failure to identify them was not recognized; and deep-seated disagreements among the president's advisers about how to proceed was neither surfaced nor resolved."[58]

As American involvement in Vietnam began to spiral out of control, the DOD kept counting: bombing strikes, enemy supply lines destroyed, body bags. None of those numbers, however, could quantify the unquantifiable: the commitment and zeal of a human enemy.

Long after the Vietnam War had ended, McNamara made this stunning admission: "We failed to recognize that in international affairs, as in other aspects of life, there may be problems for which there are no immediate solutions. For one whose life has been dedicated to the belief and practice of problem solving, this is particularly hard to admit. But, at times, we may have to live with an imperfect, untidy world."[59]

■

It took industry several more years to recognize the limitations of the analytical, quantitative revolution that McNamara had championed at both Ford and the DOD. Throughout the growth years of the 1960s, the success of American industry seemed to reaffirm the techniques the Whiz Kids had brought to Ford. "With the possible exception of General Electric, no other American corporation—not General Motors or IBM or Procter & Gamble or Coca-Cola—could boast a more stellar reputation for attracting and training men of finance than Ford," wrote John Byrne. By the early 1980s, 250 alumni from Ford's Finance Department had moved into the executive suites of other companies. Rockwell International, Zenith, American Motors, Firestone, and Xerox Corporation all came to be run by finance men trained at Ford. Yet the social vision that McNamara had promoted at Ford had long since been lost.[60]

The men McNamara and Lundy had trained knew no more about copiers, tires, televisions, or computers than they had known about automobiles. They brought a one-size-fits-all financial orientation to each new company. They dissected and translated every activity from marketing tires to developing copiers into the Esperanto of costs and profits. In the process, they eviscerated corporate cultures and left a host of companies exposed to the product and market savvy of foreign competitors, especially newcomers from Japan.

One of the most famous infiltrations of Ford finance men occurred at Xerox in the late 1960s. When Archie McCardell, a seventeen-year veteran of Ford's Finance Department, joined Xerox, he subjected the copier maker to the same minute financial analysis that the Whiz Kids had brought to Ford. He put another Ford finance veteran, Jim O'Neill into the top engineering and manufacturing post at Xerox, even though O'Neill had never designed a car, let alone a copier or computer. O'Neill, who once suggested replacing metal copier hinges with cheaper ones made of plastic, was quickly derided within the company as an accountant with no feel for product, let alone innovation. "O'Neill's financial background, belief in management by the numbers, and concern for control made him virtually intolerant of risk—a perspective fundamentally opposed to novel technology," wrote Douglas Smith and Robert Alexander in *Fumbling the Future*, a book about one of the greatest missed opportunities in U.S. business history—how Xerox lost the lead in personal computers.[61]

It was certainly a disadvantage when it came to seizing Xerox's greatest innovation since Joe Wilson invented xerography: the Alto, a personal computer that Xerox developed long before either Apple or IBM produced a PC. When Xerox back-burnered the Alto, the decision reflected a corporate culture that had been entirely co-opted by finance. It reflected a vision of finance and control that tackled only what was already seen with technology already established through development, manufacturing, and marketing systems already in place. Such a world view could exploit leadership only when leadership already existed; it could suck value only from the already profitable. In the 1970s, it arguably could work at Xerox for copiers, but certainly not for word processors or computers. Under the influence of management by numbers alone, Xerox introduced equipment [that] followed instead of led, while rejecting products like the Alto, which had every promise of leadership.

An Alto computer in 1976 might not have been a financial success. So what? Neither was the Model A Copier of the early 1950s. Joe Wilson okayed the Model A Copier because he had faith in xerography. When the Model A failed . . . [h]e insisted that he and his colleagues learn from the mistake by discovering how to design a better office copier the next time. By failing to bring the Alto to market, Xerox lost much more than money or opportunity. They lost faith—in themselves, in their past, and in their future.[62]

Indeed, during the 1970s, Xerox not only forfeited the personal computer, it also lost its edge in copiers. In late 1979, Xerox discovered that the Japanese were *selling* copiers for less than it cost Xerox to *build* them. Not only did Japanese copiers beat American copiers on price, they also beat them on quality.[63]

The same scenario played itself out in industry after industry. Once invincible copier companies, automakers, and producers of consumer electronics found themselves under assault from agile product- and market-savvy foreign competitors. The crisis swept across the heartland like an unforgiving tornado, carrying market share, jobs, and eventually whole companies in its wake.

At first, U.S. manufacturers blamed the low wage rates of the rivals, the strong dollar, and even unfair trade practices. Only gradually did it dawn on U.S. companies that in their obsession with numbers, core management values had gotten lost. In the 1980s, the hubris of the McNamara revolution was replaced by a search for the old values that had made the companies Henry Ford and Joe Wilson had built huge successes in the first place: product, innovation, and quality. Only now, with a new era of foreign competition, the stakes were higher than ever. Nor could a business culture long fed on the romance of technology and quantitative methodologies easily change its ways.

I think it significant that in more than a quarter of a century since Maslow's death, there has been no sign of a decline in his reputation, whereas Freud's and Jung's are heavily bullet scarred. This, I believe is because there is a sense in which Maslow has still not come into his own. His significance lies in the future and will become apparent in the 21st century.

—Colin Wilson[1]

Doug McGregor was a gardener. He grew people.

—Richard Beckhard[2]

Abraham Maslow and Douglas McGregor

From Human Relations to the Frontiers of System Dynamics

To technologists and managers, the end of World War II marked a clear triumph of both American technology and managerial methods. The logistical accomplishments that had been pioneered during the war by men like Robert McNamara and his Whiz Kids were embraced by the business community, helping to fuel a decades-long romance with quantitative methods and technological solutions to managerial problems (see Chapter 5).

To many social scientists, by contrast, it was difficult to view war's end as a triumph in any meaningful sense of the term. Nazism, world war, and the Holocaust all pointed to a cancerous blot on society and human nature. Moreover, a number of the leading social scientists suspected that capitalism itself was the root cause of the tragedy.[3]

Ironically, beginning in the early 1930s, Nazism had led many of the world's most prominent social scientists to seek refuge in the United States. The New School for Social Research alone had recruited over a dozen Europeans, making New York City the number one safe haven for intellectual refugees. Ejected from their Old World ivory towers, the Europeans transformed the social sciences in the United States and brought a range of disciplines and perspectives to bear on the practical problems of the war years, including military morale, psychological warfare, and food rationing.

Among the most prestigious of this group of intellectuals were the émigré psychologists who, after the war, would help revolutionize everything from education to management. These émigrés, including Erich Fromm, Kurt Lewin, Max Wertheimer, and Alfred Adler, represented a particularly diverse field of interests and psychological approaches. But they shared two common traits: First, by dedicating themselves to understanding mental processes, they shared an almost messianic drive to create a more just and equitable world. Second, as most of the émigré psychologists (with the possible exception of Lewin) were influenced by Freud's "biological determinism," which viewed the seeds of people's neuroses ingested, almost literally, with mother's milk, they tended to focus their work on curing mental dysfunction as the means of bettering society.[4]

It was this milieu that Abraham Maslow, a promising young experimental psychologist, encountered when he arrived in New York City in 1935. Unlike his contemporaries, Maslow was not a refugee. A native-born Brooklynite, he had completed his graduate work at the University of Wisconsin before returning to New York.

Maslow was, however, a Jew. Although he had been a star student on the Madison campus, he had been rejected from scores of jobs before he finally landed a research fellowship at Columbia University. Both Maslow and his colleagues, who urged him to change his first name for a less Hebraic moniker, attributed his difficulties in finding a job to the xenophobia and anti-Semitism that pervaded American campuses during the Depression. (Unlike his brothers, who had all changed their names, Maslow adamantly refused.)

Maslow's encounter with the émigré community would have a profound influence on his thinking. His exposure to the Europeans would prompt him to meld the "hard-nosed" experimental research he had done in Wisconsin with his emerging interest in the more illusive realm of human motivation.

Yet Maslow's Weltanschauung differed significantly from that of many of his European contemporaries, for he was a consummate idealist. While painfully aware of the prejudice that surrounded him, he had a defiantly optimistic view of human nature. Unlike most of his European elders, he eschewed the prevailing practice in psychology of analyzing and studying mental dysfunction. Instead, he was convinced that the secret to understanding mental well-being was by seeking out and probing the *healthiest* minds and best-balanced personalities he could find.[5]

Maslow would become known as the father of Third Force, or humanistic psychology, a movement that was quite distinct from—and often at odds with—both the behaviorist and Freudian movements. He considered both Freudian and behaviorist psychology to be half-truths. Specifically, he rejected the behaviorist notion that at birth humans are essentially blank slates on which society and experience imprint psychological makeup and personality, just as he rejected Freud's conception of man's innate selfishness and egotism. Maslow attempted to synthesize the two—hence the moniker Third Force—by drawing on the behaviorist notion that environment can influence behavior while acknowledging Freud's emphasis on the importance of biology and the notion that humans are imprinted from birth with certain innate motivations and emotions.

Fundamentally, Maslow believed in human beings' innate capacity for goodness. "Throughout much of his life, Maslow argued for a new philosophy of humanity to help recognize and develop the human capacity for compassion, creativity, ethics, love, [and] spirituality," according to the editors of *Maslow on Management*, the republication of Maslow's seminal book on management, *Eupsychian Management*. Thus, his interest in motivation inevitably led him to seek out subjects whom he considered "self-actualizers" and ultimately to the study of the nature of human potential itself.[6]

Later in his career, Maslow came to view mystical and spiritual experiences as closely linked to unrealized human potential, an interest that would make him a counterculture icon.[7] However, what lent Maslow's theories such force was the fact that much of his work was grounded in empirical research and informed by a lifelong commitment to scientific inquiry. "He did not spew forth this new approach in psychology without much thought, rigorous testing, hypothesizing, and debate," wrote his editors in *Maslow on Management*. "Thus, his work has powerfully affected managerial theory, organizational development, education, health care and science as well as psychology."[8]

A career academic, Maslow did not turn his attention to the business world until the last decade of his life. Yet already in the 1950s, years before he became aware of how his research could affect management, his work on human motivation was embraced by the human relations movement, including Douglas McGregor at MIT, the pioneers in organization behavior at Harvard, as well as such big-picture thinkers as Peter Drucker. By the 1960s, even as he became an icon of the counterculture movement, his ideas were being put into practice by some of the country's most pioneering executives.

■

The apostle of human potential and self-actualization came of age in a dysfunctional household, in the immigrant jungle that was Brooklyn during the years following World War I. Abraham Maslow was the son of Russian immigrants who had started a cooperage business in Brooklyn. From an early age, he was acutely sensitive to the "pervasive and intense" anti-Semitism of the times, which was characterized by the youth gangs that roamed the patchwork quilt of ethnic neighborhoods

around his Brooklyn home. His innate sensitivity was particularly attuned to the emotionally charged atmosphere of the Maslow household.
He was acutely aware of the deterioration of his parents' marriage. He
resented his father's frequent absences. And he developed an abiding
hatred of his mother, whose Old World superstitions he considered petty
and backward.[9]

It didn't take long for Maslow's powers of perception and aversion to
violence to crystallize into a lifelong intellectual interest in humanism
and social reform. His social conscience was first pricked in high
school, when he read the novels of Upton Sinclair. Wrote Edward
Hoffman, Maslow's biographer, "Through Upton Sinclair's muckraking
novels, Maslow became a democratic socialist in political outlook and
idealistically committed for the rest of his life to working for a better
world."[10]

As a Jew, the child of estranged parents, and an intellectual in a community of largely uneducated immigrants, Maslow came to think of
himself as a perpetual outsider, a role that helped fuel his interest in
philosophy and eventually in psychology. In 1926, after completing
high school in Brooklyn, he won a scholarship to Cornell University,
one of the few Ivy League schools that reserved some places for Jews.
There he discovered a more refined and institutionalized form of anti-
Semitism than the gang violence he had encountered on the streets of
Brooklyn. Cornell's fraternities and even its school paper, *The Cornell
Sun*, systematically excluded Jews. He left Cornell after just a year,
transferring first to City College of New York and finally to the
University of Wisconsin, where he would eventually earn a Ph.D. in psy-
chology.

It was at City College that Maslow experienced his second important
intellectual epiphany. One of his philosophy professors recommended
that he read several books on psychology, among them *The Psychologies
of 1925*, a book of essays that introduced Maslow to the work of John
B. Watson, the founder of American behaviorism. While Maslow rejected many of behaviorism's tenets, he was attracted to Watson's effort
to harness the new science of behavioral psychology to fight racial prejudice, ethnic snobbery, and even the corporal punishment of children.[11]

City College was, however, too close to home. Maslow had fallen in
love with his first cousin Bertha Goodman, a relationship of which his
parents thoroughly disapproved. To get away from his parents and to
give his relationship with Bertha a cooling-off period—even Maslow
thought they were still too young to marry—he decided to change
schools once again. This time he set his sights on the University of
Wisconsin.

The Madison campus was a decidedly progressive place. Under the influence of Governor Robert La Follette, the school had developed a reputation for both academic excellence and academic freedom. During the Depression, it also became a hotbed of leftist radicalism. Yet Maslow's work there was shaped by the decidedly pragmatic behavioralist and experimental orientation of the Psychology Department. Even then, he was drawn to such topics as the aesthetics of music appreciation—an interest the faculty thoroughly discouraged. Instead, after receiving his master's degree, he apprenticed himself to Harry Harlow, who was widely known as the "monkey man" for his groundbreaking investigations into primate behavior and learning.

Maslow served first as Harlow's research assistant and then as his doctoral student, conducting innovative research on the behavior of monkeys. Maslow's research, it turned out, would have long-term implications for his theories of human motivation. For two years, he spent much of his time at Madison's Vilas Park Zoo, where he took copious notes of primate eating habits, mating rituals, and dominance behavior. It was while watching the monkeys that Maslow made an intriguing discovery. Seeing them munch on peanuts and other treats, Maslow realized that he was observing the distinction between appetite and hunger. Monkeys, he realized, exhibit a healthy appetite for treats such as peanuts and chocolate, even after their hunger has been sated. His conclusion was that researchers working with primates would have to take into account the difference between hunger and appetite as a motivating factor. It would be several more years, however, before he would apply these insights to human behavior and develop a comprehensive theory of human motivation.[12]

The University of Wisconsin, it turned out, was not an ideal laboratory for delving into the messier terrain of human wants and needs. While Maslow had long been interested in philosophy, one of the foundations of psychology, most of his colleagues at Madison were not. Moreover, according to Edward Hoffman, Maslow's biographer, Maslow's midwestern professors had been "parochial, sometimes even xenophobic, in disparaging his interest" in such Europeans as Freud, Adler, and the Gestalt psychologists. Although Maslow would ultimately reject the Freudian preoccupation with neurosis, he was drawn to Freud's interpretation of the role of unconscious sexual desire in human motivation. He was equally intrigued by Adler's seemingly contradictory focus on the striving for power as the source of human drive.[13]

In 1933, Maslow discovered a way to test out Freud's and Adler's theories using his observations of monkeys. At the Vilas Park Zoo, he had accumulated data on both sexual and dominance behavior in simians.

He thought that by probing the "delicate balance of dominance and sexual status" in humans, he would be able to learn more about the "vexing problems of human sexual and social relations." Maslow's later studies of self-actualizing people could be traced back to his interest in the dominance behavior among monkeys.[14]

Maslow completed his Ph.D. in 1934, at the height of the Depression. Searching for a job in the 1930s was bad enough. Doing so as a Jew trying to break into academia's old-boy network, in an atmosphere of escalating xenophobia that excluded Jews from most established institutions, was almost impossible. After scores of rejections, he caught the attention of Edward L. Thorndike, a prestigious educational psychologist at Columbia University. Thorndike had won a $100,000 grant from the Carnegie Foundation for an ambitious study aimed at using psychological theory to develop scientifically based social policies relating to such problems as poverty, illiteracy, and crime. Thorndike offered Maslow a fellowship to work on his study. Maslow's assignment was "to determine the relative percentages of hereditary versus environmental influences concerning a variety of human social behaviors."[15]

Before long, however, Maslow found himself bored and dissatisfied with the work. "Temperamentally, he was incapable of persisting in any activity that he disliked," said Hoffman. (Before moving to Columbia, Maslow had enrolled in medical school but had dropped out after just one semester.) It wasn't so much that he disliked his work at Columbia, but he disagreed with Thorndike's premises. Believing that almost all human endeavors involve a mixture of genetic and cultural factors, he found it difficult if not impossible to parse out which behaviors were hereditary and which were learned.[16]

Although protégé and mentor had few common interests, Thorndike recognized Maslow's genius. Soon after arriving at Columbia, Maslow took a battery of intelligence and aptitude tests, many of which had been pioneered by Thorndike, and received one of the highest scores ever recorded—his IQ, for example, was 195. Maslow's feat prompted Thorndike to pledge his support to Maslow for "the rest of his life." Though the older man disapproved of Maslow's interest in dominance and sexuality, he kept his promise.[17]

While he was still at Columbia, Maslow began to seek out the community of émigré psychologists who had found their way to New York City, two of whom—Alfred Adler and Max Wertheimer—became important influences. Maslow met Wertheimer at the New School's University in Exile, which became known as the Graduate Faculty for Social and Political Science. In Wertheimer, a founder of Gestalt psychology, Maslow encountered a genuine intellectual soul mate. Gestalt psychology rested on the proposition that human cognition is greatly reliant on the perception of wholes, or "gestalts." Rather than learning from trial and error, as the behaviorists insisted, humans achieve true leaps of understanding when they have what Wertheimer called an "Aha!" experience. The whole, Wertheimer postulated in what has become a popular axiom, is always bigger than the sum of its parts.[18]

Wertheimer's eccentric personality also appealed to Maslow. For example, Wertheimer was given to leaping onto his desk to punctuate a point and to playing on the floor with his children even when his colleagues were present—behavior that seemed to belie his Old World Germanic upbringing. In his classes and conversations with Maslow, Wertheimer urged his younger colleague to learn from the "unmotivated" qualities of playfulness, wonder, and aesthetic enjoyment, arguing that "psychology is much too preoccupied with goal-seeking behavior." Years later Wertheimer and Ruth Benedict, who had overcome the handicap of partial deafness to do her research, would become models of what Maslow considered "self-actualizing" individuals.[19]

Most important, in a rare departure from many of his fellow refugees, Wertheimer believed that most people possess an essential goodness and decency. "Are there not tendencies in men and in children to be kind, to deal sincerely [and] justly with the other fellow? Are these nothing but internalized rules on the basis of compulsion and fear?" he asked rhetorically. If so, it was the urgent duty of social scientists to understand and develop these innate tendencies.[20]

During this same period, Maslow sought out Alfred Adler. Maslow had been intrigued by Adler's work ever since his days in Wisconsin, when he had tried to prove Adler's theory of dominance and sexuality by studying those traits in monkeys. When Adler emigrated to the United States officially in 1935—he had divided his time between Austria and the United States until Hitler came to power—he set up an open-house class on Friday evenings at the Gramercy Hotel.[21]

Maslow was one of his first students. Most significantly from Maslow's point of view, Adler believed that environmental factors play a major role in affecting human behavior. For example, one of Adler's favorite pastimes was improving the academic performance of children who had been dismissed as "intellectually backward" because of their low IQ scores. He did this by therapeutically building up their self-esteem. Thus, he argued, improving social institutions could improve the performance of individuals—an insight that had particular resonance for human relations pioneers in management.[22]

■

Maslow's work on human motivation received another, seemingly un-likely impetus when he won a research grant to study the Blackfoot Indians in 1937. He had been interested in anthropology since his student days at Wisconsin. At Columbia, he had befriended Ruth Benedict, who was at the forefront of cross-cultural research. Benedict combined such disciplines as psychology and anthropology and brought a multi-disciplinary, cross-cultural perspective to the social sciences.

It was Benedict who encouraged Maslow to go "into the field" and who sponsored his grant application with the Social Science Research Council. Maslow spent the summer of 1938 among the Blackfoot Indians studying "dominance and emotional security" among members of the tribe. Maslow was taken with the Blackfoot culture, especially its generosity and synergy. It was this experience, more than any other, that convinced him that people have certain inner needs that were unrecognized by Freud and antithetical to the capitalist notion of Economic Man driven largely by material wants. Among the Blackfoot, Maslow recognized people's innate need to experience meaning and a sense of purpose in life.[23]

By the beginning of World War II, Maslow had moved from Columbia to Brooklyn College, a predominantly Jewish institution, and was about to abandon his focus on dominance and sexual behavior and to embark on a completely new direction in his research. (In 1937, Thorndike had tried to get him a job with another university, but once again he had been turned away because of being Jewish.)

The disparate influences Maslow had received from Adler, Wertheimer, and Benedict, from his weeks among the Blackfoot, and from the renewed fighting in Europe crystallized one afternoon shortly after Pearl Harbor, in a single epiphany. This is how he remembered the experience: "I was driving home and my car was stopped by a poor, pathetic parade. Boy Scouts and fat people and old uniforms and a flag and someone playing a flute off-key. As I watched, the tears began to run down my face. I felt we didn't understand—not Hitler, not the Germans, not Stalin, or the Communists. We didn't understand any of them. I felt that if we could understand, then we could make progress. . . .

"It was at that moment that I realized that the rest of my life must be devoted to discovering a psychology for the peace table. That moment changed my life."[24]

■

Seized by a new sense of social mission, Maslow was determined to develop "a comprehensive theory of human motivation."[25] He wanted to understand not only why so many people had rallied around Hitler and Stalin but, more generally, what mankind wanted from life. He wanted to comprehend the factors that constituted happiness and a sense of fulfillment.

Maslow revisited the work of his fellow psychologists, Adler and Freud in particular. He reviewed the work of anthropologists such as Benedict, Margaret Mead, and Gregory Bateson. He became convinced that for all the differences in individual cultures, humanity shared certain common desires and goals. In 1940, he had coauthored a book with Bela Mittelman entitled *Principles of Abnormal Psychology*. To the bemusement of his colleagues, he had insisted on writing a chapter on normal personalities. In it he identified such traits as self-esteem, self-knowledge, the ability to receive and express love, and the ability to question the rules of one's society as prerequisites of a healthy psyche.[26]

Yet, Maslow was shocked by the dearth of research on the psychology of healthy individuals. With "the world plunged in war," he was determined to study relatively well-balanced individuals and develop a comprehensive study of human motivation. In 1954, he published *Motivation and Personality*, which developed his theory of human motivation built on two seminal papers that had been published a decade earlier. Of these two papers, "A Theory of Human Motivation" became his most influential paper. His theory, according to Hoffman, "largely replaced the Freudian, the behaviorist" theories, and has come to inform a host of other fields ranging from marriage counseling and psychotherapy to theology and business management.[27]

At the heart of Maslow's theory was what he referred to as "the hierarchy of human needs." He saw five levels of motivation:

1. Physiological needs: in the workplace, this might mean a dry and comfortable place to work.
2. Safety needs: the desire to work in a safe environment;
3. Social needs: the desire for a sense of belonging to an organization or community;
4. Self-esteem needs: a yearning for respect; and finally,
5. Self-actualization: the need to achieve one's full potential.[28]

While all people are born with such basic needs as food and shelter, as well as the emotional yearnings for safety, love, and self-esteem, Maslow argued that these needs are only the foundation of a pyramid of higher aspirations. As he put it, "It is quite true that man lives by bread alone—where there is no bread. But what happens to man's desires when there *is* plenty of bread and when his belly is chronically filled?

"At once other (and 'higher') needs emerge and these, rather than physiological hungers, dominate the organism. And when these in turn are satisfied, new (and still 'higher') needs emerge, and so on. This is what we mean by saying that the basic human needs are organized into a hierarchy of relative prepotency."[29]

Once needs have been satisfied, Maslow clearly implied, they no longer serve as motivators of behavior. The existence of altruism, he explained, is the result of needs that have been largely fulfilled, especially in childhood, with a resulting development of a healthy character.

At the pinnacle of Maslow's need hierarchy was the desire for achieving self-fulfillment, or what Maslow referred to as "self-actualization." Wrote Maslow, "We may still often . . . expect that a new discontent will develop, unless the individual is doing what he is fitted for. A musician must make music, an artist must paint, a poet must write, if he is to be ultimately at peace with himself. What a man *can* be, he *must* be. This need we may call self-actualization. . . . It refers to man's desire for self-fulfillment, namely to the tendency for him to become actually in what he is potentially: to become everything that one is capable of becoming."[30]

■

Maslow's work on human motivation struck an immediate chord among the successors to the human relations movement, chief among them Douglas McGregor at MIT. "You might be interested to know that I used your *Motivation and Personality* with a group of seventeen senior executives in a seminar here at MIT this fall," wrote McGregor to Maslow in 1956. "We had a long discussion of the implications of your self-actualization concept and it was quite clear that the whole idea not only made sense but fired their imagination because of its implications for industry."[31]

Maslow's impact on McGregor was so great, in fact, that it served as an important catalyst for McGregor's first book, *The Human Side of Enterprise*, which itself became a classic in human relations. Although by then both Maslow and McGregor lived in and around the Boston area and corresponded periodically, they didn't actually meet until the 1960s. In management circles, however, their names have become virtually intertwined.

Maslow and McGregor came from very different worlds, both culturally and intellectually. While Maslow was at heart a researcher and scientist, McGregor was a practitioner—though he maintained his Ivy League affiliations throughout his career. Yet intellectually, the two men ended up in very much the same place. McGregor was born in Detroit,

Michigan, the scion of a long line of strict Scottish Presbyterian ministers. His grandfather, who had been a preacher, had died while digging the foundations for a mission known as the McGregor Institute, which served indigent men (and which eventually closed during the Depression). In 1915, Douglas's father, Murray McGregor, became the lay preacher and director of the mission, where as many as seven hundred homeless men "low on the totem pole of human dignity" slept and took their meals. Douglas grew up in the mission, helping out after school and during summer vacations. It was at the mission that Douglas learned to play the piano and sing gospel songs and where he listened to the fire-and-brimstone lectures of his father, who was "weighed down by the social pathology of the men he sought to save," convinced of their core sinfulness.[32]

For a time, Douglas thought he, too, would become a preacher. But while he shared his father's compassion for the lost souls of the mission, he rebelled against Murray McGregor's pessimism about human nature and developed instead a firm conviction in the essential goodness and strength of each individual. Years later, the tension between Murray McGregor's pessimism and Douglas's optimism would play themselves out in McGregor's celebrated management dichotomy: Theory X and Theory Y.[33]

After earning a college degree at Detroit City College (which later became Wayne State), McGregor earned a doctorate in social psychology at Harvard, where he also taught briefly. In 1937, he moved to MIT and helped found the Industrial Relations Department. Except for a six-year stint as the president of Antioch College, he stayed at MIT until his untimely death in 1964.

McGregor, however, never became a conventional academic. For one thing, he published relatively little—*The Human Side of Enterprise*, his only major book, was published in 1960, twenty years after he joined the university. Then, too, in the 1930s and 1940s MIT encouraged its faculty to work in industry, a focus on practice that suited McGregor's practical nature.

Beginning in the late 1930s, McGregor's work followed the path of Mayo and Roethlisberger, focusing on labor-management relations. McGregor soon shifted his focus from the shop floor to broader questions of human relations management. According to Marvin R. Weisbord, a management consultant who wrote about McGregor, McGregor was perhaps the first industrial psychologist to emphasize the strategic importance of personnel policies, including the role of culture, systems, and training. (Of course, Chester Barnard had touched on these issues in the 1930s in *Functions of the Executive*.) McGregor's clients came to include Standard Oil of New Jersey, Bell of Pennsylvania, and General Mills. It was at General Mills, while working with Dewey Balch, the vice president of personnel, and a fellow psychologist, Richard Beckhard, who had been recruited to MIT by McGregor, that he coined the term "organization development" to describe an innovative bottoms-up approach to cultural change—possibly the first attempt to consciously change a company's organizational culture.[34]

One of McGregor's most celebrated consulting arrangements was with Union Carbide, in the early 1960s. Together with the company's industrial relations manager, John Paul Jones, McGregor helped set up an Industrial Relations Department. "Jones was especially mindful of McGregor's prediction that using full human potential in organizations would stand or fall on the ability to work successfully with groups." About the impact of the O.D. Department at Union Carbide, in the early 1960s, *Fortune* wrote, "Organization Development's group programs offer no panacea. . . . But O.D. finds itself with more work than ever, and even if it never took on another job its residual influence would be immense. Practically everybody of consequence in the company is tolerably familiar with Jones's ideas."[35]

Unlike Maslow, McGregor developed real practical experience as a manager. During World War II, he served a brief stint as the temporary labor relations manager at Dewey and Almy Chemical Company, which employed 1,500 workers and produced sealants, football bladders, and organic chemicals. At Dewey, McGregor tried to institute a collaborative approach to resolving labor-management differences relating to such wartime policies as the elimination of work stoppages. But despite a long tradition of paternalism at the company, the efforts, according to McGregor, "failed miserably, quite probably because the management representatives were defensive and somewhat antagonistic. Worker suggestions were accepted but not carried out." The failure may also have been due to the reluctance of McGregor, who was known as a gentle coach and facilitator, to exercise strong leadership.[36]

■

Indeed, McGregor's greatest strength may have been his ability to recognize and foster innovative ideas and people. Warren Bennis, who met McGregor as a student at Antioch and followed his mentor back to MIT in the 1950s, says that McGregor was "a born innovator, a born experimenter. . . . [I]t may be that his greatest and most permanent achievement was to create an atmosphere" in which people were "stimulated to question and challenge continually. . . . If there was anything he was trying to overcome or destroy, it was the institutional habit of talking about the virtue of democracy while running affairs autocratically."[37]

Like Carnegie Mellon during the same period, under McGregor's gentle guidance the Sloan School of Management's Industrial Relations Section became a lightning rod for important new ideas in human motivation and leadership that were percolating among both psychologists and management experts. McGregor had recruited Edgar Schein, an expert on organizational culture, from Harvard. He also brought Mason Haire, an expert on organizational change who had left MIT for Berkeley, back to the Sloan School. In the basement of MIT's Lever Building, Leo Moore, an expert on labor and the workplace, ran an industrial laboratory, complete with a machine shop, where he and his students experimented with work simplification and job enlargement. Among the experts whom Moore invited to speak to the class were W. Edwards Deming and Joseph Juran. In the aftermath of World War II, the two quality experts had already been discovered by the Japanese, who hoped to use their quality expertise to rebuild Japanese industry. However, it would take the United States several more decades to embrace them (see Chapter 7).[38]

Down in the same basement, working on an entirely separate project, McGregor and Alex Bavelas, who would become a prominent psychologist, conducted a psychological laboratory, where they studied groups of managers through two-way glass. These studies in so-called group dynamics were a continuation of work that had been done by Kurt Lewin, a respected émigré psychologist whose innovations, such as the concept of T-groups (training groups) would have a seminal—if sometimes controversial—influence on the human relations movement.[39]

Lewin was one of the first, and perhaps the most important, of McGregor's recruits. In 1946, he helped Lewin launch MIT's Research Center for Group Dynamics, which was moved to the University of Michigan after Lewin's death.[40]

A small, sharp-featured man, Lewin shared with McGregor an interest in applying psychological theories to real human situations. It was Lewin who coined the memorable phrase "Nothing is as practical as a good theory."

Even as scientific management experienced a resurgence after World War II, Lewin's methods became a powerful countervailing force in helping to legitimize sociopsychological management concepts. "Lewin's action research on leadership and participation rank with the twentieth century's great social achievements," wrote Weisbord.[41]

Lewin had earned his credentials in the academic center of Germany, the University of Berlin. Lewin was a maverick in almost every respect. As early as 1910, he became interested in studying subjects such as human motivation, emotions, and sentiments that were considered highly unorthodox at the time. At a time when few women could even gain admittance to European universities, many of his most noted disciples were women. And he alone among Berlin's Gestalt school was interested in industrial management. Indeed, his interests were so eclectic that during the course of his career he studied child behavior, social services, war research, and community development. His overriding concern, says Chris Argyris, who developed the foundations of the so-called Learning Organizations at Harvard, was "How do you make social science become basic and socially actionable? How do you create a better life? And a greater sense of justice and competence?"[42]

Lewin's groundbreaking work on the psychology of work began in 1920, shortly after Frederick Winslow Taylor's death. Contrasting the difference between farm work and factory work, Lewin noted the salutary effects of farming, which, unlike industrial work, engaged "the whole person." The advent of new farm equipment, which would segment the work of farmers, would, Lewin predicted, cause new problems. Lewin proposed that psychologists leave the laboratory and team up with farmers to conduct experiments using farm implements such as hoes to improve work methods. Nothing could have been more outrageous to the Herr Professors of the German university system than Lewin's suggestion, which he meant both literally and figuratively, that psychologists should get down in the dirt and dig.[43]

A year later, Lewin wrote a follow-up piece entitled: "Humanization of the Taylor System: An Inquiry into the Fundamental Psychology of Work and Vocation," in which he suggested that psychologists and efficiency experts team up to enhance both productivity and satisfaction. "The worker wants his work to be rich, wide and Protean, not crippling and narrow," he wrote. "Work should not limit personal potential but develop it. Work can involve love, beauty and the soaring joy of creating."[44]

Lewin and his followers espoused a radically pragmatic approach to researching and reforming both individual and group behavior. Lewinians eschewed conventional academic research methods, such as surveys and dispassionate interviews. Instead, they developed a hands-on, learning-by-doing approach.

After emigrating to the United States, Lewin became a leading proponent of the powerful role that social groups play in influencing a person's emotional and mental well-being. He also developed the concept of "force field analysis" to analyze the factors working for or against change. For example, in trying to reduce teenage smoking, peer pressure might be a force preventing change, while education on the hazards of smoking would be a force favoring change. The goal is to achieve a state of equilibrium between the "pushing" and "restraining" forces.[45]

Eventually, Lewin and his followers pioneered so-called group dynamics, which became a central concept of organization reform. As Art Kleiner, author of *The Age of Heretics* wrote, Lewin argued that "[y]ou cannot know an institution until you try to change it, and you cannot change it without reflecting on its purpose."[46]

Lewin's first major breakthrough came in the late 1930s, after he had left Nazi Germany for the United States. Working as a child psychologist at the University of Iowa's Child Welfare Research Station, he met Ronald Lippitt, a graduate student who would become both his protégé and principal collaborator. Lippitt was interested in the relationship between individual and group behavior. He devised a plan to study how different management styles affect group behavior. Having just left Nazi Germany and seeing "grim echoes" of Nazism in American colleges, with their rigid quota systems, which limited the number of Jews, Catholics, and ethnic groups, on campus, Lewin's reaction to Lippitt's proposal was "deeply personal." During the course of discussing the project, Lippitt and Lewin coined the phrase "group dynamics."[47]

For the study, Lippitt organized groups of middle-class public school boys into groups of five, with each group headed by a college student. He instructed each group leader to behave in one of three distinct leadership styles: laissez-faire, autocratic, and democratic. Lewin filmed each group.

The researchers found that the democratic groups worked best; they fostered tolerance, generosity, conscientiousness, and what generally would be thought of as "adult" behavior in its members. By contrast, the laissez-faire and autocratic environments produced frustration and cynicism, in the case of the former, and excessive obedience or destructiveness, in the latter. "There have been few experiences for me as impressive as seeing the expression on children's faces during the first day under an autocratic leader," wrote Lewin. "The group that had formerly been friendly, open, cooperative, and full of life, became within a short half-hour a rather apathetic-looking gathering without initiative."[48]

What's more, when the leaders switched groups, the behavior of the group changed radically to adapt itself to the new leadership style. Interestingly, the groups that had been led by an autocratic leader adapted more slowly to a democratic style. Concluded Lewin,

"Autocracy is imposed on the individual.... Democracy he has to learn!"[49]

Lewin and Lippitt discussed their findings with Margaret Mead. Out of those conversations developed another groundbreaking research project. What the boys' club experiment showed about leadership and the impact of management styles on the climate of work groups, a new study involving Iowa housewives and food rationing during World War II would do for participative management.

The study began when Lewin and Mead teamed up on a project aimed at reducing civilian consumption of rationed foods, especially meat. Mead argued that men ate whatever their wives cooked; therefore, it was the wives who made the primary decisions about what foods to purchase. Having discovered that wives served as the "gatekeepers" to the household pantry, Lewin set up a comparative experiment, dividing the survey participants into two groups. One group was exhorted by a nutritional expert on what women "should" purchase, based on a food's availability and nutritional content. A second group was "given the facts" relating to both what foods were available and which were in short supply and asked to negotiate a consensus.[50] The study produced two important insights. First, it revealed that the group whose decisions were based on consensus changed its food-buying habits much more radically than the group that was merely exhorted to change, thus establishing a core Lewinian principle: "We are likely to modify our own behavior when we participate in problem analysis and solution and likely to carry out decisions we have helped make." Second, the identification of "gatekeepers" as the key wielders of influence in groups proved exceptionally insightful and would become a cornerstone of team-building efforts for decades to come. Weisbord notes that Lewin "was never an ideologue of mindless participation."[51]

The two Iowa studies were clearly complimentary. Together, Lewin, Lippitt, and Mead had hit upon a theory of organizational change based on the assumption that a productive workplace depends on both group skills and the self-knowledge of the individuals within the group. They further recognized the potentially symbiotic relationship between individuals and groups—i.e., that group skills can further self-knowledge and vice versa.

In a culture that values individuals above all else, this conclusion was almost subversive; for the Lewinians argued that the group was key to shaping individual behavior "at least as much as the members determine the values of the group." Indeed, Lewin considered the Horatio Alger myth "as tragic as the initiative-destroying dependence on a benevolent despot." As he once said to his friend Lippitt, "We all need

continuous help from each other. Interdependence is the greatest challenge."[52]

The notion of interdependence has since become central to
American management. It is at the heart of team-based approaches to
management, including the quality movement, the learning organization, and virtually all of participative management. It is also at the root
of the relatively new science of system dynamics.

After the war, Lewin's approach to participative, action-oriented research was extended to industry. Alfred Marrow, another of Lewin's
graduate students, agreed to conduct experiments in group dynamics
with the women working at a new pajama factory owned by his family's
company, Harwood Manufacturing, in rural Virginia. Alex Bavelas, who
was also a graduate student at the time, sought to involve the workers
in finding ways to improve output to "create useful knowledge about the
processes of change itself." Instead of attempting to engineer "one best
way," Bavelas engaged both high and low producers in group discussions about various production techniques. "Not only did people learn
efficient practices from one another, they removed the barriers to
change by deciding together what to do," wrote Weisbord, noting that
Harwood experienced productivity increases as great as Taylor's. The
Harwood experiments also confirmed Lewin and Mead's earlier observations that including "gatekeepers" in any change process is a key to
its success.[53]

The Harwood experiments, with their shop-floor group meetings, became the inspiration for *The Pajama Game*, a Broadway musical and
major motion picture. Yet Lewin insisted that the successes at Harwood
did not represent a management panacea. "Managers rushing into a factory to raise production by group decisions . . . are likely to encounter
failure," wrote Lewin. Explains Weisbord, "Involving people was not a
'technique.' It was the bedrock of social learning, requiring goal focus,
feedback, leadership and participation by all the relevant actors."[54]

Lewin had one other important opportunity to test out his theory of
group dynamics. In 1946, with the flood of GIs returning from the war,
racial conflicts erupted in several northern cities. In response, a
Connecticut state agency, with funding from the National Conference of
Christians and Jews, decided to hold a conference on race relations.
Leland Bradford, who was with the National Education Association's
adult education division, which was to provide discussion leaders for
the conference, contacted Lewin for help.

Nothing could have suited Lewin better than the opportunity to put
his ideas to work fighting prejudice. Lippitt joined Lewin in this project, as did Ken Benne, another young psychologist whom Lewin and

Lippitt had gotten to know during the war. The workshop, which was held in Bridgeport, a working-class city just west of New Haven, brought together fifty participants, from schoolteachers and social workers to businesspeople and housewives. The two-week project became the catalyst for a decades-long experiment in changing group behavior.[55]

The project itself was built on an accepted therapeutic device: participants gathered in small groups to role-play potentially difficult interracial relationships, led by group leaders. In the evenings, the staff, including group leaders and observers who watched the daytime sessions, would gather to discuss the groups' progress. Participants in the groups were permitted to attend the evening sessions but were neither obliged nor expected to do so. But one night toward the end of the two-week experiment, Lewin's team experienced a collective epiphany when a group of participants passed by Lewin's room, overheard the trainers discussing the day's sessions, and stopped in to listen. During the course of the conversation, one of the four, a social worker, recognized herself in Lippitt's description of a participant "who is customarily the most backward and hesitant" but who had recently shown signs of being a "very active and verbal leader." The participants, including the social worker, agreed that her behavior *had* actually changed. "I was aware too that I was much more in the swim of things this afternoon than I had been before," she said. "I surprised myself several times the way I spoke up and found myself enjoying it."[56]

Lippitt's observation seemed to indicate that through the group dynamic, an individual could unconsciously adopt a role-play personality. What's more, Lewin thought that the social worker's participation in the analysis of her own transformation during the evening session provided a useful solution to a common problem in psychological research: how to overcome the biases of both the interviewer and the subject to achieve more accurate and reliable answers. "[A]s the staff and participants continued their talk about the day's session," he noted, "the barriers between them dissolved. . . . When the social scientists got it wrong, the participants corrected them; when the participants lost sight of the larger perspective, the social scientists gently drew them back to equanimity."[57]

The Bridgeport group, Lewin concluded, had stumbled across a new principle with wide application in the analysis and treatment of group behavior. This was a new type of therapy group designed to understand and treat social dynamics, not individual neurosis. Lewin and the trainers called their discovery a T-group (training group). T-groups, which were leaderless, were based on the notion of "action research," in which participants served as both guinea pigs and researchers; the T-groups would produce behavior, analyze it, generalize from it, and finally look for ways of applying what they had learned.[58]

The Bridgeport group published a paper on the session that came to be widely heralded in psychological and educational circles. The Office of Naval Research and the Carnegie Corporation helped fund further research on T-groups, and the National Education Association provided staff. To apply for further funding, the Bridgeport group formed a division of the NEA, based in Washington, D.C., which it called the National Training Laboratories for Group Dynamics. On Lewin's suggestion, the NTL founders set about finding an isolated location where T-group participants could get together away from the cares of their day-to-day lives. NTL's "cultural island," as Lewin called it, became the Gould Academy campus in Bethel, Maine. (Along parallel lines, Carl Rogers had developed similar small-group training programs at the University of Chicago at about the same time.)[59]

In February 1947, before the plans for NTL were complete, Lewin suddenly died in his sleep. "The timing of his death gave NTL's birth a mythic stature," wrote Kleiner.[60] For years to come, NTL held workshops each summer in Bethel, attracting a who's who of the human relations and psychological communities. Maslow, Chris Argyris, and Warren Bennis, for example, all passed through NTL as either participants or trainers. McGregor also continued to make MIT a center of T-group activity.

Although NTL survives to this day, in the 1960s it underwent both a leadership crisis and an ideological split. NTL began to suffer from a certain "anti-intellectual arrogance," says Chris Argyris. "In my estimation, there was a lack of interest in contributing to learning and executive education. It wasn't asking important questions" anymore. As NTL became more of a political base focusing on diversity issues for minorities and women, many of its most prestigious participants, such as Ed Schein and Argyris, began to withdraw.[61]

Even as Lewin was doing his groundbreaking research on group dynamics, McGregor was busy recruiting another maverick to MIT. During World War II, McGregor had spent two summers in Pittsburgh, at U.S. Steel, observing the work of Joseph P. Scanlon, the originator of one of the most promising efforts to introduce participative management to the shop floor, known as the Scanlon Plan. The son of poor Irish immigrants, Scanlon was a onetime prizefighter, cost accountant, steelworker, labor leader, and pioneer in union-management cooperation.

In some respects, McGregor and Scanlon couldn't have been more different. McGregor was tall and thin, all legs and arms; his tweed jackets and ubiquitous pipe gave him a quintessential professorial air.

Scanlon, by contrast was short and dark, with the muscular physique of the welterweight champion he once had been. Years later, McGregor cited Scanlon, along with Lewin and Charles Kettering, GM's maverick head of R and D, who had served as a trustee of Antioch College while McGregor was its president, as the men who had influenced him the most.[62]

McGregor met Scanlon just as the labor pioneer was attempting to mediate a historic agreement between the management of U.S. Steel, which was under pressure to increase production during World War II, and Philip Murray, the notoriously distrustful head of the United Steel Workers. Under the influence of Scanlon and Clinton S. Golden, a machinist and labor leader who believed in "industrial democracy," union-management collaboration flourished at U.S. Steel between the late 1930s and the end of World War II.

What became known as the Scanlon Plan got its initial impetus from Golden. A onetime follower of Eugene Debs, Golden had come under the influence of Harvard's Elton Mayo in the 1920s and endorsed efforts at union-management collaboration that were pioneered by the Machinists Union in the same decade. Such early cooperative programs got a bad name in labor circles because they coincided with the corporate efforts to marginalize the unions' influence, in part by developing paternalistic policies such as pensions, profit sharing, and safety programs.

The Depression, however, revived unionism and paved the way for mavericks such as Golden and Scanlon. Scanlon first came to the attention of union leadership during the Depression, when he took the lead in trying to help fellow workers eke out a subsistence living. He hustled local businesses for seed and fertilizer so that unemployed workers could at least plant enough produce to subsist on, as well as lumber to burn for heat in the winter.

Scanlon, who had once worked as a cost accountant in the late 1920s, joined Empire Steel in Mansfield, Ohio, in the 1930s. During the height of the Depression, the company was forced to file for bankruptcy. In 1937, as it was in the throes of reorganizing itself and unable to increase wages, a labor committee from the plant appeared at Golden's office in Pittsburgh, asking for advice. Recalling his experience with labor-management cooperation plans in the 1920s, Golden suggested that the company tap the know-how of its workers. Scanlon, who was the union local president, devised a systematic plan for eliciting employee suggestions. "The company put the ideas into practice and substantially reduced costs," wrote John Hoerr in *And the Wolf Finally Came*, on the decline of the U.S. steel industry. "Within months, Empire became solvent and granted its workers a wage increase. Later, it inaugurated a productivity bonus designed by Scanlon."[63]

Golden was so impressed by Scanlon that in 1938 he brought the Irishman to Pittsburgh and put him in charge of helping other troubled companies and their union locals develop participation programs. It is here, according to Hoerr, that labor and management reached a historic crossroads and management passed up the opportunity to develop a cooperative and mutually synergistic relationship with labor.

Within the steel industry, the success of the participative model set forth by Scanlon depended on reconciling two deeply antagonistic forces: union leadership and management. On the union side, the advocates of industrial democracy had to win over Philip Murray, who, as a ten-year-old boy, had quit school to work alongside his father in the Scottish coal mines. In the mines, Murray learned two things: first, that "the difference between death and living was a very narrow line"; second, a deep suspicion of management that penetrated his being like particles of fine bituminous coal dust. According to Harold Ruttenberg, who became an adviser to Murray during World War II, the USW chief "could never bring himself personally to cooperate and collaborate with the capitalists and their 'factotems,' as he called them."[64]

Yet Murray was an idealist. He overcame his suspicions of cooperative programs, at least during the war, even agreeing to coauthor a book with Morris Cooke, a "liberal" Taylorite, entitled *Organized Labor and Production*, which was published in 1940. Another book, *The Dynamics of Industrial Democracy*, written by Golden and Ruttenberg and published in 1942, outlined a blueprint for industrial peace based on labor-management cooperation, including Scanlon's work.

Even as participative programs led by Scanlon improved productivity throughout the steel industry, labor initiatives ran up against the brick wall of management intransigence. Management's prejudices against organized labor, reinforced by decades of Taylorism, were simply too strong to overcome. In times of crisis, such as World War II, the government would invariably solicit the help of organized labor, thereby "validat[ing]" labor's own view of its importance to society. "At such times, the hopes of union leaders that they will be given a voice in national affairs have swelled like their expanding chests," wrote Hoerr. "However, the actual influence gained by labor has been pitifully small in comparison to that granted industry leaders, especially during the two world wars."[65]

Management's eagerness to protect its prerogatives was seen most clearly in its initial rejection of an innovative proposal by Walter Reuther, a founder and leader of the UAW, to build five hundred planes

a day during World War II by converting auto plants to airplane production—a rejection that apparently stemmed from nothing more than
his status as a union man. Reuther had commissioned skilled workers
throughout the United Auto Workers to conduct a survey of the machine tools that would be available for wartime production. Based on
the feedback he received, he established that just 10 percent of the
equipment scattered throughout the UAW's plants would need to be
converted to defense production to accomplish the goal. His plan called
for "pooling machine tools and dies among manufacturers." After the
bombing of Pearl Harbor, he and his plan became a cause célèbre when
critics, some inside the government, asserted that Reuther's plan could
have been "a Godsend for MacArthur and his boys, to say nothing of the
lads on Guam, Wake and points East." While parts of Reuther's plan
were eventually adopted, attempts by both Reuther and Murray to give
labor a say in production planning for the war were repeatedly re-
buffed.[66]

Indeed, the cooperative efforts within the steel industry quickly fell
apart following the war. First, the industry, worried about an impending
recession, refused to significantly increase wages, which had been
capped throughout the war. This refusal resulted in a massive strike at
all manufacturers in 1946, which only exacerbated the already corro-
sive relationship between management and labor. Murray, certain that
his worst impressions of management had been realized, abandoned the
push for greater labor participation in shop-floor management.[67]

In 1946, McGregor, who had gotten to know Scanlon during the war,
when he had spent two summers observing Scanlon's work in
Pittsburgh, recruited Scanlon to MIT. "If Phil [Murray] had supported
Joe" and pushed for greater cooperation with management, Scanlon
would never have left the USW, says Carl Frost who worked at MIT at
the time and eventually became a follower of Scanlon. As things stood,
Scanlon became one of McGregor's most unlikely recruits to MIT.[68]

At MIT, where his backers included McGregor and George P. Shultz,
who was then a young labor economist, Scanlon continued to make significant contributions to industrial relations throughout the 1950s. For
the next several years, he conceived a variety of ways to increase rank-
and-file participation, to measure more equitably the productivity improvements made by workers, and to pay them commensurately. He also
continued to consult with companies and unions.

During his lifetime, a number of small and medium-sized companies
adopted the Scanlon Plan. After his death in 1956, two of his colleagues, Frederick G. Lesieur and Carl Frost, continued his work.
Among the best-known poster children of Scanlon's were Herman

Miller and Donnelly Corporation, which makes modular windows and mirrors. Yet Hoerr reported that by the 1960s, in major companies such as U.S. Steel, Scanlon's name had been virtually forgotten. Scanlon tackled only one small piece of the collaborative puzzle—that of the relationship between rank-and-file workers on the shop floor. It must be concluded that the disappearance of the Scanlon Plan was a result not so much of Scanlon's failure as of a failure of will on the part of both management and union leadership.[69]

■

If nothing else, the gathering under the same roof of such men as Lewin and Scanlon, as well as McGregor's younger recruits, such as Warren Bennis and Edgar Schein, would have secured McGregor an important place in management history. In today's parlance, McGregor was a quintessential facilitator whose gift for recognizing—and fostering—innovative ideas was almost as great as his ability to bring people together. "McGregor was a wonderful observer" who "could sit for hours with his lanky body at ease," asking just the right questions at just the right times, says Carl Frost, recalling McGregor's role in a particularly acrimonious debate between some union men and one of Scanlon's clients.

This incident involved a visit to Boston by the executives and union representatives of Baldwin Locomotives. At the time, Baldwin's diesel engine business had taken a beating, and the company was struggling to revive the business, even as it sought to resolve the increasingly acrimonious labor relations at the plant. Scanlon had arranged for Baldwin's union representatives and executives to visit a local company that had instituted the Scanlon Plan.

In the evening, Scanlon and the visitors from Baldwin congregated at the Harvard Club, where McGregor had organized an informal reception. McGregor sat at one end of a large wooden table, nursing his usual martini, while Scanlon sat at the other end. The Baldwin people sat on either side: management on one side, union men on the other.

The cocktail hour began pleasantly enough with the union men "joshing" management for having taken the overnight train from Baltimore and arriving in Boston exhausted, while the union representatives had flown to the meeting and arrived refreshed. The evening soon degenerated into a "donnybrook," recalls Frost, with executives and workers "calling each other names" and becoming generally "pretty loud and unpleasant." Unobserved by his feuding guests, McGregor slipped away with his martini and a plate full of cheese and crackers to a corner armchair, from which he observed the scene. "When the guests realized that their host had left, they were very embarrassed," says Frost. The room suddenly became quieter, and "Doug said, 'Now that you know all this' "—referring to whatever the point of contention was at the moment—" 'What are you going to do about it?' It was such a salutary thing to do. It completely changed the atmosphere in the room. There was no pontification. No reviewing [the issues.]" Just a simple question: "What are you going to do now?"[70]

It was not unlike the way McGregor insisted that industrial psychology courses be taught to undergraduates. No textbooks were allowed. New professors, such as Frost, were instructed simply to go into the classroom and inquire of their students, "What day is it today?"[71]

More conservative educators might shake their heads. But by the late 1940s, thanks in large part to the influence of both Lewin and Scanlon, McGregor had become convinced that group dynamics could enable people to transform their thinking and to learn life-changing behavior in a group setting that fostered open communication.

During his six-year stint at Antioch, McGregor tried to put his ideas about openness and participative management to work. At his first assembly meeting, for example, McGregor shocked his audience when he announced that he "valued his four years in analysis more than his four years as an undergraduate." He envisioned Antioch as a laboratory of true democratic participation, one that would be "a genuine program of research, with ourselves as subjects." He organized groups of students, faculty, and even janitors in small groups to conduct "goal discussions." Initially, many faculty members resented McGregor's "Madison Avenue manipulations" at a school that already, in the 1940s, had pioneered such participative concepts as including students on curriculum and disciplinary committees. Before long, however, McGregor helped transform the school, forging closer ties between the school and the community, creating a more cross-disciplinary curriculum, and experimenting with new methods of teaching and learning.[72]

By the time McGregor returned to MIT in 1954, his experience at Antioch had helped crystallize his critique of American management. He had come to the conclusion that "the way a business is managed determines to a very large extent what people are perceived to have 'potential' and how they develop." Most people strive to be productive, he believed. Echoing Barnard, he argued that corporations have yet to learn how to harness the natural drive of their employees to serve both its own ends, let alone those of each individual.

The force of this insight, in combination with Maslow's work, became the foundation stone for *The Human Side of Enterprise*. Beginning in 1957, McGregor wrote a series of papers and lectures that were greatly influenced by Maslow. "In a talk which I gave here at MIT last spring I drew heavily on your ideas about motivation," wrote McGregor on the occasion of sending Maslow a copy of the lecture. "I hope you will approve in general of the way I have used your thinking to strengthen some of my own. The implications of your theory of motivation for management philosophy and policy in industry are indeed significant."[73]

At about the same time, McGregor published an indictment of conventional performance appraisals in the *Harvard Business Review.* "An Uneasy Look at Performance Appraisal" had its roots, at least in part, in Maslow's ideas of self-actualization, and would foreshadow one of the most controversial—and insightful—indictments of modern management practice (see Chapter 7).

Elaborating on those ideas, McGregor later wrote: "Even if we possessed methods enabling us to do a perfect job of selecting young men with the capacity to become top executives, the practical gain for industry would be negligible under today's conditions. The reason is that we have not learned enough about the utilization of talent, about the creation of an organizational climate conducive to human growth."[74]

In 1960, McGregor distilled the essence of these ideas in a slim, readable volume entitled *The Human Side of Enterprise.* In it, he argued that the common practices and assumptions of management were based on a faulty premise. Management assumed that people would work only under conditions of "external coercion and control." The prevailing theory of management, he argued, saw employees as fundamentally unambitious, as desiring control and avoiding responsibility. He called this approach Theory X.[75]

For management, Theory X turned out to be a self-fulfilling prophecy. McGregor recognized the tremendous improvements in working conditions since the turn of the century, at all levels of the corporation. Drawing on Maslow's hierarchy of needs, he argued that by satisfying the safety and security needs of its employees, management had actually succeeded in creating higher-order needs.

It was those higher needs for self-fulfillment that management had failed to satisfy, according to McGregor—to its own detriment, as well as that of employees. "[T]he fact that management has provided for these physiological and safety needs has shifted the motivational emphasis to the social and the egoistic needs," he wrote in *The Human Side of Enterprise.* "Unless there are opportunities *at work* to satisfy these higher-level needs, people will be deprived; and their behavior will reflect this deprivation."[76]

In the absence of opportunities to achieve self-actualization on the job, the employee focuses his attention on the rewards management does provide—most of which, ironically, satisfy his needs *only when he leaves his job.*" Chief among these are vacation time, medical benefits, and raises. "Although money has only limited value in satisfying many higher-level needs, it can become the focus of interest if it is the only means available," wrote McGregor.[77]

Among McGregor's greatest insights—one that resonates to this day—was his contention that after people's basic needs have been satisfied, "carrot-and-stick" reward systems are wholly inadequate for satisfying higher-level needs. Picking up this same thread in 1968, Frederick Herzberg wrote a famous *Harvard Business Review* article that referred to money as a "hygiene factor": not enough of it causes distress, by itself it has little to do with job satisfaction.[78]

In American business culture, pay for performance is older than scientific management itself and would not be easily discredited. Indeed, the corporate star system is closely related to the mythic notions of rugged individualism and individual achievement that are as much a part of American culture as the Wild West. In practice, the corporate star system *seems* to work beautifully as long as companies are making so much money that they can give most of their employees a "merit raise" or bonus. However, when adverse business conditions swamped the United States in the 1980s, decades after McGregor wrote *The Human Side of Enterprise*, salary budgets shrank as quickly as U.S. market share in the face of foreign competition and exposed just how destructive "incentive pay" could be. During this period, one of the first in recent history when bonus and salary pools were so small that most employees didn't qualify for a merit raise, employee morale plunged. Eventually, a handful of companies, among them GM, American Cyanamid, and, most recently, Xerox, dusted off the arguments of both McGregor and Herzberg and took a new look at both incentive pay and performance appraisals. (The inspiration for the most recent rethinking of incentive pay schemes came from the quality management movement, in particular the work of W. Edwards Deming, who combined statistical and motivation theory to devise his own objections to pay for performance; see Chapter 7.)[79]

At the root of McGregor's objections to conventional notions of pay for performance is the conviction that money, by itself, is a poor substitute for an environment that is conducive to motivation. In place of the command-and-control imperative of Theory X, McGregor proposed an "integrative" approach to management that he called Theory Y (which drew, in many respects, on Mary Parker Follett's conception of integration; see Chapter 2). By integration, he meant "the creation of conditions such that the members of the organization can achieve their own goals *best* by directing their efforts toward the success of the enterprise." He continued, "Theory Y assumes that people will exercise self-direction and self-control in the achievement of organizational objectives *to the degree that they are committed to those objectives*."[80]

Theory Y entailed a fundamental change in the implicit contract between employees and employers. The traditional employment relationship hinged on the assumption that individuals will submit to the will and control of an employer. By contrast, Theory Y's conception of integration and self-control assumed that "the organization will be more effective in achieving its economic objectives if adjustments are made, in significant ways, to the needs and goals. . . . The assumptions of Theory Y imply that unless integration is achieved *the organization will suffer*."[81]

The impact of McGregor's work is best illustrated by the influence it had on Jay Forrester, one of the foremost computer experts in the country and the father of system dynamics, whom McGregor met in 1956, after Forrester abandoned computer science and joined the Sloan School of Management.[82]

Harnessing his knowledge of servomechanisms and feedback systems, Forrester used complex computer models to simulate how systems such as inventories and production interact to produce cycles of high and low unemployment. At the root of Forrester's idea lay the belief that most business systems are far too complex for humans to solve intuitively. McGregor's contention that American management was based on a "faulty mental model" of its employees, says Forrester, illustrated another way in which managers' mental models were the source of serious business difficulties. McGregor's thesis fit perfectly with Forrester's contention that, because of the limits of human cognition, management's mental models—including Theory X and the picture of a fundamentally unambitious, submissive workforce—were sometimes dramatically off base.[83]

Intrigued by McGregor's work and wishing to extend his own work in system dynamics, Forrester, in the spring of 1964, discussed with McGregor ways to create a computer simulation model of T-group sessions, wherein they would literally map out the processes by which people change their views and opinions. The ultimate goal was to form a universal model of group decision-making.[84]

That summer, McGregor died of a heart attack. Forrester began to write a paper entitled "A New Corporate Design," which he has continued to revise over the years. "It was my intention to go beyond *The Human Side of Enterprise* and to erase the notion of the subordinate, superior relationship" in industry, he says. "Companies talk about entrepreneurialism and capitalism, yet most major corporations have the organizational characteristics of socialist countries. They have central ownership of resources, authority to assign people, and they subjectively evaluate people, all of which are contrary to the concept of entrepreneurial capitalism."[85]

After McGregor's death, Forrester went on to develop computer simulation models that were used to design and test managerial systems. His work inspired many of the present leaders in the field of system dynamics and, together with that of Deming and Maslow, would come to influence a new generation of management experts, including Peter Senge, whose focus shifted to learning organizations[86] (see Chapter 7).

In the aftermath of McGregor's death, however, Forrester's management research became a footnote to a much broader body of work that has applied system dynamics to everything from problems affecting the environment to municipal government. Yet Forrester has never completely abandoned his interest in McGregor's work; in his most recent revision of "A New Corporate Design," he has developed an audacious new corporate structure that, he says, would dispense with command-and-control hierarchies by adapting "the U.S. Constitution to the corporation."

■

Significantly, *The Human Side of Enterprise* was rooted in Maslow's assumption that self-actualization is key to both individual and, ultimately, organizational health. Together, Maslow and McGregor's work marked a substantive departure from the human relations school of Mayo's day, when the focus was on "making people *feel* important [author's emphasis]." By contrast, McGregor, and later Maslow, when he turned his focus explicitly to the problems of industrial organizations, believed it was important "to *make* people important [author's emphasis]," by both listening to and acting on employees' concerns.[87]

After the publication of *The Human Side of Enterprise*, Maslow returned McGregor's earlier compliments. The two men had met for the first time through Andy Kay, the maverick founder of Non-Linear Systems (NLS), a California electronics company, who was enamored of the work of both men. Discovering on a trip to Boston in 1960 that these two pioneers of industrial psychology had never met, Kay picked up a phone, made sure McGregor was in his office, and drove Maslow to MIT to meet McGregor. Years later, after McGregor's untimely death, Maslow wrote a lecture entitled "The Human Side of Enterprise," instructing his students, "I would like you to see [McGregor's book] in the way that I do as a first step in the direction of a new kind of thinking for the next century. . . . The whole application of our new knowledge of human nature to the general problems of society and of human organization."[88]

For Maslow, *The Human Side of Enterprise*, together with the maverick management practices at Kay's company, opened up a new world. A visit to Kay's company, in 1962, helped open his eyes to both the problems of industrial management and the tremendous opportunities for synergy between his ideas and the most innovative management practices then being espoused by McGregor and Drucker, among others. Ultimately, it led Maslow to shape his notes into *Eupsychian Management*, which became his only book on management and was a classic in its own right.

Maslow's journey began during the summer of 1962, when Andy Kay invited him to spend the summer near his company's headquarters in northern California. Maslow would receive a large consulting fee in return for talking with Kay and visiting NLS's plant once a week. Kay, the son of eastern European immigrants, had first begun tinkering with chemicals and electronics as a teenager. Trying to reproduce Nikola Tesla's experiments in rocket propulsion in the basement of his parents' home, he nearly blew his leg off. He went on to earn his undergraduate degree at MIT and following World War II worked for the Jet Propulsion Laboratories. In the early 1950s, he launched NLS, which developed the first commercially built digital voltmeter. He became famous in 1980 for launching Kaypro Computer, one of the first U.S. companies to commercially market desktop computers.[89]

Kay's entrepreneurialism extended beyond technology. Not long after launching NLS, he began experimenting with new management methods. Noticing that the workers at the end of his production line seemed happier than the ones who had little or no contact with the finished product, he concluded that workers crave a sense of "closure," of completing a job well done. Although NLS already had a reputation for producing high-quality products, he embarked on a radical management experiment. Relying on Maslow's *Motivation and Personality*, he set out to create a workforce of "happier and healthier employees." As his employees gained the benefits of self-actualization, he believed, they would also become more productive.[90]

By the time Maslow visited NLS, Kay's transformation was complete. The assembly line had been dismantled, and the workers had been organized in teams of six to seven, with each team being responsible for the entire process of manufacturing, including assembly, inspection, and debugging. The teams set their own work hours, as well as the production schedule. There were no time cards. Moreover, NLS paid 25 percent more than the prevailing wage and was among the first companies to offer its employees stock options. NLS clearly was reaping the benefits of a satisfied workforce. Turnover and customer complaints had plunged, while sales and productivity were soaring.[91]

It was in the aftermath of his visit to NLS that Maslow began reading *The Human Side of Enterprise*. He also discovered Peter Drucker's *The Practice of Management*. "I had never before had any contact with industrial or managerial psychology, so the possibilities for general psychological theory hit me with great force, as I read first the books of Drucker and McGregor that were used as 'textbooks' at Non-Linear," he wrote at the time. "I began to understand what Andrew Kay was trying to do there, and I read on voraciously in this fascinating new field."[92]

Over the course of several weeks, Maslow dictated his thoughts into a tape recorder. His observations covered a spectrum of issues from entrepreneurship, which he saw as a form of self-actualization, to the psychology of leadership. He also incorporated Ruth Benedict's concept of synergy, which she had developed in a series of unpublished lectures in 1941 and which was then virtually unknown outside Benedict's inner circle. Maslow defined synergy as an all-for-one culture that led to the "resolution of the dichotomy between selfishness and unselfishness." In a synergistic culture, he noted, "the more influence and power you give to someone else in the team situation, the more you have for yourself." Maslow's contention was that where "selfishness and unselfishness are mutually exclusive," it is the sign of "a poorly developed culture."[93]

The concept of synergy, which Maslow had personally encountered in his observations of the Blackfoot Indians, became central to his organizational theories. Through the example of NLS, which he viewed as a high-synergy environment, he saw the possibility of fusing the interests of both workers and the entire organization through "enlightened management."[94]

Maslow's notes eventually became *Eupsychian Management*, a readable, impressionistic masterpiece. He coined the term "Eupsychia" to define a "culture that would be generated by 1,000 self-actualizing people on a sheltered island" and to help answer the questions that defined his core preoccupation: "How good a society does human nature permit? How good a human nature does society permit?" In the words of Warren Bennis, Maslow approached his material "like a swashbuckling Candide, that is with a powerful innocence that is both threatening and receptive to widely held beliefs."[95]

To Maslow, the "work life" opened up a particularly rich arena for applying his ideas about Eupsychia. He believed that industry would serve as "the new laboratory" for creating "high human development." This was of course, a logical extension of the views he had long since formed about self-actualizing individuals, a view that "the only happy people . . . are the ones who are working well at something they consider important."[96]

Maslow wrote in *Eupsychian Management*, "I gave up long ago the possibility of improving the world or the whole human species via individual psychotherapy." Next, he had turned to education as the best way of "reaching the whole human species." During his California journey, he had taken another step: "Only recently has it dawned on me that as important as education is perhaps even more important is the work life of the individual since everybody works. If the lessons of psychology . . . can be applied to man's economic life, then my hope is that this too can be given a eupsychian direction, thereby tending to influence in principle all human beings."[97]

Maslow considered it a "remarkable validation" of his theory that such esteemed management experts as Drucker and McGregor had arrived at the same view of human nature as he had. What makes *Eupsychian Management* so remarkable is that he offers an insightful critique, based on his own psychological expertise and an attempt to interject realism and complexity into ideas dominated by idealism and ideology. For example, he points out astutely that Drucker's management principles work only for an individual relatively high up on the need hierarchy—that is, individuals whose most basic needs are already satisfied. Hence, he argues, Drucker "slurs the necessity for selecting the right kind of individuals for his management principles to work. There are many people in the world . . . for whom Drucker's management principles will simply not work at all. So also for the human relations stuff and for the personnel stuff. They forget that there are many people in the world for whom those principles will fail, people who are too sick to function in an enlightened world."[98]

Drucker's philosophy, Maslow implies, assumes a much healthier society than exists even in the United States. His principles, for example, do not apply to "most American Negroes," because they "do not live under good psychological conditions," i.e., in a world without fear and in which their basic needs for safety and belonging have been fulfilled. "We must be conscious that we are fortunate, that we are graced, or we shall not be as realistic and as flexible as we must continue to be in a world in process, a world in flux," he wrote.[99]

The notion of continuous improvement—for people, for organizations, and for society—is very much a part of Maslow's thinking. Implicit in his view is the idea that both individuals and organizations must pass through levels of enlightenment before achieving Eupsychia. There are no quick fixes. Self-actualization is hard work.

This is especially true, he argued, because "everything is related to everything else" in a complex network that resembles not a linked chain but "a spider web or geodesic dome in which every part is related to every other part." What he sensed intuitively is what Jay Forrester would call a dynamic system. And in a dynamic system "everything is related" and improvement must occur throughout in order to achieve lasting change.[100]

Wrote Maslow, "This is what I get vaguely uneasy about in the reading on management, namely a certain piety, certain semireligious attitudes, an unthinking, unreasoning, a priori kind of 'liberalism' which frequently takes over as a determinant, thereby to some extent destroying the possibility of maintaining the necessary sensitivity to the objective requirements of the actual, realistic situation."[101]

Eventually, in the wake of America's romance with quantitative methods, Maslow's work faded from view. But in the early 1990s, his only book on management resurfaced, first on the Internet and later in print. The revival of *Maslow on Management* is a testament to the long-term importance of Maslow's insights into the nature of human behavior and human potential, which once again are helping to frame debates about everything from incentive pay to employee motivation.

Just as important, some of today's most successful new companies, such as SAS Institute, a much-lauded software developer in North Carolina, have become 1990s poster children for the theories of Maslow and McGregor. SAS, a $750 million, privately held company that develops software programs that are used to gather and analyze large amounts of data, looks and behaves like a company that truly believes its employees are its most important asset. Trust and teamwork are the mantra of the company, which, for example, has eliminated performance appraisals and places no limits on the number of sick days employees can take—to care for either themselves or family members who are unwell (see Chapter 7).

The influence of Maslow and McGregor is undoubtedly greatest in the field of organizational development. However, it is a testament to their ideas that they influenced such diverse thinkers as Peter Drucker, W. Edwards Deming, and Jay Forrester. Even Marvin Bower, the man who built McKinsey and Company, the influential management consulting firm, became a devotee of humanistic management late in life. If managers would actually put the lessons of *The Human Side of*

Enterprise to use, rather than just giving it lip service, "command-and-control managing would have expired long ago," Bower wrote in his most recent book, *The Will to Lead*. Yet Theory Y is a concept that many of McKinsey's clients, which, after all, represent the country's corporate mainstream, are still unlikely to endorse.[102]

Wherefore I perceive that

there be nothing better

than that a man should

rejoice in his own work.

—Ecclesiastes

W. Edwards Deming

The Prophets of the Quality Movement and the Learning Organization

When W. Edwards Deming, that larger-than-life, curmudgeonly oracle of American management, died in 1993, he seemed to take the quality movement with him. That same year, Michael Hammer and James Champy published *Reengineering the Corporation*. With its call for Tayloresque systems experts who would parachute into companies and cold-bloodedly root out waste regardless of the human cost, Hammer and Champy's book was the archetypal anti-Deming tract. It also became an overnight best-seller.

The king is dead. Long live the king!

Even before Deming's death at age ninety-three, the movement he inspired wheezed along as fitfully and defiantly as Deming himself, who made it through the last of his famous four-day seminars only with the help of an oxygen inhaler and frequent rests.

Yet even though the Q-word was purged from management lexicons, Demingism and the quality movement have left a lasting mark on American industry. For one thing, while total quality management (TQM) per se fell out of style, Six Sigma, the quality strategy pioneered by Motorola, made a comeback in the late 1990s. Most recently, GE launched what *Business Week* calls "the largest quality initiative ever mounted in Corporate America."[1] While Deming always bridled at the goal-oriented—as opposed to process-oriented—approach implicit in the moniker "Six Sigma," which refers to fewer than 3.4 defects per million operations, few serious quality programs today, by whatever name, fail to incorporate Deming's ideas.

In Detroit, the cradle of America's TQM, where the auto companies have long enjoyed a love-hate relationship with Deming, the roots of the movement are still deep. To be sure, in the early 1990s, J. Ignacio Lopez de Arriortua, GM's controversial supplier chief, made headlines by hounding GM suppliers and seemed to make a mockery of Deming-inspired efforts to build cooperation with vendors. Similarly, by 1997, Ford had abandoned its "Quality is Job One" advertising slogan in favor of "Better Ideas Driven by You."

Still, just a few months before his death Deming was asked to midwife the product development meetings of the 1995 Lincoln Continental, which would revive that car marque and break a number of product development records. And throughout the industry, the customer-focused, team-driven approach to product development and production, which had its roots in Deming's teachings and was exemplified by the Taurus and Saturn automobiles, have permanently changed Detroit's manufacturing culture—if not as radically as Deming, or even some automotive mavericks, would have wished.

Similarly, at Xerox, a restructuring in the early 1990s prompted speculation that the company had finally abandoned its much-vaunted quality movement in favor of reengineering. In fact, restructuring at the document company was accomplished largely with what one insider calls "inside QITs" (quality improvement teams) of "young high-potential managers" who were plucked from a variety of departments within the company, not by outside consultants. New employees are still trained in Xerox's leadership-through-quality process, a team-based decision-making system that got its start during the early 1980s as Xerox's answer to TQM. As of the late 1990's leadership through quality still shaped key decisions at the company—not just on quality but on everything from engineering to diversity.[2] Now many other companies that endured a crash diet of reengineering and downsizing, only to find their energy sapped, are returning to management principles that bear a strong resemblance to Demingism. In particular, the efforts to enhance organizational learning have many important principles in common with Deming's teachings.

The quality movement and learning theory grew out of a common zeitgeist and have come to be two of the most radical challenges to the traditional scientific management tradition. "Deming always talked about a new economic age. That was his term, and he said that the principles by which success is going to be determined in this new economy will be different," says Peter Senge, a leading proponent of the learning organization who met Deming in about 1990 and developed an intense dialogue with the quality guru in the last years of his life. In fact, the learning organization, as Senge defines it, encompasses "almost exactly" three of the four cornerstones of Deming's theory: understanding systems, the theory of knowledge, and what Deming refers to as psychology (intrinsic motivation, or what Senge calls "personal mastery").[3]

Where Deming and the learning theorists differ is in the scientific traditions that inform their work. Deming's philosophy has its roots in statistical theory, which involves a stochastic analysis of processes—in particular, the measurement and analysis of how variation can erode the quality of both products and processes. By contrast, Senge, a protégé of Jay Forrester, built his theory on an understanding of dynamic systems.[4]

(It's interesting to note that the relationship between Senge and Deming was a complex one. Deming, who had a tendency to surround himself with acolytes and often had a confrontational relationship with the most independent of his followers, frequently treated Senge rudely. Although Deming wrote an endorsement of Senge's *The Fifth Discipline*, at the last minute he demanded that the endorsement quotation be removed from the book.[5] Whether Deming really soured on Senge or whether—as so often happened in Deming's circle—one of his acolytes took advantage of Deming's age and vulnerability to turn the nonagenarian guru against Senge is unlikely ever to be known.)

The power of Deming's philosophy initially derived from the competitiveness crisis in which U.S. business found itself in 1980. In the long term, the significance of his work stems from the fact that it was one of the first explicit attempts to reconcile the technological and humanistic dialectic in American business. Deming coupled the technological (an understanding of systems and the use of statistical technique to improve mechanical processes) with the humanistic (an intuitive feel for the organization as a social system and a collaborative, democratic vision of management). The holistic quality of Demingism continues to present one of the most prescient philosophical challenges to management.

Deming was, in fact, the unlikeliest of management gurus to rise to prominence in the United States. A physicist and statistician by training, he had the single-focused personality of an Einstein. Both the humanistic and scientific strands of his quality philosophy can be traced back to the same root idea, a profoundly simple statistical observation about how processes work: all processes are subject to some level of variation that is likely to diminish quality. Variation is the enemy of quality; yet it is as inevitable and ubiquitous as gravity.

What makes variation a particular nuisance is that the culprit comes in two distinct guises: "common" causes and "special" causes. Special causes are the product of special circumstances, a temporary glitch in a system—the malfunction of a single piece of machinery, for instance. Because of their opportunistic nature, special causes are *unpredictable;*

thus, they can wreak havoc with a process and give management no basis on which to predict the quality level of a company's products. They can, however, be identified and eliminated by workers who have been properly trained to analyze the process.

Common causes of variation, on the other hand, are more difficult to isolate because they are inherent in the system. As such, they are, by definition, *predictable*. While they can never be fully eliminated, they allow the process to function with a predictable level of variation. Thus, a company that has only common causes to contend with in its processes will produce products of a predetermined level of quality to which it can peg warranties, product claims, and prices. Common causes also represent the greatest opportunity for long-term improvement.[6]

To the casual observer, the two types of variation may be difficult to distinguish; yet, if they are mixed, a bad situation can become worse. Consider this analogy: A car is rolling along a highway. While its driver may be steering a "straight" course, there will in fact be tiny variations— an inch to the right, two inches to the left. But essentially his performance is acceptable because he is driving within the control boundaries of the system—his car and his driving ability—which together roughly coincide with the two lines that define his lane. (The widths of traffic lanes are roughly analogous to control boundaries because they are based on how close to a straight line the average automobile and driver can remain over time, assuming the car has passed registration requirements and the driver knows how to drive and remains alert.)[7]

Now imagine that after a few hours of driving, the car suddenly crashes. The car has gone out of control. It may be assumed that the system itself is now "out of control." If the driver is still rolling along that same relatively straight highway, the crash may have been due to special causes, such as faulty brakes, a patch of ice, or drowsiness on the part of the driver.[8]

But what if the driver had turned off the main highway onto a winding mountain road? An analysis of the number of crashes on a narrow, winding road may show that a certain number of crashes (i.e., defects) per month are part of the system; that is, the probability of crashes on the winding road is statistically higher than that on a straight highway; moreover, the number of crashes on the winding road is predictable. The highway patrol can estimate, with a fairly high degree of accuracy, the probability that a certain number of crashes will occur each year.

To reduce the number of crashes, the highway patrol will have to institute certain changes in the system. The solution might involve widening or straightening the road, installing a traffic light or speed bumps, and/or changing the signage. Determining which solution is safest and most cost-effective will require input from several parts of the system, including the government department in charge of road maintenance, highway engineers, and possibly construction crews. Notice that eliminating such common causes as poor visibility or the road's narrowness constitutes an improvement of the system itself, while putting salt on the road—in the case of a special cause such as iciness—does not.[9]

Determining the root cause of the accident also requires analysis, not just gut reaction. Without analysis, the presence of ice on the mountain road, even if it was not the cause of the accident, might lead a casual observer to conclude, erroneously, that ice was the culprit. Gut reaction, in this case, could be the main cause of future accidents because the system itself—the configuration of the road—will remain unchanged.

It's also important to note that the boundaries of stability are *not* arbitrarily determined; they are dictated by the system itself. To analyze the boundaries of a system and the levels of variation, Deming taught his followers to use statistical methods, including a so-called control chart that was first devised by AT&T's Walter Shewhart.[10]

Most companies have come to embrace the quality expert's technological tool kit. It includes statistical process control (and the use of control charts), so-called Taguchi methods, simultaneous engineering, and so on. These tools are all designed to reduce variation, control processes, and ultimately improve the entire system.

Deming, however, understood that technology wasn't enough to tackle the quality problems and the complexity of a human organization. For one thing, no one was better equipped to resolve systemic problems, in Deming's view, than the people who work with the system on a daily basis and who know it best (certainly not the experts of Taylor's or Hammer and Champy's conception). Insights into the system and useful ideas for changing it, Deming believed, had to percolate up from the bottom of the organization. For that to happen, management would have to shake up the hierarchy (if not eliminate it entirely), drive fear out of the workplace, and foster the intrinsic motivation of its employees.

Thus, Deming was as much of a revolutionary as Maslow. Coming from two entirely different disciplines, statistical theory and psychology, they came to very much the same conclusions. Unlike Maslow, however, Deming spent decades attempting to transform major corporations.

While many companies were quick to seize on the statistical techniques with which his name first became associated, Deming's most insightful clients understood that his ideas amounted to a tectonic shift in management thinking. Deming probably never studied the work of Maslow and McGregor or Mayo and Roethlisberger in any systematic way. But he was a voracious reader and surrounded himself with psychologists and experts in personnel management, who would have been familiar with the ideas of his forebears. Well into his nineties, he began to study system dynamics. He never stopped learning; organizations, he believed, had to keep learning too.[11]

■

Deming's charisma and the sense of conviction he brought to his work had a great deal to do with his success. Despite his often imposing personality, he possessed a personal humility that endeared him to the Japanese, who adopted his teachings as the foundation for their quality movement following World War II. Indeed, Deming's brand of humility was particularly appealing to the Japanese; it was based on a deeply religious awareness of the relative insignificance of any single human being in God's universe, as well as a healthy respect for foreign cultures and ideas. By the 1950s, Deming was so beloved in Japan that he was hailed as "the most famous and revered American in Japan in the postwar years"—with the possible exception of General Douglas MacArthur.[12]

Despite his fame in Japan, at home Deming labored in relative obscurity, teaching statistics, working for government agencies such as the U.S. Census Bureau, and as a consultant for decades. It wasn't until the early 1980s, when U.S. manufacturers found themselves unable to compete against a surge of high-quality foreign imports, that they began to search for the secret of Japan's success and discovered Deming and the quality movement. Even then, Deming's rise to prominence was due largely to the desperation of many American companies, for the certitude and forcefulness with which he advocated his quality philosophy were often mistaken for arrogance and alienated many U.S. executives.

Deming was already an octogenarian when he got his first, storied invitation to help revive the sputtering fortunes of Motown. Responding to an urgent appeal from Donald E. Petersen, then the new president of Ford Motor Company, he swept into Detroit like a tornado that had spent eighty-one years gathering strength.[13]

During the next few years, Deming proceeded to rip the lid off of the prevailing assumptions about the reasons for the United States' competitiveness problems, heedless of whom he might offend along the way. "Why can't America compete?" Deming would ask a roomful of senior automotive executives in a rumbling baritone. The problem was *not* Japan's low labor costs, he assured them; by the 1980s, Japan's wages had reached parity with those in the United States. Nor was it the spanking new factories in places such as Toyoda City. Nor was it the soft yen, which gained in strength and reached an all-time high against the dollar in the late 1980s. Standing before a room full of executives, steel-blue eyes glowering under a shaven pate, fingers caressing the tiny emblem in his buttonhole, Deming's answer would emerge in the rising crescendo of an oncoming train: "The aaanswer iiis—MANAGEMENT!"[14]

Detroit learned quickly that Deming was not a polished boardroom diplomat. Handed the microphone at a gathering of senior auto executives at a meeting of the Society of Automotive Engineers, Deming gave Jim McDonald, then president of GM, the dressing-down of his career, publicly accusing him of responsibility for "85 percent of GM's quality problems." For the next few years, product managers at GM would practically put their careers at risk when they smuggled Deming into their meetings.[15]

Deming's legendary tantrums weren't the product of poor people skills, however. He was always courtly in the presence of women, whether colleagues or waitresses, charming and respectful in the presence of his intellectual peers (with occasional lapses as he grew older), and invariably patient and supportive in conversation with blue-collar workers or anyone he thought was genuinely interested in learning. He saved his wrath for senior executives because it was senior management alone, he believed, who had the power to change the system. To do so, executives would have to learn to take criticism and see the error of their ways.

If they weren't interested, Deming was happy to return to the basement office of his modest Washington, D.C., home. He had no interest in making money. Fame held only slightly greater appeal. What drove him was a messianic belief in the correctness of his vision.

Donald E. Petersen, Ford's president, also believed in it, and took up Deming's challenge. Petersen discovered Deming in 1980, after the airing of NBC's famous documentary *If Japan Can, Why Can't We?* At the time, Ford had begun to hemorrhage red ink, thanks to foreign competition and decades of slavish devotion to short-term financial figures. During a three-year period beginning in 1980, Ford's losses totaled $3.26 billion.[16]

That Christmas, Bill Scollard, Ford's head of manufacturing, took a copy of the NBC documentary home with him to review over the holidays. Seeing the video again convinced him to dispatch a small group of middle managers to Deming's home in Washington and to invite the aging quality expert to come to Detroit. After numerous entreaties, Deming agreed to meet with Ford, but only after Ford had guaranteed him an audience consisting of its thirty top executives, including Petersen.

The executives present at the first meeting with Deming came to constitute the genealogy of Deming's influence at Ford. They included

Scollard; Lewis C. Veraldi who became the father of the Taurus; Harold "Red" Poling, who was then head of North American Automotive Operations (NAAO) and would soon be named president; and Louis R. Ross, who would succeed Poling as head of NAAO. (Ford veterans note that it was only the statistical aspects of quality management that appealed to Poling, who was a classic command-and-control executive.)[17]

Indeed, Ford had turned to Deming only reluctantly. Had Scollard seen another way to effect the sort of radical change that Ford needed at the time, he surely would have seized on it. Although Petersen would develop an unusually close affinity for the octogenarian, the Ford managers continued to be frustrated by Deming's theoretical, academic approach. "My interest was in applications," said Scollard, years later. "It was clear we couldn't do [business] the way we had previously done." But how was Ford to translate Deming's philosophical pronouncements into applications?[18]

At one point, Scollard even enlisted the help of the Union of Japanese Scientists and Engineers (JUSE), the quality organization that had invited Deming to Japan in 1950 and that came to award the Deming Prize. But collaborating with the enemy, as the Japanese were then widely perceived, was even less palatable to Ford than dealing with an unconventional and irascible guru, such as Deming.

To the extent that Ford's managers were hoping for a quick fix, they were to be sorely disappointed. From the beginning, Deming refused to deal directly with automotive quality and insisted on talking about Ford's management philosophy and corporate culture. The Ford men expected to hear about cars, about how to transform manufacturing plants that were turning out automobiles with at least 4.5 "things gone wrong" per car, according to one of Ford's traditional quality indices, into operations that could produce trouble-free vehicles. Instead, Deming's often theoretical lectures and Socratic questioning led Ford to go far beyond quality in the traditional sense of defect reduction. Deming exhorted the company to look at the entire company as an interdependent system. He pushed for a more collaborative relationship with suppliers, a renewed focus on customers and market research, a commitment to teamwork and employee training, and a new contract with employees based on trust, not fear.[19]

Deming's influence at Ford reached the highest levels of the company. By 1983, Petersen and Deming settled into a cozy routine of monthly breakfast meetings where they discussed everything from the company's reward systems to how the company defined quality.

Yet Deming's legacy at Ford was a complicated one. Although he was not successful in many of his efforts, in particular persuading Ford to abandon its pay-for-performance approach to reward systems, he did inspire important change in the company's goals and values. "In the Japanese culture, when you talk about philosophy, they pick it up and try to work with it as such. At Ford, when you talk about a philosophy, that has a tendency to just sail out" the window, explains Fred Simon, the former head of Lincoln Continental, who worked with Deming in the early 1990s. "Give Ford a tool, like statistical process control, and they'll grab right on to it. That's the easy part. After a while you go as far with [the tool] as you can. The hard part is changing how you think about work."[20]

For a small cadre of Ford managers, including Simon and Petersen, Deming planted the seeds of a long-term shift in their philosophical approach to management. For the rest of the company, he inspired a new way of thinking about the company's structure and objectives—in particular, its relationships with its suppliers and customers.

Deming's most immediate impact was to shift Ford away from a definition of quality based on such negative measures as warranty costs and defects per vehicle and toward a focus on customer satisfaction. Explained Petersen,

> [An] interesting thing that came out of our introspection and thinking was a realization that a great deal of what we were using as our measures of quality were [ones] that were convenient for us, because in engineering [there] would be certain ways we could measure things . . . whereas what it should be is an approach where the entire focus of your definition of quality is driven by the customer, and the customer's wants and needs. And it wasn't until [then] we made that transition and got ourselves all thinking in terms of the customer, and what it takes to provide to our customers the best possible products and services that meet fully the customer's wants and needs over the lifetime of those products and services at a cost that represents real value. Then at that point you have achieved quality, true quality.[21]

In many respects, Deming tapped into the deep misgivings that managers already had about Ford's production methods. In 1979, in the aftermath of the Pinto disaster (see Chapter 5), Lou Ross was put in charge of car product development, with an express mandate to do something about Ford's product problems. Ross didn't need an outsider like Deming or a product disaster like the Pinto to convince him that there was something fundamentally wrong with Ford's product development process. A few years earlier, after returning from an assignment in Brazil, he had gone shopping for a company car for his personal use; he had been dismayed to find that in Ford's entire product line, there was none that really interested him. Soon after taking on his new job as head of product development, Ross convened a novel car "clinic" designed to test customers' reactions to Ford cars already on the road.[22]

What he learned was that just because customers couldn't identify specific problems with a given car didn't mean that they actually liked it. For example, in a test of the Ford Granada, satisfaction among customers who reported *no* problems with their cars was only 75 percent. "We wanted to get to ninety-five percent customer satisfaction," said Ross. "So we said, there's something missing." That something was the *je ne sais quoi* that distinguishes a car people love to drive from one that is merely acceptable.[23]

Realizing that the company knew very little about what its customers specifically wanted in a vehicle, Ross convened a quality strategy committee. In early 1981, about the time Ross sat in on his first meeting with Deming, fifty top executives at NAAO met for an eight-hour meeting, and divided into three groups to focus on three crucial strategic issues: group one would focus on learning more about what customers wanted; group two would figure out how to change the product development process to meet the customers' demands; and group three would develop culture and reward systems to support the efforts of groups one and two.

For months, the executives met in their teams for fifteen to twenty hours a week in addition to their normal forty-hour work schedules. Initially, everything hinged on the information produced by group one, which launched the first of Ford's in-depth focus groups, in which customers were asked to critique every Ford vehicle then on the road. In the collaborative spirit inspired by Deming, Ford corralled one hundred fifty to three hundred designers, engineers, and product developers, as well as hourly workers from manufacturing, to attend Ford clinics in Chicago and Los Angeles, as well as a clinic in Atlanta where customers were asked to explain what they liked about foreign cars.[24]

A deeper commitment to quality and customer satisfaction also meant fundamental changes in operating procedures. For example, it meant jettisoning a policy common to several units at Ford—one that had been a legacy of the bean counter era—that subjected engineering improvements to a minimum two-to-one quality improvement payback ratio. Thus, an innovation that cost one dollar would have to generate at least *two dollars* in savings. The biggest problem with this way of measuring costs was that the company "focused only on savings that the company could identify through its cost control system," explained Larry Sullivan, who served as quality warden for Ford's supplier organization. "It didn't look at savings in terms of owner loyalty and repurchase intentions, which can't be factored into the cost control system."[25]

The most sweeping policy change, however, addressed one of Deming's greatest criticisms of the company: its adversarial relationship with suppliers. One of the first Ford executives to meet with Deming in January 1981 was Sullivan. Over breakfast one morning preceding a four-day seminar held by Deming in Miami, Sullivan outlined his idea for a series of Deming seminars for the company's suppliers. Deming seemed "immediately interested," recalled Sullivan. "He had never worked with a large group of suppliers."[26]

Sullivan would launch a monthly training and education program on Deming's ideas and the virtues of statistical thinking that would in turn spark a dramatic change in the relationships between automakers and their suppliers throughout the Midwest. In February 1981, after his first meeting with Ford's top executives, Deming helped Sullivan outline a program for all Ford suppliers. The first session, taught by Deming and David Chambers, a retired professor of statistics from the University of Tennessee, was held at Ford and was attended by thirty managers representing ten supplier companies. Thereafter, Ford held one seminar every month throughout 1981. By the beginning of the following year, demand was so great that two seminars were scheduled each month.

The success of the seminars prompted Ford to spin off its training activities into a separate organization, the American Supplier Institute (ASI). As an independent association, ASI became the center of quality training for all three automakers and their suppliers.[27]

Ford's new vendor policies extended far beyond offering training through ASI and determining internal policies on design and outsourcing. They also illustrated the collaborative imperative that Deming was so instrumental in introducing to American industry.

Even as ASI was being created, Ford was taking related steps to translate its quality commitment into a management policy that would also include its internal divisions. To start with, the company would slash the number of its suppliers, both internal and external, and develop stronger links with those who could meet the company's new quality standards. The number of engine parts suppliers, for example, would be slashed from a peak of about nine hundred during the 1970s to just two hundred by the late 1980s.

To winnow its supplier base, Ford instituted the Q-1 Preferred Quality Supplier Program, a set of rigorous standards and examinations its suppliers would have to pass. Suppliers who qualified for Q-1 status would become the elite corps of Ford's supplier base, exempt from many of the inspections conducted by the company's quality cops. Eventually, the Q-1 suppliers would become Ford's only suppliers.

To qualify as a Q-1 supplier, a vendor had to demonstrate "the commitment and active support of the supplier's management to pursuing never-ending improvement in quality." Topping the list of specific qualifications was a supplier's ability to control product quality through the use of "Statistical Process Control [SPC] on selected product characteristics or [processes] that are significant to part function, fit, durability or appearance." Finally, before a supplier got a Q-1 rating, several Ford departments—including Product Engineering, Purchasing, and Supplier Quality Assurance, as well as the division(s) that would ultimately use the supplier's parts—would have to agree unanimously that the supplier had met the requirements.[28]

The Q-1 program made suppliers partners in the design process and broke the "Chinese wall" that traditionally had blocked collaboration between Ford and its vendors. In the compartmentalized world of Detroit, where warring departments traditionally spent as much time building ramparts against one another as in building cars, engineers worked on component designs in high-security design studios that even fellow Ford employees found difficult to penetrate. Moreover, because suppliers were treated as commodities, to be discarded when they had outlived their usefulness, companies such as Ford lived in fear that their suppliers might learn something about a design that could be taken to a competitor. Once completed, designs were handed over to Ford's suppliers as faits accomplis, with little opportunity for revision. The possibility of drawing on the expertise of vendors was simply unthinkable. Consequently, while a design might be an auto engineer's ideal from a functional point of view, it was often designed with little regard for the part's manufacturability. As a result, the designs for engines, as for most other auto components, were often difficult to build, prone to quality problems, and susceptible to cost overruns.

What the Q-1 program made possible was "simultaneous engineering"—a collaboration between Ford and its suppliers on specific parts. Thus, for example, the collaboration between the Ford plant that made 3.8-liter V-6 engines for such vehicles as the Taurus and its engine parts suppliers did more than improve the quality and cost of the engines themselves; it led Ford to develop a new, more efficient engine *design*.

Today Ford suppliers still must qualify for the Q-1 program. Meanwhile, ASI has expanded far beyond the automotive industry and now provides training for such companies as Motorola, Hewlett-Packard, and Xerox.[29]

ASI and Q-1 have inevitably led to the sort of collaboration that has changed both the organizational relationships in, and the culture of Detroit. Yet the approach of both institutions is inherently technical, focusing on the *science and technology* of quality improvement.

Deming's own background, as well as the widespread popularity of statistical process control, led his critics and rivals to dismiss him as a "mere statistician." While from his earliest days at Ford, he insisted that all his clients hire "master statisticians," his own focus was increasingly on improving the company as a social system. In meetings with everyone from Petersen to production workers, Deming would hammer away at the four main themes that were encompassed by the 14 Points, Deming's mantra. These four themes, which encompassed what Deming referred to as his system of "Profound Knowledge," were:

1. Appreciation of the system (i.e., the interdependence of all the organizational units that work to accomplish the goals of an organization).
2. Knowledge of variation (i.e., understanding what variation can reveal about the capabilities of the system).
3. Understanding the theory of knowledge.
4. Psychology (intrinsic motivation).

Of the four, it is Deming's theory of knowledge that is the most elusive. This theory is derived from the work of C. S. Lewis, who taught that knowledge is built on theory, observation of the past, and predictions of future outcomes. Explained Deming, "Rational prediction requires theory and builds knowledge through systematic revision" based on the comparison of the predicted outcome with the observation of actual outcome. By contrast, he asserted that "[I]nformation, no matter how complete and speedy, is not knowledge. Knowledge has temporal spread. Knowledge comes from theory. Without theory, there is no way to use the information that comes to us on the instant."[30]

One of Deming's favorite analogies involves Chanticleer, the barnyard rooster:

"Chanticleer had a theory. He crowed every morning, putting forth all his energy, flapped his wings. The sun came up. The connection was clear: His crowing caused the sun to come up. There was no question about his importance.

"There came a snag. He forgot one morning to crow. The sun came up anyhow. Crestfallen, he saw his theory in need of revision."[31]

American industry is full of Chanticleers. But coming up with valid new theories for complex problems is no easy task. Perhaps the most controversial tenet of Deming's philosophy is his opposition to traditional performance appraisals and merit pay. Although he was by no means the first expert to question American management's obsession with pay for performance, he was one of its most visible and radical opponents.

Companies, Deming believed, do not need to manipulate people into doing well. If management does a good job of hiring employees and creating an environment conducive to hard work, most people will jump at the chance to take pride in their work. Of course, there will always be fluctuations in performance—human beings, after all, aren't automatons. Deming understood that an employee with a sick child, a toothache, or some other "special cause" problem may not function at peak performance all the time. However, a management that creates a well-designed system won't have trouble getting good performance out of its employees over the long haul. Deming believed that the desire to find "joy" in work—what Maslow would call intrinsic motivation—is fundamental to human nature. Employees want nothing so much as to be given the chance to demonstrate their abilities and potential for achievement.

For decades, social scientists have tried to chip away at the granite-like certitude of compensation experts. Douglas McGregor questioned the validity of conventional pay-based reward systems. And in the 1960s Frederick Herzberg referred to money as a "hygiene factor." Most recently, Jeffrey Pfeffer of Stanford University argues that even as compensation becomes "more variable" due to the use of stock options and bonuses applied throughout the organizational hierarchy, "much of the conventional wisdom about pay today is misleading, incorrect, and sometimes both at the same time. The result is that business people end up adopting wrongheaded notions about how to pay people and why." In his new book, *The Human Equation: Building Profits by Putting People First*, Pfeffer identifies six misleading myths that inform compensation policy, among them that labor costs are a significant portion of total costs, that cutting labor costs will lower labor rates, and that individual incentive pay improves performance.[32]

In the 1980s and 1990s, Deming emerged as one of the most ardent opponents of incentive pay, arguing that tying performance targets to dollar rewards actually *harms* overall performance. By clinging to a grading system, Deming argued, management perpetuates one of the principal impediments to achieving high-quality performance and high-quality products and services: "The merit rating nourishes short-term performance, annihilates long-term planning, builds fear, demolishes teamwork, nourishes rivalry and politics."[33]

Moreover, Deming argued that pay for performance is intrinsically unfair because it ascribes to the people in a group differences that may be caused totally by the system they are working in. If management is doing its job correctly in terms of hiring, developing employees, and keeping the system stable, most employees will perform around a mean—that is, they will perform as well as the system permits. Deming contends that within a stable system, most fluctuations in individual performance *over time* will be attributable to natural variations in the system. Moreover, it is almost impossible to measure the contribution of a single individual within a system that is subject to the vagaries of numerous other variables.

If pay for performance is such a problem, why hasn't this become more apparent in practice? In fact, pay for performance seems to work beautifully during good times, when company budgets are fat and there is enough money available to give most employees a "merit raise" or bonus. The problems with incentive-based pay are exposed during bad times, such as the recession of the early 1980s.

During a recession, pay for performance becomes a zero-sum game that produces more losers than winners. As budgets tighten, companies naturally want to cut down on raises. Under traditional appraisal systems, that is most easily done by requiring managers to grade their minions on a bell curve. But bell curves, which rate people relative to one another and ensure that some are always "losers," fail to reflect the likelihood that in a typical goal-oriented work group a large number will be high achievers and incremental differences are often meaningless. For example, at one electric utility with a mandatory bell curve, the manager of a competent group of five found that the only way to meet the rule without being unfair to his staff was to institute a "designated dummy" system in which employees take turns getting demerits.

Consider what happened at IBM during the early 1990s, when Big Blue instituted a strict bell curve. With its profits declining and competition on the rise, IBM wanted to make sure that all its employees were pulling their weight. So the computer giant made it easier for its employees to be fired. Under one of the most intricately structured appraisal systems in the nation, 10 percent of Big Blue's vaunted workforce would get a flunking grade in their annual reviews that year, for many the first step toward dismissal. Another 10 percent, deemed by their bosses to be superstars, could earn bonuses of $50,000 or more.[34]

At the same time, IBM said it was not abandoning its no-layoff policy. The new system, the company insisted, was not related to its efforts to eliminate twenty thousand jobs in 1992. "In the competitive world we're in, we can't drag along folks who aren't" making the grade, said Walton E. Burdick, senior VP of personnel at IBM.[35]

Because IBM is known for hiring only high achievers, allotting low ratings to a set percentage of the workforce was widely regarded as unfair by both compensation experts and employees. John Raudsep of Towers Perrin, a management consulting firm, said at the time that IBM risked "destroy[ing] the credibility and effectiveness of their appraisal program."[36]

For all the evidence against pay-for-performance schemes, they remain as popular as ever. According to a survey by *Fortune*, the number of companies using individual incentives for at least 20 percent of their workforce increased from 38 percent to 50 percent between 1987 and 1993. And the number of salespeople paid on straight salary, with no commission, plunged from 21 percent to 7 percent between 1981 and 1990.

For all the feverish efforts to defend and invent new variations on the corporate star system, American managers are dissatisfied with it. A mid-1990s study by William M. Mercer, a New York–based consulting firm, found that 73 percent of the companies surveyed had experimented with new pay-for-performance management plans; yet 47 percent of the employees surveyed said the new systems were "neither fair nor sensible," and more than half of them said they provided "little value to the company." Mercer concluded that most pay-for-performance schemes "absorb vast amounts of management time and resources and they make everybody unhappy."[37]

Similarly, a 1992 study by Towers Perrin showed that only 40 percent of the companies with pay-for-performance systems were satisfied with the results. At least some of the dissatisfaction stems from the realization that rating employees can undermine the teamwork and collaboration that companies increasingly see as keys to competitive advantage.

Then, too, there is a fundamental fairness problem that few executives want to address. In 1995 and 1996, average executive pay jumped by close to 100 percent over the 1994 level, while during the same period the pay of employees at the bottom of organizations crept up a minuscule 3 percent. Such a huge difference in pay for performance between the top of the hierarchy and the bottom is likely to inspire little more than cynicism: when the rank and file see only greed and avarice, no amount of pay for performance or empowerment rhetoric can work.

A small number of companies have looked at the evidence and decided to buck the conventional wisdom. Jeffrey Pfeffer, for example, cites SAS Institute, the largest privately held company in the software industry with 1997 revenues of $750 million, which evaluates its managers based on their ability to attract and retain outstanding talent.

Dubbed "Sanity Inc." in a 1999 cover story in *Fast Company*, SAS offices empty out at 5 P.M.—in sharp contrast to most high-tech companies, where techies pride themselves on burning the midnight oil. The company operates the largest day care center in North Carolina and a state-of-the-art gym. To encourage families to eat together, the company cafeteria is equipped with baby seats and high chairs.

SAS's approach to work is no less unusual. In an organization of five thousand people, SAS's hierarchy has only three levels and very little formal structure. Employees regularly move from leading product teams to being members of projects led by colleagues. And although the company offers no stock options and employees command salaries that are sometimes less than what they would get at the competition, turnover at SAS has never exceeded 5 percent annually; the industry average is 20 percent. "Most employees live in a world of 'FUD—fear, uncertainty and doubt,'" says John Ladley, an analyst for META Group who follows the company. SAS is free of all three. The company has "low turnover, happy employees, good cash flow, and a balance sheet with the atomic density of lead." Said Jim Goodnight, president and CEO of the Cary, North Carolina–based company, "[W]e're in the knowledge business. . . . If we get and retain and motivate the best brains, the rest—the product development, the numbers, everything else—will take care of itself."[38]

Three years ago, SAS also eliminated formal performance appraisals. "If there was a good approach to performance appraisals, we'd all be using the same one," said David F. Russo, vice president of human resources at SAS. "Since performance management companies make a small fortune reinventing the wheel every 90 to 120 days, we reached this epiphany that these things are stupid. Managers hate them. Employees hate them."

Instead of formal performance appraisals, managers are expected to have a conversation with each employee about his or her job performance, goals, and expectations three times each year. The human resources department monitors managers to make sure the conversations take place. Although SAS managers are encouraged to identify and reward top performers, Russo acknowledges that there is "not much differential in pay" among employees at the same level. "If we hire well, motivate employees, offer the right tools and the right leadership, performance should be in very much more of a rifle pattern than a shotgun pattern," he said.[39]

Even a few traditional companies have been willing to experiment with a pass-fail approach to performance appraisals. Divisions of companies as varied as Kodak, American Cyanamid, and General Motors stopped grading employees in the late 1980s or early 1990s.

The efforts at reform were probably the farthest-reaching at GM, where an experiment with pass-fail performance appraisals dates back to the mid-1980s and Deming's work with the Powertrain division. At the time, Powertrain won a partial exemption from a companywide ranking scheme similar to the one at IBM that graded employees on a curve, arbitrarily giving 10 percent of the staff a poor rating. The forced ranking scheme, instituted in 1988, was part of a nationwide attempt to tie compensation more closely to performance. At GM, as at many other companies, the system penalized individuals for the company's declining market share and implied that the fear of a low ranking would coerce employees into doing better. But GM employees say that the scheme caused morale to plunge, setting off a near revolt among managers. The strategy was gone within a few months.[40]

In its place, a number of GM units, including Cadillac, began to look toward an embryonic experiment that had been taking shape at the Powertrain division of the company's "big car" group. Powertrain executives had gotten permission for an experiment that would replace rankings with a radically different appraisal system that would reinforce a one-for-all group culture. It tied compensation not to annual appraisals but to a "maturity curve" that considered an individual's seniority, level of expertise, and the overall market for his or her services. Evaluations were based on input from peers and subordinates as well as from managers.[41]

Powertrain allowed for the possibility that an employee might truly be outstanding. But to prevent such a designation from becoming demoralizing to others, they require "consensus by acclamation; no debate." In 1991, only 5 of 1,600 employees were deemed exceptional. The no-fault appraisal and compensation plan survived three Powertrain reorganizations. As of 1999, Powertrain, which now employs 80,000 in the design and manufacturing of engines, transmissions, castings, and components, has retained some, though by no means all, of the pay and performance evaluation features enacted in the 1980s. The division no longer does formal peer reviews and performance appraisals have made a comeback because "employees felt that their leadership wasn't doing a good enough job" of explaining and negotiating performance goals, says Bill Tate, group director of human resources, GM Powertrain Group. In terms of allocating annual raises, however, the division still avoids making fine distinctions in the performance of the vast majority of its employees. Today about 15 percent of Powertrain employees receive an "exceptional" rating and about 4 percent are ranked "below average." The 80 percent of salaried employees who fall in the middle are still evaluated on the basis of a "maturity curve." Explains Tate, "It is still to some extent a pass-fail system."[42]

The system was also considered a contributing factor to the turn-around of Cadillac, which adopted it in 1989. In 1991, Cadillac moved to the number one spot among domestic auto producers on the J. D. Power and Associates customer satisfaction surveys, up from the number three spot in 1986.

Yet even companies that have come to question the wisdom of conventional appraisals and merit pay often hide behind the ingrained preferences of their employees. For example, although some Ford executives said privately that they agreed with many of Deming's arguments, the company let a committee of employees decide on a new scheme. The group, which represented a cross section of the company, voted to maintain a ranking scheme, although it suggested limiting the categories to three. In GM's Powertrain division, by contrast, the pass-fail system was the result of more than two years of planning and education.

The ardor with which Deming put forth his objections to traditional pay for performance is due to more than mere pragmatism. To be sure, he was concerned that the grading game violated the logic of systems and variation theory and failed to motivate employees over time. But on a purely visceral level he despised the manipulative nature of pay-for-performance schemes.

Deming's conviction in the potential and essential goodness of most human beings was derived from his deeply held religious beliefs and an upbringing on the American frontier that was the antithesis of industrial life. This core spirituality informed his philosophy and defined his character. It also helped account for the charismatic power he had to make converts of even his greatest skeptics.

■

Deming was born in October 1900 in Sioux City, Iowa, to William and Pluma Deming. The family lived in Iowa in modest circumstances until 1906, when they made the long train journey west and settled in Wyoming. In Cody, Ed, as he was known to distinguish him from his father, and his brother, Robert, quickly acclimated to frontier life. Living in a boardinghouse in town, they got to know the locals, including Buffalo Bill Cody, the Army scout, buffalo hunter, and founder of Buffalo Bill's Wild West Show, by sight.

A few years after settling in Wyoming, the Demings moved to a town that would come to be known as Powell, after John Wesley Powell, a Civil War veteran and anthropologist who became known as the "father of reclamation." Powell had advocated the development by the federal government of irrigation water that would attract homesteaders such as the Demings to barren lands in places like Powell. At the time, 15,237 acres of land were being parceled out to pioneering families; William Deming received a forty-acre plot near what was yet to become the town.[43]

The Demings lived their first five or so years in Powell in a tar-paper shack, where Deming's sister, Elizabeth, was born in 1909. The farm was never much of a success. William Deming, who had worked as a law clerk before moving to his homestead, continued to bring in some free-lance legal work, and Pluma Deming supplemented the family income by giving piano lessons, sometimes traveling with her children to neighboring towns. It was from his mother that Ed developed a love of music that would remain an important part of his life.[44]

But the family's best efforts, a vegetable garden, a few chickens, and a cow weren't always enough to keep food on the table. Winters, when snow would seep through the cracks and accumulate inside the house, were especially harsh. Consequently, when Ed got old enough, he made contributions to the family finances. The $1.25 he earned after school hauling kindling and coal at Judson's Hotel and the few extra dollars he got for lighting Powell's gasoline streetlamps sometimes went to buy household necessities.[45]

Deming's abhorrence of waste, his diligence, and his frugality took root during his childhood and lasted the rest of his life. He and his wife, Lola, remained in the modest Washington home near the Maryland border that they bought during the Depression. Deming's youngest daughter, Linda, even recalls her father dating the eggs in the refrigerator with a felt-tipped pen to make sure the older ones were eaten first, so none would go to waste.

As a young man, Deming led a studious, sheltered existence. Even after he left Powell, his life revolved around his studies and odd jobs. In 1917, he made the train trip to Laramie, where he attended the University of Wyoming and earned a B.S. in engineering, supporting himself with odd jobs such as janitorial work and snow shoveling. In the 1920s, he moved to Colorado, where he attended the Colorado School of Mines and the University of Colorado, from which he received a master's degree in mathematics and physics.[46]

Between his studies in Colorado and getting his doctorate in physics from Yale in 1928, Deming landed two summer jobs in a row that would make up one of the most formative experiences of his early career. His work at Western Electric's Hawthorne plant in Chicago was the only time in his career that he was employed full-time by a corporation. What he saw at Hawthorne, a plant that employed 46,000 people assembling telephone equipment, left a lasting impression on him. While

Hawthorne has been described as a relatively progressive place to work—it offered higher-than-average wages, a restaurant that dished out the same food to both workers and executives, and various savings plans—it was no utopia. The work, much of it performed by women, was monotonous. Assembling telephone relays, for example, entailed putting together a coil armature, contact springs, and insulators in a fixture and securing the parts in position by means of four machine screws, a job that took about sixty seconds and had to be repeated endlessly throughout the day. Workers regularly complained of smoke, fumes, and extreme temperatures. Deming himself described the place as "hot" and "dirty" (see Chapter 4).[47]

Such Dreiseresque conditions were completely foreign to the impressionable twenty-five-year-old. While he had experienced his share of hardship, he had been influenced by the frontier spirit and pioneer experience of his parents and his childhood. Life in Wyoming had been an unpredictable adventure in which each man attempted to shape his own destiny but in which success was often determined by external conditions: the weather, the availability of water, and the land policies of a distant federal government.

Deming had no frame of reference for the demeaning drudgery the workers at the Hawthorne plant had to endure. Thus, his ideas about companies as social systems grew out of his observations of work conditions at Western Electric. (Similarly, his statistical work echoes the experiments of Walter Shewhart, a Bell Labs statistician who pioneered the use of control charts to measure and improve the capabilities of AT&T processes, instead of relying on inspection to weed out faulty products.) In particular, he was influenced by the stark contrast between the independent, pioneer spirit of his Wyoming childhood and the manipulative nature of management as it was exemplified by the bogey—or piece-rate—system he observed at Western Electric. Ironically, it was during his stay in Chicago that the Hawthorne plant became the setting for the now-famous experiments in human motivation that were conducted under the aegis of Harvard's Elton Mayo and Fritz Roethlisberger (see Chapter 4).[48]

Years later, it was a similar, uniquely Asian version of the pioneer spirit that inspired Deming after World War II and that would turn his Japanese experience into the second major influence on his thinking. He was first summoned to Japan in 1947, just two years after the Japanese surrender, by the administration of General Douglas MacArthur. Deming was one of several U.S. experts assigned to work with Japanese statisticians to develop the national census of 1951, which was intended, among other things to help assess the level of devastation in the country after the war. (During the Depression, Deming had helped the U.S. Census Bureau pioneer statistical sampling methods.) Among the goals of the Japanese survey was an assessment of the amount of new housing that would be needed to accommodate the vast population that had been left homeless after the war.[49]

The nature of Deming's work on the Japanese census gave him a unique opportunity to travel around the country and get to know Japan. While many of his American colleagues looked with disdain on their former enemies and kept to their American enclaves, Deming went wherever he could. He toured both the cities and the countryside, and even became an aficionado of Kabuki theater, which at the time was off-limits to Allied personnel.

Deming's travels exposed him to the underbelly of Japanese postwar life. In Nagoya, he visited a railroad yard at midnight and saw dozens of homeless bedded down for the night on thin rice mats. Spotting an old man and a small boy huddled inside a nearby warehouse, he noted in his diary, "both [were] in rags, huddled around a charcoal burner, scarcely a spark left. . . . I would have given a dollar for a chocolate bar for [the boy.]" He encountered a similar scene in Tokyo, crossing a bridge over one of the numerous canals. "I spied a man, a little boy and girl, all in tatters," he wrote. "The little boy was sobbing on his daddy's knees. The little girl just sitting; looked at me with her big Japanese eyes. . . . Homeless, no doubt, and hungry; probably much else wrong also, but not much else counts. What could I do? They were not begging: I had seen only two beggars in Japan—most remarkable testimony to these people. I went back and gave him a package of cigarettes: He could barter them for food. . . . I went to my office. A thought came to me; I'll go to the Ernie Pyle snack bar and purchase some doughnuts to take to them. So I did—two dozen. It was nearly dark now and blowing chilly. I gave them the doughnuts."[50]

Deming, who as a small child had endured what was often a hand-to-mouth existence, respected—and identified with—both the pride with which the Japanese bore their misfortunes and their dogged determination to overcome their harsh circumstances. "Practically all of the area of heavy industry between Tokyo and Yokohama and in every big city is a complete blank, some concrete and twisted steel left, [yet] new wooden homes are springing up like mushrooms everywhere over the seared areas," he wrote in his diary. "The debris is practically all cleared away; what isn't being built is in winter wheat or garden." In 1988, a few months before his annual trip to Japan, he recalled that "The [Japanese] people were hopeful, happy, clean, they looked forward to another day, though they were hungry. Nothing impressed me so much as the striking contrast between the happiness of the Japanese and their devastation."[51]

The progress and dedication he saw in Japan led Deming, during a subsequent trip in 1950, to predict that "Japanese [manufacturing] quality would capture market the world over by 1955." At the time, he also wrote Kenichi Koyanagi, who was managing director of JUSE, "Let us hope and pray that 1950 may mark the rebirth of Japanese industry and much wealth and happiness for Japan! Be assured that I shall always be ready to do anything possible for you."[52]

The Japanese would soon have an opportunity to show their appreciation for Deming's respect and faith. In 1950, he was invited by JUSE to offer the first of a series of lectures on statistical process control. JUSE scheduled more than a dozen lectures from Tokyo to Kyushu, attracting thousands of listeners from both industry and government. The importance of his lectures went far beyond his ability to explain the arcana of SPC. For one thing, his self-deprecating charm (which was little in evidence in the United States in the 1980s) and his mastery of Japanese customs and manners won him a special place in the hearts of the locals long after other Westerners began pouring into Japan to help with the country's postwar recovery.[53]

Deming also had a knack for making accessible what had heretofore seemed like engineering alchemy. He used golfing analogies instead of arcane statistical theory to make his points about variation, improvement, and control. And he stressed the importance of viewing quality concepts as part of a holistic new management philosophy in which every member of an organization must play a part. He would begin his lectures with an all-encompassing vision of the role quality management would play in Japan's revival and with a sort of Calvinistic message of redemption: "We are in a new industrial age.... International trade is an essential component of peace and prosperity.... [S]tatistical techniques have brought new meaning into all these requirements of international trade."[54]

Most important, Deming recognized quality control as management's principal responsibility and as an organization's best means of identifying and anticipating the needs of customers. During his 1950 visit, Ichiro Ishikawa, the first president of JUSE and then chairman of Keidanren (the Japanese Federation of Economic Organizations), Japan's most powerful business group, threw a dinner for Deming and the twenty-one chiefs of Japan's leading industries at Tokyo's Industry Club. The meeting went so well that the participants decided to hold a subsequent one-day conference at a mountain retreat in Hakone. That conference, which attracted dozens of top managers from such companies as Kawasaki Steel and Hitachi, became a key event in winning over top Japanese management to the importance of quality management. As the late Eizaburo Nishibori, a former Toshiba executive and one of Deming's oldest friends in Japan recalled, "[Deming] told them that quality should be their top priority. That quality came before profit, because it was quality that creates profit. And he told them that only through long-range planning could they hope to build truly successful businesses."[55]

Deming lectured in Japan throughout the 1950s. His lectures stressed the crucial relationship between quality management, innovation, and customer satisfaction: "For the reliable and economical communication with the consumers and non-consumers of a product, it is necessary to carry out statistical tests and surveys. I shall now speak to you about this particular aspect of quality control, and I shall remind you that its main purpose is *re-design* of the quality of your product, and *adjustment* of the plant . . . *to meet rationally predicted changes in demand.*"[56]

To link consumer research and product manufacturing, Deming introduced what has come to be known as the Deming cycle (adapted from Shewhart's original conception). This cycle of continuous testing and improvement, Deming taught in his earliest Japanese lectures, inevitably leads to the redesign of the product on the basis of additional consumer research. The analysis inherent in this "plan, do, check, act" continuum was adapted by the Japanese to help monitor almost every process within a corporation.[57]

In fact, it became the basis of the Japanese strategic planning system known as policy deployment. As recently as the 1990s, policy deployment formed the basis of total quality control (TQC) and is the way management goals at leading companies, such as Toyota, Kansai Electric Power Company, and Fuji-Xerox, are disseminated, executed, analyzed and improved. PDCA would also help make the leap from improvement to innovation.[58]

In 1951, JUSE publicly acknowledged the contribution Deming had made by creating an eponymously named quality award. In subsequent years, JUSE parlayed the Deming Prize competition into a national event that played a crucial role in shaping Japan's management agenda and in developing what has come to be known as TQC. The TQC movement institutionalized the use of statistical analysis to control variation and to bring about improvement throughout virtually every sector of Japanese industry and in every management discipline. It also made "continuous improvement" the rallying cry throughout Japan. In 1960, in final recognition of the enormous impact that both Deming and the prize had had on Japanese industry, Deming became one of the first Americans to receive the Second Class Sacred Treasure, a medal bestowed on him by Emperor Hirohito.[59]

■

For all of Deming's success in Japan and the fame he generated in the United States, he was never fully satisfied with his impact on U.S. management. In a lecture he gave in Japan in the fall of 1988, Deming quipped, "I gave some lectures to the State Department and I told them: Do not export North American management to a friendly country." Explains Fred Simon, a former Ford Motor Company executive who was first exposed to Deming's ideas when he worked on the original Taurus and later came to head the Lincoln Continental team, "It's easy to adopt Deming's tools without adopting his philosophy." With a few exceptions, "no one at Ford was talking about the philosophy, only about controls. How do you measure, and whom do you hold accountable? Of course, you get tremendous improvement using the technical tools. But you could multiply those gains if you also applied Deming's philosophy."[60]

In the 1980s, when U.S. companies were racing to catch up with the Japanese, American Cassandras argued that Japanese management techniques wouldn't work in the United States because Japanese culture was intrinsically more receptive to collaborative management practices. As the decade progressed and American industry recovered, managers patted themselves on the back for Americanizing Japanese management innovations—that is, for successfully adapting an idea such as quality management to an essentially command-and-control corporate culture.

Yet the importance of Deming's philosophy to the information age was its radical break with many accepted tenets of management: its insistence on constant change and flexibility, its implicit faith in the ability of individuals and the informal organization to generate new ideas, its opposition to hierarchy and its trappings, and its assumption that the greatest competitive advantage would accrue to companies that help employees achieve their full potential.

But what of Deming himself? How did a quintessential American—a statistician, no less—arrive at a philosophy that is such an affirmation of human potential and that is, Senge argues, "fundamentally different from the reactive, developmental orientation of Western culture."[61]

The answers are elusive. Senge attributes Deming's humanism to his artistic orientation. From his days sitting beside his mother on the piano bench, Deming studied and composed music; well into his eighties, music remained one of his only respites from a seven-days-a-week work schedule, and you could sometimes spot liturgical music he had composed mixed in among his lecture notes. "Artists have to understand the creative process," says Senge. To a true artist, self-actualization comes from tapping into an intrinsic inner vision or aspiration. (In this sense, Senge even objects to what he terms the reactive nature of Maslow's hierarchy of needs, the notion that self-actualization can come only as a *reaction* to fulfilling lower-level needs.)[62]

Deming's religious upbringing also clearly played a role. He recognized and identified with the deep reservoirs of inner strength and the penchant for learning that he saw in the Japanese.

Whatever the roots of Deming's personal transformation, Senge, for one, believes that, at least in this regard, we must become more like the Japanese. The goal- and control-oriented Western culture, he believes, has much to learn from the "generative," learning-oriented culture of the East. To develop a "generative," as opposed to adaptive, learning, he argues, managers must develop the interpersonal skills of the learning organization.[63]

While proponents of the learning organization disagree with a few of the tenants of Demingism, the two movements are part of the same continuum. Like the quality movement, the learning organization has both technical and humanist roots: for its scientific foundation, it draws on Forrester's theories of system dynamics; for interpersonal skills, it is a direct descendant of the psychological tradition of Lewin, Maslow, and McGregor.

Moreover, the movement's most visible spokesman, Peter Senge, is a self-avowed disciple—though not an uncritical one—of Deming. Deming's quotations are liberally sprinkled throughout his writings. What was missing from the quality movement, according to Senge, was a way to operationalize the behavioral changes that are needed for continuous change and learning. Building primarily on the work of Forrester, Argyris, and Deming, the theorists of the learning organization have sought to fill this behavioral gap.

Like Deming, proponents of organizational learning believe that competitive advantage depends on the ability of organizations to constantly change and reinvent themselves. "The rate at which organizations learn . . . may become the only sustainable source of competitive advantage," said Ray Stata of Analog Devices.[64] One major impetus behind organizational learning was the development of "planning as learning," at Royal Dutch/Shell in the 1970s. The concept, which was pioneered by Arie De Geus, who was head of planning for Royal Dutch/Shell at the time, involves developing detailed alternative scenarios of the future. The idea is to make people sensitive to the first indications of unanticipated changes and flexible enough to react to developments that might run counter to management's preconceived ideas about the future. This ability to constantly evolve and improve depends in turn on the extent to which organizations can foster learning, collectively as institutions and individually as members of an organization. Learning, in this sense, is *not* synonymous with information gathering. It involves being open to new ideas and points of view and shedding both conscious and subconscious prejudices. It is also the antithesis of complacency. "Learning occurs between a fear and a need," wrote Kofman and Senge.[65]

The learning theorists base their philosophy on the conviction that the major threats to human society and institutions are much more subtle and insidious today than they were in the past. Environmental destruction and the erosion of our educational system, for example, have replaced war and pestilence as major threats to modern society. New threats require not only new remedies but also new ways of thinking about society itself. "[T]he main dysfunctions in our institutions—fragmentation, competition, and reactiveness—are actually by-products of our success over thousands of years in conquering the physical world and in developing our scientific industrial culture. So, it should come as no surprise that these dysfunctions are deeply rooted. . . . Fragmentation, competition, and reactiveness are not problems to be solved—they are frozen patterns of thought to be dissolved," argued Peter Senge and Fred Kofman.[66]

Senge identifies five "disciplines" that are the foundations of organizational learning. Unlike many management principles, they are fundamentally "personal" disciplines that require quite literally both a personal transformation on the part of members of an organization and a collective transformation. The disciplines, which Senge outlined in his best-seller, *The Fifth Discipline*, are:

• *Personal mastery.* This is a variation on what Maslow called self-actualization. Senge's concept of personal mastery also encompasses the notions of "creative tension" between a desired future and current reality, as well as Deming's idea of continuous improvement (or, in this case, self-improvement). Man has an innate desire to achieve his full potential, a drive that most traditional hierarchical organizations, by definition, thwart—there is room at the top for only a relative handful of high-potential employees. Personal mastery is based on the conviction that there is a mother lode of untapped creative potential that an organization can mine only if it achieves alignment between the personal aspirations of individuals and the goals and visions of the organization.[67]

• *Building a shared vision.* This is a political process, a way of galvanizing collective aspirations. "When there is a genuine vision (as opposed to the all-too-familiar 'vision statement'), people excel and learn, not because they are told to, but because they want to." Organizational vision is the sum of individual aspirations and insights.

• **Mental models.**   Following a theory of reflection and inquiry developed by Chris Argyris and Donald Schön, the practice of working with mental models involves articulating and recognizing deeply ingrained assumptions, generalizations, and images that shape our perceptions of the world and how we take action. According to Shell's De Geus, "[I]nstitutional learning is the process whereby management teams change their shared mental models of the company, their markets, and their competitors. For this reason we think of planning as learning and of corporate planning as institutional learning." Adds Senge, "The discipline of working with mental models starts with turning the mirror inward; learning to unearth our internal pictures of the world to bring them to the surface and hold them rigorously to scrutiny." It is a process whereby "people expose their own thinking effectively and make that thinking open to the influence of others."[68]

• **Team learning.**   Teams are the "fundamental learning unit" in modern organizations. The basis of team learning, according to Senge, is "dialogue . . . the capacity of members of a team to suspend assumptions and enter into a genuine 'thinking together.' " In Senge's definition, dialogue is akin to the sort of conversation that is the creative lifeblood of modern science.[69] In sharp contrast to the image of the lone scientist as creative genius, the most complex problems of our era—the revolution in quantum mechanics, for instance—grew out of a series of profound conversations, such as those that percolated in Heidelberg around the seminars of Max Born and James Franck, and others around Niels Bohr in Copenhagen. Moreover, like the collaboration between Joe Mayer, a noted chemist, and his wife, Maria Goeppert-Mayer, a Nobel laureate in physics, breakthroughs in science, as in business, increasingly grow in a multidisciplinary context. (Maria Mayer attributed her Nobel Prize–winning breakthrough in so-called spin-orbit coupling to the experimental perspective she learned from her chemist husband.)

Because of the complexity of most business systems and the speed with which they change, the ability to tap the insights of many individuals is more important than ever. The purpose of dialogue, in this sense, is to transcend the knowledge of any single individual and to achieve leaps of creative insight that would be difficult for any one person to achieve alone.

Team learning, however, also requires the capacity to overcome the barriers to constructive discussion. Chief among these impediments are what Chris Argyris calls "defensive routines," the myriad ways in which we try to avoid conflict and embarrassment, whether by self-censorship, "smoothing over" disagreements, or lashing out at challengers. Senge points out that systems thinking is "especially prone to evoking defensiveness" because, by definition, both the source of (and the solutions to) problems are found within the policies and strategies of a given system, rather than in some "outside" enemy.[70]

Even scientists now find that they have to break loose from their circumscribed disciplines and reach out for insights in new fields. Thus, breakthroughs in such areas as game theory, system dynamics, and systems analysis are the products of an expanded dialogue involving experts in a variety of disciplines that, in the past, would have been unlikely to collaborate.

• *Systems thinking.* This conceptual framework, which Senge drew from Jay Forrester's work, is the fifth discipline. It involves creating a series of mental models for navigating the complex systems in which we live and work and making sense of the intricate patterns of interrelated events and actions that influence every endeavor. (Senge adopted the term "mental models" from Forrester and adapted it to Argyris's work.) Although Senge says that systems thinking is no more important than the other disciplines, it is the theoretical foundation of the organizational learning philosophy, much the way the theory of variation is the cornerstone of quality management. "Without a systemic orientation, there is no motivation to look at how the disciplines interrelate."[71]

Senge's major insight is the realization that systems thinking alone cannot achieve long-term organizational change without the interpersonal skills encompassed by the other four disciplines. "Systems thinking without the discipline of mental models loses much of its power," Senge wrote; entrenched mental models will thwart both insights that might be gleaned from systems thinking and the changes that might result from it.[72]

■

To foster and conduct research on learning organizations, Senge, a lecturer at MIT, established the Organization Learning Center (OLC) at MIT in 1991. (In 1997, the center was spun off as the Society for Learning Organizations, or SOL, an independent not-for-profit organization.) Among the center's participants were Edgar Schein from MIT; Daniel Kim, the founder of Pegasus; Bill Isaacs, a theorist on dialogue, and some twenty member companies, including Harley-Davidson, Ford, AT&T, Pacific Bell, and National Semiconductor.

Taking a page from Kurt Lewin, Senge and his colleagues believe in "action learning," the proposition that learning comes from doing and vice versa. Like a theater troupe or orchestra, Senge argues, in an article co-authored by Fred Kofman, an organization must move continuously between "a practice field and a performance field."[73]

The center's first pilot project was indirectly a continuation of the work Deming had been doing at Ford. It started in 1991, when Fred Simon was put in charge of building a completely new Lincoln Continental and reviving a brand name that, with just 25,000 vehicles sold annually in recent years—less than half the number of Cadillacs during the same period—had all but faded out of the market.

Simon, who had worked on the original Ford Taurus and had developed a keen admiration for Lewis C. Veraldi, who headed that project, was determined to rekindle some of the collaborative magic that had made the Taurus such a success. "I was tired of the way [most Ford] programs were run," he recalls. "The constant bickering. Constant surprises. Parts that turned up late because we didn't hear about the problems until the last minute."[74]

Simon knew that achieving a more cooperative work environment wouldn't be easy, given Ford's operating procedures. For one thing, Ford kept careful track of engineering problems during the product development phase, and engineers were under tremendous pressure to minimize those problems. One corporate rule of thumb dictated that there should be no more than two hundred unresolved "engineering concerns" at any one time. If the number rose beyond that—which was not unusual on a complete redesign, such as the 1995 Continental—engineers hid the problems and tried to resolve them without notifying management and other members of the design team. By trying to resolve issues alone, however, an engineer working on the engine, say, might inadvertently create problems in the power train that wouldn't become apparent until the end of the design process. Thus, a problem that could have been resolved for about $25,000 early in the design process could cost as much as $30 million to resolve at the end of the process, especially if it involved changing hard tools, such as dyes. Thus, about 10 percent of a typical $1 billion new-product launch was devoted to fixing engineering problems. Last-minute problems not only were costly, they could adversely affect the quality of the final product.[75]

Bringing design and engineering problems out into the open early in the design phase was key to Simon's strategy—and one long advocated by Deming and long since adopted by the Japanese. To do so, Simon was determined to "get all these people together and get them to see each other as people rather than as job descriptions. I felt that if we learned to call each other by name, we wouldn't want to let each other down."[76]

Since 1991, Deming had been meeting monthly with managers from Continental, among the few clients he still met with privately. Yet when one of Simon's lieutenants, Nick Zeniuk, suggested inviting Senge to facilitate a more open dialogue, Simon was adamantly opposed. "There was no way I was going to let some academic tell me how to run my program," he recalls.[77]

Eventually, Simon succumbed to the persuasion of Zeniuk and Vic Leo, a staff executive involved with higher-level management training, who pursuaded him to bring Senge to Ford. One evening in late 1991, Simon and several of his managers flew to Boston and met with the learning organization pioneers at what was then still MIT's Organizational Learning Center. The group included, among others, Senge and Argyris, who, though on the Harvard faculty, also served on OLC's and, later, SOL's board.

That meeting sparked a pilot project that would become important to both Senge's group and the Lincoln Continental team. For Senge, it was an opportunity to prove that the theory and tools of organizational learning could work in an operational setting—a new product with a finite beginning and end. For Ford, the MIT group offered an opportunity to achieve the "softer," collaborative innovations that Deming had long been advocating at the company.

Over the next several months, members of the MIT team would meet once a month for about one and a half days with Continental's leadership to help open communications and resolve the psychological and emotional issues that were getting in the way of honest exchanges and problem solving. Simon says he knew almost immediately that bringing in the MIT team was the right decision, for it was at the first meeting with a facilitator from OLC, Bill Isaacs, who was working with the group on the need for greater openness, honesty, and respect that the manager in charge of manufacturing stood up and said: "I'm ready to do it." Then, pointing a finger at the finance manager, he erupted, "But she'll never work that way!"[78]

Distrust was at the root of the conflict. The finance manager saw herself as the "controller," explains Simon, whose first job at Ford was as a bean counter in the finance department. Her assumption was that "these people are irresponsible; they don't care about cost. If I as finance person don't control the budget, they'll give away the store." By contrast, manufacturing and engineering believed that finance was supposed to be providing a service, "making sure we know the real implications from a cost perspective." By working out their "mental models" with the help of Daniel Kim, an expert in product development and organizational learning, and getting at the underlying concerns of both finance and manufacturing, the two were able to work out their differences, says Simon.[79]

Deming had long been exhorting managers to "break down barriers" and to seek "transformation." It was OLC, however, that introduced a series of concrete tools for doing just that—for dissecting what Chris Argyris called the "mental models" and "defensive routines" that interfere with open communication. The question that Argyris tries to get both individuals and teams to ask is: What is it *we* do that gets others to react the way *they* do? The tools for getting at the answers include the following:

• *The left-hand, right-hand columns.*   During the course of an actual meeting, fold a piece of paper in half and, in the left-hand column, write what you are thinking about the other people at the meeting and what they are saying. In the right-hand column, write what you yourself say out loud. The discrepancy between the two columns will help reveal "the personal biases that get in the way of real work."[80]

• *The ladder of inference.*   By climbing down the following ladder, you discover why you behave the way you do and thus can keep yourself from jumping to the wrong conclusions:

> • I take ACTIONS on my beliefs.
> • I adopt BELIEFS about the world.
> • I draw CONCLUSIONS.
> • I make ASSUMPTIONS based on the meanings added.
> • I add MEANINGS (cultural and personal).
> • I select DATA from what I observe.
> • I OBSERVE data and experiences (as a video tape recorder might capture them).

• *System maps.*   Derived from Jay Forrester's diagrams of complex dynamic systems, system maps are simplified and free of mathematics and computer models. Says Simon, "It lets people understand at a more intuitive level what is going on." The diagrams are based on the idea that systems have predictable dynamics that evolve over time, based on positive and negative feedback loops that Forrester borrowed from electrical engineering. The idea is to understand how accelerating processes and balancing processes interact, even in social systems like corporations.[81]

■

These learning tools helped Continental to resolve the bulk of its engineering problems early in the design process and to achieve several product development milestones. The quality and customer satisfaction reports on the Continental surpassed those on any other North American luxury car and matched those of the best imported luxury car in the North American market, according to the National New Car Buyer Study. The new-model Continental was ahead of schedule and under budget. Indeed, Simon had slashed the budget for late engineering changes by more than a half, to $27 million, saving $65 million. Most of the savings turned into pure profit on the final product. (Initially, the finance department had argued that it was impossible for Simon to push it below about $95 million.) In the end, Paul Nolan, the plant manager of the Continental said of the project, "It was the smoothest launch I've ever seen."[82]

Yet for Simon and Ford, the changes at Continental could not be viewed as an unalloyed success. The philosophy and techniques espoused by SOL were considered subversive by Ford's command-and-control hierarchy. On the one occasion when Simon had tried to explain to his supervisor what he was doing, the man had responded, "That's OK, as long as it doesn't interfere with your real job." Ultimately, Simon and other Ford colleagues wondered whether Simon's early retirement was due to the unorthodox practices he encouraged at Continental. (At one point, Simon's team was even accused of being a cult.)[83]

Indeed, Simon's experience at Ford illustrates one of the initial disagreements between Deming and Senge and the difficulty of expanding small innovations in one isolated unit onto the organization as a whole. Deming always insisted that real change had to be driven from the top, with the full backing and understanding of the CEO. Senge's prime concern, at least initially, was in sparking grassroots change; he argued that looking to senior management is little more than a cop-out for lower-level managers not to take effective action. "[T]he basic assumption that only top management can cause significant change is deeply disempowering," he argued. "Why then in the 'age of empowerment' do we accept it so unquestioningly? Isn't it odd that we should seek to bring about less hierarchical and authoritarian organizational cultures through recourse to hierarchical authority?" (Eventually, the experience at Continental brought Senge to the view that leadership has to come from several points in the organization.)[84]

This debate was revisited during the original 1992 meeting at MIT between the Ford team and OLC. While Argyris, taking what would have been Deming's side, insisted that the CEO should be brought in from the beginning, Simon sided with Senge. "I think it would have been impossible to get top management on board from the beginning," he reflects. "Red [Poling, the CEO] was command and control. I don't care what the papers say about him, that's the kind of guy he was." Poling had loved the technical side of Deming's teachings, the statistical aspects, says Simon. "Red loved that . . . because it [seemed to mean] more controls. . . . What he missed was Deming's philosophy."[85]

By opting largely to exclude senior management from his decision-making processes, Simon would have to endure a public hazing from fellow managers and superiors that was at times, as he put it, "terrifying." His most unsettling moment came during the first engineering review with senior management.

At the time, Simon together with the managers of all other new-product launches at Ford, met in a conference room at NAAO's headquarters in Dearborn, Michigan, to give a status report to the assembled senior executives, including the executive vice president for NAAO. During the course of the meeting, the manager in charge of new-product launches rated how well each new-product launch was doing. The rating was based largely on the number of unresolved engineering problems that were then outstanding. The projects with the fewest problems were marked with a green flag; the worst cases were marked with a red flag.[86]

In keeping with Simon's efforts to bring all engineering problems to the surface early in the design process, at the time of the launch review the Continental had a record *five hundred* "unresolved" engineering concerns. When the time came for the Continental's review, the manager in charge of new-product launches stood up, pointed at Simon, and said that the new Continental wasn't red, "it's purple. Not only is it purple," he added, "he's too stupid to know how much trouble he's in." He concluded by saying, "No program can recover from this number of engineering concerns!"[87]

Simon confesses that he then briefly "slipped into [his] old style" of management. His engineers hunkered down and wrote fixes for every engineering concern; within a week, Continental was down to just fifty concerns. Then Continental created a "hidden system." For the corporate reviews, engineers would hide problems as they traditionally had done; but inside the Continental team, the problems were to remain open. Not long after instituting the hidden system, Simon got a letter of congratulations from the head of product development for clearing up all the unresolved engineering concerns. Simon enlarged the letter and hung it in his office. "Isn't that sad," he says. "We got congratulated because the bigger system didn't know what was going on—that we had created a hidden system."[88]

Nor did it help Simon's career that the success of the Continental launch validated his subversive management tactics. In 1994, he took early retirement. Some months after he had left Ford, one of his friends, Iva Wilson, was talking with Simon's former supervisor, who happened to be her neighbor in Ann Arbor, about the Continental. When the supervisor sounded negative about both Simon and the project, Wilson said, "But you can't deny the results. They achieved exceptional results."[89]

"Yes, they did," responded the supervisor. "But think of how much better they could have been if they hadn't been fooling around" (with all that organizational learning stuff).[90]

Concludes Simon, "Results don't change mental models." Simon's assumption that the results alone would win management over were "naive," he says in retrospect. "It's a trap I see more and more often. By not finding a way to enlist management's support and understanding," he says, he inadvertently created an "us versus them" situation, triggering "defensive routines." Thus, he created a psychological situation in which management, to defend its own position, *couldn't* acknowledge that his way might have been right. He has since come around to the view that there "had to have been a way to invite senior people in to understand the process and to reflect on whether the results we achieved were caused by the things we were doing." Simon, who now runs his own consulting business in Michigan, still isn't sure how that can be accomplished. In a classical bureaucratic irony, Simon, like other executives who took an early retirement package, have been banned from ever working at Ford again. Ford wants to make sure that its executives don't meet their downsizing targets by showing employees the (front) door and then rehiring them as consultants via the (back) door. Implicit in Ford's rule is the understanding that retired managers, such as Simon, have valuable institutional knowledge that smart managers who remain at Ford will want to tap. In fact, some Ford managers have maintained their ties with Simon. And a number of units, including product development groups, Powertrain operations, and Visteon, a parts division, are pursuing a number of organizational learning initiatives.[91]

Many learning organization advocates implicitly minimize the importance of top-management involvement, thus creating a false dichotomy. There is abundant evidence that line managers and the "informal" organization can achieve powerful results *for a time*. Rarely, however, do they succeed in the long term in the face of even tacit opposition from management. The Continental team succeeded despite the Ford hierarchy. But because he didn't have management's backing, Simon's example could serve as a disincentive to more faint-hearted managers at Ford. (Senge argues, however, and quite rightly, that top-management commitment without grassroots change leads to "top-management impotence.")[92]

It is a sad fact that for all the rhetoric about collaborative management, at the vast majority of companies empowerment today remains as elusive a concept as it was when Maslow wrote about NSL thirty years ago. While managers often espouse empowerment in theory, in a pinch they fall back on the command-and-control model that they know best. Employees, not surprisingly, are often ambivalent and distrustful of empowerment programs. To complicate matters further, says Argyris, "The change programs and practices we employ are full of inner contradictions that cripple innovation, motivation, and drive." Such contradictions, he says, are inevitable because even the most Eupsychian organization will have some top-down controls. The key, he argues, is to bring these contradictions to the surface. "Otherwise a credibility gap will be created that can pollute the organization for many years to come."[93]

Thus, empowerment, like self-actualization, is hard work. True empowerment begins with commitment. And commitment, as Argyris points out, "is not simply a human relations concept." While many companies and managers have mastered "external commitment"—i.e., compliance—they have not succeeded in inspiring "internal commitment." Internal commitment is, by definition, "participatory and very closely allied with empowerment."[94]

Commitment building is also a gradual process. Not surprisingly, commitment and management continuity are often closely linked. At companies that have maintained a high degree of management continuity, there is a greater opportunity for knowledge and learning to circulate throughout the organization. It is no accident that companies such as Xerox, where a corporate vision and commitment to that vision have been built over time, it is often top management that seeks to find ways of tapping the knowledge and learning deep within its ranks. The communities of practice developed at Xerox can be seen as part of this process (see Chapter 3).

The no-win situation in which Simon and, ultimately, Ford found themselves in the aftermath of the Continental project goes to the heart of two major dilemmas that face established organizations: first, the problem of gleaning, and acting on, new insights about how psychological factors impact the human side of enterprise, especially in a corporate culture with deep mechanistic and hierarchical roots; and second, the difficulties of effecting meaningful change on a large enough scale to make a long-term difference.

Simon is hopeful that the seeds planted by Deming and OLC will gradually change Ford's culture. He points out that the members of his Continental team have since scattered throughout Ford, planting the seeds of learning elsewhere in the organization, much the way Simon had brought the lessons he had learned from the Taurus, a decade earlier, to the Continental. Indeed, Simon credits Petersen, who, he says, "worked really hard" to turn Ford's militaristic, tell-the-chief-only-what-he-wants-to-hear culture into one that was "more open and fair" and "encouraged more communication." It is a testament to Petersen, he says, that "the culture had moved far enough along that we couldn't go all the way back."[95]

In its tussle with both quality management and organizational learning principles, Ford's story, like that of many organizations, is one of two steps forward and (at least) one step back. Yet the stakes couldn't be higher. If a study conducted by Royal Dutch/Shell in the 1970s is correct, most corporations are destined to die out in as few as forty years (see Epilogue). Only the ability to learn and to change in significant ways will give them a chance to defy the biological clock that ticks for companies, much as it does for humans.

So far, the story of the quality movement has been one of incremental changes—a little teamwork here, some long-term contracts with suppliers there, a *very small number* of companies significantly transformed. While many executives intuitively understand the need for radical change, they are fundamentally conservative. Thus, such innovative experiments as the Continental are misunderstood and often unappreciated.

The philosophy encompassed by Deming's quality movement and the learning organization pioneers is a radical one. It assumes that change must come from both collective *and* individual empowerment. New ideas and strategies can emerge from almost any part of the organization. Power resides with individuals, who have the ability to *persuade* and *facilitate* change, rather than a mandate to dictate. As Phil Carroll, the former CEO of Shell Oil, puts it: "Perhaps my real job is to be the *ecologist for the organization.* We must learn how to see the company as a living system and to see it as a system within the context of the larger systems of which it is a part. Only then will our vision reliably include return for our shareholders and a social vision for the company as a whole.... The name of the game is giving up power." Or, as Saul Alinsky, the pioneering community organizer, once put it, "The most effective community organizer is he who is invisible."[96]

Economics was always special: it was self-contained; it was the queen of the social sciences; it played hardball. . . . Herb Simon and others at Carnegie Mellon joined economics and organization theory to pry open what had been a black box . . . to examine the business firm in more operationally engaging ways.

—Oliver Williamson[1]

Herbert A. Simon

The Needle and the Haystack

In May 1997 in New York City, Gary Kasparov, the reigning world chess champion, faced the most formidable rival of his career. After five tense games, Kasparov's opponent launched a sixth-game blitzkrieg. In just nineteen moves, the chess match was over. Kasparov had lost. The winner was Deep Blue, an IBM computer.

A few hundred miles away, in Pittsburgh, Herbert A. Simon—the Leonardo da Vinci of the information age—heard the news with no small amount of satisfaction. Years before, Simon, a chess aficionado, pioneer of artificial intelligence and cognitive psychology, renegade economist, and management pathbreaker, had predicted that a computer would beat the world's leading chess master by 1967. In the intervening years his rivals had gloated that at last one of Simon's arrogant assertions had been proven wrong. But of course it hadn't. He was just off by a few decades; it had taken longer than he had anticipated for the process of trial and error and innovative programming to teach the computer to become a grand master.[2]

To a chess master—and to Herb Simon—winning or losing isn't everything: it's the strategy and the learning that matter. One game lost can produce new insights that will lead to future victories. The fun is in the decision making.

Small wonder that Herbert Simon approached life much the way he would a particularly challenging game of chess. Since his days as a young graduate student at the University of Chicago during the turbulent years of the Depression, he had reveled in the complexities of the times and the multiplicity of ideas that surrounded him. A polymath, he sampled a multitude of academic options—not with a predetermined game plan but with a combination of logic and instinct that brought success with almost every move.

Simon's choices frequently drove him in seemingly contradictory directions. In the space of just a quarter of a century, his peripatetic intellect would take him from political science and economics to cognitive psychology and computer science. In the end, he became a pioneer in each of these disparate disciplines, winning the kudos of each new profession. (In addition to winning the Nobel Prize in Economic Science, he holds the Turing Prize for computer science and the first National Medal of Science awarded for work in the behavioral sciences.) He once noted, "When I did sense something exciting and fundamental, I sniffed my way toward it and became involved in it almost without plan or forethought."[3]

What Simon would later call his "biased random walk" inevitably led to the core preoccupation that would define his eclectic career: the riddle of human decision making. "I expect that I was always ambitious to contribute to the solution of central problems in science, but I started out my career with little knowledge of the geography of science or my location in it," he recalls. "I did tend to home in on the Big Questions: I read the Great Books assiduously, I found Whitehead and Russell, I dug into the work of Walter Pitts and Warren McCulloch on the application of Boolean logic to the nerve networks and Claude Shannon on switching circuits as soon as I learned of it." James G. March, who refers to Simon as an intellectual "interloper" rather than an "imperialist," said, "[H]is record exhibits such breadth and versatility that it would clearly be pretentious were it not so distinguished."[4]

During the course of a career that has spanned more than half a century, Simon's work on organizational theory was a relatively short chapter. His interest in administrative decision making began during the 1930s, when he was studying political science at the University of Chicago. It continued through a few years of government research, most of it involving cost-benefit analyses of Works Progress Administration programs. And it extended briefly into his career at what was then the Carnegie Institute of Technology, where he helped found the Graduate School of Industrial Administration (GSIA). Ultimately, Simon virtually abandoned the field as he was swept up by the revolution in cognitive science and artificial intelligence in the late 1950s and 1960s.

Simon's insights about how the limitations of human thought affect the functioning of organizations produced a crucial nexus between economics and organizational theory. His ideas flew in the face of the neoclassical economists' view of human beings as wholly rational decision makers, as well as their vision of a firm as little more than a vehicle for a wholly profit-maximizing entrepreneur. Thus, when Simon's ideas about organizational decision making, specifically what he called "bounded rationality," won him the Nobel Prize in Economic Science

in 1978, it was to the surprise—and in some cases the outright dismay—
of a number of leading economists.

Simon saw man as an economic actor bombarded with choices and
decisions but possessing only finite information storage and processing
capabilities. According to Simon, people are "intendedly rational, but
only limitedly so." He saw man's struggle to digest avalanches of information and to compensate for their inability to take in all the available
choices by selecting "good enough" options, rather than the "optimal"
solutions postulated by neoclassical economists.[5]

Simon's theory of the firm was based on four main ideas: First, organizations are not the abstract, one-dimensional entities often depicted
by economists. Rather, they are entities of tremendous complexity made
up of diverse individuals and interests, all of which are held together by
a variety of "deals" and coalitions, ranging from, say, explicit employment contracts to implicit agreements between departments and colleagues and what Chester Barnard called "inducements" and
"contributions."[6]

Second, contrary to the assumptions of classical economics, organizations are not provided with a complete list of alternatives and complete knowledge about the consequences of their decisions and actions.
As Barnard put it in a letter critiquing Simon's groundbreaking book,
Administrative Behavior, "[I]n an extremely high proportion of decisions it is impossible ever to determine which alternative was or would
have been better. The situation is like that of the explorer who sets a
distant mountain peak as his immediate goal; of the various alternative
routes by which he guesses that he might reach it, he can, in fact, traverse only one and he never can know whether the one he selected was
the better, although under some conditions he may be able to make a
fair guess." Like explorers scaling a particularly difficult peak, companies must constantly search for alternatives, information, and knowledge; thus, to understand how organizations make choices, one must
understand how they conduct this search process.[7]

Third, rather than searching for optimal solutions, organizations use
targets, or aspiration levels—i.e., a safe path up a mountain that will get
climbers there before the weather changes—to distinguish between outcomes that are "good enough" and those that are not.[8]

Fourth, much human behavior, both inside and outside organizations, involves following rules, rather than rationally calculating the expected consequences of a given action.[9] For example, one implicit (and
sometimes explicit) rule in business is to stick with a tried-and-true
vendor, rather than search for a new one every time supplies need to be
purchased, even if, in theory, there may be a better or cheaper vendor

out there somewhere. The reason is that, all things being more or less equal, finding a better vendor takes time and work and involves inherent uncertainties (i.e., information about suppliers is imperfect and limited), whereas the arrangements worked out with the existing vendor are familiar and relatively safe—in short, good enough.

Simon's work built on Chester Barnard's *Functions of the Executive* (see Chapter 3) in two important respects: first, in recognizing the complex alliances and deals that make up organizations and the need to "motivate participants by balancing inducements and contributions" and second, in recognizing the behavioral implications of limited knowledge and alternatives. Simon also emphasized the importance of process and helped establish an entirely new way of looking at organizations and at management—as "a problem-facing and problem-solving" machine designed to "cop[e] with the limits of man's abilities to comprehend and compute in the face of complexity and uncertainty."[10]

Bounded rationality and the "behavioral theory of the firm," which was pioneered by Simon's cohorts Richard Cyert and James March at Carnegie Tech, created a bridge between economics and organizational theory. The shift from *coordination*—a relatively straightforward tactical process—to the more complex and subtle problems of *decision making* and *motivation* implicit in Simon's theory affected the way employee/employer relations were conceived, the role of knowledge and information in the performance of firms, and the trends in legal theory and government regulation.[11]

The often brilliant simplicity of Simon's insights was, however, usually obscured by his almost equal devotion to the rigors and elegance of mathematics. He was committed to moving organizational theory out of the province of ideals and precepts and onto the same scientific footing as engineering and medicine. He strove to explain and prove his theories in mathematical language, not sound bites that would be picked up by the business press. (It is important to note that unlike Taylor and McNamara, Simon was not interested in using quantification to wring greater efficiency out of organizations; rather, he wanted to study human behavior in organizations, using all of the modern tools of empirical and mathematical analysis to aid his research.)

Today Simon's work is far less known to laymen than that of other management philosophers. The biggest problem with Simon's work, quips Peter Drucker, who otherwise admires his colleague, is Simon's penchant for "too many footnotes"—most of them laden with mathematical proofs. Literally hundreds of academic treatises that Simon has written during his career serve as a monument to his primary passion.[12]

Ultimately, Simon may be remembered as much for his pioneering work in artificial intelligence and cognitive psychology as for his work on bounded rationality and administrative theory. In the arcane world of cyberscience, it doesn't matter if mere mortals don't understand your ideas as long as other scientists can translate them into software programs and electronic circuitry. An electronic problem, once solved, can be replicated in unlimited numbers of computers. Organizations, however, are not programmable in the same way computers are. Simon understood better than most people both the limitations of human decision making and their profound effect on organizations. But while he was a keen observer of the problem, he did not have the interest or the inclination to grapple with solutions (though he did help pioneer the expert systems that would become key to problem solving in industry).

Since his student days at the University of Chicago during the Depression, Simon was always torn between his desire to tackle problems that had relevance to the real world and his penchant for arcane analysis. He was clearly drawn to the messy realities of human administration. Unlike many of his fellow management philosophers, he did work as both a manager and an administrator for several years, during which he is said to have demonstrated a taste—if not much talent—for organizational politics and bureaucracy.

Yet, Simon's greatest preoccupation has been the life of the mind. As a young man, he sharpened his brain on chess, books, music, and entomology the way many of his contemporaries toned their bodies on the athletic field. As an adult, he has made a sport of picking apart the theories of fellow scientists, regardless of whether their field of study is physics or economics, political science or psychology. Similarly, he has made it a point of honor to teach himself the native language of each new country that he visits; today he has a rudimentary knowledge of close to twenty languages, including Chinese and most of the European languages. He learned the languages, he says, "because they were there," and because they are "more fun" and "more useful" than crossword puzzles or cryptograms.[13]

In his dealings with his fellowman, the prophet of bounded rationality operates on the assumption that his decisions are, if not wholly rational, at least superior to those of other mortals. As an administrator and academic Olympian, a matter-of-fact conviction that he is smarter than almost everyone else led Simon to adopt an authoritarian approach with his colleagues. "He had this attitude that 'we'll make the most progress if we organize and do exactly what I tell them,' " says Phil Bromley, a former student and ardent admirer.[14]

His authoritarian streak is matched only by his often biting candor. "Economics has made almost a positive virtue of avoiding direct, systematic observation of individual human beings while valuing the casual empiricism of the economist's armchair introspection," he wrote in one of his frequent barbs at the economics profession.[15]

Simon's determination to speak his mind and to pursue his goals in a professional context, even at the risk of offending his colleagues, is rooted in his desire to know, not (primarily) to feed his ego or his bank account. He simply loves to argue and refuses to lose verbal jousts—even, according to one colleague, if he has to embellish the details to prove his point.

Those who are closest to Simon, including graduate students and family members, acknowledge his argumentative streak but treasure him for his thoughtfulness, insightfulness, and caring. His graduate students are, to a remarkable extent, united in their recollections of a mentor who was always supportive, even when they disagreed with him. Indeed, the work of his closest colleagues and protégés constitutes a miniconglomerate in intellectual innovation—due in no small part to his interest in and involvement with their work. Yet while he makes himself available to friends and colleagues and the odd inquiring writer, he has never sought out—and rarely attracted—publicity outside academe.

It's ironic that the pioneer of human decision-making theory should have proven himself so clumsy at navigating the less rational side of his colleagues' feelings and motivations. Simply put, he can't resist playing "mind games"—both in earnest and in fun.

■

Simon's own penchant for learning and analysis was evident from an early age. As a boy, he "learned that he was different than the others." For one thing, young Herb was left-handed and color-blind—a fact that may have thwarted his early interest in biology. He was also a Jew, a social handicap that often bothered him. And he was smarter than his comrades, a mixed blessing that occasionally isolated him from his peers but was, at the same time, "important to him."

Though not exactly antisocial, as a young man he was introverted. Although he had a brother, Clarence was five years older, making Herb "nearly an only-child." Having been skipped over three semesters in school, he was also by far the youngest in his class. So he spent long hours by himself, collecting stamps and teaching himself how to play chess, seated at a board with a chess book propped up by his elbow.[16]

Simon's boyhood was spent in Milwaukee, Wisconsin, in a middle-class German neighborhood. Until he went to college, he lived in an extended family populated by his parents, his older brother, a grandparent or two, and the family maid in a large, immaculately kept house.

On warm days, Simon enjoyed sitting out on the stoop that overlooked Juneau Avenue. From there he could watch the daily parade of Harley-Davidson workmen who lived in the neighborhood and trooped past his house on the half-mile walk to and from the company's main plant, their metal lunch boxes swinging at their sides. The Davidsons themselves lived just a few blocks away in one of the mansions on Highland Boulevard. Around the corner was the residence of Dan Hoan, the Socialist mayor of Milwaukee, whose long-standing stewardship of the town vested the term "socialism," in young Herb's mind, with "a very mild and benign meaning."

Even as a boy, Simon showed the instincts of an autodidact and a polymath. In the well-ordered Simon household, where the children were spared most chores—the Nobel laureate says he still doesn't know how to make a bed—he had plenty of opportunity to explore his interests. He roamed the public library and the museum, which were housed together in a building three miles from his home, a trip he frequently made alone on foot. He got to know every room of the museum and eventually befriended Hy Rich, a graduate student in entomology who worked at the museum. For several summers, Simon would spend long hours at the museum working as a volunteer and occasionally scouring the streams of Milwaukee for specimens.[17]

As a child, Simon was closer to his mother, Edna Merkel Simon, than to his father, who was a somewhat stern German émigré. From Edna, who was an accomplished pianist, Herb learned to play the piano proficiently—Edna's Steinway dominates her son's living room to this day. The considerable influence of his father, Arthur Simon, an electrical engineer and inventor with numerous patents, entered his son's consciousness only gradually. As an engineer, Arthur Simon's main work was designing complex switch gears used to control mining machinery, theater lighting systems, lathes, and battleship gun turrets. In his spare time, Arthur Simon tinkered in his basement workshop, where he built, among other things, the first radio on Juneau Avenue with his young son Herb watching.[18]

Years later, servomechanisms would play an important role in Herb Simon's forays into both artificial intelligence and operations research. It was in 1948, while he was teaching at the Illinois Institute of Technology, that it "gradually dawned on" him that he had been "a closet engineer" since the beginning of his career.[19]

Arthur Simon was also an intellectual. And his library, laden with books on analytical geometry, calculus, and physics, as well as the literary classics, planted the intellectual seeds for the autodidact that Simon was by nature. On cold Saturday afternoons, Herb would read plays such as *The Comedy of Errors*. During family holidays, which were spent in the north woods of Wisconsin, he pored over Dante's *Inferno* and Milton's *Paradise Lost*. Among his father's books, he discovered *The Federalist Papers* and a text on psychology. By the age of twelve, he later boasted, he had taken "his education entirely [into] his own hands."[20]

In 1933, at the height of the Depression, Simon won a scholarship to the University of Chicago, where he would encounter a world in social and intellectual ferment. In those days, the University of Chicago campus was a hotbed of leftist politics and ideological debate among Trotskyites and Stalinists, socialists and New Deal Democrats. A new behavioral, multidisciplinary approach to research and education was also reshaping the social sciences at the school.

Initially, Simon had planned to major in economics. But he wasn't fond of the rigorous rules he encountered in academia. When a calculus professor insisted that Simon attend classes, he responded by quitting the classroom altogether; in the future, all of his study of mathematics would be self-taught. And upon learning that a major in economics required him to take an accounting course—a subject he deemed too dull to merit his attention—he switched his major from economics to political science.

Simon, it was clear, was an inveterate nonconformist in everything from his political views to his academic theories. While still in grammar school, he published a letter in the local paper in defense of atheism. By the time he arrived at the University of Chicago, he considered himself "more or less a socialist." Said Simon, "I was (and am) a New Deal Democrat, probably imprinted by Franklin Delano Roosevelt's inaugural address." And years later, in building his career, he eschewed big-name Ivy League affiliations, preferring to be a big fish (or a whale, as it turned out) in a relatively small pond. For Simon, there was "no greater pleasure than being the underdog, unless it was the pleasure of being the winning underdog."[21]

Simon was still an undergraduate student at the University of Chicago, working on a practical piece of social science research, when, for the first time, he bucked conventional wisdom in a big way. At the time, he was studying a classical budgeting problem in the administration of public recreation in Milwaukee. The "problem"—or rather, his view of it—broke new ground in both economic and administrative theory.

It all started in 1935 with the search for a term paper topic for a course in municipal government. Simon's professor at the time, Jerome

Kerwin, had been studying the relationships between city governments and schools. Kerwin suggested that Simon return to Milwaukee to study the administration of the local playgrounds, which was divided between the school board and the Parks Department.

Simon arrived in Wisconsin to discover that there was a high degree of tension and disagreement between the school board and the Parks Department on how the budget for the playgrounds should be disbursed. At first blush, the problem seemed like a classical budgeting dilemma. The gist of the problem was to figure out how to allocate funds between two divisions of the municipal government that had overlapping responsibilities for the city's playgrounds. At the root of the problem was the fact that while the Playground Division was responsible for construction of the playgrounds, it was the Extension Division of the school board that was responsible for supervising both maintenance and recreation activities at the playgrounds.[22]

For several weeks Simon acted as a reporter, interviewing administrators with both the school board and the Parks Department. The textbook economist's solution to the budgeting dilemma, he realized, would have been to divide the funds so that each dollar spent for park maintenance would produce the same return as each dollar spent for the salaries of recreation leaders.[23]

Yet the more he talked to the administrators in each department, the clearer it became that *no one* was viewing the decision through such a rational economic lens. "They weren't equating marginal thises and thats," he recalls. "I was thinking hard and trying to figure out how to explain each group standing up for what it was familiar with. I lived in the world. I saw that people get attached and loyal to things." He realized that those preferences and loyalties usually weighed more heavily than wholly rational, bottom-line considerations.[24] By virtue of the different cultures of each division, as well as the rules and values they subscribed to, the two groups couldn't agree on the amount of money that should be earmarked for maintenance. "It is . . . understandable that the Playground Division, whose work has been the construction of the physical facilities, should consider it a false economy to inadequately provide for the maintenance of those facilities," wrote Simon. What's more, the Playground Division had used an experimental approach to construction that had led to higher-than-expected maintenance costs.[25]

To the Extension Division of the school board, which had subsisted for years on a shoestring budget, the Playground Division's idea of prudent spending seemed like an extravagance. Faced with the sudden new financial obligations of the new facilities, the Extension Division preferred to "minimize the costs of maintenance so as not to divert funds from supervisory activities."[26]

Recalled Simon, "Was I surprised at their ignoring accepted economic theory? Perhaps, initially, but on reflection, I didn't see how it could be done. How were the values of better activity leadership to be weighed against the values of more attractive and better-maintained neighborhood playgrounds?"[27]

Herein lay Simon's conundrum: "How do human beings reason when the conditions for rationality postulated by neoclassical economics are not met? Investigating further, I thought I could see a rather simple pattern. Those who were organizationally responsible for playground supervision wanted more money spent for leadership; those who were responsible for the physical condition of the playgrounds wanted more spent for maintenance." Generalizing, he realized that people cope with complex problems and organizational issues by identifying with the goals of their own departments.[28]

One answer to the Milwaukee conundrum was that each group made choices based more on the *habits* and *values* of each department, rather than on the basis of some logical formulation. "When people don't know how to optimize, they may very well be able to satisfice, to find good enough solutions," he wrote. "And good enough solutions are often to be found by heuristic search through the maze of possibilities."[29]

Simon saw the problem as one of human decision making and "bounded rationality." In 1945, close to ten years after conducting the study in Milwaukee, he would publish *Administrative Behavior*, a study of the role of decision making in organizations, which had its roots in the Milwaukee study.

Of course, in 1936, Simon, who had never worked in an organization and had barely even studied them, knew he had a great deal to learn. While Kerwin thought highly of Simon's analysis, he wondered aloud why Simon had confined himself to describing organizations rather than evaluating them. Simon's response was that he had had no idea how to go about doing such an evaluation.

To learn, Simon enrolled in a course on "Measuring Municipal Government," which was taught by Clarence Ridley, a leading expert on the subject. The course led to a long collaboration between Simon and Ridley.

At about the same time, Simon became Ridley's research assistant and the coauthor of several leading papers on municipal government. An engineer by training, Ridley was a pioneer when it came to municipal government and had served as city manager of Bluefield, West

Virginia, before becoming an academic. While teaching at the University of Chicago, Ridley also became director of the International City Managers Association, the leading organization for city managers (that is, the administrators of cities that are run by a city manager form of government, as opposed to a mayoralty). At a time when the financial plight of cities had made measuring public services a subject of keen national interest, Ridley launched the *Municipal Year Book*, a project that Simon worked on—which enabled managers to benchmark their city services against those of other municipalities.[30]

To Simon, Ridley was the very model of an effective administrator. Ridley, in fact, was a member of the small pantheon of men whom Simon considered his role models, including Simon's father, Charles Merriam (the chairman of the University of Chicago's Political Science Department), Chester Barnard, and Franklin Delano Roosevelt.

Seeing Ridley at work, Simon became convinced that the one hope for *expanding* human rationality was through enlightened administration. "Watching him, I came to understand that well-managed organizations are powerful instruments for achieving socially important goals, and not yokes around the necks of their members," he recalled, ". . . a view quite opposed to popular folklore in our society, which commonly sees them as dehumanizing bureaucracies."[31]

Simon's own interest in cities was fueled not only by the Depression and his work with Ridley but also by Charles Merriam, who had made public service a key focus of the curriculum. From Merriam, he absorbed a commitment to the empirical approach to political science, including the study of human behavior, psychology, and the full spectrum of social sciences.

Up until Merriam's time, the study of political science had been informed largely by moral philosophy. By contrast, Merriam, who had run for mayor of Chicago in 1911 (and lost), believed in empirical research. Merriam conducted such groundbreaking studies as *Non-Voting* at least a decade before public opinion polls became part of the American political process. Merriam was concerned with developing new data-gathering methodologies, such as statistical sampling, and new ways of understanding the *intentions*, rather than just the *actions*, of individuals.[32]

The deepening economic crisis of the Depression had fostered a surge in new ideas and efforts at improving government administration. Many of these efforts centered around Chicago. In the winter of 1930, Louis Brownlow, who had served as an official in the Wilson administration and was an expert on public administration, set up the Public Administration Clearing House with backing from Luther Gulick and funding from the Spelman Fund under Beardsley Ruml. (A few years later, Brownlow, together with Gulick and Charles Merriam, would be appointed by President Roosevelt to the President's Committee on Administrative Management, which proposed improvements in the organization of the federal government.) PACH was a consortium of national professional organizations, such as the American Public Works Association and the International City Managers Association.[33]

Brownlow had chosen Chicago as a base instead of Washington, partly because the Windy City was home to a number of government service organizations. He wanted to be near the locus of ideas on public administration, which were then percolating at the University of Chicago. Ruml also moved to Chicago to take over the deanship of the Social Science Division at the University of Chicago.

Here at teatime on the second floor of the university's new Social Sciences Building—Ruml had raised the funds for the building as part of his theory that related ideas in education and management should be housed in a common physical space—the diverse ideas that so attracted Simon were steeped along with the tea in a large samovar. "One went in, put down a nickel, picked up a cup of tea and a cookie, and plunged into the maelstrom of conversation," Brownlow recalled. "In 1933 the conversation was almost always about immediate crises."[34] The preoccupations of the Depression rubbed off on Simon. In 1937, together with Bill Cooper, a friend who would go on to become a colleague and sometime professional rival, and Dorothea Pye, a fellow graduate student and secretary in the Political Science Department whom he would soon marry, Simon formed the Progressive Club. With its prime focus on local government, the club got off to a running start when it succeeded in recruiting as charter members such academic stars as Charles Merriam, Jerome Kerwin, and Paul Douglas. Herb and Dorothea also joined the Hyde Park Independent Voters, which supported antimachine candidates for city office, and canvassed the Fifth Ward for their candidate.[35]

Giving voice to the political passions that informed his youth, Simon wrote in a 1995 edition of *Public Administration Review*, "The attractions of libertarianism . . . will fade in the face of the world's great social problems of population, of environment, of energy, of peace. . . . [W]e will learn that government plays an essential and honorable role. . . . No lesson needs so much to be taught today as the lesson that democracy requires politics, and that human society requires social programs and effective administration of these programs."[36]

In addition to Roosevelt-era democratic values, under Merriam's influence Simon absorbed the "commitment to the proposition that political science was science." Along with that commitment went a belief in a multidisciplinary approach to learning that "made the whole university, and all of the methodologies present in it, available to the students of political science." Such disparate fields as sociology and survey methodology, psychology and mathematical economics, and econometrics were all free game to Merriam's students in the study of political processes and human behavior.[37]

It was at this time, too, that Simon first stumbled across Chester Barnard, whose influential book *The Functions of the Executive* was published in 1938. "Organizations, it appeared, could be understood by applying to them what you knew of human behavior generally," says Simon. The "phenomena of loyalty and identification," for example, were apparent everywhere—in school, in Barnard's corporation, in the Milwaukee Parks Department and School District. "It even occurred to me that the mediating role I had sometimes played as a boy, when misunderstandings arose between my mother and grandmother, was not wholly unlike the role of the foreman as 'man in the middle,' " he wrote, referring to another groundbreaking study in organizational behavior, *Management and the Worker* by Fritz Roethlisberger and William J. Dixon (see Chapter 4).[38]

Under the influence of both Ridley and Merriam, as well as Barnard's book and the Milwaukee study, Simon began to formulate an idea for his doctoral thesis. The thesis, which eventually would be rewritten and published as *Administrative Behavior*, was to analyze the decision-making processes in organizations.

Simon's doctoral thesis, however, would be written far from the fountainhead of ideas at the University of Chicago. In late spring of 1938, he was still working for Ridley when he won a Rockefeller Foundation grant to continue some studies of local government that had been started in Berkeley, California, by the Bureau of Public Administration as part of a "white-collar" WPA project. A few months earlier, he had married Dorothea. Together the newlyweds set out on a cross-country train trip to Berkeley, where they lived for the next three years.

At Berkeley, Simon undertook a series of studies that sought to show how quantitative empirical research could contribute to the understanding and solution of municipal problems. Although he was already at work on his thesis, most of his California papers were pioneering studies in cost-benefit analysis rather than bounded rationality. The first study, for example, sought to determine how large the caseloads of social workers should be for the most effective operation of the agency.

Although they had little to do with his later work, the California studies also gave Simon his first chance at hands-on administration on a large scale—an experience he learned to relish. As director of administrative measurement studies, he was responsible for a staff of more than fifty employees, most of them WPA workers. When he was studying the State Relief Administration, the number of employees climbed to several hundred.

Simon enjoyed outsmarting local bureaucrats. At the time, the SRA was embroiled in a political donnybrook, the result of both internecine rivalries within the Democratic Party as well as battles between Republicans and Democrats in the state legislature. Simon didn't hesitate to move in and fill the vacuum created by the political tempests. As he recalls of one of the projects that frequently took him to Los Angeles, "More than once we arrived at one of our district offices on a Monday morning to find that the director had been fired. We would then proceed down to the state headquarters, also in Los Angeles, pound on the desk, and demand (and get) the director's reinstatement. The political situation was so confused that no one knew what authority we had, and those momentarily in charge assumed we would not be so peremptory if we had none."[39]

Simon clearly relished the exercise of authority. Although after the California years he never spent much time away from academia again, he would, throughout his life, play a variety of advisory roles in government. For example, he served as a consultant to the Bureau of the Budget during World War II. He also served on the President's Science Advisory Committee (PSAC) under both Johnson and Nixon.

With each foray into bureaucracy, Simon demonstrated an uncanny skill at pushing his own agenda. In a letter to Simon about his leadership of a PSAC panel on auto emissions, William H. Drury of the Massachusetts Audubon Society wrote, "I enjoyed the opportunity of observing your leadership of the discussions. In your hand that is an art, but for some reason your adeptness doesn't lead to suspicion on the part of the led. It has been a chance to become wiser about the so-called operations of the government."[40]

It was, however, through Simon's work on the Economic Cooperation Administration (ECA), which was responsible for implementing the Marshall Plan after the war, that his role in a real organization and his theories about decision making converged most fully. At the time, there were six alternative approaches to how Marshall Plan funds should be disbursed in Europe. Simon, who was part of a core staff of administrators who were present at ECA's birth in 1948, felt strongly that the allocation of funds should be based on negotiations with a unified Europe through a central Paris office, as opposed to, say, bilateral negotiations with individual countries. Even then, says Simon, he believed in the concept of a European union.

To champion their own viewpoint, Simon and his colleagues drafted a document entitled "Basic Principles of ECA Organization," which described the mission of ECA as *they* defined it. The group then disseminated the document as ECA grew into an agency of more than seven hundred people. Noted Simon, "Our policy document never received any official approval—that would have taken months and much compromise—but it was widely circulated, giving each new person who entered the organization a specific picture of what it was about." Thus the "Basic Principles" served as an instrument of the informal organization.[41]

In effect, the memo provided ECA's incoming administrators, who were new at their jobs and who faced the complex task of funneling aid to Europe quickly, a plausible (good-enough) plan. "The idea behind the document was that a relatively brief draft memorandum of some two thousand words *might* gain some circulation in the agency, that it *might* actually be read by a few influential people, and that a few of the central concepts *might* be absorbed and influence future thinking."[42]

Simon, for one, also relied on the probability that this good-enough solution would short-circuit the search for alternatives. Circulating through ECA in what must have seemed like an official form and in the absence of rival documents (at least in the early stages of the organization), it must have carried added weight. Wrote Simon, "This conception of the program served as both a weapon and a motive for the competitors in the power struggle that went on in this, as in every burgeoning organization. Units that fit the conception could use it to claim a larger place in the program."[43]

In 1942, after completing his work at Berkeley, Simon accepted a teaching job at the Illinois Institute of Technology. He was glad to return to Chicago. Living on the South Side of Chicago (in the same building as Milton Friedman), he once again thrived on the intellectual life of the city.

It was during this period that Simon undertook his "reeducation" in economics. At the urging of Cooper, who was teaching at the University of Chicago at the time, he joined the Cowles Commission for Research in Economics. At the forefront of postwar developments in mathematical economics and econometrics, the Cowles Commission brought together many of the men who would go on to win the Nobel Prize in Economic Science during the two decades after it was established in 1969, including Kenneth Arrow, Tjalling Koopmans, and Franco Modigliani.[44]

To Simon, the Cowles seminars, which were held once a week, represented the best of the "invisible college" that not only had nurtured his intellectual development but also would foster his ability to pursue decision making across the borders of numerous scientific disciplines. "The typical scientist is not a guy who doesn't show up at meetings," he remarked years ago. "He participates. Science is not only the invention of ideas, but the propagation of ideas."[45]

Long after his involvement with the Cowles Commission had ended, Simon stayed close to many of its members. Jascha Marschak and Tjalling Koopmans, in particular, became lifelong friends. And it was through Simon and Cooper that Modigliani came to Carnegie Tech in the 1950s. Many of Simon's former Cowles Commission colleagues, including Koopmans, Marschak, and Arrow, also later turned up at the RAND Corporation, which was home to the earliest research on computers and artificial intelligence (see Chapter 5). It was also undoubtedly through his Cowles Commission associations that Simon's name was kept before the Nobel committee long after he had shifted his focus away from economics.

In the spring of 1945, Simon sent Chester Barnard, whom he had never met, a copy of his manuscript. Barnard's response made it clear just how important *Administrative Behavior* was to become in the world of organizational theory. "This is the first book on administration I have read that I think is valuable," wrote Barnard to Simon, applauding Simon's attempt to build a theory of decision making. Paraphrasing the philosopher A. N. Whitehead, Barnard added, "[I]t is impossible to get anywhere with bare facts without a theory since without a theory there is no basis for determining what facts are relevant and evidential." During the next several months, Barnard poured over *Administrative Behavior* sentence by sentence, sending Simon a lengthy critique of his work. Barnard eventually wrote the foreword to the book. The two men met just once, probably in Chicago when Barnard was traveling through the Windy City.[46]

While *Administrative Behavior* won kudos in academic circles following the war, the field of public administration, with which the book was identified, had fallen out of vogue. Thus, it was not until Simon moved to Carnegie Tech a few years later that he encountered a group of academics with whom he could pursue further research on the ideas he had first laid out in *Administrative Behavior*.

With the publication of *Administrative Behavior*, Simon assumed a position of power at IIT. By 1946, at the age of thirty, he took over the reins of the Department of Political and Social Sciences. In 1947, with the publication of *Administrative Behavior*, he was promoted to full professor.

Given his new position, Simon was not eager to leave IIT. But in 1948, Bill Cooper, who had recently joined the Carnegie Tech faculty in Pittsburgh, invited Simon to give a seminar, the first of several recruiting overtures from Carnegie's newly formed Graduate School of Industrial Administration. Arriving on campus in midwinter, Simon was pleasantly surprised by the university's verdant surroundings, which were in sharp contrast to Pittsburgh's reputation as the "Smoky City." Henry Hornbostel's stately Palladian buildings were set against a winter white backdrop, with snow-covered Schenley Park visible in the distance. Simon soon became convinced that the "financial resources of GSIA could launch, much sooner than at IIT, the sort of empirical research on organizations that seemed the logical sequel to *Administrative Behavior*."[47]

The upheaval of the 1930s and 1940s had paved the way for a number of important new movements in economics and organizational theory. The length and virulence of the Depression, which had defied all conventionally held rules of classical economics, had brought about a crisis in the economics profession and paved the way for the theories of John Maynard Keynes. Keynesianism—the notion that government fiscal policy could regulate aggregate demand and mitigate major cyclical swings in the economy—fit in neatly with the University of Chicago's interest in government policy. (Though the subject was taken up by the Cowles Commission, it did not begin to have a major impact on the University of Chicago until after Simon had graduated.)[48]

World War II had also spawned operations research, and in the aftermath of the war businesses and academics were experimenting with transferring those tools to peacetime applications. The behavioral sciences were flourishing, nourished in part by the publication of Barnard's *Functions of the Executive*, Roethlisberger and Dixon's *Management and the Worker*, and Simon's *Administrative Behavior*.

Another important trend was the search for new avenues of research that would prevent the world—the United States, in particular—from falling back into economic chaos. The Depression and war production had transformed virtually every sector of economic activity since the 1920s. Yet the world seemed dangerously short of the knowledge that was needed to guarantee economic growth and security. And, as the end of World War II ushered in the Cold War, international tensions remained high. "If war should break out again, it was argued, the United States would need to remobilize its economy almost overnight," according to a study by the Graduate Management Admissions Council. "Research was needed to determine how to do this better than it had been done between 1941 and 1944."[49]

Viewed with the benefit of hindsight, the 1950s now seem like a "golden age" of opportunity for business. At the time, however, the beginning of the Korean War, a new Red scare, a galloping arms race, and the steady escalation of the Cold War made Americans feel less secure than ever. H. Rowan Gaither, head of the Ford Foundation during most of the 1950s, spearheaded multimillion-dollar research grants for the study of American business, justifying the investment, at least in part, as a way to fight communism. Gaither's goal was nothing less than the achievement of "quantum improvements" in U.S. management: "If we are to achieve a better realization of democratic goals within the United States and for the peoples of the world, our domestic economy must stand as an example before the world as a strong and growing economy characterized by high output, the highest possible level of constructive employment and a minimum of destructive instability."[50]

The stage was set for pioneering a new era in management. Moreover, it was particularly suited to an approach that drew both on the rigorous quantitative analysis that had been key to successful military production and deployment during the war and on the emerging theories of human behavior that were "percolating" in the social sciences, especially at the University of Chicago. (Of course, as many U.S. industries, and universities and even the tacticians of the Vietnam War would later discover, quantitative methods were not a panacea for management.)

Thus, it was not surprising that when William Larimer Mellon gave $6 million to establish a new business school at Carnegie Tech in Pittsburgh in 1949, the founders of GSIA tapped Herbert Simon and several of his former colleagues from the University of Chicago. Under the leadership of George Leland Bach, a University of Chicago–trained economist, GSIA aimed to "address the needs of practitioners and to develop, nearly from scratch, a new, scientifically grounded academic discipline."[51] And who better to help establish such an eclectic approach to business and economics than the intellectual "fly-by-nights" from the University of Chicago?

To a core group of neoclassical economists who already were at work at Carnegie Tech and would be incorporated into GSIA, Bach sought out a small cadre of innovators who would introduce a host of countervailing disciplines and perspectives. Chief among Bach's recruits was William W. Cooper, the University of Chicago–trained economist who had worked at both the Tennessee Valley Authority and, during the war, at the Bureau of the Budget, which later became the Office of Management and Budget. According to Simon, Cooper was "a revolutionary." Indeed, his approach to economics and accounting was so "offbeat" that his thesis committee at Columbia University couldn't understand it and refused to grant him a Ph.D. Yet his contributions to economics and management came to be so widely recognized that his lack of a "union card" never got in the way. Recalled Simon, "Most people . . . just supposed he had one."[52]

Cooper became a prime innovator in the burgeoning field of operations research, which applied quantitative tools to managerial problem solving and expert decision making and first came into use during World War II. In particular, he pioneered the field of linear programming. In the business world, he was best known for successfully applying linear programming to improving the efficiency of the oil-refining process; this replaced the rule-of-thumb expertise that petroleum engineers heretofore had used. Cooper's expert system evaluated the various grades of petroleum and the cost of producing them at any given time, and came up with the optimum mix for achieving a desired quality at the lowest cost.

Years later, quantitative methods would be used in everything from tactical warfare to planning corporate strategy, sometimes with disastrous consequences (see Chapter 5). But in the 1940s, quantitative methods were the shining new scientific solution to the messiness—and limitations—of human organizations and decision making.

More so than either Simon and Cooper, Elliott Dunlap Smith, another of "Bach's boys," was a Renaissance man where business education was concerned. Although Smith had been a member of the Yale Economics Department, most of his scholarship had been in the application of new psychological knowledge to the problems of business administration. He had also spent more than a decade at the Dennison Manufacturing Company, serving both as personnel manager and as a division manager.[53]

The final addition to the GSIA team—and a ballast to both the neoclassical economists and the innovators from Chicago—would be a Harvard Business School man. Melvin Anshen, who joined GSIA in the early 1950s, had taught marketing and policy at Harvard and was a proponent of the case method. While his subject and approach to teaching differed radically from those of the rest of GSIA's senior team, he found common ground with his colleagues in the government work he had done during World War II. Like Bach and Cooper, Anshen had worked in Washington during the war, conducting statistical work and studying material allocations at the War Production Board. (Bach had been with the Federal Reserve and later the Hoover Commission, and Cooper had been at the Bureau of the Budget.)[54]

Together, "Bach's boys" made a formidable team. "Almost none of the founding fathers of GSIA (except Provost Smith) had extensive backgrounds in management or business education," recalled Simon. "We were social scientists who had discovered in one way or another that organizational and business environments provide a fertile source of basic research ideas, and who therefore did not regard *basic* and *applied* as antithetical terms. Accurately or not, we perceived American business education at that time as a wasteland of vocationalism that needed to be transformed into science-based professionalism, as medicine and engineering had been transformed a generation or two earlier."[55]

In the summer of 1949, Herb, Dorothea, and their three children moved to Pittsburgh. They bought a house just a mile from Carnegie Tech (the institute became Carnegie Mellon University in 1967) where they would live for the next forty years.

Throughout the early 1950s, Simon collaborated with Richard Cyert and James G. March to build on his original work on bounded rationality. Together with a handful of graduate students, the GSIA team pursued a series of empirical studies, including ones that analyzed the decision-making process in several companies, trying to shed light on decision-making behavior in firms on both the individual and the group level. Significantly, said March, "the studies were not part of a grand project scheme, but grew out of the ideas that were floating around" at the time. They probed the difficulties organizations encounter in selecting the problems they plan to tackle during any given point in time. They sought to understand the way organizations reconcile the myriad inconsistent goals and conflicts of interest within firms. And they analyzed the search for alternatives. In 1958, March and Simon published *Organizations*, the first major harvest of their joint research. In 1963, Cyert and March published the principal fruit of that collaboration, *The Behavioral Theory of the Firm*, a book that drew on, and gave extensive credit to, Simon.[56]

By introducing the idea of bounded rationality and uncertainty into the management equation, Simon, March, and Cyert shifted the focus of the management philosophers from organizational theory to behavioral theory. If much of the analysis of organizations thus far had concerned itself with the problem of *coordinating* specific tasks and complex institutions—using either the "visible hand of management" or the "invisible hand of the market"—bounded rationality and the behavioral theory of the firm focused the spotlight on *decision making*. In particular, they were interested in the factors that affect employees and groups of employees as they make decisions in a world limited by their ability to absorb and process information. And they were interested in the implications that such behavior had for the way in which firms are organized.

One of Simon's most significant observations was the importance of premises, habits, and "ordinary rules of behavior" in shaping human choices and decisions. First, he likened the way that people typically set agendas to a two-bin inventory system: "For each need or want there is an 'order point' and an 'order quantity.' " When inventory levels are low, the Order Department typically reorders the depleted merchandise unless some other emergency has deflected its attention. Second, he said, both group and individual decisions are influenced subconsciously by the conditioning of habit. Wrote Simon, "Once a habit has been established, the mere presence of the stimulus tends to release the habitual behavior without further conscious thought.... This is a point that has far-reaching implications for organization."[57]

In a humorous adaptation of Simon's favorite metaphor for the limitations of human decision making—the search for a needle in a haystack—March explained Simon's theory as follows:

> The standard metaphor for the theory reflects both the simplicity of the ideas and the memories of a Wisconsin boyhood. Consider a farmer confronting a haystack and deciding what to do with it. To make a decision in purely classical form, he would want to know (among other things) all of the contents of the haystack, all possible uses of each of the contents and combinations of them, and the probability distribution over all possible consequences of each. Simon observed that few farmers behave in such a way. A more typical farmer reduces the size of the problem. He notices that his shirt needs a button, and considers looking for the sharpest needle in the haystack. That seems a difficult thing to do, so he decides to look for any needle good enough to sew a button. But then he remembers an old family rule that shirts needing buttons should be hung in the laundry. So he does that. Simon's great contribution was to point out that decision making in economic organizations is more like hanging a shirt in the laundry than looking for the sharpest needle in the haystack.[58]

Motivation was another important subtext of Simon's work. But Simon's concern was not with morale and motivation in the inspirational sense. "High morale is not a sufficient condition for high productivity, and does not necessarily lead to higher productivity than low morale," wrote March and Simon in *Organizations*. "One would not predict that 'satisfied' rats would perform best in a T-maze. Similarly, there is no reason for predicting that high satisfaction, per se, motivates a given individual to conform to the goals specified by the hierarchy."[59]

People are clearly much too complicated to respond in a predictable manner to simple carrot-and-stick manipulations. Similarly, organizations, with their myriad employees and systems, existing within a changing and uncertain environment, can never fully grasp the consequences, both intended and unintended, that follow from specific actions and policies of management. Simon recognized the important role played by the informal organization and informal communication systems precisely because it is in this sphere that organizational objectives and personal goals meet or collide. He also recognized the importance of organizational loyalty and identification in helping the administrator narrow his choices to fit organizational aims; organizational identification, after all, had held the key to the playground dilemma in the Milwaukee study. Similarly, he saw the problems that organizational loyalties can cause: "The principal undesirable effect of identification is that it prevents the . . . individual from making correct decisions" when the subgoals of, say, a department or division with which he identifies should be "weighed against other values outside that area" but are not.[60]

Most provocatively, Simon and Company recognized that understanding the processes of human decision making, search, and aspiration levels was necessary not only for survival and productivity but also for innovation. "We are concerned with the switching mechanisms by which organization members shift their attention from their more regular concerns to the search for new alternatives," wrote March and Simon in *Organizations*. More recently, creativity, intuition, and how experts think has become a key focus of Simon's work in cognitive psychology.[61]

What Simon began as a relatively theoretical formulation in *Administrative Behavior*, Cyert and March sought to detail with empirical studies in *The Behavioral Theory of the Firm*. In 1953, they began a series of in-depth studies of the decision-making process, seeking to describe some of the properties and rules that characterize certain types of decisions. For example, the authors studied the branch plant of a heavy manufacturing company in the aftermath of an accident in which one worker was killed; they observed management's decision-making process as it evaluated various strategies for improving safety standards, including a proposal to purchase new equipment. The authors uncovered a textbook case of bounded rationality, including conflicts of interest, the hidden agendas of different departments, the dissemination of misinformation, and the generation of wildly variable cost estimates.

Ultimately, *The Behavioral Theory of the Firm* was not so much a definitive theory as a beginning of the sort of empirical research the authors felt was needed to develop a meaningful understanding of organizations. The authors amassed further proof that organizations are, at best, "adaptively rational" entities that are capable of "learn(ing) from . . . experience."[62]

The authors acknowledged that, by necessity, the book was something of an abstraction of the complex situations they encountered within each organization. Yet, wrote Cyert and March, "The justification lies in our . . . hope that the data will provide a start for empirical research in an area of extensive ad hoc theory."[63]

One of the most provocative outcomes of this work, which in and of itself served as empirical proof of the role of bounded rationality, was the theory of organizational slack, which was developed by Cyert and March. Organizational slack, in essence, is the difference between a company's performance and its potential performance, which is defined by various organizational inefficiencies such as excess expenditures, suboptimal technologies, and unexploited opportunities. "Slack arises both because there is conflict within an organization and [because] different parts of an organization seek to realize their own objectives," sometimes at the expense of the overall goals of the firm, explains March.[64]

Slack also arises because organizations "satisfice"—that is, they look for alternatives that meet their targets rather than optimize by looking for a single best alternative. Slack has two major consequences, explains March: "First, slack contributes to performance smoothing. In this regard it functions very much like energy reserves in human and other species. When things are going poorly, an organization can improve performance by cutting into the slack. As a result slack buffers the organization from adversity by providing an emergency reserve of potential performance. On the other hand, when things are going well, slack is accumulated. In effect, potential performance is stored for possible future use.

"Second, slack protects organizational experiments and diversity from central observation and pressure. When slack is high, control is loosened and projects of local interest can be undertaken."[65] One classic example is the skunk works that many companies establish, using departmental budget surpluses to fund projects that haven't received official sanction.

The problem of developing a theory of decision making would seem to be hopelessly confounded by the nearly infinite variety of decisions and the circumstances on which decisions can be predicated. Yet Cyert and March undoubtedly began to lay the groundwork for beginning to understand the key behavioral elements that influence the process. For example, to understand decision making, they believe, one has to understand the process of search, including the conditions under which search will be intensified. In effect, they showed how decision-making processes tend to favor short-term, familiar solutions, rather than long-term, new solutions. For one thing, organizations don't try to anticipate the future by searching for alternatives all the time; rather, they "monitor for problems and react to them."[66]

Wrote Cyert and March, "In general, we predict that a firm will look first for new alternatives or new information in the area it views as most under its control. . . . Organizational choice is heavily conditioned by the rules within which it occurs." According to this hierarchy of control, the authors predicted that cost considerations will come first, demand estimates will come second, and organizational objectives will be left until last. The reason is that objectives involve the "whole environment" of the firm and are, therefore, the least controllable. Costs, by contrast, are internal to the firm and relatively easy to reduce. And demand is external and *may* be predicted. In addition, the authors argued that how individuals and organizations perform relative to their aspiration levels has a keen influence on decision making, especially on their willingness to take risks. Thus, search is biased by "the training, experience, and desires" of those who are conducting the search.[67]

While work on the behavioral theory of the firm was relatively short-lived at Carnegie, Simon's core idea and Cyert and March's explication of it flourished elsewhere, spawning a rich legacy of thought that has fundamentally changed everything from economics and organizational theory to antitrust policy and the law. Bounded rationality is, for example, at the root of so-called resource-based or knowledge-based approaches to corporate strategy (see Chapter 9). Because bounded rationality sees knowledge as a scarce resource, competitive advantage, according to the resource-based view, flows from an organization's idiosyncratic, difficult-to-imitate resources, such as 3M's legendary competence with sticky tape. "In dreaming up businesses as diverse as 'post-it' notes, magnetic tape, photographic film, pressure-sensitive tapes, and coated abrasives, the company has brought to bear widely shared competencies in substrates, coatings, and adhesives and devised various ways to combine them. What seems to be an extremely diversified portfolio of businesses belies a few shared core competencies," wrote C. K. Prahalad and Gary Hamel in their famous 1990 Harvard Business School article, "The Core Competence of the Corporation."[68] This resource-based view, which seems particularly relevant to technology companies, has been championed by David Teece at Berkeley and popularized in management circles by Prahalad and Hamel.[69]

Another offshoot of bounded rationality that has had perhaps the farthest-reaching impact is so-called transaction cost economics. In its interdisciplinary approach, the theory is a true brainchild of Carnegie. "While *The Behavioral Theory of the Firm* has been described as the intersection of economics and organization theory, transaction cost economics works from the intersection of law, economics, and organization," says Oliver Williamson, a protégé of Simon and Cyert in the early 1960s. To Williamson, the principal lesson of bounded rationality is that "all complex contracts are unavoidably incomplete" precisely because humans are incapable of taking into account all possible contingencies. By linking bounded rationality to the law, transaction cost economics has been instrumental in moving contract law away from a legalistic, letter-of-the-law approach to one that includes contract law as a flexible framework. In other words, by recognizing that no contract can anticipate all contingencies and circumstance (and trying to do so would be uneconomical), Williamson argues that the *intent* of an agreement can be as important as the letter. In contrast to both classical economists and the behavioral theorists, however, Williamson argued that organizations neither maximize nor satisfice; what they really strive to do is to *economize* (see Chapter 9). Recognizing the mind as a scarce resource, managers attempt to deploy cognitive capacity effectively and to mitigate contractual breakdowns, according to Williamson.[70]

Finally, bounded rationality created a foundation for the evolutionary theory of the firm put forward by Richard Nelson and Sidney Winter. Neither Nelson nor Winter was closely linked to Carnegie (though Nelson did teach at GSIA for one year in 1960). However, based in large part on Simon's work and the behavioral theory of the firm, Nelson and Winter adopted one of the most compelling evolutionary analogies to explain how firms behave, arguing that they are strongly influenced by their histories and the routines they have developed. (Milton Friedman had seized on the evolutionary analogy when he referred to "natural selection" to explain how firms that come closest to profit maximizing are the fittest and most likely to survive. Edith Penrose, a respected economist, however, put a dent in this argument when she pointed out that for natural selection to work, there must be heritable characteristics— i.e., behavior that isn't purely accidental but is replicable over time.) "There has to be some equivalent to the genetic constitution or genotype, such as the structural characteristics, routines or culture of the firm, which fixes, determines, moulds or constrains the phenotype in some way," argued Geoffrey M. Hodgson.[71]

To explain why some firms flourish, while others that are superficially similar don't, Nelson and Winter argued that organizations nurture routines and patterns of behavior that are both hearty and self-perpetuating. Although not as sturdy as genes, these routines help firms retain skills, knowledge, and the sort of core competencies that enable a company such as 3M to consistently come up with innovations that other companies with comparable R-and-D budgets can't match. Moreover, Nelson and Winter argued that winning evolutionary traits do not necessarily involve profit maximizing. Rather, they include technical competencies and policies (such as those of 3M), hiring and firing procedures, inventory and production management, and procedures for setting business strategy.[72]

Moreover, Nelson and Winter recognized that much business behavior is not routine but fundamentally *innovative.* Borrowing another concept from evolutionary biology, they developed a theory of economic mutuation and built it on the concept of "search" developed by Cyert, March, and Simon. The evolutionists argued that profitable firms tend to maintain their routines and don't search for alternatives. By contrast, when profitability suffers, they search for alternative strategies and routines—new approaches to R and D, new personnel policies, and so on—that will restore profitability. Thus, Nelson and Winter provide a powerful insight into how managerial routines affect culture and performance, as well as the conditions under which organizational learning can take place.[73]

■

A more fertile decade in the life of an academic institution than the 1950s at GSIA can hardly be imagined. Yet for all the creative dialogue that nourished the pioneers at GSIA, tensions soon emerged between the disparate factions—in particular, between the neoclassical economists and the behavioralists. Recalled Williamson, "The astonishing thing about Carnegie is that it joined two very fundamental and seemingly incompatible strands. . . . The one dealt with bounded rationality, organization theory, and behavioral economics. . . . The second strand dealt with rational expectations and efficient markets."[74]

Tension also developed between the behaviorists and the operations researchers. It soon became clear that Cooper and Simon couldn't agree on a proper focus for business school research, especially what the balance between empirical research and quantification should be. Simon felt that Cooper's operations research group was overly fascinated with "abstract mathematical techniques," was "too formal and one-sided," and lacked an appreciation for the need for empirical research within firms that he and Richard Cyert and James March were advocating. Indeed, the debate at GSIA proved to be a preview of the struggle that would ensue on campuses and industries across the nation.

At GSIA, the crisis reached a boiling point in the summer of 1951, when the economists and operations researchers decided to unite against the behavioralists. One July evening, Cooper confronted Simon at a bar in the Shadyside section of Pittsburgh. He accused Simon of bullying his colleagues and using his position at GSIA to intimidate the faculty who disagreed with him, and urged him to resign as chairman of the Industrial Management Department.[75]

Simon did not resign. And by most accounts the tension persisted for, at least, two years. Ultimately, noted Simon, "The problems that created the crisis did not wholly go away; they were built into the fabric of the GSIA mission. . . . Keeping the balance of the scientific and the professional, of the economic and the behavioral, was an arduous job. . . . [It was] very much like mixing oil with water. . . . Left to themselves, the oil and water will separate again. So also will the disciplines and professions. . . . [B]y hard work we managed to keep GSIA pretty well emulsified, at least until the 1960s."[76]

The core issues were soon obscured by the sideshow of a recurring duel between Simon and Franco Modigliani. On the face of it, the Simon/Modigliani jousts should have been the stuff of good intellectual repartee, precisely what the two men had come to enjoy during their years on the Cowles Commission—the two future Nobel laureates and their families had, in fact, become friends after the Modiglianis had moved to Pittsburgh.

Modigliani's monetarist and Keynesian macroeconomist ideas were diametrically opposed to Simon's. The disagreements between Simon and Modigliani, however, were based as much on style as on substance. During the 1950s, young faculty members quickly learned that if they were giving a talk at one of GSIA's weekly faculty seminars, "there had better be only one piece of chalk in the room." Incoming faculty soon discovered that few faculty seminars attended by both Simon and Modigliani would last more than a few minutes. In no time at all, "Franco or Herb would stride up to the front of the room, grab the chalk and give an entirely different seminar," recalls one faculty member. "There were knock-down-drag-out fights between Modigliani and Simon. Herb comes out of the University of Chicago tradition. If he gets into an argument, he will win it, even if he has to make up the numbers." The feuding didn't stop, until Modigliani left GSIA for MIT, several years before he won the Nobel Prize. (While many of the neoclassical economists at Carnegie blamed Simon for Modigliani's departure, others point out that the exodus that swept up March, Cooper, and Bach, among others, was a natural outcome of "an academic nova that self-destructed by virtue of its own excellence," as well as heavy recruiting by other big-name institutions.)[77]

Indeed, Simon's love of argument—regardless of the subject or the setting—was legendary. Recalls Lester Lave, another colleague, "At one time, before Simon had become famous, he had the habit of coming into the GSIA cafeteria, choosing a table at random, and introducing himself to the others at the table. He would turn to them and say, 'Tell me about your research.' Herb would listen for two minutes and then announce: 'Unfortunately, you're wrong.' And then he would hold forth on whatever the subject was—physics, say—and see how long he could maintain his position.

"To Herb it was great fun, a mind game," says Lave. "Pretty soon people knew who Herb was, and they wouldn't let him sit down. Herb never intended it to be hostile or obnoxious. He was just having fun. 'Why isn't everyone else?' he'd wonder."[78]

Simon won many of his intellectual jousts. But in the end, the number crunchers and the economists won the war—to the long-term detriment of GSIA. He found it increasingly difficult to get appointments for his doctoral students. It didn't help that he refused to temper his arguments or veil his contempt for mainstream neoclassical economics. "I was prepared to preach the heresies of bounded rationality to economists . . . in season and out," he said. In the end, GSIA became inhospitable to all views but those of the neoclassical economists, a legacy the school would come to rue as age, ill health, and new preoccupations diminished the role of the behaviorists, leaving a vacuum at the school.[79]

For Simon, scientific debate has always been as much a part of life as breathing. Even at home, the conversation would start as soon as Simon returned from work in the evening; sitting in the kitchen while Dorothea fixed dinner, Simon would regale his wife with his latest ideas. Dorothea, who holds master's degrees in both political science and education and has coauthored numerous academic papers with her husband, including one on learning theory, is easily up to the repartee. Indeed, when Simon proposed to Dorothea, he did so only after extracting a promise from her that she would learn calculus. Although it took several years, she eventually lived up to her promise.[80]

The conversations, which frequently turned into debates—would continue at the dinner table. "It got to be a joke in our house," recalls

Katherine Simon Frank, the eldest of Simon's three children. "There always had to be a bookcase with an encyclopedia, a good dictionary, the World Almanac, bird books, tree books, maps, and atlases near at hand. In conversation things came up, and you had to be able to answer the questions. You couldn't *not* know the right name or the right date. There was always someone jumping up from the dinner table" to check a reference. Questions about homework would spark fresh discussions. Before a typical evening was over, Simon would inevitably sit down to his mother's Steinway, which still sits in the couple's living room, and play, more often than not, one of the "B's": Bartók, Beethoven, Brahms, or Bach. Recalls Katherine, "I loved to go to bed hearing the vague wisping sound" of the piano wafting up the stairs.[81]

It was also during this "communal time" that Simon could sit for hours near the parlor window, memorizing vocabulary and the basic rules of grammar of whatever language he happened to be studying at the time. Then, balancing a work of literature (written in its native language) on one knee and a dictionary on the other, he would painstakingly master it. "He told me once," says Katherine, "that when he gives a lecture in a foreign country he delivers at least the first sentence in the native tongue." His passion for learning languages was "a way of connecting with people wherever he went" and yet another way to generate new conversations.[82]

Yet Simon's combativeness in the workplace eventually lost him his strongest allies within GSIA. At the same time, his interest in decision making had diverted his attention to the nascent field of artificial intelligence.

■

In January 1956, Simon arrived at a class he was teaching on mathematical modeling in the social sciences and could hardly contain his excitement. To his startled students, he announced, "Over Christmas vacation Allen Newell and I invented a thinking machine." It was, he later observed, the most important event in his life as a scientist.[83]

Four years earlier, Simon had been serving as a consultant to the RAND Corporation when he met Allen Newell, a brilliant young computer scientist. Newell and Simon shared a love of mountain hiking and a fascination with decision making. Their encounter quickly developed into a close friendship and years-long collaboration.[84]

The two men met at RAND during an ambitious experiment in group decision making for which Newell had secured funding from the Air Force. The experiment involved building a full-scale simulation of an Air Force Early Warning Station. Newell worked on the experiment with

J. C. Shaw, a systems programmer. Together they demonstrated that a computer—even a crude one—could generate not just numbers but symbols, in this case representing location points on a two-dimensional map.

Simon who was serving as a consultant on Newell's experiment and who had followed the developments in computer technology ever since his days at the University of Chicago, was hooked. In the summer of 1954, he taught himself to program IBM's first stored-program computer, the 701. And Newell and Simon discussed the possibility of using a computer to simulate "all sorts of information processes," including human thinking.[85]

Newell already had made plans to move to Pittsburgh to work with Simon on organizational research and to complete his Ph.D. Now he abandoned his plans to do industrial research and planned instead to do his doctoral research on programming a chess machine in collaboration with Simon and Shaw.

The focus of the research eventually changed from chess to geometry and, ultimately, to logic. The ensuing Logic Theorist program used so-called heuristics, or rules of thumb, rather than just algorithms to prove mathematical theorems. "In effect, they incorporated Simon's concept of 'bounded rationality'—involving the use of shortcuts not necessarily limited by the rules of formal logic—into computer operations. With this program . . . Newel and Simon were able to show that computers could do something that looked like independent thinking: making judgments, millisecond by millisecond about what data are relevant and which rules to follow."[86]

The trio also developed the first so-called list-processing languages for the computer; these embodied most of the ideas contained in object-oriented programming and were direct ancestors of LISP, the standard artificial intelligence (AI) language that was developed by John McCarthy in about 1960.

■

Simon was about to undergo another major shift in his lifework. Even as departmental politics were pushing him away from GSIA, his new interest in AI was pulling him toward computer science and cognitive psychology. In 1960, he took a sabbatical at the RAND Corporation. By the time he returned to GSIA a year later, Lee Bach had resigned his deanship, and Dick Cyert, who had headed the undergraduate Industrial Management Department, had taken Bach's place.

Cyert's tenure as dean of GSIA accelerated Simon's separation from the school. Despite the role Cyert had played in developing the behavioral theory of the firm, Simon accused the new dean of allowing himself to become "bedazzled with mathematics and formal methods." Increasingly, Simon found himself in the minority, battling a faculty that was more and more intolerant of nonquantitative research. It was not, however, until 1970 that he made a formal break with what he perceived as the "excessive formalism and shallow mathematical pyrotechnics" of GSIA and moved his office to the Department of Psychology. But long before then, he "worked hard to make sure there was room elsewhere on the campus for economists of other persuasions," in particular, at the School of Urban and Public Affairs and in the College of Humanities and Social Science, which was home to the Department of Social and Decision Sciences.[87]

In 1978, eight years after leaving GSIA, Herb Simon received a phone call from a former Swedish student, Sven-Ivan Sundquist. It was mid-October, and Sundquist was calling to tell his mentor about a chance encounter he had had that day with a member of the Nobel committee, who had hinted broadly that Simon had been selected to receive the next prize in economic science. Simon knew that a final academy meeting would take place the following day, a Monday, ending at noon local time, after which phone calls would be placed to recipients around the world. "I found myself a bit tense and exhilarated during the rest of the afternoon," he later recalled.[88]

Of course, no one is ever wholly surprised at receiving the Nobel Prize. For at least a year, Simon had known that he was on a shortlist and had done some "campaigning" for the prize. He concedes that he devoted "perhaps 5 percent more" of his time to economics than he otherwise would have.[89]

A less self-assured person might have wondered if Sundquist might not have misinterpreted the conversation or, at the very least, would have lost some sleep. Not Simon. He went to bed early that Sunday night, got a good night's rest, and was up and dressed by 6 A.M., when the call came in on Monday morning. He spent much of the day on the phone that morning, responding to an endless stream of well-wishers. He did, however, take off enough time to turn up promptly for his Monday classes.

The journey to Sweden would be the occasion for a family vacation. Dorothea and his children, Kathie, Peter, and Barbara, were all there. So were Menachem Begin and Anwar Sadat, who were the controversial winners of the Nobel Peace Prize that year, and Isaac Bashevis Singer, who won the literary honors.

In Pittsburgh, it was as if the Pirates had won the pennant. Letters poured in not only from the mayor's office but from a wide array of

Pennsylvania officials, as well as from academicians and administrators from local colleges and universities. Echoing the heartfelt admiration of numerous students and former students, Ed Feigenbaum, a professor of computer science at Stanford, sent his mentor an e-mail soon after hearing the news from Stockholm: "My student encounter with you was the turning point of my intellectual life. . . . It seems to me as I write this, to be somewhat odd that as the world is expressing its gratitude to you for your contributions to its science and thought, I am once again expressing to you my personal gratitude for your contributions to my personal science and thought!" Even Mrs. David Hughes, Simon's first secretary at GSIA some thirty years earlier, couldn't wait to pen a note of congratulations, remarking in a spidery, elderly hand on her lingering "fondness" for her former boss.[90]

Kudos percolated up out of Simon's distant past. "One of the unexpected bonuses of the past week, as surprising as the award itself, and equally gratifying, were the many messages that took me back to places far away and times long ago," Simon wrote to old family friends from Wisconsin. In another acknowledgment, of a letter from his former high school English teacher, he wrote, "The life of a teacher has been deeply satisfying to me and my choice of it was surely influenced by the model of the high school and college teachers I liked and admired."[91]

By contrast, among economists the news was greeted with decidedly mixed feelings, to say nothing of surprise. Many of the most noted economists, including Robert Solow, at MIT, sent their "enthusiastic" and seemingly unequivocal congratulations. Sidney Winter, the pioneer of environmental economics, hinted at the astonishment that swept through the economic community: "Perhaps someone instructed the [Nobel] Committee in the moral of the Nine Dot Problem: Go a little way outside the box and an easy and satisfying solution may be found. Those of us who find the standard economics box a bit cramped are enormously pleased at the Committee's insight and boldness."[92]

Nowhere were the feelings of ambivalence, and even dismay, clearer than in the reactions of some GSIA colleagues. While Richard Cyert, in his official remarks, compared Simon to Aristotle, GSIA students arriving to class on Monday morning were greeted by economics professors who lectured them on why "Herb *shouldn't* have won the prize," recalls Phil Bromley. Indeed, Bromley got his degree in 1981 in the School of Urban and Public Affairs because by then there would have been no hope for one of Simon's students to pass muster with a thesis committee dominated by GSIA economists.[93]

Simon was well aware of the animosity against him, but if it bothered him, he let his sense of superiority overcome the slights. "Many economists and most media folk thought I was an outsider, an unknown who had been selected by some fluke," he wrote in his autobiography. He went on to eviscerate his enemies, noting, first of all, that he was "the fifth most frequently cited economist (in leading economics journals) during the 1950s."[94]

Economists who saw him as a usurper, said Simon, were "simply ignorant of the sociology of the economics profession." He goes on to note that the most "salient fact in postwar history of economics was its sudden conquest by mathematics and statistics. . . . If you examine the list of Fellows of the Econometric Society in 1954, fifteen years before the first Nobel Prize in economics was awarded, you will find the names of 20 of the first 27 prize winners." The year 1954 was, of course, the year Simon joined the society. "So, far from being an outsider, I was a duly certified member of the Econometric Mafia, much better known to my fellow members . . . than to the rank and file of the profession," he concluded. "If I was an outsider to the economics profession as a whole, I was an insider to its elite."[95]

Yet to the mavericks who came out of Carnegie, GSIA is still remembered fondly as a rare, "infectious place" precisely because it accommodated, at least for a short time, an extraordinarily eclectic mix of great men (they were almost exclusively men) and great ideas. In the words of Jacques Dreze, who was a student in the 1950s: "Never since then have I experienced such intellectual excitement." To other students, such as John A. Dimling, Simon was, well, the sharpest needle in an extraordinary haystack. Paraphrasing Simon's own favorite metaphor, Dimling wrote to Simon on the occasion of his Nobel Prize: "As I proceed from one haystack to the next, looking not for the sharpest needle but for one sharp enough, it occurs to me that even a satisficing strategy will occasionally produce the sharpest needle. . . . I suspect my experience at Carnegie, due in considerable part to your presence there, was one time I found the sharpest needle."[96]

Rarely in the history of the world has an institution grown to be so important and so pervasive as the corporation in such a short period of time.

—Alfred Du Pont Chandler[1]

Alfred Du Pont Chandler and Alfred Sloan

The Historian and the CEO

For the American corporation, the beginning of history—that is, a written record of its evolution and culture—is a relatively recent phenomenon. With a few exceptions, most notably Chester Barnard's *Functions of the Executive,* which was published in 1938, American management became truly conscious of itself only after World War II. It was in 1946 that Peter Drucker wrote *Concept of the Corporation,* an in-depth analysis of General Motors and the first study of its kind. It says something about how managers saw themselves immediately after the war that both Drucker and Donaldson Brown, the CFO of General Motors, had grave misgivings about the publishability of Drucker's project. "I don't see anyone interested in a book on management," said Brown at the time.[2]

In fact, both *Concept of the Corporation* and Alfred Sloan's *My Years at General Motors,* which was written in the 1950s, became must reading for executives in the postwar years. (GM's legal department would not, however, release Sloan's book for publication until 1964.) These books were joined by a growing number of writings on management, including March and Simon's *Organizations* and William H. Whyte Jr.'s *The Organization Man.*

Practitioners and theorists also began to shine a light on the work of the CEO in planning corporate strategy. Edith Penrose, a respected economist, wrote *The Theory of the Growth of the Firm,* which debunked the notion that there is a limit to the size that companies can achieve as long as organizational growth is accompanied by an appropriate change in corporate structure. H. Igor Ansoff, a general manager of the Lockheed Electronics Corporation, wrote *Corporate Strategy* in 1965, developing his concepts "out of frustration with planning as the naive extrapolation of past trends." And the Harvard Business School began publishing *Business Policy: Text and Cases*, which had grown out of a Business Policy course that, under various titles, had been taught at the school for decades.[3]

Yet the man who emerged in the 1960s as perhaps the foremost student of strategic change and decision making in large companies was Alfred D. Chandler.

Soon after World War II, Chandler had begun to study the inner workings of big corporations in what would become a lifelong quest to develop a theory of big business. For Chandler, who helped Sloan write *My Years at General Motors*, this insider's look at the giant automaker was just one small building block in a massive, decades-long effort to understand the strategies and structures of big corporations. By 1962, when he published *Strategy and Structure*, Chandler had immersed himself in the operations of hundreds of companies. Chandler's brilliance, says Thomas McCraw, a Harvard business historian and Chandler protégé, is his ability to "explain the sea to the fish who swim in it."[4]

Chandler's background put him in an ideal position to serve as the Boswell of American capitalism. Born into the du Pont clan—though he was not a blood relation (as a child, Chandler's mother, Carol, had been virtually "adopted" by the du Ponts following the death of her father, William Ramsey, a DuPont Company executive)—Chandler gained access to internal DuPont documents that would give him a rare window on the decision making that shaped the world's foremost chemical giant. Those documents helped Chandler write the definitive book on the rise of E. I. DuPont de Nemours and Company in which Chandler extols DuPont's transformation from a family-run business into a bureaucratically controlled enterprise. Years later the DuPont connection also helped him with an introduction to Alfred Sloan and far greater access to GM documents than Drucker had enjoyed. Then, too, as the scion of a prominent East Coast family who came of age during the Great Depression, Chandler was imbued, from an early age, with the sense of awe for the power and importance of history.

■

The summer of 1933 marked a milestone in the Chandler family history, though one that was markedly different from the changes faced by most of their countrymen at the height of the Depression. Like millions of Americans, Alfred Chandler, Sr., who was better known as Ralf, had lost his job as treasurer and VP of sales with the Bellanca Aircraft Company in Wilmington, Delaware. After Bellanca went out of business, he ran a bus company until it, too, failed. Finally, he had to resort to managing the considerable fortune of his mother-in-law, the formidable Lena Ramsey, who was known as "Nana" by her grandchildren.[5]

The weather that summer reflected the mood of the country. On the first day of July it began to rain, and it went on raining for twenty-three of the next thirty days. The Chandlers, Carol and Ralf and their five children, were comfortably ensconced in the family's summer residence at Nantucket. To prevent the kids from destroying the house, Ralf tried to divert his fidgety brood with a favorite pastime: geography lessons. A large globe stood in the living room and served as a useful prop. An expert storyteller, he "lulled [the] rabble into a peaceable mob with imaginary wanderings and dreams of other worlds."[6]

Tempers in the Chandler household ran short that summer. One rainy July afternoon, as the children set off firecrackers in the sitting room fireplace, Ralf, who had loved to fly Bellanca's single-engine propeller planes, paced the room restlessly. Staring at a favorite 1815 map of the United States that hung over the sofa, he suddenly announced, "This is the last year in our family life that we can all be together for a trip as one unit, off to sail the seas and explore the world."[7]

Though a family inheritance had cushioned the Chandlers from the worst blows of the Depression, they too had had to tighten their belts. When Ralf had lost his job, the Chandlers had moved into Dalhousie, Lena Ramsey's estate in Wilmington. The trip, he knew, depended on funding from the family matriarch. Though it was a rainy, blustery day, Ralf packed up the kids and took the ferry to Hyannis, on the mainland, and from there to a house Nana had rented for the summer. To almost everyone's surprise, Nana, reasoning that the trip would save on private school fees, quickly agreed to the enterprise—and announced that she, too, would join the sailing party.

Ralf wasted no time in preparing for the journey, planning every detail like a Jules Verne character off on a great adventure. During the coming weeks, the living room floor was transformed into "a rising wave of specifications for sloops, schooners, brigantines, yawls and ketches" that had been mailed by ship brokers. Every other surface, including the sofa and tables, was covered with maps, atlases, and back issues of *National Geographic*. At last Ralf found a schooner called the *Blue Dolphin*, and a captain who would keep to the budget that Carol had worked out. Ralf dispatched his wife to Boston to purchase a year's worth of provisions, including sixty pounds of coffee, several cases of butter, one hundred pounds of sugar, and thirty-eight pounds of roast beef and sirloin steak.[8]

The children would be educated on board, and so the Chandlers packed books on algebra, Latin, history, literature, and poetry—among them Samuel Taylor Coleridge's "Rime of the Ancient Mariner," Alfred Thayer Mahan's *The Influence of Sea Power upon History, 1660–1783,* and Herman Melville's *Moby-Dick,* which Nana read out loud to the children.

Finally, the *Blue Dolphin* and a party of fifteen, including family and crew, were ready to set sail. Ralf and the older boys set off for Gloucester, Massachusetts, to fetch the boat. The women and smaller children boarded the ship when it docked in the bay next to Nana's rice plantation in South Carolina.

As they viewed the *Blue Dolphin* at anchor for the first time, on a hot September day, the younger Chandler children stood mesmerized atop the dunes facing Winyah Bay. Beyond the waving green palmettos shimmering in the southern sunlight stood a proud hundred-foot schooner, the wind whipping its three flags. From the stern flew the "blood and guts" (because sailing under the Canadian colors would save on taxes); from the foremast, the pennant of the Nantucket Yacht Club, navy blue with a single star; and on the mainmast, a swallow-tailed, pale-blue-and-white pennant specially devised by Ralf for the occasion that was to be the Chandler house flag. On the deck stood Admiral Ralf Chandler, resplendent in a white yachting cap with a blue sun visor, white pants, and a blue flannel jacket with a Nantucket Yacht Club button pinned to the lapel. (Ralf's sartorial splendor was a far cry from the duck pants, worn blue cotton jacket, and battered cotton hat in which his children were accustomed to seeing him.)[9]

The Chandler clan ran through the dunes, sprinkled with small cactuses, to the waiting ship. Flushed and disheveled and singing "Hail to the Nantucket Yacht Club," the only rallying song they all knew, the Chandlers set sail for a yearlong journey.

Decades before hotels and tourists invaded the Caribbean, the Chandlers island-hopped through the Antilles, savoring the local cultures and exploring caves that had been occupied by the pirate Bluebeard. Columbus Day was spent on San Salvador Island in the Bahamas, the first island spotted by the explorer on his journey to the New World. In Haiti they visited the Palais Sans-Souci, climbed the Citadelle Laferrière, and read *Black Majesty* by Henri Cristophe, the builder of the citadel. Using Mahan's text as a guide, they "re-fought" the battles between the English and the French for control of the Caribbean. They sailed through the Panama Canal to the Galapagos Islands. And on their return trip through the Panama Canal, they docked the *Blue Dolphin* next to Jack Morgan's *Corsair,* then the most famous yacht in the world. Seeing all the children on the smaller boat,

Morgan invited the Chandlers aboard, where Ralf found himself re-united with Junius Morgan, Jack's son and an old Harvard classmate. Nana, who didn't like Morgan because she thought of him as a robber baron, initially refused to board the *Corsair*, prompting another lecture from Ralf about how Morgan's father, J.P., had actually been in-strumental in helping to rescue the country from earlier crashes. Throughout the journey, recalls Ralf's son Alfred Chandler, Jr., "My fa-ther kept on this running commentary about history. He had a great sense of history, of the continuity" of historical events.[10]

■

Alfred Du Pont Chandler was fifteen years old when he embarked on this family adventure. The journey—its optimistic defiance of the Depression, its adventurous itinerary, its eccentric cast of characters—would all imprint on him a lifelong love of history. At night, sleeping under the stars on the deck of the *Blue Dolphin*, "Alfie" would regale his brothers and sisters with the invented adventures of Wrinklebelly, about a team of children who survive a holocaust in the New York sub-way and go on to explore a devastated world. (Wrinklebelly was actually the nickname for Willie, the fourth Chandler sibling, on whom the char-acter was modeled.)[11]

As a teenager, Alfred Jr. was "not an impressive boy to meet. He eas-ily camouflaged himself in a group," recalls his younger sister, Caroline (Nina), who, however, would lay awake nights, mesmerized by her brother's Wrinklebelly stories, which have been passed down in the Chandler family like an especially beloved heirloom. Of medium height and build, Alfred Jr. hunched over when he stood, "moved in a loose-jointed shuffle," and mumbled when he talked. But, recalls his sister, "if Alfie was excited about an idea he was working out, you were face to face with the beauty, dazzle and power of electricity. He would grow so excited that tears of joy and passion filled his eyes. He talked faster and faster until he was almost incomprehensible. Running all through his talk was a bubbling humor."[12] In his seventies, Chandler has retained many of his personal idiosyncrasies—the stoop, the marbles-in-the-mouth elocution, the gentle, unassuming manner—and a fiery passion for his subject.

Chandler followed the path he seemed destined for as a young man. Just as Ralf had planned, after the trip, Alfred enrolled at Philips Exeter Academy and followed his forebears to Harvard, where he was deter-mined to study Civil War history. Later, he would say he had known "for as long as I can remember," that history was his calling.[13]

Chandler, however, was not destined to become a specialist in early

American history. Instead, another chapter of family history intervened. As a graduate student at Harvard, just after the war, he discovered a trove of letters and papers that had belonged to his great-grandfather Henry Varnum Poor. A founder of Standard & Poor's Corporation, which provides financial information and comparative bond ratings, Chandler's great-grandfather had been a journalist, reformer, and pioneering financial analyst. For most of his life, he had focused on one industry—the railroads—and chronicled, in great detail, their evolution and relative financial health. In the process, he had become one of the most reliable and detailed chroniclers of the profound economic changes that had shaped the country at the turn of the century.

Finding such a gold mine in his own attic—actually, that of his great-aunt Lucy Poor, with whom he was living at the time—established the course that Chandler would pursue as a business historian. Chandler's Ph.D. dissertation became a biography of his great-grandfather. Building on Poor's detailed accounts of the railroads, the dissertation also provided a dynamic map of the turn-of-the-century economic landscape and how it had been transformed by the Iron Horse. Equally important, Poor's newspaper clippings, which covered decades of news about the railroads and his notes on everything from freight rates to the financial conditions of individual companies, established the pattern of Chandler's own work as a historian. From then on, forensic financial analyses, comparative studies, and day-to-day investigations of his subjects became Chandler's own preferred modus operandi.

Out of such mulch grew the foremost analyst and apostle of large, vertically integrated corporations and a father of corporate strategy. In the years after the discovery of Henry Varnum Poor's papers, beginning in the 1960s, Chandler wrote a series of masterpieces of comparative business history. In *Strategy and Structure*, he probed the origins of diversification in four major corporations and argued that "structure follows strategy." His axiom both helped explain the growth of America's greatest corporations and gave impetus to the field of corporate strategy. In *The Visible Hand*, for which he won the Pulitzer Prize in History in 1978, he challenged neoclassical economic wisdom by arguing that the "invisible hand" of the market has been replaced by the visible hand of management in allocating resources within modern industrial economies. And in one of his last major books, *Scale and Scope*, which, according to Thomas K. McCraw, a business historian at Harvard and editor of *The Essential Alfred Chandler*, "represents the culmination of Chandler's long quest to chart the evolution of modern industrial enterprise," he argues that the "first movers" in capital-intensive industries kept their competitive advantage only if they made three key strategic investments: first, in large scale, high-speed production; second, in distribution; and third, in a management structure that could plan, coordinate, and monitor the company's vast operations.[14]

Despite the coincidence—and advantages—of his birth, Alfred Du Pont Chandler insists that the DuPont connection had only a tangential impact on his career. Indeed, Chandler is fond of pointing out that, unlike the Chandlers, the Wilmingtonians—with the exception of Pierre S. du Pont—"had very little sense of history" at all.[15]

Even so, his family—an awareness of the connections of his forebears, the Chandlers and the Canbys, to the East Coast establishment—as well as a passion for history that was passed down from his adventurous and well-read father and the 1933 journey on the *Blue Dolphin*, all left important marks on Chandler.

■

Alfred was born at Dalhousie in 1918, while Ralf was fighting in France during World War I. It was characteristic of Ralf's approach to life and to the study of history that as an officer on the front lines in France, he relieved the monotony and stress of endless bombings by setting up a school house for enlisted men, noncommissioned officers, and officers in an abandoned freight car. During lulls in the fighting, seated in a wreck of an armchair he had salvaged from some rubble, Ralf would hold forth on algebra and geometry. What enthralled his audience the most, according to Nina, who kept a diary of her family's yearlong journey on the *Blue Dolphin*, were Ralf's histories of the French towns they had marched through and of the exploits of Charles Martel and Charlemagne. (In fact, Ralf was no armchair soldier; he was cited for bravery after rescuing men who were literally drowning in mud following a bombardment.)[16]

The Chandlers were prominent Yankees from Massachusetts. The first Alfred Du Pont Chandler, Ralf's father, had helped found the town of Brookline, Massachusetts, and become its first selectman. Both Ralf Chandler and his father had been educated at Harvard.[17]

Carol, on the other hand, had grown up in the backyard of the du Pont estate in Wilmington. Her father, William Ramsey, had been a young engineer at E. I. DuPont de Nemours & Company who quickly rose in the ranks and eventually became acting chief engineer, director, and vice president of the company. Ramsey moved his family to Guyencourt, then little more than a station on the Reading Railroad, to an estate he called Dalhousie, after his ancestors' Scottish castle. When he died at the age of fifty-one, he left Nana with five small children, a fortune in DuPont stock, and real estate holdings that included both Dalhousie and a working rice plantation off the coast of South Carolina.

Nana herself was descended from a Quaker family that had settled in Wilmington long before the du Ponts came over from France. The Canbys' flour mills predated the du Pont gunpowder factories, though they stood beside each other on the Brandywine River. The du Ponts, Nana always said, were just a little bit "nouveau."[18]

It was undoubtedly Ralf Chandler who had the greatest influence on his son. Alfred was just six years old when Ralf gave him a copy of Wilbur Fisk Gordy's *Elementary History of the United States*, a book written for sixth-graders and replete with twenty-five maps and hundreds of illustrations. Alfred immediately sat down and read the book. Later, he claimed to have read it through nineteen times in all.[19]

As an undergraduate at Harvard, Chandler majored in history. For his senior thesis, he chose a topic close to home—close, that is, to his grandmother's plantation in South Carolina. Its subject was "The [Gubernatorial] Campaign of 1876 in South Carolina." The thesis "foreshadow[ed] the characteristic Chandler method," says McCraw. First, by exploring the dramatic end of Reconstruction in South Carolina, Chandler zeroed in on his favorite leitmotif: the process of historical change. Then too, in researching the paper, he used his now-famous forensic approach to historical research and his interest in sociology. To write the thesis, not only did he use archival materials, he traveled to South Carolina to interview people who had been living during the period and read daily copies of the *Charleston News and Courier*. And he began the thesis with a map of the counties of the state, showing the percentages of black and white voters in each district.[20]

Chandler graduated from Harvard in 1940. Like his classmate John F. Kennedy, he then joined the U.S. Navy. (In an old photograph of the Harvard sailing team, Alfred sits two seats away from his teammate, the future president.) As with so many members of his generation, World War II proved to be another seminal influence. "Chandler found himself in the midst of one of the greatest national mobilizations in history," wrote McCraw in an unpublished article. "The whole undertaking produced feats of organizational innovation unprecedented in human experience—and, for Chandler himself, an unforgettable example of the morphology of change within giant organizations—the subject that later became his consuming preoccupation as a scholar."[21]

Chandler's most significant wartime experience occurred relatively late in the war, when, as an interpreter of aerial reconnaissance photographs, he was called upon to analyze German and Japanese territory before, during, and after Allied bombing runs. "During his training at the photo interpreters' school, it became clear to him that strategic bombing often failed to achieve its goals of crippling the enemy's industrial capacity," because it simply forced factories "underground," wrote McCraw. "Only if supply lines were severed or sources of energy knocked out would production capability be destroyed."[22]

These lessons were later absorbed by Chandler into his work on logistics, industrial production, and key sectors of national economies. They also reinforced his interest in change. "Years later, he revisited the very same questions that had occupied him as a 26-year-old naval officer: 'How were things done at a certain time, how were they done later, and what had happened to cause the change?' "[23]

After the war, Chandler intended to pursue his career in southern history, and enrolled at the University of North Carolina. But he soon abandoned the subject and returned to Harvard, still unsure of his field of specialization.

At Harvard, he found himself drawn, once again, to the sociologists, chief among them Talcott Parsons. In particular, Parsons's argument that the structure of institutions reflects their purpose would become a key theme in Chandler's work.

Two other aspects of Chandler's Harvard experience influenced him profoundly. First, he became involved with the Research Center for Entrepreneurial History, which had been started by the economist Joseph Schumpeter shortly before his death. He also came under the influence of Arthur Cole, an economist who helped build Baker Library and who was a great advocate of cross-disciplinary scholarship. The cross-disciplinary focus of the center, which attracted historians, sociologists, and economists, particularly appealed to Chandler. The monthly seminars were "interdisciplinary in the best sense," he recalled, noting that it was not until years later that he realized "just how much there was in this nexus in Cambridge."[24]

Then there was the discovery of Henry Varnum Poor's papers. After Chandler's return to Harvard, he had trouble finding a home for his growing family in Cambridge's tight postwar housing market. He had married Fay Martin, whose father was a prominent Virginia banker and whose uncle ran *The Virginia Pilot*, a Norfolk newspaper. So the Chandlers, together with their young daughter, Dougie, moved into the two-family house in Brookline that belonged to Alfred's great-aunt Lucy Poor. It was in a storeroom of Aunt Lucy's house that Chandler discovered the papers of Henry Varnum Poor, Lucy's father and his own great-grandfather.

Henry Varnum Poor's life spanned nearly a century, from 1812 to 1905. For close to four decades, beginning in 1849 until the Interstate Commerce Commission was established in 1887, Poor edited and published a number of railroad journals. As the editor of the *American Railroad Journal,* and later the *Manual of Railroads of the United States,* Poor filled the need for "accurate and reliable investment data" for a burgeoning class of publicly traded corporations. As a journalist, reformer, and financial analyst of railroads whose life and career spanned the most dynamic period of economic change in American history, Poor became the foremost authority on America's iron arteries with a unique view of the U.S. economy.[25]

What made Poor's work—and Chandler's treatment of it—so special is how, by training a spotlight on the railroads, both men succeeded in illuminating the evolution of big business in America. The financing of the railroads required infusions of vast sums of private capital, a development that created, for the first time, "a sizable investment class in the United States." Management of the railroads, in turn, demanded the creation of big corporations with a nationwide scope. Poor understood the historical importance of the railroads: "A history of these works is a most interesting chapter in the history of the country, and better than anything else illustrates the force and practical character of our people."[26]

Over time, Poor compiled detailed histories of 120 different railroad companies, replete with statistical data and organizational information. Poor's reports constituted, according to Chandler, "the first major attempt to record the past activities of important units of an industry." Poor made it a point to scrutinize the financial practices of railroads, especially those that sought funding from the New York money markets. For example, he criticized the Erie Railroad, which was at that time the darling of investors, for its "loose financial practices," specifically for acquiring too much debt, for using debt to pay out dividends, and for failing to provide adequate financial disclosure to the shareholders and money markets. By 1852, mortgage bonds had become a popular security in the New York market. "Too popular, Poor thought. He now began to worry about the dangers of a boom in railroad bonds and a resulting overexpansion in railroad construction," wrote Chandler. "With this in mind he turned from assisting the promoters and companies issuing the bonds to serving the firms and individuals purchasing them."[27]

Poor's influence was such that in 1855, John Murray Forbes, who financed the Burlington Railroad, "instructed his staff to be more cooperative with Poor" lest "he cut our stock down 5 percent by his confounded article."[28]

As a financial analyst, Poor developed a number of statistical tools and financial innovations. For example, he devised comparative ratios on everything from repairs and expenses to profits and total expenditures. And he constantly exhorted railroads and legislatures to produce more accurate data.[29]

Poor's reporting innovations came to be widely adopted. Poor understood the costs of railroad construction, in particular the industry's reliance on fixed assets, such as equipment, buildings, and real estate. Fixed assets, in turn, necessitated a change in sound capital structure and would, for example, permit the railroads to carry a much heavier debt burden than would be considered prudent for other businesses. However, the railroads also needed more accurate ways of measuring their fixed assets, including depreciation, renewals, and obsolescence.[30]

In his analysis of railroad administration, Poor even foreshadowed many of the twentieth-century debates on management, including those involving the separation of management and capital. Poor recognized that the railroads had little to learn from the management of typical factory operations of his day, which were usually contained within one or two buildings and could be inspected relatively easily. The railroads, in short, "demand[ed] wholly new methods of management." To solve the problem of adequate supervision, Poor at first advocated a strict hierarchical structure, with a clear division of labor. Such a system, he felt, would create a "thorough and uniform system of reporting to assure accountability and communication" throughout an organization. Indeed, the railroads emulated the command-and-control structure of the military, which was adopted by other companies, too.[31]

However, toward the end of the 1850s, Poor recognized the dangers inherent in such a bureaucratic structure. For individual middle managers, he sensed the potentially deadening effects of being small cogs, with a "fixed position and a fixed salary," in a large bureaucratic machine. He recognized the potential territorial conflicts of different departments within a large organization, and he understood the need for highly competent leadership, without which "the whole organization could break down."[32]

Poor worried that professional managers wouldn't share the interests of their owners. As Chandler wrote, Poor was concerned that "managers, not having the incentives that come from operating and developing one's own property and from receiving the full rewards for extra ability and effort, would be content with mediocre or even worse performance. The owners—the stockholders—not having the knowledge necessary to understand the intricacies of railroad management . . . were naturally unable to spot maladministration or suggest any useful reforms."[33]

Poor's concerns about the potential conflict of interest between managers and owners presaged the concerns over management legitimacy that came to the fore during the 1920s and 1930s and led to changes in strategy and structure at companies such as DuPont and GM.

Indeed, Poor's chronicle was the cornerstone of what would become Chandler's overall theory of big business. The key ingredients were contained within Poor's analysis of the railroads: the need for public financing and financial markets and the development of large nationwide corporate organizations that would "demand wholly new methods of management" and gave rise to a new cadre of professional managers. Wrote McCraw, "Overall, Chandler's biographical study of Poor represents an initial grain of sand around which he constructed, layer by layer over the next forty years, an enormous pearl of sustained scholarship."[34]

Sparked by his research on Poor, Chandler developed a lifelong interest in studying American industry and the American corporation. His approach to economic history was shaped, in turn, by the sociological and behavioral approaches to history that he had absorbed at Harvard by studying the relationships among different groups of people, the decision-making processes of their leaders, and the "institutional arrangements" within which decisions are made.

This sociological view was reinforced by Chandler's experience reviewing the work and papers of four disparate men, Theodore Roosevelt and Dwight D. Eisenhower, whose presidential papers he helped to edit, and Pierre du Pont and Alfred Sloan, about whom he would write extensively. "[A]lthough Roosevelt and Eisenhower, and du Pont and Sloan, concerned themselves with very different types of problems, the processes by which decisions were reached and actions implemented had many similarities," he wrote. "Theirs were usually group decisions based on a vast flow of information, and synthesized by offices within the enterprise . . . [and] an extensive bureaucracy which could turn and shape them. For this reason Sloan's day-to-day activities were closer to Eisenhower's than they were, say, to those of John Jacob Astor or even Cornelius Vanderbilt; Eisenhower's were much closer to Sloan's than to those of Andrew Jackson or even Ulysses S. Grant."[35]

Chandler assembled the "brick wall" of his theory of big business out of close studies of dozens of companies. Two of the most important bricks in his construction were his studies of E. I. DuPont de Nemours and General Motors. In about 1955, he had begun researching the book that, in 1962, would be published as *Strategy and Structure*. The project took him to Wilmington to examine the DuPont corporate papers, which included copies of every meeting of the operating committee, minutes of board meetings, and countless compilations of industry statistics. It also helped bring him to the attention of GM's Alfred Sloan, who enlisted Chandler's help in writing his autobiography and, in the process, gave him access to vast troves of GM documents.[36]

This worm's-eye view of corporate decision making led Chandler to part company with traditional economic historians and the prevailing view of the omniscient entrepreneurial decision maker. In analyzing the railroads and the decision making of presidents and CEOs of large organizations, he saw that it was the bureaucrats, vast numbers of "unidentifiable employees," who played a pivotal role in influencing the executive decision-making process. The growth of national markets had spawned large multifunction enterprises. To meet the needs of a growing consumer market, companies had integrated vertically, especially their manufacturing and marketing functions, while at the same time branching out into related product areas.[37] Both vertical integration and diversification increased the complexity of organizations and decision making and spawned a vast cadre of middle managers.

As Chandler studied the changes at GM and DuPont, he noticed that diversification and vertical integration presented a conundrum for management. Most large enterprises, at the turn of the century, were managed through "centralized, functionally departmentalized structures"—what is now referred to as "U-form organizations." (The "U" stands for "unitary.") Wrote Chandler, "[T]he dominant centralized structure had one basic weakness. A very few men were still entrusted with a great number of complex decisions." The complexity of diversified business put an "intolerable strain on existing administrative structures." Moreover, because most of these administrators spent their careers in "a single functional activity," they had little understanding of the myriad needs and problems in other parts of their companies.[38]

Chandler also observed that the nature of management decision making changed dramatically with the development of new technologies. This was especially true of technologies that fostered the speeding up of production. "As long as the processes of production and distribution depended on the traditional sources of energy—on man, animal, and wind power—there was little pressure to innovate," he wrote. "By 1910, the *threshold* of a new administrative development was being raised in those industries which came into the orbit of the two new generators of power, the internal combustion engine and the electrical motor." At the factory level, it was these changes that had given rise to scientific management and Frederick Winslow Taylor's attempts at rationalizing production.[39]

In the 1950s, Chandler trained his lens on the administrative revolution that these forces had unleashed on middle and top management. To research *Strategy and Structure*, he harnessed his vast comparative techniques to study the administrative changes at literally dozens of major corporations and then zeroed in on a detailed comparison of GM; DuPont; Sears, Roebuck; and Standard Oil.

These four companies had diversified early and were the "most important innovators" of what he termed the "multidivisional" (or M-form) type of organization. What's more, each of the four had developed a decentralized administrative structure at about the same time, in the 1920s. "What is important for this study is that the executives of these four began to develop their new structure independently of each other and of any other firm. There was no imitation. Each thought its problems were unique and its solutions genuine innovations, as brand new ways of administering great industrial enterprises."[40]

As his research on *Strategy and Structure* progressed, Chandler "realized that the overload in decision making at the top was indeed the reason for creating the new structure. But the need did not result from the larger size of the enterprise *per se*. It came rather from the increasing diversity and complexity of decisions that senior managers had to make." By contrast, Henry Ford was able to expand the size of his business considerably without a comparable increase in complexity, because he concentrated on a single product.[41]

Chandler's thesis was that "different organizational forms result from different types of growth." Moreover, he argued, strategy is driven by dynamic changes in the competitive climate of industries, in technologies, and in the national economy. Finally, "once a firm had accumulated large resources, the need to keep its men, money, and materials steadily employed provided a constant stimulus to look for" new products and new markets.[42]

In the case of DuPont, size and complexity inexorably led to a change in structure. "One reason, perhaps, why General Motors and du Pont met and answered their organization problems early was that in 1920 and 1921 their operating problems were larger and more complex than those of most contemporary American industrial enterprises," wrote Alfred Sloan.[43]

World War I served as a catalyst for the strategic and structural changes at DuPont. To meet the growing need for explosives, the company undertook a major expansion of its operations, including manufacturing more of its own raw materials, such as sulfuric acid and alcohol. Faced with excess capacity at the end of the war, it decided to expand into a range of new products, including paints and dyes.

Diversification put new stresses on management. "[E]xecutives with experience primarily in explosives were making decisions about paints, varnishes, dyes, chemicals and plastic products" with which they had little or no experience, according to Chandler. Moreover, the new products required "different types of standards, procedures and policies." In particular, products such as household paints, unlike chemicals and explosives, were sold directly to consumers and raised new problems relating to advertising and distribution—even the possibility of "opening retail outlets," with which DuPont had no experience.[44]

Restructuring, however, didn't follow seamlessly from strategic change. At DuPont, as at most companies, it almost always was precipitated by crisis; without crisis, Chandler noticed—in an observation that almost certainly was influenced as much by Herbert Simon's behavioral perspective as by his access to company documents—executives were often so overwhelmed by operating problems that they failed to see the need for restructuring (see Chapter 8). Under its old U-form structure, many of DuPont's new businesses, such as paints and varnishes, turned out to be money losers, even during years of peak demand. When depression hit in 1920 and 1921 and DuPont discovered that each of its businesses, except explosives, was losing money, the top executives finally were won over to the need for restructuring.

Thus, an important corollary to Chandler's thesis was that "growth without structural adjustment can lead only to economic inefficiency." As he wrote, "Unless new structures are developed to meet new administrative needs which result from an expansion of a firm's activities into new areas, functions, or product lines, the technological, financial, and personnel economies of growth and size cannot be realized."[45]

As Chandler would learn, the depression of 1920 and 1921 revealed the financial and structural weakness of the patchwork quilt of businesses that William S. Durant had assembled under the GM umbrella. Contrary to popular wisdom, the structural and strategic transformation at GM, while every bit as profound as DuPont's and similar to it in many ways, evolved quite independently of that of the Wilmington firm. Wrote Alfred Sloan, in a passage of *My Years with General Motors*, "Both managements at the time were in fact independently concerned with the problems of organization, and both eventually adopted principles of decentralization. But they proceeded from opposite poles. The DuPont Company then was evolving from a centralized type of organization, common in the early days of American industry, while General Motors was emerging from almost total decentralization. General Motors needed to find a principle of co-ordination without losing the advantages of decentralization."[46]

■

Chandler came to the attention of Alfred Sloan following the publication of Chandler's article "Management Decentralization: An

Historical Analysis," which presaged some of the themes he would explore in *Strategy and Structure*. The article was first noticed by John McDonald, a journalist who had just begun working with Sloan on the latter's book. McDonald suggested bringing Chandler in as an adviser on the project, initiating a unique collaboration between the preeminent historian of corporate strategy and the archetypal CEO.

Chandler took the train to New York and spent two days "convincing management that I was OK." It was one time that "the Wilmington connection . . . helped," he notes with a typical combination of understatement and self-deprecating humor.[47]

Chandler, however, wanted the collaboration to be on his terms. "Sloan just wanted to talk the way he had with Drucker," recalls Chandler, referring to Peter Drucker's 1946 opus, *Concept of the Corporation*. "I said we couldn't." Chandler knew that Donaldson Brown, who had been treasurer and director of du Pont and later VP of finance at GM, and was right-hand man to both du Pont and Sloan, had a good memory; he also knew that "Sloan did not. I'd ask him about this and this and this. And he'd say: 'Did I do that?' " What's more, Chandler had seen the records that had been kept by Pierre du Pont, who had become a chief investor in and president of GM during the 1920s. Says Chandler, "I knew just how good the GM documents [probably] were."[48]

After winning over Sloan's army of lawyers, Chandler discovered that GM's documents had been filed in alphabetical order, a form in which they were of little use to a historian searching for patterns of change and strategic decision making over time. He then insisted that the documents be refiled, this time in chronological order, and copied in triplicate. One set of documents would be sent to Chandler in Cambridge, another set to Sloan, and a final set to McDonald.[49]

Chandler's insistence on the official written record proved fortuitous both for Sloan's book and for *Strategy and Structure*. The early chapters of Sloan's book, especially the one on the copper-cooled engine, were strongly influenced by Chandler and would never have come to light without the official record. "The final draft of Sloan's autobiography evidences a historical perspective that it would otherwise have lacked," wrote McCraw, noting that Chandler's chapter on General Motors also benefited from the collaboration with Sloan. (It's worth noting that after Sloan's death, GM burned most of his papers; thus, Chandler's copies of the GM documents, which are now housed at Harvard's Baker Library, are among the best surviving records of Sloan's reign at GM.)[50]

The GM documents gave Chandler a rare glimpse of the inner workings of a corporation. Through them he saw Sloan's influence on the annual model change and the development of return on investment as a key financial yardstick by which to judge the performance of the company's divisions. The minutes of the executive committee also revealed the level of "openness" and "disagreement" that Sloan fostered among his executives. Most important, it exposed the long internal debate among Sloan, DuPont, and Charles Kettering, GM's maverick head of R and D, over the development of the copper-cooled engine. It also gave Chandler an unprecedented opportunity to witness the mind of one of the century's leading CEO strategists.[51]

After a long line of maverick automotive entrepreneurs, including Henry Ford and William Durant, who brought together a number of different car marques under the GM umbrella, Sloan would pioneer a federalist organization structure, complete with checks and balances. Sloan called his predecessors "personal types of industrialists" who "injected their personalities, their 'genius,' so to speak, as a subjective factor into their operations with the discipline of management by method and objective facts." If Ford was an "extreme centralizer" and Durant an "extreme decentralizer," Sloan was the *ur*–organization man.[52]

Sloan was born in New Haven, Connecticut, in 1875. When he was still a boy, Sloan's father, a coffee and tea merchant, moved his business and his family to Brooklyn. Young Alfred grew up in Brooklyn, where he acquired the accent that marked his speech even as a CEO. After earning a B.S. degree in electrical engineering from MIT, he went to work for the Hyatt Roller Bearing Company. "I could not know then that through Hyatt I had entered one of the headwaters of General Motors," he wrote.[53]

When Hyatt developed financial problems in the late 1890s, Alfred's father helped raise $5,000 to keep the company afloat, on the condition that his son help manage Hyatt for at least six months. Under Sloan, who became general manager, Hyatt began to thrive. To expand Hyatt's customer base, Sloan began to solicit business from the fledgling auto companies and succeeded in selling Hyatt's antifriction bearings to a number of them. One company that proved to be an especially hard sell was Cadillac, which at the time was run by Henry Leland and became part of GM in 1909. To Leland, "quality was . . . God," recalled Sloan. "I had trouble at first, in the early 1900s, in selling Mr. Leland our roller bearings. He then taught me the need for greater accuracy in our products to meet the exacting standards of interchangeable parts."[54]

At the turn of the century, even as Frederick Winslow Taylor was preaching the marvels of scientific management to companies throughout the Philadelphia area, Alfred Sloan was cultivating the pioneers of the auto industry. Once a month, on Saturday nights, he would make the trip to Flint, Michigan, to meet with men such as Walter Chrysler and Charles Nash. There, amid the horses, wagons, and carriages of farmers who had driven into town for their weekly shopping and night out, a "small society of automobile and parts producers" got together for drinks and shop talk on Saginaw Street, the main street of Flint.[55]

It was at these get-togethers that Sloan probably first met William Durant. In 1916, Durant, who was in the process of consolidating General Motors, made an offer for Hyatt. When Sloan and his directors agreed to sell the company, Durant incorporated Hyatt into a new enterprise known as United Motors Corporation, which included, among other companies, the electrical equipment firm that came to be known as Delco. Sloan became the president and chief operating officer of United Motors, broadening his business horizons, for the first time, beyond "a single component of the automobile." Two years later, Sloan and John J. Raskob, who had come from du Pont to become the chairman of GM's finance committee, sold the assets of United Motors to GM.[56]

Sloan joined GM as vice president in charge of the United Motors' accessories companies and as a director and member of the company's executive committee. Sloan realized almost immediately that GM was in a state of disarray. "Mr. Durant did not have a sound concept of accounting as such and did not realize its great significance in administration," he wrote. "I was particularly concerned that he had expanded General Motors between 1918 and 1920 without an explicit policy of management with which to control the various parts of the organization." GM's myriad divisions regularly battled one another for funds, and different members of the executive committee backed whatever pet projects they liked best. Appropriations for plant expansions were made without holding divisions accountable for their expenditures or making a systematic analysis of the actual needs of the corporation. The divisions spent lavishly, and requests for further appropriations continued to be met by the executive and finance committees, neither of which "had the needed information or the needed control over the divisions."[57]

GM's haphazard administration reached a crisis point in 1920, when "the bottom dropped out of the automobile market." The slump of 1920 revealed that Durant had gone heavily into debt, using his sizable holdings in GM stock as collateral. The financial debacle precipitated Durant's resignation from the company. To keep the creditors at bay, the du Ponts took over a sizable chunk of Durant's holdings. By 1921, DuPont would increase its GM holdings to 36 percent of the company's total common stock. Thus, began a new era at GM, one that would be dominated by the considerable organizational skills of Pierre S. du Pont and Alfred Sloan.[58]

Once the immediate financial crisis had been averted, du Pont and Sloan faced a sweeping reorganization of GM. Much of that reorganization would be based on an "organization study" that Sloan had drafted in 1919. The key objective of the study was to provide an answer to the haphazard nature of GM's organization and to "find a principle of coordination without losing the advantages of decentralization."[59]

Sloan's study was in many respects an unusual and highly original undertaking. Wrote Sloan, "I had not been much of a book reader, and if I had been, I understand that I would not have found much in that line in those days to help; and I had no military experience."[60]

Instead, Sloan borrowed a page from his days as head of United Motors. Recalling how he had coordinated the highly diversified business that came under the United Motors umbrella, he was determined to achieve a comparable "happy medium . . . between the extremes of pure centralization and pure decentralization." On the one hand, he wanted to "maximize decentralization of divisional operations," while at the same time "limit[ing] the responsibility of divisional chief executives in the expression of 'proper control.' "[61]

In the interests of coordination, Sloan set up a number of centralized functions and policies to help rationalize the work of the divisions and to achieve synergy within the corporation. For example, Donaldson Brown devised a system of standard accounting, including the principle of return on invested capital. "By placing each division on its own profit-making basis, I gave the general office a common measure of efficiency with which to judge the contribution of each division to the whole" rather than the cost or cost-plus basis on which divisions passed materials from one division to the next. The executive committee also devised a product policy, redefining each of its six divisions by price category to avoid overlap among the divisions. Thus, for example, Chevrolet became the low-priced model that would compete against the Ford Model T. And high-end Chevys were phased out. One objective of the product policy was to minimize duplication and internal competition between different divisions by rationalizing the models produced by the divisions.[62]

Sloan's plan created a deliberate tension between "maximized decentralization" and "proper control," and its success depended on achieving a proper balance between the two. It was a balance that would, in later years, frequently elude the company; GM's troubles during the 1980s, for example, could often be traced back to the executive committee's eagerness to overrule division executives without, however, having an adequate understanding of the market and its customers.

By contrast, GM's success owed much to Sloan's genius for using his executive power judiciously, while maintaining a thorough understanding of both the marketplace and every facet of the company's business. Even as CEO, Sloan was known for visiting dealers regularly to learn firsthand how customers received GM products. He also fostered an open exchange of ideas. Wrote Sloan, "I never minimized the administrative power of the chief executive officer in principle when I occupied that position. I simply exercised that power with discretion; I got better results by selling my ideas than by telling people what to do. Yet the power to act must be located in the chief executive officer."[63]

However, Sloan discovered early on that developing an organizational principle can be vastly easier than following through on it. As Chandler began to work with Sloan on his autobiography and to review the documents that had been sent from Detroit, he discovered one striking omission from Sloan's version of events: the problems that had developed soon after the reorganization in connection with "a revolutionary car" that was to have an air-cooled engine designed by Charles Kettering, GM's maverick head of R and D. As Sloan later confessed, "[F]or most of the first definable period of the new administration . . . we departed from and even violated those first principles. In other words, the logic of the mind and the logic of history were not of the same order."[64]

In theory, the air-cooled engine, which was also known as the copper-cooled engine for the copper fins that channeled cool air to the engine, was superior to conventional water-cooled models. The new design had the benefit of using fans to keep the engine from overheating, rather than the "cumbersome radiator and plumbing system of the water-cooled" models, which added to the weight and cost of each vehicle. Kettering and Pierre S. du Pont both favored the new design as a replacement for the conventional water-cooled engine and "wrote [letters] back and forth behind Sloan's back." Sloan remained skeptical about whether the technical difficulties with the new engine could be ironed out quickly enough for it to be used in upcoming vehicles.[65]

For two and a half years, beginning shortly after the reorganization, the copper-cooled engine was the central focus of debate by the three most powerful men at GM. Yet when Sloan decided to write the story of his years at GM, "[t]he one thing [he] didn't want to talk about was the copper-cooled engine," recalls Chandler.[66]

Under Chandler's gentle coaxing, the story of the copper-cooled engine finally emerged. The problem, as Sloan later defined it, was one of "conflict between the research organization and the producing divisions, and of a parallel conflict between the top management of the corporation and the divisional management." In particular, the executive committee, led by Pierre du Pont's bullish prospects for the air-cooled car, decided in favor of testing the air-cooled technology. Once its merits had been proven, the executive committee wanted a four-cylinder air-cooled car to be adopted as a replacement for Chevrolet's lowest-priced model, the 490, as well as a slightly higher priced, six-cylinder model for the Oakland Division.[67]

While the Oakland Division was relatively enthusiastic, the executive committee's decision was strongly opposed by the Chevrolet Division's management. K. W. Zimmerschied, the general manager of Chevrolet, had developed a new body for the 490 and made improvements in the existing water-cooled engine and wanted to delay development of a four-cylinder air-cooled engine, presumably because the bugs still hadn't been worked out of Kettering's design.[68]

The executive committee overruled the division heads at Chevrolet and authorized "a kind of pilot operation" to begin producing air-cooled cars at the GM Research Corporation in Dayton, Ohio. This created something of an organizational crisis. "[W]ho was adviser to whom on production: Research to the car division or the car division to Research?" Zimmerschied wanted to know. Recalled Sloan, "The difficulty lay not only in the question of whether the decision regarding the new car was sound, but in how to get it carried out where it had to be carried out, namely, in the divisions. In extenuation of what was done, I should say that this was the first time, to my knowledge, in the history of General Motors that intimate co-operation was called for between the Research Corporation and the divisions on an important problem, and no established means existed by which this co-operation was to function."[69]

One result of Chevrolet's objections was that Kettering, faced with a relatively hostile Chevrolet and a receptive Oakland, chose to test the six-cylinder car first. In the fall of 1921, the first air-cooled cars were tested at the Oakland Division in Pontiac, Michigan. The test was a failure.

Although a copper-cooled Chevrolet was hailed at the New York Automobile Show of 1923, the few copper-cooled Chevys that were on the road continued to have problems. In the wake of the failure of the copper-cooled engine, in May 1923, Pierre du Pont, who had pushed the technology from the beginning, resigned from the presidency of GM. Sloan succeeded him, and one of his first decisions as president was to suspend production of cars with the copper-cooled engine.

An interesting footnote to the story is that Sloan, the quintessential organization man, understood the value of a maverick like Kettering. To prevent Kettering from resigning over the copper-cooled engine debacle and to give him time to continue developing the technology, Sloan set up an official skunk works, "a kind of copper-cooled car division." Kettering would have the opportunity to work out the technical problems involved in manufacturing a car and, once the technical work was done, market the cars he produced.[70]

The copper-cooled engine did eventually die. Wrote Sloan, "I don't know why. The great boom was on and meeting the demand for cars and meeting the competition with improved water-cooled car designs absorbed our attention and energies."[71]

By making room for Kettering's maverick genius, however, GM was able to capitalize on one of the auto industry's greatest innovators. Kettering went on to develop high-compression engines, nontoxic refrigerants, the two-cycle diesel engine, with which GM revolutionized the railroads, and a host of other innovations.[72]

From a strategic point of view, "[t]he significant influence of the copper-cooled engine was in what it taught us about the value of organized cooperation and co-ordination in engineering and other matters," wrote Sloan. "It showed the need to make an effective distinction between divisional and corporate functions in engineering, and also between advanced product engineering and long-range research. The copper-cooled-engine episode proved emphatically that management needed to subscribe to, and live with, just the kind of firm policies of organization and business that we have been working on. Altogether the experience was to have important consequences in the future organization of the corporation."[73]

Concluded Sloan:

> If I have any opinion today, it is that Mr. Kettering may have been right in principle and ahead of his time, and that the divisions were right from a development and production standpoint. In other words, in this kind of situation it is possible for the doctors to disagree and still all be right. From a business and management standpoint, however, we were acting at variance with our doctrines. We were, for example, more committed to a particular engineering design than to the broad aims of the enterprise. And we were in the situation of supporting a research position against the judgment of the division men who would in the end have to produce and sell the new car. Meanwhile, obsolescence was overtaking our conventional water-cooled models and there was nothing in the official program to protect their position.[74]

■

It was only with the great economic expansion during and after World War II and the increase of "systematic research and development" that the modernized, decentralized corporate structure became widespread. Yet to Chandler and other observers of corporate history, the success of GM and DuPont served as living proof of Chandler's theory of big business and the validity of M-form organizations: "[T]he new structure left the broad strategic decisions as to the allocation of existing resources and the acquisition of new ones in the hands of a top team of generalists. Relieved of operating duties and tactical decisions, a general executive was less likely to reflect the position of just one part of the whole." At the same time, "the new structure left the divisional executives to run the business, while the general officers set the goals and policies and provided overall appraisal.[75]

The M-form structure had additional advantages. The mechanisms for communicating information between divisions and top management created a "steady flow of detailed reports" on every aspect of a division's performance and provided both divisional managers and top executives with "a useful and continuing check on operating results and achievements."[76]

Significantly the M-form structure also provided "a place to train and test general executives." Noted Oliver Williamson, "It is perhaps ironic that at the very time the M-form innovation was beginning to take hold, widespread concern over the failure of the modern corporation to satisfy legitimacy tests was first expressed." By building managerial competence and accountability to the managerial process, the M-form organization actually "restor[ed its] integrity," which the U-form organization had begun to lose.[77]

In detailing the evolution of strategy and structure at America's major corporations, Chandler's book helped give birth to the field of "corporate strategy" and a booming business in strategic consulting. Marvin Bower, the legendary leader of McKinsey & Company, for example, says his firm repackaged Chandler's M-form concept and marketed it to clients around the world. *Strategy and Structure* also served as a catalyst for the publication *Strategic Management Journal*, which was first published in 1980 and became a leading research journal in the field.[78]

It helped that *Strategy and Structure* "came out at a critical time," says Chandler. The early 1960s was a period of great ferment in both strategy and organization theory. For example, even as Chandler was putting the finishing touches on his work, Edith Penrose published *The Theory of the Growth of the Firm* (1959). Although Penrose is little known outside academic circles in the United States—she and her husband were forced to emigrate to the United Kingdom during the McCarthy era—her book has been a key influence on organization theory. She argued that, contrary to neoclassical wisdom, there is no intrinsic limit to the size that companies can achieve. Corporations, she argued, can always diversify into new and unrelated product areas, an option that neoclassical theory, which assumes that a firm is tied to a given set of products, doesn't take into account. However, in what has become known as the "Penrose Effect," Penrose also argued that "a firm is prevented from growing as fast as it may like because there is a very distinct cost of rapid growth" in the form of market *and* managerial diseconomies. As she wrote in a passage that echoes Chandler's views, written at almost exactly the same time, "The conclusion that the limited capacity of the individual will limit the size of firms has not . . . been supported by events. . . . On the contrary, the big firms appear extremely successful and there is no evidence at all that they are managed inefficiently when enough time has been given them to *make the adjustments and adaptations of their administrative framework appropriate to increasing size.*"[79]

■

Chandler's work proved to be very influential. In particular, *The Visible Hand*, which built on the foundation of *Strategy and Structure*, has shaped what is widely known as "institutional economics." The field involves the study of how institutional change affects industrial organization in the economy. While Adam Smith saw the dominance of the "invisible hand" of market forces in allocating goods and services, Chandler argued that the visible hand of management will often "internalize transactions," especially in manufacturing and marketing, "in an effort to speed the processes of production and distribution." Moreover, he argued, the advantages of "internalizing" such business activities as distribution and marketing "could not be realized until managerial hierarchies had been created."[80]

Finally, *Scale and Scope*, which was published in 1990, marked, according to Thomas McCraw, "the culmination of Chandler's long quest to chart the evolution of modern industrial enterprise." In it, Chandler comes closest, said McCraw, to elaborating a "historical theory of big business that any scholar has achieved." The book, which examines hundreds of industries in Germany, the United Kingdom, and the United States, made the following observation about the modern industrial enterprise: major industrial corporations have clustered in industries with certain characteristics.

First, they clustered in industries in which high-technology production processes made it possible to exploit *"the unprecedented cost advantages of the economies of scale and scope."* These tended to be capital-intensive, rather than labor-intensive, industries, in which investment in new plant and equipment greatly increased the "ratio of capital to labor involved in producing a unit of output." In these industries, these large-scale, low-cost producers operated at a much greater cost advantage than smaller, labor-intensive producers. (Many of these companies were in process industries, such as food, oil, and chemicals, as opposed to, for example, textiles, apparel, and printing, in which economies of scale and scope could not be achieved as readily by increased investment in plant and equipment.)[81]

Second, as these capital-intensive producers grew in scale (volume), scope (diversification), and complexity, they also began to invest in their own distribution networks. "When a manufacturer's volume attained a scale that would reduce the cost of transporting, storing and distributing his products to the level of that achieved by the [independent] wholesaler through volume economies, the intermediary lost his cost advantage," wrote Chandler.[82]

Third, scale and scope demanded a managerial structure that could plan and supervise these far-flung enterprises.[83]

■

Chandler's work left a particularly strong mark on Oliver Williamson, the apostle of "transaction cost" economics. *"Strategy and Structure . . .* had a massive influence on my understanding of managerial discretion," he wrote.[84]

Williamson had discovered that "organization form matters" and that institutions matter, even in economics. In *Markets and Hierarchies*, which was published in 1975 to widespread acclaim, Williamson argued that much of the economic activity that used to take place in the marketplace involving myriad small producers has come to be performed by a large and often vertically integrated (M-form) corporation that functions like a "miniature capital market." Specifically, the M-form organization can do a better job of approximating the "goal pursuit and least-cost behavior" normally associated with neoclassical profit maximization than the more traditional U-form organization, according to Williamson.[85]

In Williamson's world, it is the comparative cost of a given transaction that determines whether the transaction will take place inside a corporation or in the marketplace—i.e., whether a manufacturer will decide to purchase its raw materials from an outside supplier or produce them. While traditional economists argue that economic man seeks to optimize and Herb Simon argues that he "satisfices," Williamson contends that what economic man (and woman) really does is *economize* on transaction costs. (Indeed, Williamson is strongly influenced by Herbert Simon. The condition of bounded rationality and the related problems of uncertainty and opportunism on the part of managers were incorporated into transaction cost economics for purposes of assessing whether a given transaction should be "internalized" or take place in the marketplace; see Chapter 8).

Williamson's argument had widespread implications for antitrust law—the subtitle of *Markets and Hierarchies*, "Analysis and Antitrust Implications," hints at it. Williamson, who served a one-year stint as a special economic assistant to the head of the U.S. Antitrust Division in the Johnson administration, argued that, contrary to traditional economic doctrine, firms that engage in complex, long-term contracts can have economizing as well as the more familiar and overworked monopolizing purposes ascribed by orthodoxy. For example, antitrust suits filed against both Schwinn and GTE, in the 1960s and 1970s, respectively, centered on efforts by both companies to impose resale restrictions on their franchisees. Williamson contends that both companies were motivated by a (legitimate) effort to protect a brand name, rather than a monopolistically driven desire to restrict the functioning of the market. Though Schwinn lost its case before the Supreme Court in 1967, GTE won ten years later in a decision that, according to Williamson, retroactively vindicated Schwinn.[86]

Institutional economics has had an uphill battle winning acceptance of its definition of the firm as an organizational entity, as opposed to a technological one defined by a mix of inputs and outputs. However, Williamson, strongly aided by Chandler, created the framework that "enabled economists for the first time to say something about the *efficiency* properties of different organization forms."[87]

■

By the end of the twentieth century, it had become fashionable to view the traditional hierarchical organization as painfully out of date. Flatter, "virtual" organizations have come to be seen as the structure needed for global, fast-changing, knowledge-based industries. Silicon Valley entrepreneurs are the heroes of the new millennium.

To Alfred Chandler, on the other hand, the big corporation is still king. In his latest, yet-to-be-published book, "Paths of Learning: The Evolution of High Technology Industries," an exhaustive exploration of the evolution of high-technology industries, it is still the well-established corporations—IBM, DuPont, and Merck—that come out on top. This fact alone is likely to make the book highly controversial when it is published early in the next millennium.

In "Paths of Learning," Chandler argues that the competitive strengths of firms are based on "product-specific capabilities" involving both technological and managerial strengths. His arguments build on the knowledge-based strategy and core competency arguments of such theorists as Prahalad, Hamel, and Teece. These capabilities, according to Chandler, are learned and are "embodied" in a unique organizational setting. He views high-tech firms "less as a unit which carries out transactions . . . and more as a repository of learned product-specific knowledge."[88]

These knowledge-based capabilities play two pivotal roles in Chandler's framework: First, they are the "learning base" for product and process improvement. Second, they create powerful barriers to entry. Notes Chandler, "Once an industry became firmly established, the new entrants into that industry were rarely start-up firms."[89]

One of Chandler's chief examples involves IBM and how its technology came to dominate the computer industry. In sharp contrast to IBM's image as a lumbering giant that missed out on computer graphics and was late in developing minicomputers, Chandler outlines how Big Blue surged ahead of the competition in *both* mainframes and personal computers. The two keys to IBM's long-term success, according to Chandler, were the technological knowledge base it developed with the 360 and 370 mainframe models, its organizational and marketing know-how, which dates back to 1913, and the development of its business tabulating machines for a worldwide market. (IBM's highly successful 650 computer [1954] was a transistor-powered punch-card tabulator.)[90]

Chandler's IBM story begins in the early 1960s, when the company pioneered a series of innovations in both hardware and software that Chandler calls "probably the most ambitious, complex, costly and successful example of product development and commercialization in history." As IBM's 360 and 370 computers developed a huge lead on those of the company's European and Japanese competitors, its European rivals attempted to develop a computer compatible with the 370 system but failed.[91]

The Japanese were luckier. Gene Amdahl, the lead designer of IBM's computers, left the company and searched for investors who would pony up the $40 million to produce his own System 370. Fujitsu, with the help of the Japanese government, jumped at the chance to acquire 20 percent of Amdahl's company and, along with it, IBM's know-how. Meanwhile, as if in a frantic global relay race, Siemens contracted with

Fujitsu to purchase, on an original equipment manufacturing (OEM) basis, a computer based on Amdahl's technology. Via a series of licensing and supplier arrangements, the world's other leading computer companies, including Olivetti, Bull, and NEC, all acquired products based on IBM's technology. Writes Chandler, "By the early 1980s, the European and Japanese competitors so closely followed the IBM path that all but two were making almost exact copies of IBM's System 370 and the two others were producing IBM-compatible systems."[92]

Yet despite the proliferation of clones, IBM remained the most powerful, and most profitable, company in the industry, according to Chandler. "Although IBM's competitors had caught up during the 1970s," he writes, by the 1980s Big Blue's revenues were twice those of all of its U.S. competitors *combined*. By 1985, they were three times that amount.[93]

IBM's knowledge base also helped ensure the company's success in the PC market, according to Chandler, even though it launched its first entry *three years* after the industry's pioneers, Apple, Tandy, and Commodore did. Moreover, its recruitment of Intel and Microsoft, which produced the chip and the operating system for IBM's PC, created two new innovative giants with the scale, scope, and knowledge base to dominate their industries.

To catch up with the PC upstarts, IBM jump-started its now-famous PC operation in Boca Raton, Florida, far from its Armonk, New York, headquarters. In the interest of speed, the company made three fateful decisions that would transform the PC market: First, it used an "open architecture" that would not be protected by patents; by creating an open system, it both opened the door for scores of competitors and start-ups and revealed "an almost unanticipated mass consumer market for computers." Second, it purchased a relatively cheap Intel chip. Third, it subcontracted the operating system to a relative upstart, Bill Gates at Microsoft.[94]

IBM's pivotal role, according to Chandler, was in revealing an enormous, and heretofore unrecognized, consumer market for PCs. By becoming the only full systems company, the company was able to reinforce its lead in large and medium-sized computers. It was even able to outpace Digital Equipment Company, which ran almost even with IBM during the mid-1980s in the production of minicomputers (medium-sized machines). "In mainframes only IBM had the resources and capabilities to make successfully the necessary transition that its own PC had forced," writes Chandler. "In 1994 it was still the industry's largest revenue producer. . . . It was, according to Datamation, the number one producer in large and mid-range systems, peripherals, and software (with revenues of $11.5 billion as compared to Microsoft's $4.5 billion), and number two in workstations and personal computers."[95]

Chandler stresses, however, that bigness is not enough. In consumer electronics, RCA was in a position comparable to IBM in the development and commercialization of radio and TV. In the late 1960s, however, RCA turned to markets where it had few product-specific capabilities. First it attempted and failed to develop a computer mainframe system similar to IBM's. Then it became a conglomerate. In the early 1980s, RCA collapsed, and with it went the U.S. consumer electronics business. The Japanese, led by Matsushita and Sony, quickly dominated the industry worldwide.

For Microsoft and Intel, the alliance with IBM was also pivotal. Without it, Chandler implies, these companies could not have developed the sort of crucial knowledge base that enables a handful of companies to dominate an industry. Through their alliance with IBM, says Chandler, "Intel and Microsoft had the opportunity to exploit the economies of scale and scope in much the same grand manner as the first-movers in oil, steel, gas, rubber, tobacco and motor vehicles had done decades before. Even more important, that franchise made them masters of the industry's continuing paths of technological innovation and continuing paths of learning, in semiconductors, operating systems, and applications software. For after 1985 the opportunities for start-ups in the personal computer industry came from marketing rather than technological innovations."[96]

By setting up IBM as a model of big-business success, however, Chandler has exposed himself to a wave of criticism. "Even Lou Gerstner [IBM's CEO] would disagree with Chandler's assessment of IBM" in the mid-1990s, says Pankaj Ghemawat, a fellow strategist at Harvard. Indeed, Gerstner took over in 1993 to reverse an eight-year-long slide. Chandler has become "excessively enamored" with his own monolithic theory, according to his critics.[97]

In fact, the brick wall of Chandler's theory remains largely intact. Not even the critics of the M-form organization have come up with an alternative. While Prahalad and Hamel's *Harvard Business Review* article on core competency is an attack on the M-form organization for missing out on the competencies that are shared across divisions, it did not come up with an alternative organization form. Ghemawat says that the M-form organization may have problems, but we "don't quite know the solutions yet."[98]

To Chandler, big will always be beautiful. There is little in Chandler's work, for example, that would hint at the disasters that befell big business in the 1970s and 1980s; he attributes these, in retrospect, to an unfortunate obsession with short-run financial returns that represent "managerial capitalism gone to seed." At the end of the twentieth century, Chandler's worldview is still very much influenced by Ralf Chandler, that quintessential "nineteenth-century rational optimis[t]," who saw the world as getting "better and better all the time."[99]

Thomas McCraw pointed out that throughout his work, Chandler maintains the value-free rationalism of his era. Chandler is not interested in the "human side of enterprise"; nor is he interested in the political process and the impact of government regulation on business. Indeed, Chandler implies that "the state has played only a minor role in the rise of industrial capitalism," according to McCraw. Chandler's view is very much that of the dispassionate interpreter viewing the aerial reconnaisance photographs of the enemy.[100]

Yet for all of his detachment and single-focused vision, it is impossible to come away from Chandler's work without a sense of the overwhelming power of the corporation, its unparalleled role in creating American prosperity, and the unique institutional character of each corporate giant.

*Transaction cost economics also builds on the work of Ronald Coase, who nearly forty years ago argued that markets and hierarchies are "alternative methods for coordinating production." Coase, winner of the 1991 Nobel Prize, established the field of institutional economics by asking the seminal question "Why are there firms?" Although Coase never fully answered the question, he provided "a subtle critique" of the neoclassical theory of the firm and provided "an extremely fruitful impetus for new thinking." Coase was also the first economist to argue the importance of differential transaction costs in determining the mode of economic organization. And he is the patron saint of the law and economics movement.[101]

Drucker has this ability to make you sit forward when he talks. Drucker gets to the edge. And then, instead of mush, he gives you thoughts that are large. They are books.

—Jack Welch, CEO,
General Electric[1]

Peter F. Drucker

The Big Idea Man

One of the first meetings Jack Welch scheduled after being named CEO of General Electric was with Peter F. Drucker. The meeting was arranged by Welch's predecessor, Reginald Jones, and took place in January 1981 in GE's Manhattan offices. Drucker and Welch would seem to be unlikely soul mates. For one thing, the Austrian intellectual who speaks in a slow, measured Viennese baritone and the working-class boy turned CEO (at age forty-five, the youngest CEO in GE history) who speaks in a rapid-fire Boston brogue would hardly seem to share the same language at all. Yet after little more than an hour, Welch was hooked.

"There's a Henry Kissingerness about him," he recalls. "He's mastered that gravitas." The accent; the slow, measured delivery; the gravelly voice and intense eyes: "People like that capture your attention. You listen." And then there are the Big Questions. Explains Welch, "I like people who can give you simple, straightforward things."[2]

It was at that first meeting that Drucker asked one of the two Big Questions that would occupy Welch during the next several years: " 'If you weren't already in this business, would you choose to get into it now?' You could write a book and not learn as much as you would from that question!" says Welch.[3]

Welch knew from experience—he had run businesses that were leaders and businesses that were laggards—that it was easier to run a leader. In bad times, "the leader might catch a cold, but number three or four gets pneumonia." Drucker had crystallized something that Welch knew in his gut but had never articulated: it would help lead Welch to shed any business in which GE could not be number one or number two. This led to a massive restructuring that eliminated scores of businesses and one in four jobs. It was a strategy that helped boost GE's market value from $12 billion in 1981 to $330 billion in 1998 and that won

Welch, first, the appellation "Neutron Jack" and eventually a reputation as possibly the "greatest" corporate leader since Alfred Sloan.[4]

If you weren't in this business, would you be in it today? "That question resonates in every discussion we have here," says Welch. "It's an incredibly simple, straightforward way to think through a lot of business entries. That's not a slogan, it's much more than a slogan. It describes a selling environment and your behavior in that selling environment."[5]

Sharp; simple; direct; boiling a problem down to its essence. "I try to do that," says Welch. "Drucker, he's the master of doing that. I'm the lightweight."[6]

That 1981 meeting was not the last time Welch would summon Drucker. The consultant would return to GE several years later to pose another "Big Question" that GE would invest several more years in trying to answer. It was a role Drucker was used to; he had advised at least two GE CEOs before Welch came onto the scene. His first stint as a consultant to GE had begun in the early 1950s. That was nearly a decade *after* he had done a historic study of General Motors—the first of its kind on a major U.S. corporation.

Like the astute journalist he was at the beginning of his career—before he became one of the foremost analysts of the American corporation—Drucker had a unique ability not only to sniff out the important events and trends in corporate management and to conceptualize them provocatively but to be there, on the front lines, when historic changes were taking place.

Just three years after emigrating to the United States, Drucker had gotten permission to conduct a sweeping analysis of the structure and management of General Motors, which he published as a book a year after the war. *Concept of the Corporation*, which appeared a decade before Alfred Sloan's *My Years at General Motors*, was, in fact, the first attempt to conduct a comprehensive analysis of a major corporation. It was quickly embraced by the new cadre of management students and became required reading for students of both government and management throughout the country. With his classic sense of drama and self-promotion, Drucker said of his own book that it "established the discipline of management . . . [and] for better or worse, set off the 'management boom' " that has gripped America ever since. To a great extent, he was correct.[7]

Riding the success of *Concept of the Corporation*, Drucker came to the attention of the men who were reshaping GE following the war. Thus, he became a key adviser on what would be one of the most famous, and most imitated, restructurings in American corporate history, one launched by CEO Ralph Cordiner in the 1950s. That experience provided fodder for his next major opus, *Management,* the first major textbook on the subject of management.

On the strength of raw intelligence coupled with a sharp and eloquent pen and tongue, Drucker became an adviser to America's leading CEOs and a preeminent social and business critic. Over the years, he has written close to two dozen books and hundreds of articles. In the process he invented the term "management by objectives," if not the idea behind it; he identified the importance of the "knowledge worker" earlier than almost anyone else; and he advocated a customer-driven approach to management at a time when most American companies were complacent in the knowledge that consumers were grateful for any products they could find.

Looking back, Drucker has arguably been the most popular management philosopher of the century. Though his sweep has been far too broad to pigeonhole him in either the human relations or the scientific management camp, his ideas are informed by a core belief in both the importance of the corporation as a defining institution of American society and the need for a corporate social contract.

No revolutionary, Drucker is an apostle of great corporations. His great strength is his ability to absorb vast amounts of information, to see patterns in what would appear as a jumble of chaotic events, trends, and economic indicators, and to anticipate—and articulate—each new zeitgeist. His life is also a testament to the American Dream, the ability of an enterprising immigrant both to succeed in his adopted country and to reinvent himself.

■

In Drucker's case, the American Dream was on fast forward from the moment he set foot in New York City, in the sweltering summer that preceded Pearl Harbor. While everyone else readied for war, Drucker launched quite a different campaign: he got his first job working for Henry Luce, writing and consulting for *Time* (later he would serve as a consultant and freelancer for *Fortune.*) By 1942, he was en route to GM headquarters in Detroit. No sooner did he finish *Concept of the Corporation,* at the end of the war, than he set his sights on the West Point of capitalism, on the banks of the Charles River.

In May 1946, Drucker sent a copy of his new book to Elton Mayo, who was by now an éminence grise at Harvard Business School, with a letter noting his intellectual debt to Mayo. "Only one chapter—the third—deals specifically with the problems to which you have devoted so much time and study, but the whole book is based on the principles you have worked out and tries to use the approach to economic prob-

lems which you have pioneered," wrote Drucker, who was then teaching at Bennington College (see Chapter 4).[8]

Several more letters followed. By Christmas of that year, Mayo agreed
to meet with the young Austrian writer in his offices at Harvard. What
had begun as a meeting of minds now turned into something of a mating dance. Drucker, it was clear, was interested in a job at Harvard.
During the discussion in Mayo's office, the subject had been raised—
somewhat obliquely—but no concrete offer had been made. By the
spring, Drucker decided to press the point. "I have become more and
more convinced that the people who have started to work on the basic
social problems of an industrial society have an obligation to teach the
men whose actual performance will decide whether we are going to
have a free industrial society or not, i.e. the future executives," he wrote
Mayo in March 1947. "At the same time, I have become aware that the
young men in management are desperately anxious for such teaching. I
would not have believed it possible for the reprints of my Harper's series to sell almost eight thousand copies, largely to men in junior executive positions. . . . I hope this explains why I now venture to write to
you that I would be very much interested indeed in an opportunity to
work at the Harvard Graduate School of Business Administration."[9]

Drucker, however, wanted to make sure that he did not appear as a
supplicant, pointing out that Mayo had taken "the lead," that the subject of Drucker's own future plans had been raised first by Mayo. "I have
felt very acutely that I was ingenuous to the point of rudeness during
the conversation we had in your chambers before Christmas. . . . It
seemed to me that you . . . were asking about my future plans and that
I turned away this question in a manner which I hope did not offend
much. . . . There was however a good reason for my reluctance to follow
your lead. It was not only that I felt that a discussion of my plans would
make it appear as if one of the main purposes of my visit had been to
discuss a job for myself—which was very far indeed from my intent."[10]

As long as the subject had come up, though, Drucker wanted to make
clear that he would come only if an attractive enough offer were made.
"Because my position and my income here [at Bennington] are those of
a senior man . . . I would not feel able to consider a position elsewhere
unless it were a senior job—whatever that may mean concretely—with a
compensation commensurate for such a job."[11]

Years later, Drucker claimed, "I'm the only person who has said no
[to Harvard] four times." Drucker also says he said no to Princeton.
"No," on second thought, isn't quite accurate. "If I had wanted to, if I
had shown any great interest, I would have gotten [an] offer," he says.
What is clear is that in the coming years, his name surfaced again and

again at leading academic institutions around the country. He was put forward for an appointment at Yale but was ultimately vetoed. He was also a "main competitor" for an appointment at what was then Carnegie Tech, but that too failed to materialize.[12]

In retrospect, it is not surprising that as a young man in his mid-thirties, Drucker could not help but flirt with the leading academic institutions of his adoptive country. In the end, however, he was forced to recognize that he did not fit in. "I love to teach, but I've never wanted to be in academia," he says with the clarity of hindsight. "I'm not an academician by temperament."[13]

It is one of the more peculiar twists in Drucker's life and work that the man who has become the most revered management philosopher of the last several decades never found a place for himself at a premier business school. As both a philosopher and a social critic, he considered himself to be both above the fray and apart from it—a bystander, as he calls himself. At a time when the new direction of business education was analytical and quantitative, he deliberately kept himself apart from the mainstream. Even as Herbert Simon and his colleagues were filling their manuscripts with equations and footnotes, Drucker kept his books and articles free of both and made his prose defiantly readable. Then, too, while his personality—a combination of European charm and intellectual hauteur—easily won over corporate executives, it alienated many academics.

In the end, Drucker did accept an appointment at New York University. Although the Manhattan-based private university is now considered among the top business schools in the country, in the years following World War II it was a far cry from Harvard. It primarily offered finance and accounting courses to GIs who attended classes part-time in a ramshackle arrangement of rented classrooms scattered around the Wall Street area.

What NYU gave Drucker was the freedom to write and consult. It was during his years at NYU that he became an adviser to David Rockefeller, then CEO of Chase Manhattan Bank, and to the General Electric Company at the very time the company was undergoing a sweeping reorganization that became a model for American industry.

To his academic critics, Drucker has never been much more than a "journalist," the most scathing indictment that can be leveled at an academic. To journalists, many of whom eagerly lap up every well-turned phrase from Drucker's impressive lexicon, he can be an "unspeakably rude" consultant with the hauteur of a head of state.

To his admirers, however, Drucker is "perhaps the most perceptive observer of the American scene since Alexis de Tocqueville." Earlier and more clearly than anyone else—with the possible exception of Chester Barnard—he captured the essence of the century: the importance of the corporation as the defining *social* institution of our time. In two books, one written before World War II and the other published in 1942, Drucker blamed fascism for the collapse of Europe's spiritual and social order and the failure of *both* European capitalism and socialism. The supremacy of economic values assumed under capitalism, and the view of man as first and foremost an *economic* actor, was clearly wrong. At the same time, socialism had failed to abolish the class system or to mitigate the class warfare that had been exacerbated by capitalism. In an industrial society, according to Drucker, even though the business enterprise produces economic results, "it is not entirely, or even primarily, an economic institution." Instead, the enterprise becomes a "human and social" institution.[14]

As a consultant to many leading U.S. corporations, Drucker not only won the confidence of the century's leading capitalists but can claim credit for some of their successes—as well as some of their failures. Decades before marketing and customer focus became mantras of modern management, he understood that the "enterprise has to be market-driven," a conviction that became a leitmotif of his consulting engagements.[15]

Drucker has worn the test of time so well that even many of his erstwhile critics and natural adversaries have come to admire him—if somewhat grudgingly. Herbert Simon, for example, the ivory tower's quintessential academician, concedes that he was "not impressed" by Drucker when he first met him in Pittsburgh in 1949. Today, however, Simon seems surprised by his own admiration for Drucker. "Drucker is not a theorist in the strict sense, but he's a shrewd observer," says Simon, who had the opportunity to observe Drucker's influence firsthand when they were both on a World Bank Committee delegation in China and credits him with getting the Chinese to "reconcile" such capitalist notions as the separation of management and ownership with Communist dogma. Alfred Chandler also speaks admiringly of Drucker: "He's not a historian, but he's very important. He's sensible and a good synthesizer. There's no bad stuff in Drucker." That's more than he will say about other contemporary management theorists who have achieved guru status.[16]

Though hardly a journalist by any late-1990s conception of the term, it is a moniker Drucker wears proudly. Drucker is, if nothing else, a great storyteller; it is his grasp of metaphor, drama, and the unexpected twist ending that lends his insights such powerful effect. For Drucker, consulting has always been the "laboratory" for his writings and ideas. Teaching is his "hobby." It is writing, however, that he describes as his "compulsion neurosis."[17]

■

Drucker recounts one story of his youth with great gusto. He was twenty years old, working as a securities analyst in Frankfurt, when he wrote his first econometric paper, a model of the New York Stock Exchange, which proved "with impeccable assumptions that the New York Stock Exchange could go only up." The study, which was published in a prestigious European journal, came out two days before the great stock market crash of 1929. "That's when I stopped—or tried to stop—making predictions," he quips.[18]

Cloaked within the self-deprecating humor of the anecdote, this story serves a number of narrative purposes. It establishes Drucker's intellectual precociousness and his credentials as an analyst. It shows that, had he wanted to, he could easily have become a member of what Herb Simon calls the "econometric mafia." And it tells us, in effect, that as something of a polymath, he could have done anything—that the path he has trod has been entirely of his own choosing.

That path, in fact, has been one of a twentieth-century prophet—a man who has built a reputation on interpreting the times and, yes, predicting the course of future events. Even as a child, Drucker was drawn to philosophically challenging subjects. Knowing that he would one day be expected to attend university—not a foregone conclusion in continental Europe—sixteen-year-old Peter decided to test his intellectual mettle on a piece of academic research. When his uncle Hans Kelsen, who later went on to become a leading legal scholar at Berkeley, told him that explaining the rationale for criminal punishment was the most difficult problem in legal philosophy, young Peter decided to "go to work on criminal punishment and to write the *definitive* book" on the subject. With the help of a family friend, Count Max Traun-Trauneck, who was an administrator at the Austrian National Library in Vienna, Drucker gained access to a small room where he read a who's who of moral philosophy, including Aristotle, Thomas Aquinas, Jeremy Bentham, and David Hume.[19]

The result of this effort was vintage Drucker, as it combined scholarship, synthesis, and a totally contrarian conclusion: "It took me only a few weeks of baffled reading to come to the conclusion that all these great men must be tackling the wrong problem. If a dozen explanations, all starting with totally different but self-evident premises, reach the same conclusion, then, elementary logic would argue, they are all rationalizations rather than explanations, and beside the point. The point, it seemed to me, was not punishment at all. . . . What needed explanation was the existence of crime—and that I knew to be well beyond my powers."[20]

Peter Ferdinand Drucker embarked on his journey in the best place for rearing intellectuals and philosophers during the early part of the century: Vienna. He grew up amid a genteel milieu of Habsburgian civil servants and intellectuals, a world peopled with outsized personalities of the waning, fin-de-siècle empire. Smart and precocious, he was reared on the precarious precipice of Modernism, infused as it was in Vienna with a potent brew of intellectual creativity, political angst, multiculturalism, and anti-Semitism.

Drucker's own identity, which he has woven into a rich tapestry of memory, remains curiously entangled in the Old World, prewar "Atlantis" into which he was born and which he couldn't wait to leave behind. It is an identity as intricately structured as a fine Gobelin tapestry with hidden welts and weaves, shadowy details, and subtleties of color. From his youth, he always preferred the company of his elders—the older, "wise" men and women who together with his parents, Caroline and Adolf Drucker, made up his world. "I had never liked being young, and detested the company of delayed adolescents."[21] His world was peopled with larger-than-life characters: men of letters, such as Hugo von Hofmannsthal and Arthur Schnitzler, who were his parents' "best friends"; men such as Sigmund Freud, who ate lunch at the same cooperative restaurant during the food shortages of World War I as the Druckers and vacationed near the same Alpine lake ("Remember today," his parents told young Peter when he was introduced to Freud. "You have just met the most important man in Austria, and perhaps in Europe"); and such protofeminists as his "aunt" Trudy, the only woman doctor of her time to become a chief of staff and director of a European hospital, and Genia Schwarzwald, who founded Vienna's first college preparatory school for girls.[22]

Last but not least, there were his parents. Caroline, whom he resembles most, came from a well-to-do family but was orphaned as a child. One of Genia Schwarzwald's first prep school students, she was both attractive and intelligent. She was also strong-willed, argumentative, and independent. And she was a natural ally of her oldest son. Peter had a younger brother, Gerhart, who makes only cameo appearances in his brother's memoirs and who belonged, presumably, to the young people whose company young Peter largely disdained. "My mother and I never had to [explain] anything to each other," says Drucker. "We saw things exactly the same [way]."[23]

Adolf, the father of the bard, was another matter entirely. Drucker recalls an almost saintly figure, a "great man" of such boundless integrity that he had a tendency to turn friends into "worshipers." Indeed, young Peter held his father in such high esteem that he felt almost destined to disappoint him. We were "so different, we found it almost impossible to understand each other," he recalls. "Our relations were not bad, but until I turned thirty they were not good."[24]

In particular, Adolf's concerns about his son's future centered on Peter's decision to enter the world of commerce. "There is nothing my father would have liked more than for me to be respectable," quips Drucker. And at the turn of the century, respectability meant a career in the civil service, academia, or one of the gentlemanly professions: the law or medicine. (It couldn't have helped Peter's frame of mind that Gerhart was set on attending medical school.) To this day, there is no more respectable designation for a Viennese gentleman than "Herr Doktor," which covers anyone with a degree in medicine, the law, or a university professorship. Despite his misgivings, Adolf helped his son find a position in the business world.[25]

Yet Adolf could be as calculating as he was honorable. Even as a young man, when Peter embarked on his first job in Germany as a trainee in an export firm in Hamburg, the elder Drucker admonished his son, "Unless you get a doctorate, you'll never amount to anything. And [if you go to work] you'll never get a doctorate." It was all the challenge Peter needed. Just to show his father how wrong he was, he enrolled at Hamburg University to study for a law degree soon after arriving in Hamburg. "It was not until years later that I realized he knew perfectly well what he was doing," he recalls. "He was shrewd enough to know that I could not resist that kind of challenge."[26]

Befitting a man who couldn't wait to leave his homeland and who later embraced America as the only place where he ever felt truly at home, Drucker's recollections of his roots and his childhood resemble nothing so much as a Middle European Horatio Alger story. There is an artfulness to his recollections. Coming from a world in which nothing was so important as lineage, he describes his forebears as a distinguished Protestant clan that lost its fortune in the stock market crash of 1873, becoming "dirt poor" overnight. Thus, Adolf had to go to work at age eight, tutoring the son of a wealthy Jewish banker; eventually he earned a doctorate and became a prominent civil servant. Indeed, in typically Austro-Hungarian fashion, in Drucker's stories the friends and countrymen of Jewish ancestry are always described as such: "Hofmannsthal was a half Jew," he says. "Schnitzler was one hundred percent Jewish."[27]

Judaism, anti-Semitism, and Jewish self-hatred were a leitmotif of fin-de-siècle Vienna. From the writings of Ludwig Wittgenstein and Carl

Schorske's *Fin de Siècle Vienna* to Drucker's own memoirs, they are a defining theme of the times. Writing about a close friend of the family who became a high official in Austria's Ministry of Finance, Drucker noted, "[T]he family had already made the big step toward assimilation into the successful bourgeoisie. An uncle . . . had moved to Vienna and become one of the city's leading lawyers and the first Jew to head the Vienna Bar Association." This same man, he noted, "was by no means the only European Jew who turned anti-Jewish to resolve his own inner conflicts. Marx held very much the same opinions. And both Freud in Vienna and Henri Bergson in France could only come to terms with their own Jewish heritage by turning against it."[28]

What of Drucker's own Jewishness? In his memoirs, Adolf Drucker is described as a Protestant and Freemason. Caroline's father, we are told, was a British subject. Drucker himself is a practicing Episcopalian. He has never been to a Jewish wedding or a bar mitzvah. Not until he was well into his eighties did he attend the Jewish funeral of an old friend. "Of course," he concedes when asked, "there is no Austrian of my class [i.e., intellectuals, civil servants] who doesn't have Jewish relations." Who they are, where they came from, or how many generations back they go, he doesn't volunteer.[29]

Given Drucker's Viennese roots and his interest in the taxonomy of friends and acquaintances, it is a strange—and telling—omission from his own official record. The careful editing of his identity is the one chink of vulnerability in an armor of intellectual and ethical certitude. It undoubtedly has its roots with his parents, who constructed a fortress of bourgeois Protestant respectability to protect themselves and their children.

Even after emigrating to the United States, Drucker would have been grateful for the abridged version of the Drucker family history. For example, he found that in 1940s America, the sublet agreement for a house in a respectable suburb such as Bronxville, New York, required a recommendation from a minister. In a small American town, credit at the bank depended on showing up at church regularly. And Jews were systematically excluded from the academic and corporate circles to which Drucker sought access. Nevertheless, the ambiguity of his own identity is the one residue of old Europe from which America's most prescient philosopher has never shaken himself free.

■

From the age of fourteen, Drucker knew that he wanted to "get out of Vienna and out of Austria altogether, as soon as [he] possibly could."[30] He set off for Hamburg in 1927, soon after his graduation from the gymnasium (high school). Having deemed his experiment in academic research on the problem of criminal punishment a failure, he pressed his father to find him a business internship away from Vienna. The job was the first in a series of positions he held until he emigrated to the United States in 1937. A year after moving to Hamburg, he became a securities analyst in Frankfurt. While working full-time, he continued studying for his doctorate in international law, which he earned in 1931. About the same time, he began moonlighting as a professor.

Drucker lost his analyst's position during the stock market crash of 1929, when he embarked on a career that—to hear his detractors tell it—has dogged him ever since: he became a journalist.

■

The beginning of the 1930s, a catastrophe for Europe, was a heady time for young Peter Drucker. Not yet twenty-four, he seemed to have reached the pinnacle of his career. He worked first at the *Frankfurter General-Anzeiger*, an afternoon newspaper. Soon thereafter, he was offered a leading editorial position with a newspaper in Cologne, as well as a lectureship—a prestigious, though unpaid, "Dozent" position—at the local university. And though he was not a German citizen, he was already the youth chairman of the most promising anti-Nazi party, a predecessor of today's CDU, the Christian Democratic Union.[31]

But these were turbulent times in prewar Germany. In July 1932, the Nazis gained 37.4 percent of the vote, making them the largest party in the Reichstag. That November, the Nazis' vote dropped to 33 percent. But fear of the Communists, who gained ground during that election paved the way for Hitler's grab for power on January 31, 1933. For Drucker, success suddenly carried an unbearably high price: assuming the Cologne lectureship would automatically mean accepting German citizenship, something Drucker says he was not willing to do under the current regime. Then, too, as one of the "most prominent young people" in Germany and one of the few who was not a leftist, he was offered a job as press secretary to the Foreign Office by the Nazis.

Drucker already had decided to make a clean break with Germany. As a sort of insurance against being seduced by the Nazis, he had written a monograph on Friedrich Julius Stahl that was a veiled anti-Nazi manifesto. Stahl, a Jew by birth, was "perhaps the only political philosopher German Protestantism ever produced," wrote Berthold Freyberg, an old friend of Drucker's, in an essay on his friend. "A staunch conservative, [Stahl] rejected absolutism and created the legal foundation for constitutional monarchy.

"One reason why Drucker chose this remarkable and little understood figure for his first political analysis was, of course, precisely because this great spokesman of conservatism in nineteenth-century Germany had been of Jewish origin. The very choice of such a subject in those days was a manifesto and a courageous . . . attack on Nazi propaganda. The essay was immediately understood as a complete rejection of Nazism and was banned within a few weeks after its appearance."[32]

■

As a young man—an "unbearably arrogant young pup," as he describes himself—Drucker had known when to quit. A few weeks before his planned departure from Germany in 1933, Drucker got a visit from a newspaper colleague who had joined the Nazi Party and who asked for Drucker's help in protecting his fiancé, a young Jewish woman. In the course of their conversation, the colleague voiced grave misgivings about the "madmen" he was encountering in the inner circles of the Nazi Party. When Drucker urged his colleague to follow his example and leave the country, the man retorted heatedly, "You just don't understand, Drucker. . . . I'm not clever, I know that. Don't you understand that I want power and money and to be somebody? That's why I joined the Nazis early on. . . . And now I have a party membership card with a very low number and *I'm going to be somebody!*"[33]

As he let the man out of his apartment, Drucker was seized by a sense of foreboding: "Suddenly I had a vision—a vision of things to come, of the horrible, bloody, and mean bestiality that was descending on the world. There and then I beheld as in a dream what was later to become my first major book, *The End of Economic Man*. I felt an almost irresistible urge to sit down and start typing. But I repressed it and started packing instead. I was on the train to Vienna by the following noon."[34]

Some two decades later, in a mock commencement address written for *Fortune* under the subheading "The Importance of Being Fired," Drucker gave some unlikely advice to newly minted graduates from the country's leading business schools. "Getting fired from the first job is the least painful and least damaging way to learn how to take a setback," he wrote. "Nobody has ever lived who has not gone through a period when everything seemed to have collapsed and when years of work and life seemed to have gone up in smoke."[35]

■

In 1933, Drucker set off to make a new life for himself in London. It was there that he ran into Doris Schmitz, a young woman whom he had known slightly in Germany and who later became his wife. With the help of family friends, he got an introduction to Freedberg & Company, a venerable merchant banking firm, where he worked as an analyst and economist for the next few years. As in Vienna and Frankfurt, he quickly sought out the most illustrious intellectual circles. Every week, for example, he took the train to Cambridge University to attend John Maynard Keynes's seminar. He also befriended Noel Brailsford, a controversial writer thirty years Drucker's senior, who wrote for a number of eminent publications, including *The New Statesman* and *The Manchester Guardian*, and whom Drucker adopted as his wise man in exile.[36]

As a sanctuary from Nazism, Drucker's sojourn in London—especially his three years working at Freedberg & Company—served another important purpose: it helped reinforce his conservative, nineteenth-century liberal Weltanschauung. Freedberg & Company had been founded by Ernest Freedberg, whose family had been bankers in Germany and who, during a sojourn in South Africa in the late 1800s intended to cure his tuberculosis, had become banker to Cecil Rhodes, another sufferer of the dreaded disease. "A good deal of the fun at Freedberg & Company . . . lay in the knowledge that I was watching a near-extinct species: the nineteenth century private banker as Balzac had best described him," he wrote. "I felt very much the way an anthropologist must feel when he observes one of our 'living ancestors,' a tribe of Amazon Indians, perhaps, going about their hunting and trapping, unaware of the bulldozers only a few miles away already laying down the super-highway that will destroy their Stone Age civilization."[37]

What impressed Drucker the most was "the shrewdness, wit and integrity" of Freedberg. Years later, he would observe that the "gun slingers of the go-go stock market of the 1960s . . . had little of the wisdom that made small-town provincial Ernest Freedberg realize that any management that promises 10 percent growth in both profits and sales for years ahead is either crooked or stupid or both."[38]

Drucker, however, was bored by banking. Nor did Britain feel like home to the Druckers. "There was no future for us in England; we didn't belong," says Drucker sixty years after emigrating to the United States. "The kind of work I've done—the kind of career I've built—in this country, we probably could only make in this country. No other country in the world would have accommodated a maverick like me."[39]

Drucker likes to say that he always started at the top. "If I had started at the bottom, I would never have gotten anywhere."[40] In the rigid class structure of prewar Britain, an Austrian intellectual with a thick Viennese accent and a hint of Jewish ancestry could never start at the top. Then, too, Drucker has always had an uncanny knack for seeing the shape of future events—and the future clearly belonged to America.

When Peter and Doris Drucker sailed for the United States in April 1937, the manuscript of *The End of Economic Man* was packed in their luggage. The Druckers arrived in Manhattan in the middle of a record-breaking heat wave. The Midtown hotel where they stayed was just east of where the Eighth Avenue subway line was being built. So in addition to enduring torpid temperatures that never dipped below ninety degrees even at night, they were kept awake by the endless cacophony of jack-hammers working on the construction just outside their windows. Almost immediately, the two immigrants fled to a sublet in Bronxville, a suburb just north of the city.[41]

But if the heat and noise of New York City seemed overwhelming, everything else felt just right. "Both of us, from day one in this country, were at home," recalls Drucker.

Once again, Drucker adapted easily to his new surroundings. Until war broke out in Europe, he continued to work as a freelance journalist for several European publications and to do some "asset management" work for Freedberg & Company. By 1939, when war cut him off from his European connections and his main source of income, he picked up regular assignments from *Harper's* and the *Saturday Evening Post*. He was teaching economics and statistics at Sarah Lawrence College in Bronxville. He was even able to turn down a job at *The New York Times* because he didn't want to become "a cog in a machine."[42]

The publication of *The End of Economic Man* also brought Drucker to the attention of Henry Luce, who approached Drucker about coming to work for Time, Inc. Over lunch at a fashionable New York restaurant with Henry and Clare Boothe Luce, who was "visibly bored" by the discussion, Luce probed the Austrian immigrant about coming to work for *Time* as the magazine's foreign news editor. Drucker was to replace Laird Goldsborough, the controversial foreign editor who had advocated appeasement of the Nazis and had praised Francisco Franco.[43]

While he had his misgivings about group journalism, the prestige and princely salary offered by Luce had their appeal. Ultimately, says Drucker, his chances at *Time* were undermined by the "internal intrigues," "backbiting," and "feuding" that were endemic to Time, Inc., and that for a time were directed at Drucker by *Time*'s "communist cell."[44]

Drucker, who had predicted the Hitler-Stalin nonaggression pact in *The End of Economic Man*, undoubtedly became a target of 1930s Communists. However, the notion of a Communist cabal in the editorial ranks of *Time*—one strong enough to sway Luce, an autocrat who was known for doing as he pleased—stretches the bounds of credibility. It is much more likely that, ever the maverick, Drucker didn't fit into the *Time* culture any more than he would have succeeded as a cog in the works of *The New York Times*. (Indeed, Drucker says of Sarah Lawrence, the only other institution where he was working at the time, "I didn't like Sarah Lawrence, and Sarah Lawrence didn't like me.")[45]

Instead, Drucker went to work on the tenth-anniversary issue of *Fortune* magazine. He took on occasional consulting assignments for *Time* but never a permanent position.

Drucker's considerable ambition had not yet taken on a specific shape. "I had a pretty good idea of what I *didn't* want," he says. It wasn't until 1941, when he had lunch with Lewis Jones, the president of Bennington College, that Drucker "fell" into the job that would set him on an academic course. Bennington had just gotten one of the numerous grants then being assigned by the Rockefeller Foundation for research in the social sciences. Jones had come to New York in search of a social scientist to join the faculty. Over a free-ranging discussion at lunch, Drucker recommended Karl Polanyi, an eccentric Hungarian intellectual whom he had first met in Vienna when Polanyi was an editor at *The Austrian Economist* (*Der Österreichische Volkswirt*). Suddenly, Jones stopped in midstream. "Come to think of it, how would you feel about joining us?" he asked Drucker.[46]

"Ten minutes later, I was signed on," says Drucker. "I told him I just needed to check with my wife."[47]

To hear Drucker tell it, he had spurned *The New York Times* and turned down Henry Luce. He had demurred when Harvard and Princeton approached him about a job. (Even before his discussions with Mayo at the Harvard Business School, Drucker says, he had been "approached" by Harvard's Littauer School.) At the start of World War II, a full-time job with the Board of Economic Warfare was "changed into a far more satisfying—and productive—part-time consulting relationship." Writes Drucker: "I neither functioned well nor felt happy as a cog in a bureaucratic machine."[48]

How was it that suddenly, in just ten minutes, the urbane Austrian decided to join the Bennington faculty and retreat to a sleepy, snowy Vermont village? For one thing, he says, "I was given the freedom to teach whatever subjects I thought I needed learning in: political theory and American government, American history and economic history, philosophy and religion."[49] Then too, in a small pond he could be not only a big fish, but an unfettered one as well.

Drucker spent the next seven years at Bennington. From then on, he maintained affiliations with one academic campus or another, building what eventually became the most recognized—and possibly the most respected—name in management. He had not yet completely abandoned his Ivy League ambitions. Yet Drucker, who would soon become the guru of large organizations, proved defiantly incapable of finding a permanent place for himself within a large institution. He was destined to remain on the fringes of the academic, if not the corporate, world.

It is telling that of all the places in the world where he would ever live, it was Bennington that the cosmopolitan intellectual considered "most nearly home." The Druckers' third and fourth children were both born in Bennington. (The Druckers' eldest child, Kathleen, had been born about a year after the Druckers arrived in the United States.) The bucolic college town, whose surroundings may have reminded him of the hills and woods around Vienna, appealed to Drucker, who is an avid hiker. Then, too, Bennington closed for the three coldest winter months—partly to save fuel, partly to give its students real-world work experience. The winter hiatus gave the Druckers the chance to spend time in New York, to avail themselves of the city's cultural institutions, and to work at the Columbia University library.[50]

After moving to Bennington, Drucker began searching for a research project on the "political and social structure of industrial society . . . 'the anatomy of industrial order.' "[51] The project would be something of a sequel to his latest book, *The Future of Industrial Man*, in which he had first argued that the corporation—and, by implication, the modern organization—is "the representative social institution" of our society. Audacious and contrarian, *The Future of Industrial Man* was written during the summer of 1940, just before the United States entered World War II, a period when few Americans or Europeans could think about anything but survival, let alone a well-reasoned blueprint for post-Nazi society.

In his book, Drucker dissected the evil that was sweeping Europe and found the root of the problem in "rationalist Liberalism," which, he argues, is "fundamentally . . . totalitarian" because it "believes in the absolute and sovereign state."[52] It is only the *Christian*, religious-based liberal movement, rooted in Edmund Burke, that is truly "free and antitotalitarian" and that offers an alternative to absolutism, according to Drucker. It is the Christian roots of American social philosophy, with its emphasis on the "uniqueness of the individual," he later wrote, that make America's society at once "the most materialistic and the most idealistic."[53]

Drucker then proceeded to put forward his ideas for reclaiming the values of what he terms the "Anglo-Saxon liberalism of the 19th century" and to explore a new, legitimate foundation for political and social integration. The locus of this integration, he argued, would be large business enterprises, through which the principles of legitimate gover-

nance and the individual's "status and function" in society would be realized.[54]

Drucker was reacting in large part to the alienation of the worker in
industrial society, a theme already sounded by Elton Mayo and Fritz
Roethlisberger and in the literature of the times, both American and
Austrian. In *Concept of the Corporation*, which he began researching in
1942, he wrote that in "modern industrial society the citizen must ob-
tain both standing in his society and individual satisfaction through his
membership in the plant, that is, through being an employee.
Individual dignity and fulfillment in an industrial society can only be
given in and through work." In addition, he believed that a free society—presumably through its large corporations—must provide "full employment" and some protection for the individual against "the vagaries
of the marketplace."[55]

Indeed, it was *The Concept of the Corporation* that helped to cement
Drucker's reputation as a management philosopher. In it, he analyzed
General Motors through the lens of a social scientist, bringing together
perspectives from political science, sociology, and philosophy, as well as
economics. He examined the company in all its complexity, from the
plant floor to policy making in the executive suite. Ultimately, he sought
to interpret GM's role against the "broad canvas of social beliefs and
promises" invested in big business by American society. While the book
became a required text in leading universities, in courses from political
science to business, Drucker's broad-brush approach served to alienate
him further from academia.[56]

Shortly after the publication of *The Future of Industrial Man*,
Drucker got a call from General Motors and was invited to meet with
Donaldson Brown, the vice president of finance, who was known as "the
brains of GM." Brown had been brought to GM in 1921 by Pierre du
Pont, to establish the carmaker's financial and statistical controls. "I've
read your book," said Brown. "We in GM have been working on the
things you're talking about—on the governance of the big organization,
its structure and constitution, on the place of big business in society,
and on principles of industrial order."[57]

Drucker went to Detroit in 1943, just as the company was in the
throes of wartime mobilization, and spent eighteen months studying the
company's management policies and organization. It was his first inside
look at management. "When I got to General Motors, I knew nothing
about management," he later conceded. The experience confirmed the
bias toward large organizations, decentralization, and customer-focused
marketing that would surface in his later work.[58]

Concept of the Corporation built on Drucker's assertion that "[t]he emergence of Big Business . . . as a social reality during the past fifty years is the most important event in the recent social history of the Western world." The book reaffirmed his belief in the corporation as the "representative institution" of American society and his belief that the corporation "must hold out the promise of adequately fulfilling the aspirations and beliefs of the American people."[59]

Drucker's choice of GM as a laboratory for his research was largely a function of the fact that the auto company was willing to give him access, whereas other companies would not. Yet he was fortunate in that GM was one of the only U.S. companies at the time that had "been consciously and deliberately working at basic problems of policy and has . . . based its policy on the conception of the modern corporation as a social institution."[60]

In his book, Drucker presented federal decentralization as the model of the company's corporate structure, praising the balance of power between the executive committees that set policy and administrative systems, on the one hand, and the manufacturing divisions, on the other. Even while noting GM's exceptions to the rule of decentralization—the organization of the Fischer Body Division and, to a lesser extent, Chevrolet—he extolled the general principle of a balance of power within the company. "Central management has twofold functions under a system of decentralization. It is at the same time the servant of the divisional managers, helping them to be more efficient and more successful in their autonomy, and the boss of the corporation. . . . Above all, central management thinks ahead for the whole Corporation. It is thus differentiated from divisional management not only in power and function but in time."[61]

GM's federal decentralization was successful, according to Drucker, because it facilitated the measurement of each division against two "yardsticks" of market performance. The first was "base pricing," which involved a careful analysis of cost factors that allowed GM to determine whether a division's good results were due to efficiency or improved methods or the result of forces outside management's control. The second was market share: for GM's large, centralized component divisions, such as Fischer Body, where measuring market share was difficult, if not impossible, cost-accounting methods were used instead. But even for those divisions, he wrote, "the competitive pressure is at work all the time. . . . Thus the effects of decentralization are achieved to a considerable extent even though decentralization itself is absent."[62] His ultimate argument in favor of decentralization was that as an organizational form it was more conducive to fostering leadership than centralization. Centralized organizations, he charged, "fail to measure up to one of the most important yardsticks of institutional and administrative efficiency: they do not discover and develop industrial leaders.... In every large-scale organization there is a natural tendency to discourage initiative and to put a premium on conformity."[63]

Drucker's primary proof for this assertion was that, even during the war, central management had established maximum and minimum production orders for each division but otherwise allowed each division manager to decide "what to produce, where and how," as well as to set pricing and delivery schedules. The model was so successful that Fischer Body, which during World War II had temporarily decentralized its operations to produce a range of products from aircraft instruments to tanks, decided to maintain its decentralized organization after the war. The main reason for the change, cited by the Fischer Body management, was "[t]he need for trained and independent leaders who cannot be obtained in sufficient quantity and quality in a centralized organization."[64]

Drucker, however, recognized the problem of "isolation" in the boardroom that can keep corporation executives from being able to assess the forces buffeting their business realistically. He wrote that while "a certain amount of mental parochialism is essential for the discharge of his duties ... this parochialism of the executive imagination is also very dangerous for the corporation." (Indeed, parochialism and an erosion of the divisions' independence—and particularly of independent thinking—would in later years prove a significant problem for GM.)[65]

Most significantly, Drucker stressed GM's "unfinished business"—the way the work and jobs of individual employees were organized. The optimistic and, in many ways, naive conception of the worker as a good corporate citizen who could fulfill his need for "status and function" through his job was due in part to Drucker's observation of GM during the mobilization crisis. For during the war, plant management was, in fact, "forced to use its imagination to establish a relation between the war worker and his product, not out of humanitarian reasons but for the sake of greater efficiency." He cites the "unbelievable increase in morale and productive efficiency" that occurred when the Army brought a bomber and its maintenance crew to GM. The bomber gave the workers a chance to see the final product for which they manufactured parts and, in effect, a chance to talk to the customer—a concept that didn't gain wide currency in manufacturing until the quality movement of the late 1980s.[66]

Drucker's vision of the social benefits of corporate citizenship and federal decentralization are nowhere more apparent than in a story he recounts about a controversial production experiment at Cadillac. The story, it turns out, is more moral tale than reality and raises one troubling aspect of Drucker's remarkable legacy. For the sake of a good story, he is perfectly willing to edit—and perhaps even invent—facts. The story as he tells it, goes like this: In 1942, Cadillac's general manager, Nicholas Dreystadt, against the advice of senior management, accepted a contract to produce aircraft bombsights. Technologically, the bombsights were among the most sophisticated and delicate pieces of equipment produced during the war. Although each car division was free to bid on any military contract it wanted, GM's top brass opposed Dreystadt's move, arguing that the job was too complex and the shortage of labor at the time was insurmountable.[67]

The grumbling in the executive suite turned to outrage when, according to Drucker, GM's top executives learned that Dreystadt and his personnel manager, Jim Roche, who would later go on to become GM's president, had drafted two thousand superannuated black prostitutes to build the bombsights.[68]

Dreystadt, however, exercised his rights under decentralization to accept the contract. And he set about the work of making good corporate citizens out of the women. Since most of his new female workers were not only untrained but also illiterate, he personally machined a dozen bombsights and produced a training film that detailed the step-by-step production process.[69]

Dreystadt and his band of female outcasts proved the naysayers wrong. Within weeks, Dreystadt's workers, in what had become known as Cadillac's "red light district," had surpassed their production quotas.[70]

The tragic outcome of Cadillac's experiment ultimately undermined Drucker's theory that big business could provide the "status and function" of—let alone an employment guarantee for—its good corporate citizens. For Dreystadt was able to protect his crew only until the end of World War II. He knew that veterans returning from the war would have first preference for the jobs they had left behind. Yet for a time, he thought he might be able to take advantage of the inevitable boom in peacetime production to save some of the women's jobs after the war.[71]

Facing continued opposition from both labor and management, the women were ultimately fired. When Dreystadt learned that a number of them had committed suicide rather than go back to the streets, he was inconsolable. "God forgive me," grieved Dreystadt the good, Christian manager in Drucker's narrative. "I have failed these poor souls."[72]

But an exhaustive search for Cadillac's bombsight workers, including interviews with dozens of workers who worked at GM during the war, reveals not a shred of evidence to support Drucker's story. United Auto Workers records, including a 1943 UAW survey of employment in the auto plants by race and gender, reveal that no single plant employed more than a few hundred black women, and most had only a few dozen. Of approximately 2,200 "Negroes" employed at *three* Cadillac and Fleetwood plants in the Detroit area, less than 100 were black women, according to the UAW survey conducted in March 1943. Of those, two thirds worked as "matrons and janitresses." Jim Roche, the former personnel manager, recalls no such project, no sizable black female workforce, certainly no black hookers.[73]

For the sake of a colorful story, Drucker is willing to go too far. Yet in key respects, he was not willing to go far enough in his conception of the participative potential of labor in industry. To be sure, one of Drucker's principal criticisms of Elton Mayo was that the Harvard guru was fundamentally *manipulating* workers in the interests of management by merely creating the *appearance* of listening to their concerns. By contrast, Drucker believed it was important to actively "listen" to workers—to what they feel they need to know as well as to the problems they perceive in the workplace.[74]

After *Concept of the Corporation,* Drucker spoke highly of the efforts of Charlie Wilson, Sloan's successor, to learn more about GM workers and their attitudes toward their jobs. In doing so, however, Drucker revealed that when it comes to "human relations," he had not progressed as far beyond Mayo as he might have thought. For example, he is full of unalloyed praise for a Wilson-inspired contest entitled "My Job and Why I Like It," which surveyed a majority of GM employees, about 200,000 in all, about their jobs. Drucker described the results of the contest as "the richest research material on employee attitudes and worker values ever brought together."[75]

Not surprisingly, the survey results were stored away, never to be used again. Whom does Drucker blame? While conceding that the company found it difficult to analyze 200,000 entries, he points his finger at the union for resisting such an encroachment by management on what the organizers considered labor's terrain. In fact, the contest—and its outcome—is part of a rich legacy of failed suggestion programs and attitude surveys that have changed virtually nothing in plants across the country. In the absence of a wholehearted executive-level commitment to push decision making and participation down the line, such efforts never rise above the gimmickry—well intentioned though they may be—of countless management fads.[76]

Drucker, however, was not willing to go so far as to concede that the *average* worker, properly trained, could make a significant contribution to plant-floor management. His principal idea of giving "status and function" to workers was to create a "self-governing plant community" that would administer the community services for the plant. Such a self-governing community would decide on matters relating to plant safety, working conditions, and parking. It would not, presumably, allow the workers a systematic role in determining the efficacy of certain materials and equipment or the manufacturability of particular parts.

Drucker's idea reveals how strongly he was wedded to the notion of hierarchy. Although he is not "an elitist in the conventional sense," wrote John Tarrant, author of *Drucker: The Man Who Invented the Corporate Society*, "one may find through his thought a consistent feeling that 'everyone has his place'—with the corollary that the individual should accept his place and work to make himself effective and happy within" it. Nor is there any evidence that if such a self-governing body had been created, it could ever have been more than a palliative, let alone a vehicle for genuine "citizenship." In subsequent years, Drucker would vacillate between calling his idea about the "self-governing plant community" among his "most important and most original" and dismissing it as an "intellectual Edsel."[77]

One idea that does make an appearance in *Concept of the Corporation* and that proved particularly prescient was the need to create "equal opportunity" for advancement for the best of a company's workforce. To do so, Drucker proposed replacing the "irrational" and "haphazard" approach to promotion with clear policies, such as job rotation and training opportunities. He was fond, for example, of saying that if it hadn't been for the circumstances that had kept Walter Reuther laboring in a factory instead of giving him a chance to go to college, he could have been president of GM instead of the head of its union. (Presumably, since Drucker views unions as merely a necessary evil, this would have better served the interests of the corporation.) "The corporation simply cannot afford to deprive itself of the intelligence, imagination and initiative of ninety per cent of the people who work for it, that is, the workers. It can neither afford to reserve its executive positions for that small minority that managed to get a college degree; there simply are not enough *good* people with degrees around to satisfy the demand."[78]

It says something about the state of management, as an academic discipline, that almost everyone connected with *Concept of the Corporation* had grave doubts about its publishability. "I don't see anyone interested in a book on management," said Donaldson Brown at the time. Wrote Drucker, "I shared Brown's skepticism about the possibility of a saleable book."[79]

It was Lewis Jones, the president of Bennington College, whose assessment of the book came closest to divining its impact: while he thought it would be successful, he also predicted that it would ultimately harm Drucker's academic career. "You are launched on a highly promising academic career, either as an economist or as a political scientist," he said. "A book on a business corporation that treats it as a political and social institution will harm you in both fields."[80]

If *Concept of the Corporation* alienated academics and served to further distance Drucker from the ivy tower, it won him the respect and friendship of top executives. To be sure, the book was not widely embraced at GM. Alfred Sloan, for one, "saw no point" in it. And although Sloan didn't stand in Drucker's way, he made no reference to Drucker in his own book, *My Years at General Motors*. Ultimately, Drucker's impact on Sloan may have been profound; according to Drucker, Sloan credited *Concept of the Corporation* with inspiring him to write *My Years at General Motors*.[81]

However, Charles E. Wilson, who succeeded Sloan as president and CEO, maintained a relationship with Drucker long after Drucker had finished his GM study. One of the fruits of that relationship, which grew out of a discussion on a way to allow employees to share in the growth and profitability of the company—a subject Drucker touches on in *Concept of the Corporation*—was Wilson's plan for creating an employee pension fund that would be invested in common stock (but not in GM shares; the sums from a profit-sharing plan would be too small to be meaningful to most workers, both men agreed). Ironically, Drucker opposed the company pension fund solution on the ground that company pensions would restrain individual workers' mobility.[82]

Another possible outcome of the dialogue between Drucker and Wilson was the Supplementary Unemployment Benefits scheme, which was developed by Wilson's staff and which has since been adopted by other industrial companies. Although GM had worked on a wage guarantee during the Depression, it couldn't come up with a plan that wouldn't bankrupt it. It was his own advocacy of an "annual wage," according to Drucker, that convinced Wilson to go back to the drawing board.[83]

Concept of the Corporation became must reading in schools of government and business alike. When Ernie Breech left GM to become Ford's lieutenant, Drucker became "required reading for everyone who wanted to appear on their toes—including Henry Ford II." And Arjay Miller, one of the Whiz Kids (see Chapter 5) and the former CEO of Ford Motor Company, said, "I found it extremely useful in forming my own judgments regarding what was needed at Ford. It was, by a considerable margin, the most useful and pragmatic publication available, and had a definite impact on the postwar organizational development within the Ford Motor Co."[84]

Lewis Jones's words proved prophetic, however. An otherwise sympathetic review in *The American Political Science Review* ended by saying, "It is to be hoped that this promising young scholar will soon devote his considerable talents to a more serious subject."[85]

Drucker, of course, proved stubbornly recalcitrant. After *Concept of the Corporation*, his writings on politics shifted decisively to the burgeoning new field of management, which he had helped to popularize. Three years after the publication of *Concept of the Corporation*, he accepted a job not in the Ivy League, but at NYU.[86]

With the publication of *Concept of the Corporation*, Drucker also won a significant following in business—and nowhere more than at General Electric. During the late 1940s, Drucker had worked briefly with Fred Borch, the Lamp Division's marketing whiz who succeeded Ralph Cordiner as CEO in the 1960s. (The Lamp Division, which was the most independent in its management largely because it had been the only GE division to produce a profit during the Depression, served as something of a model for the rest of GE.) Early in the tenure of Cordiner, who became CEO at the beginning of the Korean War, Drucker was invited to GE headquarters. One of Cordiner's first acts as a chief executive had been to bring in Harold Smiddy from Booz Allen & Hamilton to set up the Management Consultation Services, which was to research and "find the principles of professionalism in management, and then to develop professional managers." It was to assist with this effort that Smiddy, in turn, approached Peter Drucker.[87]

General Electric, where Drucker spent as much as three days per week throughout the 1950s, was the largest and most intensive consulting assignment of his career. It placed him in the cockpit of what was then America's fourth largest corporation, and possibly its most respected.

As a top adviser to GE during most of the 1950s, Drucker found an ideal laboratory for his ideas. While his role at GM had been primarily that of observer, through his work at GE he demonstrated the profound impact he could have on one of the country's leading corporations and, through it, on U.S. industry as a whole.[88]

Drucker went to GE just as the company was undergoing both explosive growth and one of the most ambitious reorganizations in corporate America. He served as a chief architect of the company's ambitious management development program and as a key adviser to Smiddy on such projects as Crotonville, GE's corporate training center—one of the first of its kind—where, for many years, he was the only outsider invited to speak. He also headed a committee charged with devising GE's new compensation strategy. And he was an early and vocal advocate of a market-oriented approach to decentralization that didn't achieve full flower until Jack Welch took over as CEO in the early 1980s.[89]

While Drucker's involvement with GE was far more intense than it would be with other corporations, the assignment was typical of the role he assumes with his clients, in that he brought a big-picture, market-centered "outsider's perspective" to what was a relatively rigid, engineering-oriented corporate culture. "A great deal of the work had to do with what today you would call strategy and a great deal with introducing marketing to GE, which, except [for the] consumer goods division, saw itself as an engineering outfit and was run that way."[90]

Cordiner, who had run GE's consumer products business in the 1930s and had left the company at the start of World War II to become president of Schick and to "try out some management techniques" he hadn't been able to sell at GE, was more than ready to shake up GE's corporate culture. He returned to GE in 1943 and spent the rest of the war "thinking about the future" of the company. Though Cordiner was being groomed as the successor to Charlie Wilson (no relation to the Wilson at GM), the start of the Korean War thrust him into a leadership role earlier than anyone expected when Wilson left GE to become head of the Office of Defense Mobilization.[91]

Cordiner saw clearly that GE's reorganization was driven by two exigencies of the postwar era: first, a surge in the demand for GE consumer products, including small appliances, large appliances, and so-called brown goods, such as TVs and stereos, which had been unavailable during the war, and second, a commensurate need for *experienced* managers. Though GE's postwar management population had swollen, it was full of personnel hired during the war, many of whom "had never experienced competition in peacetime," as well as returning GIs who had not worked at GE since the beginning of the war. At the same time, the company faced the "largest quantitative demand for managers" in its history. "About two-thirds of the present jobs of Section-Manager level or above will have to be filled during the next decade by people not now in those jobs," according to one company estimate at the time. "And, it is common experience that every promotional decision at the top of an organization triggers many more moves—sometimes as many as ten—in successive lower levels."[92]

Cordiner himself put it this way in a preface to the four-volume "blue books" that were first published in 1954 at the culmination of the reorganization: "There has been a growing realization in American industry that great untapped opportunities lie in finding ways to develop more fully our human resources, particularly the managers of our business enterprises. Technological advances and the increasing complexities of managing today's and tomorrow's conditions have made manager development a necessity as well as an opportunity. Those who have been closest to this field believe that an opportunity exists in General Electric to increase productivity 50 percent in the next ten years through better management alone. . . .

"The company's decentralized plan of organization was developed and put into effect with the recognition that its benefits will not be fully realized until we have an ample supply of well-equipped 'professional' managers."[93]

The task that lay ahead of GE was even more formidable in some respects than the reorganization that had faced Sloan at GM. Thus, although the GE decentralization would become "the standard model worldwide," the company would have to fine-tune the structure for decades to come. "GM had nowhere near the problem we had in that we were building everything from aircraft engines to toothbrushes," says Hugh Estes, who worked with both Drucker and Smiddy during the 1950s. Then, too, GE's plants were scattered around the country, with each factory producing a variety of products. "We faced the realization that big works were unwieldy," recalls Robert E. Newman, another former GE executive. Major appliances, for example, were made in seven different cities across six states, in plants that, for the most part, "weren't designed for the purpose." Thus, in addition to decentralizing the company, management would have to rationalize its manufacturing operations and the product lines made at each plant.[94]

Moreover, both Cordiner and his plan were viewed with considerable suspicion within the company. That an erstwhile defector from the GE ranks—one who had led a *consumer products* company, a maker of shavers, no less—should be brought back to command a citadel of engineering was "bitterly resented" by many at GE. By most accounts, it took two years for Cordiner to win the confidence of his troops.[95]

Many GE insiders also failed to see the need for organizational change. While many managers "admitted that the inherited structure was a crazy, shapeless jumble which the business had outgrown," the prevailing attitude was "We make and sell turbines, so why bother about who does what?"[96]

Yet by 1953, Cordiner had succeeded in presiding over a profound restructuring of the company. GE's centralized bureaucracy had been split into twenty-two decentralized divisions containing about one hundred independent operating departments, which were to function as the basic units of GE's operations. The rationalization of GE's manufacturing operations had uprooted thousands of plant managers. Countless assistantships and staff positions had been jettisoned. With them had gone the morale of managers, who were reeling from the combined shocks of reorganization, the rewriting of long-familiar rules, and the promise of further changes.[97]

Cordiner's revolution was about more than just a reorganization, it was about redefining "the essence of management" and the role of the professional manager. Smiddy's group—Drucker in particular—was at the center of this effort and was charged with "push[ing] back the frontiers of the unknown, to convert rules of thumb into tested principles and practices and to transform hunch into learnable and teachable knowledge." To that end, Smiddy's team pored over the records of more than two thousand GE managers, interviewed hundreds of them, used GE business units to test new methods, and examined fifty outside companies. "General Electric's leaders propose to prove that management is a profession and that a man should not become a manager, as he does now ... largely because he has won in a game of musical chairs," wrote William B. Harris in *Fortune* magazine in 1955.[98]

Amid these fast-breaking waves of change, Drucker demonstrated a singular ability to anticipate the shifts in the currents and each new swell. He saw with remarkable clarity the challenges that lay ahead of GE in everything from consumer marketing to international expansion and was able to help the company conceptualize new business and management strategies. Hugh Estes, for example, remembers Smiddy and Drucker "breaking up the company into separate [smaller] companies." Adds Newman, "Peter Drucker was very important in trying to work out what really constituted [each individual] business."[99]

In 1954, GE held one of a series of conferences at Association Island in the St. Lawrence Seaway. Drucker was one of the key speakers at the conference. "Both the needs of the enterprise and the needs of our society demand that we learn,

"What the professional employee is,

"What he is expected to contribute, and

"How he has to be integrated into the business enterprise, and for the greatest good of society," he intoned.[100]

This was a period of "big-picture" thinking that, by 1954, resulted in "as broad a degree of decentralization as [could] be found anywhere." To help institutionalize the effort, GE published a four-volume bible outlining its management philosophy and invoking a small cadre of apostles whose ideas were key to the GE philosophy; they included Frederick Winslow Taylor, Mary Parker Follett, Ralph Cordiner, and Peter Drucker.

Drucker was the "big-picture" guy whom GE engineers needed to see, and make sense of, a turbulent future. While GE had clearly bene-fited from the surge in postwar business, "the top officers of the com-pany admit[ted] ruefully that they [had] not foresee[n]," the postwar boom and therefore had not adequately "exploit[ed] it."[101]

Cordiner was, if nothing else, a consummate planner. And Drucker was the company's resident futurist. Speaking before a group of execu-tives at Crotonville, Drucker held forth on such topics as demographic and market changes in Latin America and the shift of peasant popula-tions from the countryside to the cities. "What will it mean to businesses selling in South America?" he asked. "You're in a transportation busi-ness. Do you think the move to big cities means a new market for trans-portation? What does it mean to you?"[102]

Drucker's ability to grasp new ideas—and to inspire the confidence of the GE managers he advised—was crystallized in the role he played in helping to conceptualize GE's jet engine business. Toward the end of the 1950s, Drucker met Gerhard Neumann, a German Jewish engineer who had been known as "Herman the German" in China during World War II, where he had joined the famous Flying Tigers before becoming a master sergeant in the U.S. Army Air Corps.[103] Neumann had his own vision for harnessing the jet engine to revolutionize commercial aircraft. "Gerhard saw very early on that the jet engine, though a very different one from what you put into a single-seat fighter plane, would make mass air transportation possible," recalls Drucker. "But that meant working very closely with aircraft manufacturers, rethinking what is performance in a civil versus a military plane."[104]

"Neither airlines nor airframe manufacturers were ready for the jet." First, manufacturers weren't interested in civilian planes because the military was their main customer. Moreover, they would have to spend enormous sums of money to design a civilian jet plane that would carry several hundred people across the continent. Explains Drucker, "The aviation industry saw the jet engine as simply an engine to put into an existing propeller plane. What Neumann saw very clearly—and what made GE the leader in jet engines—was that you don't design jet engines to fit existing planes, you design optimal jet engines and then the plane around [them]. This was a very difficult [idea] to market. . . .

"I helped Neumann and his people—all of whom were technically oriented, most of whom came out of the military, to understand or try to understand the value system of potential customers, [and] also [to figure out] who is making the decisions. In retrospect, this seems obvi-ous, but in prospect it wasn't a bit obvious. Neumann came to me because he realized that that's what he himself needed. Those are the kinds of things I worked on with Gerhard."[105]

In some respects, Drucker was too far ahead even for GE. He pushed continuously—though not always successfully—to keep the new business units focused on specific markets. Cordiner's creation of more than a hundred self-governing *product* divisions "was an enormous step forward, but it was not basically [a] *market* focused" strategy, he says. The divisions were "still organized by the engineering required for each unit. It's only been since Welch that GE has organized itself around markets rather than technology. That, by the way, fitted Smiddy, who was himself an engineer."[106]

"One of my functions was to be dubious about that. My constant contribution to GE—and you won't find it in any of the [blue] books because I don't think they understood it—is that you can't impose your own internal logic on the universe . . . and this was counter to GE's basic religion."[107]

Drucker was sometimes wrong, with stunning long-term consequences. "We designed the world's most scientific compensation system, and it damn near ruined GE," he admits with self-deprecating humor. With few exceptions, U.S. companies had little at the time that could be called a compensation system, and GE's, in particular, was "a total mess." Says Drucker, "Compensation was based in part on tradition, and in large part arbitrary. The powerful people inside GE got a lot of money for their own people, [but] there was no system."[108]

In a drive to professionalize management, GE charged Drucker with heading a task force on compensation. The goal was to develop an objective yardstick against which performance, and ultimately remuneration, would be measured. Drucker's team included such up-and-comers as Reginald Jones, who became CEO in the early 1970s. The task force also conducted extensive interviews within GE and drew on Drucker's experience both at GM and consulting for Sears, Roebuck, one of the few companies that had a compensation system. "We came up with a beautiful system, which is still the foundation for [most] compensation systems—that salary and bonus are tied to the year's results"; that is, to return on investment (ROI).[109]

Because of GE's preference for developing a simple, single yardstick against which to measure compensation, Sears became the primary model for GE's compensation plan, according to Drucker. Since the 1930s, store managers at Sears had been rewarded on the basis of their one-year sales results. But as Drucker and GE soon learned, "store managers don't run businesses, they run stores, and there's a big difference."[110]

The problem was that even as GE pegged compensation of its divisions and smaller units to ROI, the reorganization gave each business unit responsibility for innovation. "What we did—in retrospect, it's obvious—was absolutely a mistake," concedes Drucker. "Innovation requires investment today without any return for a long time. [Under the new compensation plan] for a general manager to spend a penny on innovation meant taking money not just out of his own pocket, but also away from his people. So for ten years GE didn't innovate. It became apparent very soon that we had created an enormous disincentive to innovation." Neither Drucker nor GE fully grasped the inconsistency at the time.[111]

In fact, Drucker argues, he never advocated a single yardstick. He would have preferred to peg compensation to "a number of objectives," including employee morale and manager development. Ultimately, however, he was won over to GE's preference for a single performance measurement. It's telling that when Reg Jones, who had been on Drucker's compensation task force, became CEO, one of his first actions was to change the compensation plan.[112]

By then, however, the damage had been done: GE's compensation system came to be widely imitated. What Drucker learned about compensation at GE has become a key debating point among compensation experts. Thus, in *Management*, Drucker's influential textbook on the subject, he wrote, "The most damaging misdirection may result from those apparently eminently 'fair' compensation systems for the heads of decentralized divisions and businesses which relate a manager's pay directly to performance, usually to performance measured by return on investment during the calendar year. . . . [I]f return on investment or current profits are overemphasized, the managers of decentralized current profits are overemphasized, the managers of decentralized business will be misdirected toward slighting the future. . . . Compensation must always try to balance recognition of the individual with stability and maintenance of the group. No attempt at a 'scientific formula for compensation can therefore be completely successful.' "[113]

The greatest strength of GE's decentralization was what Drucker himself viewed as the salient strength of the "federal principle": as an unparalleled tool for grooming managers and future leaders.[114]

GE, however, also served as a model for "what not to do," in that the company failed to test its assumptions, including its organization design. Had the company tested its assumptions, says Drucker, it might not have subjected each of its businesses to a rigid structure made up of five key functional areas: engineering, manufacturing, marketing, accounting, and personnel. By doing so, "two things were not seen—with resulting high damage," he wrote. "First, it was not realized that some manufacturing businesses needed additional and different key functions.... One example was the computer business, where product development and customer service were far too important to be subordinated to engineering and marketing. GE's failure in the computer business had many causes, but the imposition of the functional structure of a typical manufacturing business was probably a major contributor. Second, there were some businesses that looked like manufacturing businesses but were, in effect, innovative businesses" that had no specific product or market. Typical of such arrangements were GE's R-and-D contracts for the U.S. government that might eventually develop into a product. "Yet the functions of a typical manufacturing business were imposed on them. Some of these innovative development businesses managed to survive by quiet sabotage of the official structure. The others were seriously damaged."[115]

What Drucker realized is that decentralizing what was essentially a single-product business (GM) was a much easier proposition than the challenge represented by the diversity and complexity of GE's operations. Despite the company's missteps, not even Drucker—with the benefit of hindsight—would view its reorganization as a failure. Rather, it has proven to be a work in progress.

The Practice of Management grew directly out of Drucker's work at GM and GE. *Management: Tasks, Responsibilities, Practices*, an eight hundred–plus-page tome published in 1974, builds on the earlier work and incorporates his experiences as an adviser to Chase, Sears, Roebuck, Blue Cross, and IBM, not all listed by name. (To this day, Drucker says, he names only clients that have publicly identified him first.)

Together, Drucker's experiences at GE and GM represent more than a decade of intensive involvement with two of America's major corporations. Equally important, they gave Drucker a broad purview of the industrial landscape and its challenges—from basic manufacturing and consumer marketing to high technology and product innovation. In sharp contrast to his image as a dilettante, Drucker's unique outsider/insider perspective is probably unmatched among academics and rare even among consultants.

Nor was Drucker's virtual laboratory confined to industrial companies. In 1955, when a group of bankers—vice presidents of the newly merged Chase National Bank and the Bank of Manhattan—convened for their first joint management meeting, John McCloy, the chairman of what was now the Chase Manhattan Bank, wanted an outsider to chair the meeting. He chose Drucker, who was in his mid-forties at the time, to deliver an address to the merged bank's key employees, who had been ordered to appear at the Princeton Inn in Princeton, New Jersey.[116]

For several years, Drucker had been serving as an adviser to David Rockefeller on personnel policy at Chase, whose headquarters were across the street from the NYU Business School, where Drucker was teaching at the time. Throughout the 1950s, he met with Rockefeller to discuss issues ranging from the bank's international expansion to the hiring and training of domestic personnel.

A few years later, Drucker became an adviser to Walter Wriston, the chairman of First National City Bank of New York (later Citibank). Fueled by his monthly appearances at bank headquarters, Drucker's influence on the chairman became something of a legend. In fact, says Drucker, he served as a sophisticated sounding board for the banker. "The reason Walt and I are such close friends is because he never did anything I told him," he quips, adding that Walt was a "wonderful client" because "he made up his own mind, he didn't use me as a substitute for thinking. He expected me to ask very searching, difficult questions. But I don't think he ever acted on my advice."[117]

For a polymath whose knowledge and interpretive skills are firmly harnessed to his considerable European charm and wit, the role of court adviser comes naturally. It helps that in addition to a fascination with books, Drucker possesses a journalist's curiosity about both his physical surroundings and the people he meets. During a rainstorm in the 1940s, a detour through London's Burlington Arcade, where the Royal Society was holding its annual exhibition—one on Japanese art—led Drucker to become a connoisseur.

In recent years, Drucker's life and work have come full circle. In the late 1980s, during a period of intense competitive ferment, Drucker was summoned back to GE. This time the "question" Drucker posed was more of a statement: "Make sure that your back room is their front room," recalls Welch. It was a statement that helped define Welch's approach to a wave of outsourcing. "In other words, don't you do guard services at your plant. Get someone who specializes in guard services" to do them for you. Get rid of in-house printing, in-house conference services, any business that isn't at the core of your focus. Explains Welch, "He made it very clear what a waste" it was to be in marginal activities where, inevitably, GE would put its "weakest people."[118]

Take the case of GE's central-air-conditioning business. "After I sold the business to Trane," a maker of air conditioners, says Welch, he called his old general manager. " 'How's it going?' I asked.

" 'I can't tell you how great things are,' he answered. 'Every morning my chairman tells me how much he loves air-conditioning. Every morning I woke up around you, you told me how much you hated being in the air-conditioning business.' "[119]

Make sure your back office is their front office. "That's a big deal," explains Welch. "It describes the whole restructuring."[120]

Indeed, in his tenth decade, Drucker continues to consult. He maintains contact with former clients. And he continues to gain new ones. In recent years, he has advised several universities on setting up virtual campuses and the benefits of distance learning. In 1996, he was tapped by Mark H. Willes, the new publisher of the *Los Angeles Times*, to discuss a major reorganization of the paper.[121]

Much of Drucker's focus in recent years has been on nonprofit organizations. His nonprofit clients have included universities, the Girl Scouts, and CARE. And in 1990, he lent his name to a foundation that had been spearheaded by Frances Hesselbein, the former national executive director of the Girl Scouts, and Richard Shubert, CEO of the American Red Cross. The mission of the Drucker Foundation is not to dispense money but to disseminate cutting-edge management ideas to nonprofits. While the foundation takes its lead from Drucker and the principles he has advocated over the years—such as maintaining a clarity of mission, focusing on the customer, and playing to an organization's strengths—he insisted that it draw on leading-edge management practice. While most of the foundation's funding comes from private individuals and organizations, including such companies as GE, Drucker contributed his royalties from his book *Managing the Non-Profit Organization* to the foundation. He also participates in the foundation's conferences.[122]

Drucker's interest in nonprofits was a logical evolution of both his commitment to the importance of organizations and his recognition that the corporation has failed to live up to its promise as the place where "the social tasks" of society and community can be organized. The downsizing wave of recent years not only has "destroyed the ethic of loyalty among middle managers" but has made a mockery of Drucker's assertion that employees are a vital source of knowledge, not a balance sheet item to be eliminated. Moreover, according to the American Management Association, "fewer than half of the firms that have downsized since 1990 have seen long-term improvements in quality, profitability or productivity." Says Drucker, "Corporations once built to last like pyramids are now more like tents."[123]

The mobility inherent in the new knowledge society has further undermined "community" and created, along with new opportunities for prosperity and entrepreneurship, new social problems as well. Nor has government been up to the task of creating the social services needed to make capitalism bearable.[124]

Increasingly, Drucker sees nonprofits—such as the church (including megachurches) and the Girl Scouts—as the institutions for "creat[ing] citizenship." He even foresees an expanding role for nonprofit institutions in contracting with government to accomplish social tasks. School voucher programs may be the most current example of the trend Drucker is predicting. However, with concerns about the erosion of public schools and whether public education should be subcontracted to private and religious educational institutions, voucher programs also have risks. Notes Jack Beatty in *The World According to Peter Drucker,* "There is a danger in the celebration of the social sector and its volunteerism, that the taxpayer will get the highly agreeable message that the problems of the inner city can be met without his taxes."[125]

Indeed, the clear message from the Progressive era was that while voluntarism works during good times, it is no answer to crisis. And even during the most bullish years of the 1990s, the inner city presented a crisis that demands public policy, as well as volunteerism and corporate involvement, if it is to be resolved.

Drucker's most compelling argument may be that for capitalism and democracy to survive, society must find a way to mitigate the social costs of a (relatively) free market economy. It is a lesson that has come to the fore as the United States has tried to export a free-market ideology to developing nations without advocating the social institutions (both voluntary and governmental) that have made capitalism bearable at home. That message, which Drucker has promoted for more than half a century, may prove to be his most enduring legacy.

[I]f you look at them in the light of their potential, most commercial corporations are dramatic failures—or, at best underachievers. They exist at a primitive stage of evolution; they develop and exploit only a fraction of their potential.

—Arie De Geus, *The Living Company*[1]

Epilogue

In the 1970s, Royal Dutch/Shell conducted a groundbreaking study of the life expectancy of Fortune 500 companies. The study concluded that while a few companies reach the mature age of two hundred years—and one or two have even survived seven hundred years—the vast majority expire within forty to fifty years. By 1983, for example, fully one third of the companies that had been listed in the 1970 Fortune 500 had disappeared. "Like individuals who are unhealthy and can expect an early demise, most large, apparently successful corporations are profoundly unhealthy," wrote Peter Senge in a forward to *The Living Company* by Arie De Geus, a former Shell executive who pioneered the Shell study.[2]

Schumpeterians might argue that creative destruction is the lifeblood of a healthy economy. Certainly, the creation of the high-technology sector in the United States over the past few decades has been a principal engine of economic growth. But economic and social stability depends as much on the growth and evolution of existing firms as it does on the creation of new ones. (GM, for example, still has eleven times the sales of Microsoft and twenty-two times as many employees.)[3]

If the Shell study is correct and corporations are chronic underachievers, finding the key to unlock their potential remains one of the great untapped organizational challenges. One inescapable conclusion of the study is that a century's worth of management fads has only begun to mine that potential.

Another conclusion is that the long-dominant metaphor for the corporation—that of the machine—is a root of the malaise. To think of an organization as a mechanical device is to discount the value of human creativity and the possibility that organizations can foster a sense of purpose in an almost organic sense.

People are the source of the competitive advantage and the heart of the survival instinct that drive long-lived companies. According to the Shell study, the longest-surviving companies have the following four traits:

1. They are sensitive to their environment.
2. They are socially cohesive, with a strong sense of organizational "community" and identity—that is, they foster "a feeling of belonging to a social system." While lifetime employment is not a hard-and-fast rule, management is often chosen from within, and long employee tenure is the rule, rather than the exception. At the same time, these companies are very selective about the individuals they admit into their midst, ensuring that longevity does not lead to complacency. While it may emerge that the values and needs of the company and an individual are "inharmonious," the social contract in these companies affirms "that there is at least a statistical *probability* of lifetime employment."
3. These companies are also tolerant of internal processes of change. In particular, they are "tolerant of activities on the margin: outliers, experiments, and eccentricities within the boundaries of the cohesive firm."
4. They are financially conservative and focused on preserving capital.[4]

■

The conclusions of the Shell study put a premium on trust, civic behavior, the development of individual potential, and leadership as stewardship. In other words, they mark a resounding endorsement of a stakeholder-versus-shareholder-dominated philosophy of management.

Curiously, this is a viewpoint that has worked its way into the fabric of mainstream industry. If the values of Sanity Inc. (the SAS Institute) can be written off as the eccentricities of a privately held company, it is not so easy to explain away more than a decade of experimentation that has reshaped such companies as Shell, Xerox, GM, and Ford, erstwhile poster children of scientific management. It's not that these companies have lost their appreciation for quantifiable values of efficiency, productivity, and profitability; indeed, in a world of global competition these values are more important than ever.

Rather, all these companies profess a growing acceptance of the idea that companies are first and foremost human organizations and that treating them as anything else will erode core business objectives. To be sure, much of the reengineering and restructuring of the past decade was accomplished at considerable human cost. And as a consequence, many companies found their creative energies sapped.

At the same time, the merger of the scientific and human side of enterprise has been visible across a broad spectrum of industries and management functions. And it has led, over the past decade, to unprecedented levels of experimentation, organizational learning, and improvement. These traits, in turn, are a fundamental premise of benchmarking, simultaneous engineering, and other collaborative and cross-departmental forms of product development and innovation. They are embedded in the efforts of companies such as Xerox to tap the informal organization among its frontline software designers and researchers. And they are implicit in the new, enlightened environmentalism of both Ford Motor Company and General Motors.

What sets the current thinking apart from earlier management trends—whether Taylorism, the human relations movement, Theory Y, or the financial discipline of the Whiz Kids—is that it emerged from a period of prolonged adversity that began during the mid-1970s and lasted well into the 1980s. It was then that complex hierarchical production systems based on economies of scale became "dauntingly risky."[5] The crisis gave rise to "federally" organized forms of management, in which top management is shaped by decisions of outside units, including remote divisions, suppliers, and even customers, and in which the basal unit of the organization is the team or work group. These new organizational forms led to a greater exchange of ideas and the breaking down of management silos into smaller, more flexible granaries that have a greater opportunity to exploit the reservoirs of untapped potential.

Meanwhile, in the United States, the gradual strengthening of a stakeholder management culture is reaching outside the boundaries of the corporation. Already, it has given rise to a new "democratic experimentalism" that draws on the "federalist," collaborative example of some corporations. Community policing, efforts to streamline military procurement, and experiments in social service and education reform are examples of these efforts.

Globalization, the increasing complexity of markets and production systems, and the exchange of ideas across cultures have all helped bring together the humanistic and scientific tracks of management. Viewed from the late twentieth century, which also has seen an almost unthinking glorification of free-market capitalism, this trend is at once both incongruous and meaningful. In the microeconomic sphere, heretics such as Herbert Simon long ago recognized that both individuals and firms are far more complex than the rational profit maximizers postulated by economic theory. Yet the most recent Asian economic crisis grew out of an almost naive belief in the universal efficacy of the unfettered movement of capital across borders. The aftermath has seen a tempering of laissez-faire ideology; even ardent free-marketeers are now calling for some limits on capital flows.

There is also a growing acceptance of the notion that for capitalism to succeed globally, it must be made bearable for society at large. Karl Polanyi's insight that "markets are sustainable only insofar as they are embedded in social and political institutions" is as true today as it was when he wrote *The Great Transformation* in 1944.[6] In the United States, the corporation may have failed to fulfill the role that Peter Drucker foresaw decades ago of "giving status and function" to the individual. Drucker may be correct that, at least in the United States, this role is increasingly being filled by the nonprofit sector—by churches and charities, in particular. But in the developing world, in the absence of effective government regulation and a social safety net, good corporate citizens are often the *only* local forces with the power to lend stability and legitimacy to capitalism. As Harry Pearce, the vice chairman of General Motors, recently observed, "Business is coming to realize that we are all global citizens with global responsibilities. . . . The automotive industry has a special responsibility to serve as environmental stewards, particularly in developing countries where our manufacturing footprint is becoming increasingly broad."[7]

After the fall of communism, the success of capitalism will continue to rest, to a great extent, on the example set by the corporation, and increasingly by that of the new transnational enterprise. These institutions, in turn, will be shaped by a new cadre of twenty-first-century managers and how they both view and practice the role of stewardship.

Acknowledgments

This book has been in many ways a collaborative effort. The idea for *The Capitalist Philosophers* grew out of discussions with editors Karl Weber and Peter Osnos. It was nurtured by John Mahaney, my editor; Flip Brophy, my agent; and Peter Bernstein, my friend and erstwhile editor and publisher. A special thank-you to Beth Pearson and Luke Mitchell for their patience and for helping to guide this manuscript through the long and sometimes arduous publication process.

A number of librarians and archivists were instrumental in helping with my research. I owe a special debt of gratitude to Al Bartovics, the research archivist at Harvard University's Baker Library; to Sharon Ochsenhirt and John Popplestone at the Archives of the History of American Psychology at the University of Akron; and to Nydia Cruz at the S. C. Williams Library of the Stevens Institute of Technology in Hoboken, New Jersey. Thank you also to Michael Smith, who helped me navigate the vast troves of material in the Walter Reuther Archives at Wayne State University in Detroit; to Gail Thomas, who gave me access to the papers of Mary Parker Follett and Colonel Lyndall Urwick at the Henley Management College in England; and to the archivists at Carnegie Mellon. Also, thanks to the countless librarians at the New York Public Library, the Library of Congress, and the libraries of Columbia University whose help was so valuable during the course of my research.

I also owe a special thank-you to Jim Aisner for his advice and help in getting to know many of the past and current players at the Harvard Business School; to Bruce Bunch for helping me locate historical material on General Electric; and to Chris Swaney, who introduced me to the history and faculty of GSIA at Carnegie Mellon.

I am particulary grateful to my principal subjects, especially Alfred Chandler, the late W. Edwards Deming, Peter Drucker, James March, Robert McNamara, Peter Senge, and Herbert Simon. They all gave generously of their time and, in many cases, gave me access to valuable unpublished material that helped to elucidate the ideas contained in this book. At the same time, I take full responsibility for any errors that may have found their way into the finished work. I also owe a debt of gratitude to many of the friends, colleagues, and family members of the philosophers about whom I have written; they helped me get to know my subjects and illuminate their ideas, and often led me in new and fruitful directions. They include Chris Argyris, L. B. Barnes, Richard Beckhard, Warren Bennis, the late Chris Christiansen, the late Richard Cyert, Katherine Simon Frank, David Garvin, Art Kleiner, Jay Forrester, Carl Frost, Lester Lave, Paul Lawrence, George Lombard, Thomas McCraw, Nina Murray, William Pounds, Charles Sabel, Gustave Shubert, Barbara Simon, Dorothea Simon, Fred Simon, Deborah Stevens, David Teece, Jack Welch, Oliver Williamson, and Abraham Zaleznick.

In addition, several friends and colleagues read chapters of this book or offered valuable advice. They include Simon Head, Art Kleiner, and Barbara Presley Noble. Thank you to Marta Mooney at Fordham University for advising me to look at the work of Herbert Simon, for her friendship, and for always having just the book I needed to plug a hole in my narrative. Thank you also to Jonathan Alter for his advice on the Robert McNamara chapter, and to Jimmy Pritzker for his insights into military history. Donna Rosato provided valuable research. And last but not least, thank you to my husband, Jose, for living with me and my manuscript, for reading it, and for having a discerning eye for the "paradigm."

I owe a special thank-you to the friends and family members who have helped make it possible for me to juggle family life and writing. They include Gladys Mondragon, Jimena Figueroa, Tony Gabor, and Flora and Pepe Fernandez. Most important, thank you to Sarah and Anna for being wonderful and for inspiring me in everything.

Finally, I want to express my appreciation to Terri Thompson at Columbia University, and to my new colleagues in the English Department and Business Journalism Program at Baruch College, especially Roz Bernstein, Josh Mills, Alisa Solomon, and John Todd for their support with both this book and my newest academic adventure.

Notes

1: Frederick Winslow Taylor: The Father of Scientific Management

1. John Dos Passos, *The Big Money*, volume 3 of U.S.A. trilogy (Boston: Houghton Mifflin, 1946, pp. 21–26.
2. Daniel Nelson, *Frederick W. Taylor and the Rise of Scientific Management* (Madison: University of Wisconsin Press, 1980), p. 92.
3. Ibid.; F. W. Taylor, "The Principles of Scientific Management," *The American Magazine*, 71 (5) (March 1911), p. 570. "Testimony of Frederick Winslow Taylor at Hearings Before Special Committee of the House of Representatives, January 1912," *Bulletin of the Taylor Society*, 11 (3 and 4), June–August 1926, pp. 89–191.
4. Nelson, *Frederick W. Taylor*, p. 92.
5. Ibid., p. 172.
6. Sudhir Kakar, *Frederick Taylor: A Study in Personality and Innovation* (Cambridge, Mass.: MIT Press, 1970), p. 145.
7. Robert Kanigel, *The One Best Way* (New York: Viking, 1997), pp. 382–383.
8. Ida Tarbell, "The Golden Rule in Business," *The American Magazine*, January 1915, pp. 29–83, November 1915, pp. 11–17.
9. Sanford M. Jacoby, *Modern Manors: Welfare Capitalism Since the New Deal* (Princeton, N.J.: Princeton University Press, 1997), p. 12.
10. "Testimony of Frederick Winslow Taylor Before the House of Representatives," pp. 89–191.
11. Kanigel, *The One Best Way*, p. 7.
12. Recollections of Birge Harrison, unpublished, archived at Stevens Institute of Technology, c. 1916.
13. Kanigel, *The One Best Way*, pp. 58–61, 102–105.
14. Ibid., pp. 28–29, 71.
15. Ibid., p. 88; see also Jeffrey Pfeffer, *New Directions for Organization Theory* (New York: Oxford University Press, 1997), p. 12.
16. Kanigel, *The One Best Way*, p. 91.
17. Ibid., pp. 107–109.
18. Ibid.
19. Kakar, *Frederick Taylor*, pp. 41, 52.
20. Kanigel, *The One Best Way*, p. 116.
21. Ibid., pp. 112–113.
22. Ibid., p. 118. Also Kakar, *Frederick Taylor*, p. 38.
23. Kanigel, *The One Best Way*, pp. 142–143.
24. Ibid., p. 152.
25. Ibid., pp. 160–161, 165; Kakar, *Frederick Taylor*, pp. 42–43.
26. Kanigel, ibid., pp. 16, 202.
27. Kakar, *Frederick Taylor*, p. 41.

28. Nelson, *Frederick W. Taylor*, pp. 8–9.
29. Kanigel, *The One Best Way*, p. 171.
30. Ibid., p. 281; see also, Philip S. Foner, *History of the Labor Movement in the United States, Vol. 5: The AFL in the Progressive Era, 1910–1915* (New York: International Publishers, 1980), p. 143.
31. Kanigel, *The One Best Way*, p. 164.
32. Ray Stannard Baker, "Fred. W. Taylor—Scientist in Business Management," *The American Magazine*, 71 (5) (March 1911), p. 4.
33. Kanigel, *The One Best Way*, pp. 165–170.
34. Ibid., p. 173.
35. Ibid., p. 175.
36. Ibid., pp. 199, 238–239; Charles G. Wrege and Ronald G. Greenwood, *Frederick Winslow Taylor: The Father of Scientific Management* (Homewood, Ill.: Business One Irwin, 1991), pp. 49–50.
37. Kanigel, *The One Best Way*, pp. 201–202.
38. Ibid., p. 197.
39. Kakar, *Frederick Taylor*, pp. 100–101.
40. Kanigel, *The One Best Way*, pp. 203–204.
41. Frederick Winslow Taylor, "The Present State of the Art of Industrial Management," unpublished paper, December 6, 1912.
42. Nelson, *Frederick W. Taylor*, pp. 60–61.
43. Ibid., also letter from James M. Dodge to Frederick Winslow Taylor, January 18, 1915.
44. Nelson, *Frederick W. Taylor*, p. 43.
45. Jacoby, *Modern Manors*, pp. 17–18.
46. Kanigel, *The One Best Way*, pp. 205–206.
47. Ibid.
48. Kanigel, *The One Best Way*, p. 207.
49. Tarbell, "The Golden Rule in Business," Part 1, *The American Magazine*, 78 (5) (November 1914), p. 11.
50. Kakar, *Frederick Taylor*, pp. 5–6; 100–101.
51. Kanigel, *The One Best Way*, p. 446.
52. Letter from Morris L. Cooke to Frederick Winslow Taylor, February 7, 1914.
53. Letter from A. J. Portenar to Frederick Winslow Taylor, April 28, 1914.
54. Ibid. See also letter from Frederick W. Taylor to Morris L. Cooke, May 7, 1914.
55. Kakar, *Frederick Taylor*, pp. 20–21, 93–97.
56. Henry R. Towne, "The Evolution of Industrial Management," *Industrial Management*, April 1, 1921, pp. 231–233; see also Nelson, *Frederick W. Taylor*, p. 14.
57. Letter by W. A. Fannen to Miss Mitchell, April 20, 1916.
58. Kanigel, *The One Best Way*, pp. 281–284.
59. H. L. Gantt, "A Practical Application of Scientific Management," *The Engineering Magazine*, 41 (1) (April 1911), p. 1.
60. Kanigel, *The One Best Way*, pp. 212–213, 446.
61. Ibid., p. 209; see also Edna Yost, *Frank and Lillian Gilbreth* (New Brunswick, N.J.: Rutgers University Press, 1949), p. 161.
62. Transcript of talk by Frederick Winslow Taylor, December 5, 1901, p. 95.
63. Nelson, *Frederick W. Taylor*, p. 151.
64. Ibid., pp. 79–80.
65. Ibid., p. 92; see also Kanigel, *The One Best Way*, p. 318, and Kakar, *Frederick Taylor*, p. 141.
66. Nelson, *Frederick W. Taylor*, pp. 91–92.
67. Ibid., p. 95.

68. Ibid., pp. 93–94.
69. Kakar, *Frederick Taylor,* pp. 145.
70. Nelson, *Frederick W. Taylor,* pp. 94–95.
71. Kakar, *Frederick Taylor,* p. 145.
72. Ibid.
73. Kanigel, *The One Best Way,* pp. 316–317.
74. Letter from Frederick Winslow Taylor to Morris L. Cooke, December 6, 1913; letter from Major General William Crozier to Frederick Winslow Taylor, November 26, 1913; letter from A. B. Wadleigh to Frederick Winslow Taylor, January 3, 1914; letter from Frederick Winslow Taylor to A. B. Wadleigh, January 6, 1914.
75. "Testimony of Frederick Winslow Taylor Before the House of Representatives," p. 117.
76. Kanigel, *The One Best Way,* p. 323.
77. Ibid., p. 351; see also Nelson, *Frederick W. Taylor,* p. 84, and Lewis, "The Taylor Way," pp. 419–425.
78. Lewis, ibid., pp. 419–425.
79. "Testimony of Frederick Winslow Taylor Before the House of Representatives," p. 109.
80. Transcript of talk by Frederick Winslow Taylor, December 5, 1901, p. 95.
81. Kanigel, *The One Best Way,* p. 351.
82. Ibid.
83. Letter from A. J. Portenar to Frederick Winslow Taylor, June 27, 1914.
84. Nelson, *Frederick W. Taylor,* pp. 35–36.
85. Kakar, *Frederick Taylor,* pp. 102–105; Kanigel, *The One Best Way,* p. 410.
86. Kanigel, ibid., pp. 382–383.
87. Ibid., pp. 348–354.
88. Ibid., p. 353.
89. Ibid., pp. 352–354.
90. Ibid., pp. 352–355.
91. Foner, *History of the Labor Movement,* pp. 113–116.
92. Letter from Frederick Winslow Taylor to Louis D. Brandeis, November 11, 1910.
93. Letter from Frederick Winslow Taylor to Louis D. Brandeis, undated.
94. "Testimony of Frederick Winslow Taylor Before the House of Representatives," p. 89; see also Kanigel, *The One Best Way,* p. 436.
95. Foner, *History of the Labor Movement,* p. 35.
96. Letter from Upton Sinclair to *The American Magazine,* February 24, 1911.
97. Kanigel, *The One Best Way,* pp. 448, 455; Jeffrey L. Cruikshank, *A Delicate Experiment: The Harvard Business School 1908–1945* (Boston: Harvard Business School Press, 1987), p. 58.
98. Letter from Frederick Winslow Taylor to William J. Redfield, February 12, 1912.
99. Ibid.; letter from Frederick Winslow Taylor to Henry Towne, October 30, 1911; letter from Henry Towne to Frederick Winslow Taylor, October 2, 1911.
100. "Testimony of Frederick Winslow Taylor Before the House of Representatives," p. 105.
101. Ibid.; letter from Frederick Winslow Taylor to Ida Tarbell, March 6, 1914; letter from Sanford Thompson to Frederick Winslow Taylor, September 9, 1911; Kanigel, *One Best Way,* p. 355.
102. "Testimony of Frederick Winslow Taylor Before the House of Representatives," p. 162.
103. Ibid., pp. 142–143, 152.
104. Ibid., pp. 153–156.
105. Ibid., p. 155.
106. Ibid., pp. 155–156.

107. Ibid., pp. 155–156, 157.
108. A. J. Portenar to Frederick Winslow Taylor, April 28, 1914.
109. Kanigel, *The One Best Way*, pp. 482–483.
110. Letter from Frederick Winslow Taylor to L. P. Alford, August 21, 1912.
111. Nelson, *Frederick W. Taylor*, p. 148.
112. Ibid., p. 147.
113. Ibid., p. 143; letter from Frederick Winslow Taylor to James M. Dodge, February 25, 1915.
114. Nelson, *Frederick W. Taylor*, p. 145.
115. Ibid., pp. 143–145.
116. Letter from James M. Dodge to Frederick Winslow Taylor, January 18, 1915.
117. Letter from Frederick Winslow Taylor to James M. Dodge, February 25, 1915.
118. Nelson, *Frederick W. Taylor*, p. 144.
119. Ibid., p. 145.
120. Letter from James M. Dodge to Frederick Winslow Taylor, November 3, 1910.
121. Cruikshank, *A Delicate Experiment*, p. 56.
122. Letter from Frederick Winslow Taylor to Edwin Gay, November 13, 1913; letter from Frederick Winslow Taylor to Edwin Gay, November 9, 1913.
123. Letter from Wallace C. Sabine to Frederick Winslow Taylor, June 25, 1908.
124. Nelson, *Frederick W. Taylor*, p. 188; letter from Edwin F. Gay to Frederick Winslow Taylor, May 8, 1911; Cruikshank, *A Delicate Experiment*, p. 56.
125. Letter from Frederick Winslow Taylor to Edwin Gay, January 31, 1910.
126. Franklin Taylor Clark to Frederick Winslow Taylor, February 28, 1912.
127. Cruikshank, *A Delicate Experiment*, p. 56.

2: Mary Parker Follett: The Mother of Postscientific Management

1. Lyndall Urwick, "The Problem of Organization: A Study of the Work of Mary Parker Follett," *Bulletin of the Taylor Society and of the Society of Industrial Engineers*, 1(5) (July 1935).
2. Pauline Graham, ed., *Mary Parker Follett: The Prophet of Management* (Boston: Harvard Business School Press, 1995), p. xiv; see also Charles F. Sabel and Michael C. Dorf, "A Constitution of Democratic Experimentalism," *Columbia Law Review*, 98 (2) (March 1998), pp. 267–473.
3. Graham, *Mary Parker Follett*, p. 159; see also Eduard Lindeman, "Mary Parker Follett," *The Survey*, February 1934.
4. F. M. Stawell, "Mary Parker Follett, Sidgwick Hall, 1890–1891," reprinted from the *Newnham College Letter*, January 1935; Committee on Extended Use of School Buildings, 1911–1912, "Report of the East Boston Centre," *The Women's Municipal League of Boston Bulletin*, May 1912, pp. 5–12.
5. Lyndall Urwick, "Some Americans," speech given at annual dinner of the Fellows Group, Academy of Management, Boston, August 21, 1973; author telephone conversation with Pauline Graham, 1997.
6. Recollections of Dame Katherine Furse, unpublished, 1928–33, Henley Management College archives.
7. Notes by E. Balch, 1934; e-mail from Pauline Graham to author, February 16, 1999.
8. Letter from George Follett to Dame Katherine Furse, January 25, 1934; letter from Stephen Follett to Dame Katherine Furse, March 11, 1950.
9. Notes by E. Balch, 1934.
10. Recollections of Dame Katherine Furse.
11. Letter from George Follett to Dame Katherine Furse, January 25, 1934; letter from Stephen Follett to Dame Katherine Furse, March 11, 1950; see also Lyndall

Urwick, *Dynamic Administration: The Collected Papers of Mary Parker Follett* (New York: Pitman Publishing, 1973), p. 10.

12. Letter from Stephen Follett to Dame Katherine Furse, March 11, 1950.

13. Ibid.

14. Letter from Dame Katherine Furse to Henry Dennison, January 24, 1950.

15. Albie M. Davis, "An Interview with Mary Parker Follett," draft of article to appear in July 1989 edition of *Negotiation Journal;* see also "Memorial Biographies of Former Students," Radcliffe College.

16. Davis, ibid.

17. Ibid.; see also Graham, *Mary Parker Follett*, p. 14.

18. James A. Stever, "Mary Parker Follett and the Quest for Pragmatic Administration," *Administration & Society*, August 1986, pp. 159–177.

19. Ibid.

20. Ibid.

21. Sanford M. Jacoby, *Modern Manors: Welfare Capitalism Since the New Deal* (Princeton, N.J.: Princeton University Press, 1997), pp. 20, 40.

22. Typed review of Roxbury, *The Women's Municipal League of Boston Bulletin*, in ibid.

23. Ibid.; typed notes by Pauline Graham, unpublished, 1986.

24. Lyndall Urwick, "Mary Parker Follett, 1858–1933," unpublished, May 20, 1969; notes by Pauline Graham, unpublished, 1986.

25. Ibid.

26. Eva Whiting White, "Tribute to the Memory of Mary Parker Follett," speech given at the 25th Anniversary Banquet of the Boston School Centers, October 16, 1937; see also L. Urwick and E. F. L. Brech, *The Making of Scientific Management* (London: Sir Isaac Pitman & Sons, 1963), p. 50.; Judith Merkle, "Managing Democracy: The Political Theory of Mary Parker Follett," paper given at the 43rd Annual Meeting of the Academy of Management, Dallas, Texas, August 14–17, 1983.

27. Letter from Ella Cabot to Dame Katherine Furse, June 4, 1934.

28. Notes by Pauline Graham.

29. Ibid.

30. Lyndall Urwick, "The Problem of Organization: A Study of the Work of Mary Parker Follett," *Bulletin of the Taylor Society*, July 1935, pp. 163–169.

31. Merkle, "Managing Democracy."

32. Michael C. Dorf and Charles F. Sabel, "A Constitution of Democratic Experimentalism," *Columbia Law Review*, March 1998, p. 416.

33. Stever, "Mary Parker Follett"; Merkle, "Managing Democracy"; Dorf and Sabel, ibid., p. 277.

34. Notes by E. Balch; Graham, *Mary Parker Follett*, p. 17.

35. Ibid., pp. 48–50, 53, 54.

36. Urwick and Brech, *The Making of Scientific Management*, p. 53.

37. Urwick, "The Problem of Organization." pp. 163–169.

38. Urwick and Brech, *The Making of Scientific Management*, p. 50; Graham, *Mary Parker Follett*, p. 18.

39. Graham, ibid., pp. 127–129.

40. Urwick and Brech, *The Making of Scientific Management*, pp. 52–53.

41. Graham, *Mary Parker Follett*, pp. 126–127.

42. Urwick, "The Problem of Organization," pp. 163–169.

43. Graham, *Mary Parker Follett*, p. 103. Mary Parker Follett, "The Illusion of Final Authority," *Bulletin of the Taylor Society*, 11 (5) (December 1926), pp. 243–255.

44. Ibid.

45. Graham, *Mary Parker Follett*, ibid., pp. 126, 158.
46. Follett, "The Illusion of Final Authority," pp. 243–255.
47. Graham, *Mary Parker Follett*, pp. 126, 158.
48. Jacoby, *Modern Manors*, p. 19; Urwick and Brech, *The Making of Scientific Management*, p. 52.
49. Urwick, "The Problem of Organization," pp. 163–169.
50. Graham, *Mary Parker Follett*, pp. 72, 84.
51. Ibid., pp. 109–112.
52. Ibid., pp. 81–82.
53. Ibid., pp. 117–118.
54. Urwick and Brech, *The Making of Scientific Management*, p. 64.
55. Ibid., pp. 61–66.
56. Ibid.
57. Unpublished notes of Pauline Graham, archived at Henley Management College.
58. Ibid.
59. Ibid.
60. Ibid.
61. Graham, *Mary Parker Follett*, pp. 7–8; Dorf and Sabel, "A Constitution of Democratic Experimentalism," p. 417.
62. Ibid., p. xvi.
63. Ibid., p. 4.
64. Ibid., p. xvii.
65. Ibid., pp. 7–8.
66. Lyndall Urwick, "The Truth About Schmidt," unpublished, March 23, 1972.
67. Ibid.
68. Dorf and Sabel, "A Constitution of Democratic Experimentalism," p. 267.
69. Ibid.

3: Chester Barnard: The Philosopher King of American Management

1. William B. Wolf, *Conversations with Chester I. Barnard*, ILR Paperback No. 12, New York State School of Industrial and Labor Relations, Cornell University, Ithaca, N.Y., January 1973, p. 50.
2. Jeffrey L. Cruikshank, *A Delicate Experiment: The Harvard Business School 1908–1945* (Boston: Harvard Business School Press, 1987), p. 170.
3. William G. Scott, *Chester I. Barnard and the Guardians of the Managerial State* (Lawrence: University Press of Kansas, 1992), pp. 4, 18.
4. Sanford M. Jacoby, *Modern Manors: Welfare Capitalism Since the New Deal* (Princeton, N.J.: Princeton University Press), p. 19.
5. Scott, *Chester I. Barnard*, pp. 4, 18.
6. Chester I. Barnard to Lawrence J. Henderson, August 7, 1940, Chester Barnard Collection, Carton 2, Baker Library, Harvard Business School.
7. Cruikshank, *A Delicate Experiment*, p. 154; Chester I. Barnard to Lawrence J. Henderson, July 2, 1940.
8. Jacoby, *Modern Manors*, p. 17.
9. Cruikshank, *A Delicate Experiment*, pp. 154–155.
10. Wolf, *Conversations with Chester I. Barnard*, pp. 3–4; Scott, *Chester I. Barnard*, p. 62.
11. Scott, ibid., p. 11.
12. Ibid., p. 42; John B. Miner, ed., *Administrative and Management Theory* (Aldershot, U.K.: Dartmouth Publishing Company, 1995), p. 191.
13. Scott, *Chester I. Barnard*, pp. 62–63.
14. Author interview with Peter Drucker, Claremont, Calif., 1997.

15. Scott, *Chester I. Barnard,* pp. 64–65.
16. Ibid., p. 65.
17. Ibid., p. 67.
18. Ibid., pp. 72–73.
19. Ibid., p. 69; letters from Chester I. Barnard to customers, February 1, 1933, and September 5, 1933, Chester Barnard Collection, Carton 1, Baker Library, Harvard Business School.
20. Wolf, p. 51.
21. Scott, pp. 69, 90.
22. Ibid., pp. 74–75.
23. Ibid., pp. 76–77; letter from Chester I. Barnard to W. L. Crum, chairman of the National Bureau of Economic Research, November 4, 1942, Chester Barnard Collection, Carton 2, Baker Library, Harvard Business School; Miner, *Administrative and Management Theory,* p. 189.
24. Wolf, *Conversations with Chester I. Barnard,* pp. 34–35.
25. Scott, *Chester I. Barnard,* p. 75.
26. Letter from Elton Mayo to J. H. Willits, January 17, 1923, Elton Mayo Papers, Box 7, Baker Library, Harvard Business School.
27. Scott, *Chester I. Barnard,* pp. 49, 58–59.
28. Robert Sobel, *The Age of Giant Corporations* (Westport, Conn.: Praeger, 1993), p. 67.
29. Adolf A. Berle and Gardiner C. Means, *The Modern Corporation and Private Property* (New Brunswick, N.J.: Transaction Publishers, 1991.)
30. Scott, *Chester I. Barnard,* pp. 20–21; Sobel, *The Age of Giant Corporations,*
31. Scott, ibid., p. 19; letter from Chester I. Barnard to Lawrence J. Henderson, August 7, 1940, Chester Barnard Collection, Carton 2, Baker Library, Harvard Business School.
32. Chester I. Barnard, *The Functions of the Executive* (Cambridge, Mass: Harvard University Press, 1968), p. xi.
33. Ibid., p. xxi.
34. Ibid., p. 14.
35. Ibid., pp. xi., 5.
36. Scott, *Chester I. Barnard,* pp. 98, 109.
37. Letter from Chester I. Barnard to B. D. Thomas, director of Batelle Memorial Labs, December 11, 1957, Chester Barnard Collection, Carton 2, Baker Library, Harvard Business School.
38. Barnard, *The Functions of the Executive,* p. 305.
39. Ibid., p. 115; *In Search of Excellence,* Peters and Waterman, p. 97.
40. Barnard, ibid., p. 110; Wolf, *Conversations with Chester I. Barnard,* pp. 15–16.
41. Barnard, ibid., pp. 116, 120.
42. Author interviews at Xerox and National Semiconductor, Palo Alto, Calif., 1996.
43. Barnard, *The Functions of the Executive,* p. 227.
44. Scott, *Chester I. Barnard,* pp. 116–117.
45. Barnard, *The Functions of the Executive,* p. 82.
46. Ibid., p. 144.
47. Wolf, *Conversations with Chester I. Barnard,* p. 29.
48. Barnard, *The Functions of the Executive,* pp. 93–94, 143–144.
49. Ibid., pp. 110, 144–145.
50. Ibid., p. 110; Wolf, *Conversations with Chester I. Barnard,* p. 32.
51. Scott, ibid., p. 142; Barnard, *The Functions of the Executive,* pp. 202–203.
52. Letter from James March to author, September 28, 1998.
53. Scott, *Chester I. Barnard,* p. 106.
54. Barnard, *The Functions of the Executive,* p. 196

55. Ibid., p. 282.
56. Miner, *Administrative and Management Theory*, p. 172.
57. Typed, unpublished speech, Chester Barnard, Chester Barnard Collection, Carton 1, Baker Library, Harvard Business School.

4: Fritz Roethlisberger and Elton Mayo: Two Creative Misfits Who Invented "Human Relations" (and Put the Harvard Business School on the Map)

1. Elton Mayo, *The Social Problems of an Industrial Civilization* (London: Routledge and Kegan Paul, 1975), p. 49.
2. George Caspar Homans, *Coming to My Senses: The Autobiography of a Socialist* (New Brunswick, N.J.: Transaction Books, 1984), p. 310.
3. J. H. Smith, "The Three Faces of Elton Mayo, a 'Marginal Man,' " *The Times Higher Education Supplement*, December 26, 1980, p. 9.
4. Letter from Elton Mayo to G. A. Pennock, October 28, 1929, Elton Mayo Papers, Box 7, Baker Library, Harvard Business School.
5. Letter from Justice William O. Douglas to Elton Mayo, May 30, 1946, Elton Mayo Papers, Box 7, Baker Library, Harvard Business School.
6. Fritz J. Roethlisberger, *The Elusive Phenomenon* (Cambridge, Mass.: Harvard University Press, 1977), p. 12.
7. Ibid., pp. 12–14.
8. Ibid., pp. 15–16.
9. Letter from Fritz Roethlisberger to Harold J. Ruttenberg, October 26, 1961, Fritz J. Roethlisberger Papers, Carton 5, Baker Library, Harvard Business School.
10. Roethlisberger, p. 18; Fritz J. Roethlisberger, "Roethlisberger on Roethlisberger," *Harvard Business School Bulletin*, January–February 1978, pp. 10–13.
11. Roethlisberger, *The Elusive Phenomenon*, p. 20.
12. Ibid., p. 21.
13. Ibid., pp. 21–22.
14. Ibid., p. 24.
15. Ibid., p. 25.
16. Ibid., p. 26.
17. Ibid.
18. Ibid., p. 27.
19. Homans, *Coming to My Senses*, p. 139; Mayo, *The Social Problems of an Industrial Civilization*, p. xiv; e-mail from L. B. Barnes to author.
20. Author telephone interview with Paul Lawrence, 1996; e-mail from L. B. Barnes to author.
21. Richard C. S. Trahair, *The Humanist Temper: The Life and Work of Elton Mayo* (New Brunswick, N.J.: Transaction Books, 1984), pp. 198–199.
22. Ibid., p. 36.
23. Letter from Helen Mayo to Elton Mayo, January 10, 1947, Elton Mayo Papers, Box 1, Baker Library, Harvard Business School; see also Trahair, *The Humanist Temper*, pp. 38–39.
24. Trahair, ibid., pp. 39–40.
25. Ibid., pp. 41–42, 44.
26. Ibid., pp. 44–45.
27. Ibid.
28. Ibid., p. 51.
29. Ibid., pp. 51–52.
30. Ibid., p. 57.
31. Ibid., pp. 42–43, 192.
32. Ibid., p. 59.

33. Ibid., pp. 76, 199.

34. Ibid., pp. 65–70, 79–83.

35. Ibid., pp. 66, 188; letter from Emily Osborne to Elton Mayo, October 8, 1934, Elton Mayo Papers, Box 7, Baker Library, Harvard Business School.

36. Trahair, *The Humanist Temper*, p. 81.

37. Ibid., pp. 83–85.

38. Ibid., pp. 105–107.

39. Ibid., pp. 114, 120–126.

40. Ibid., pp. 131–132.

41. Ibid., pp. 144–145.

42. Ibid., pp. 132, 152, 155, 187.

43. Ibid., pp. 149–150.

44. Letter from Elton Mayo to Beardsley Ruml, c. 1942, Elton Mayo Papers, Box 7, Baker Library, Harvard Business School.

45. Trahair, *The Humanist Temper*, p. 154.

46. Letter from Elton Mayo to J. H. Willits, January 17, 1933, Elton Mayo Papers, Box 7, Baker Library, Harvard Business School.

47. Trahair, *The Humanist Temper*, pp. 155, 157, 189.

48. Ibid., pp. 171, 175, 181–182.

49. Ibid., p. 172.

50. Ibid.

51. Letter from Elton Mayo to J. H. Willits, January 17, 1923, Elton Mayo Papers, Box 7, Baker Library, Harvard Business School.

52. Ibid.; Trahair, *The Humanist Temper*, p. 173.

53. Letter from Elton Mayo to J. H. Willits, May 14, 1923, Elton Mayo Papers, Box 7, Baker Library, Harvard Business School.

54. Letter from Elton Mayo to J. H. Willits, May 14, 1923, Elton Mayo Papers, Box 7, Baker Library, Harvard Business School.

55. Trahair, *The Humanist Temper*, p. 175.

56. Ibid., pp. 176–177, 186.

57. Letter from Elton Mayo to J. H. Willits, May 14, 1923, Elton Mayo Papers, Box 7, Baker Library, Harvard Business School.

58. Trahair, *The Humanist Temper*, pp. 171, 175, 181.

59. Jeffrey L. Cruikshank, *A Delicate Experiment, The Harvard Business School 1908–1945* (Boston: Harvard Business School Press, 1987), pp. 116, 120–121, 148–149.

60. Ibid., p. 154.

61. Ibid., p. 155.

62. Ibid., pp. 56–58.

63. Ibid., p. 164.

64. Ibid.

65. Letter from Elton Mayo to Donald K. David, August 6, 1942, Elton Mayo Papers, Box 3, Baker Library, Harvard Business School.

66. Homans, *Coming to My Senses*, p. 90.

67. Ibid., pp. 111, 113; Cruikshank, *A Delicate Experiment*, p. 164.

68. Roethlisberger, *The Elusive Phenomenon*, p. 62.

69. Mayo, *Social Problems of an Industrial Civilization*, p. xx.

70. Homans, *Coming to My Senses*, p. 90; letter from Elton Mayo to Donald K. David, Elton Mayo Papers, Box 3, Baker Library, Harvard Business School; letter from Alan Gregg to Elton Mayo, January 15, 1942, Mayo Papers, Box 7, Baker Library, Harvard Business School; letter from Elton Mayo to Ross G. Harrison, April 21, 1942, Elton Mayo Papers, Box 7, Baker Library, Harvard Business School; Reviews.

71 J. H. Smith, "The Three Faces of Elton Mayo 'a Marginal Man,' " *The Times Higher Education Supplement,* December 26, 1980, p. 9.

72. Author telephone interview with George Lombard, 1996.

73. Letter from Alan Gregg to Elton Mayo, July 5, 1942, Elton Mayo Papers, Box 7, Baker Library, Harvard Business School.

74. Wallace B. Donham, Foreword, in Mayo, *Social Problems of an Industrial Civilization,* p. xxxv.

75. Mayo, *Social Problems of an Industrial Civilization,* p. xxiv; letter from Elton Mayo to Harold Ruttenberg, March 7, 1945, Elton Mayo Papers, Box 7, Baker Library, Harvard Business School.

76. Letter from Gail Mayo to Elton Mayo, November–December 1946, Box 1, Baker Library, Harvard Business School; letter from Elton Mayo to Harold Ruttenberg, March 7, 1945, Elton Mayo Papers, Box 7, Baker Library, Harvard Business School.

77. Mayo, *Social Problems of an Industrial Civilization,* pp. 13, 19.

78. Ibid., pp. 66–67.

79. Author telephone interview with George Lombard, 1996.

80. Mayo, *Social Problems of an Industrial Civilization,* pp. xxviii, 18, 21.

81. Letter from Elton Mayo to Neville Chamberlain via W. T. Grant, November 1938, Elton Mayo Papers, Box 2, Baker Library, Harvard Business School.

82. Author telephone interview with L. B. Barnes, 1996.

83. Trahair, *The Humanist Temper,* p. 200.

84. Roethlisberger, *The Elusive Phenomenon,* p. 27, 29; Trahair, ibid., p. 6.

85. Roethlisberger, ibid., p. 33.

86. Trahair, *The Humanist Temper,* p. 200.

87. Ibid., p. 214; Roethlisberger, *The Elusive Phenomenon,* p. 35.

88. Roethlisberger, ibid., p. 37.

89. Ibid., 31.

90. Ibid., pp. 46, 48; letter from Elton Mayo to Donald K. David, August 6, 1942, Elton Mayo Papers, Box 3, Baker Library, Harvard Business School.

91. Mayo, ibid.; Roethlisberger, *The Elusive Phenomenon,* p. 49.

92. Roethlisberger, ibid., p. 49.

93. Ibid., p. 46.

94. Ibid.

95. Ibid., pp. 47–48.

96. Mayo, *Social Problems of an Industrial Civilization,* p. 64.

97. Roethlisberger, *The Elusive Phenomenon,* p. 47.

98. Ibid., pp. 47–48.

99. Ibid., pp. 163–165.

100. Ibid., pp. 50–51.

101. Letter from Hal Wright to Elton Mayo, April 25, 1932, Elton Mayo Papers, Box 7, Baker Library, Harvard Business School.

102. Letter from G. A. Pennock to Elton Mayo, March 11, 1932, Elton Mayo Papers, Box 7, Baker Library, Harvard Business School.

103. Letter from Emily P. Osborne to Elton Mayo, December 14, 1932, Elton Mayo Papers, Box 7, Baker Library, Harvard Business School.

104. Letter from Emily P. Osborne to Elton Mayo, April 11, 1933, Elton Mayo Papers, Box 7, Baker Library, Harvard Business School.

105. Letter from A. N. Whitehead to Elton Mayo, September 6, 1932, Elton Mayo Papers, Box 7, Baker Library, Harvard Business School.

106. Trahair, *The Humanist Temper,* pp. 263–264; Roethlisberger, *The Elusive Phenomenon,* p. 53.

107. Letter from Elton Mayo to Emily P. Osborne, November 15, 1932, Elton Mayo Papers, Box 7, Baker Library, Harvard Business School.

108. Letter from Emily P. Osborne to Elton Mayo, January 29, 1933, Elton Mayo Papers, Box 7, Baker Library, Harvard Business School.

109. Ibid.

110. Letter from Emily P. Osborne to Elton Mayo, May 25, 1936, Elton Mayo Papers, Box 7, Baker Library, Harvard Business School.

111. Letter from Hal Wright to Fritz Roethlisberger, January 28, 1941, Fritz J. Roethlisberger Papers, Carton 2, 1922 to 1942, Baker Library, Harvard Business School.

112. Roethlisberger, *The Elusive Phenomenon*, p. 47.

113. Ibid.

114. Letter from W. J. Dickson to Fritz J. Roethlisberger, July 6, 1943, Fritz J. Roethlisberger Papers, Carton 2, Baker Library, Harvard Business School.

115. Roethlisberger, *The Elusive Phenomenon*, p. 58.

116. Ibid.

117. Ibid., p. 90.

118. Letter from Elton Mayo to Donald K. David, August 6, 1942, Elton Mayo Papers, Box 3, Baker Library, Harvard Business School.

119. Ibid.

120. Roethlisberger, *The Elusive Phenomenon*, p. 92.

121. Howard Whitman, "United in War, Divorced in Peace," *Daily News* (New York), June 12, 1943.

122. Roethlisberger, *The Elusive Phenomenon*, p. 102.

123. Ibid., pp. 92–93.

124. Letter from Austin Grimshaw of the War Production Board to Elton Mayo, September 21, 1943, Elton Mayo Papers, Box 7, Baker Library, Harvard Business School.

125. Letter from G. A. Pennock to Elton Mayo, March 14, 1942, Elton Mayo Papers, Box 7, Baker Library, Harvard Business School.

126. Letter from Margaret Conlan to Elton Mayo, May 8, 1946, Elton Mayo Papers, Box 7, Baker Library, Harvard Business School.

127. Roethlisberger, *The Elusive Phenomenon*, p. 54.

128. Jeffrey A. Sonnenfeld, "Shedding Light on the Hawthorne Studies," *Journal of Occupational Behavior*, 1985, vol. 6, pp. 111–130.

129. Roethlisberger, *The Elusive Phenomenon*, p. 106.

130. Letter from Fritz Roethlisberger to Hal Wright, September 27, 1940, Fritz J. Roethlisberger Papers, C. 2, 1922–1942, Western Electric, XYZ, Baker Library, Harvard Business School; letter from Harold North, Swift and Co., to Elton Mayo, June 4, 1941, Elton Mayo Papers, Box 7, Baker Library, Harvard Business School.

131. Letter from J. B. Shimer to Fritz Roethlisberger, May 19, 1944, Fritz J. Roethlisberger Papers, Carton 2, Baker Library, Harvard Business School.

132. "The Mayo Weekend: Conference on Human Relations and Administration, May 10–11, 1947," unpublished notes, Box 9, Baker Library, Harvard Business School.

133. Roethlisberger, *The Elusive Phenomenon*, pp. 277–279, 297.

134. William Dowling, "Conversation with Fritz J. Roethlisberger," *Organizational Dynamics*, Autumn 1972, pp. 31–45.

135. Ibid.

136. Letter from Malcolm R. Lovell, Jr., to Fritz Roethlisberger, October 8, 1951, Fritz J. Roethlisberger Papers, Carton 2, Baker Library, Harvard Business School.

137. Malcolm P. McNair, "Thinking Ahead: What Price Human Relations?" *Harvard Business Review*, March–April 1957, pp. 15–39.

138. Ibid.; Roethlisberger, *The Elusive Phenomenon*, pp. 282–283.

139. McNair, "Thinking Ahead," pp. 15–39.

140. Ibid.

141. Letter from Mrs. Elton Mayo to Wallace B. Donham, December 11, 1947, Elton Mayo Papers, Box 1, Baker Library, Harvard Business School.
142. Roethlisberger, *The Elusive Phenomenon*, pp. 238–239.

5: Robert S. McNamara: The "Bean Counters" Usher in a New Era of Scientific Management

1. Jeffrey L. Cruikshank, *A Delicate Experiment: The Harvard Business School 1908–1945* (Boston: Harvard Business School Press, 1987), p. 223.
2. Ibid.
3. David Jardini, "Thinking Through the Cold War: Rand, National Security and Domestic Policy, 1945–1975," unpublished Ph.D. dissertation.
4. Author telephone interview with Gustave Shubert, 1998.
5. Author interview with Robert S. McNamara, April 1999.
6. John A. Byrne, *The Whiz Kids* (New York: Currency/Doubleday, 1993), p. 41.
7. David Halberstam, *The Reckoning* (New York: William Morrow & Company, 1986), p. 204.
8. Robert S. McNamara, *In Retrospect* (New York: Times Books, 1995), p. 8; Byrne, *The Whiz Kids*, p. 34.
9. Byrne, ibid., pp. 35, 40; McNamara, ibid., p. 8.
10. Byrne, ibid., p. 36.
11. Ibid., pp. 40–43.
12. Ibid., pp. 43–44; Halberstam, *The Reckoning*, p. 204.
13. Byrne, ibid., pp. 24, 49.
14. Ibid., pp. 50–51.
15. Author telephone interview with Gustave Shubert, 1998.
16. Thomas K. McCraw, ed., *The Essential Alfred Chandler* (Boston: Harvard Business School Press, 1988), pp. 4–5.
17. Byrne, *The Whiz Kids*, pp. 79–80.
18. Robert Lacey, *Ford: The Men and the Machine* (Boston: Little, Brown & Company, 1986), pp. 342–344, 355–357.
19. Byrne, *The Whiz Kids*, p. 176; Halberstam, *The Reckoning*, p. 210.
20. Byrne, ibid., p. 175.
21. Halberstam, *The Reckoning*, pp. 213, 216.
22. Author interview with Robert S. McNamara, April 1999.
23. Halberstam, *The Reckoning*, pp. 216, 238, 243, 499, 500.
24. Author telephone interview with Gustave Shubert, 1998.
25. Halberstam, *The Reckoning*, pp. 242, 245.
26. Ibid., p. 221; Andrea Gabor, *The Man Who Discovered Quality* (New York: Times Books, 1990), p. 133.
27. Gabor, ibid., p. 133; Lacey, *Ford*, pp. 581–582.
28. Halberstam, *The Whiz Kids*, p. 321.
29. McNamara, *In Retrospect*, pp. 12–13.
30. Ibid., pp. 21, 22; Jardini, "Thinking Through the Cold War," p. 197.
31. Author telephone interview with Gustave Shubert, 1998.
32. Alain C. Enthoven and K. Wayne Smith, *How Much Is Enough?* (New York: Harper & Row, 1971), p. 61.
33. Enthoven and Smith, *How Much Is Enough?*, p. 65.
34. Ibid.
35. Jardini, "Thinking Through the Cold War," p. 68.
36. Ibid., p. 197; author telephone interview with Gustave Shubert, 1998.
37. McNamara, *In Retrospect*, pp. 22–23.

38. Jardini, "Thinking Through the Cold War," p. 197; Enthoven and Smith, *How Much Is Enough?*, p. 32.
39. Jardini, ibid., pp. 165, 191, 212, 213; Enthoven and Smith, ibid., p. 11.
40. Jardini, ibid., pp. 164–165, 191–192.
41. Enthoven and Smith, *How Much Is Enough?*, p. 13.
42. Ibid., pp. 12–14.
43. Ibid., p. 15; Jardini, "Thinking Through the Cold War," p. 195.
44. Jardini, ibid., p. 201.
45. Ibid., pp. 194, 195.
46. Author telephone interview with Gustave Shubert, 1998.
47. Enthoven and Smith, *How Much Is Enough?*, p. 45.
48. Ibid., p. 1.
49. Steven Lee Myers, "Pentagon 'Maverick' Sounds Alarm," *The New York Times*, January 18, 1999, p. A15.
50. Author telephone interview with Gustave Shubert, 1998.
51. Harold P. Ford, *CIA and the Vietnam Policymakers: Three Episodes 1962–1968* (Springfield, Va.: History Staff Center for the Study of Intelligence, Central Intelligence Agency, 1998), pp. 6, 22.
52. Author interview with Robert S. McNamara, April 1999.
53. Ford, *CIA*, pp. 49–50.
54. Author interview with Robert S. McNamara, April 1999.
55. Ford, *CIA*, p. 56.
56. Robert S. McNamara with James Blight, Robert Brigham, Thomas Biersteker, and Herbert Schandler, *Argument Without End* (New York: Public Affairs, 1999), p. 352.
57. Ford, *CIA*, p. 11; author telephone interview with Jardini, 1998.
58. McNamara et al., *Argument Without End*, p. 332.
59. Ibid., p. 323.
60. Byrne, *The Whiz Kids*, p. 432.
61. Douglas K. Smith and Robert C. Alexander, *Fumbling the Future* (New York: William Morrow & Company, 1988), p. 156; Byrne, ibid., p. 433.
62. Smith and Alexander, ibid., pp. 177–178.
63. Gabor, *The Man Who Discovered Quality*, p. 188.

6: Abraham Maslow and Douglas McGregor: From Human Relations to the Frontiers of System Dynamics

1. Abraham H. Maslow, *Maslow on Management* (New York: John Wiley & Sons, 1998), p. 3.
2. Author interview with Richard Beckhard, New York City, 1997.
3. Edward Hoffman, *The Right to Be Human* (Comack, N.Y.: Four World Press, 1997), p. 97.
4. Author interview with Warren Bennis, Los Angeles, 1998.
5. Hoffman, *The Right to Be Human*, p. 52.
6. Ibid.; Maslow, *Maslow on Management*, p. 3.
7. Hoffman, ibid., p. 41.
8. Maslow, *Maslow on Management*, p. 2.
9. Hoffman, *The Right to Be Human*, pp. 2–3.
10. Ibid., p. 15.
11. Ibid., pp. 33–34; author telephone interview with Edward Hoffman, 1998.
12. Hoffman, Ibid., p. 44.
13. Ibid., p. 57.

14. Ibid., p. 62.
15. Ibid., pp. 71–72.
16. Ibid., p. 65.
17. Ibid., pp. 71, 74.
18. Ibid., pp. 90–91.
19. Ibid., pp. 92–93.
20. Ibid., p. 94.
21. Ibid., p. 104.
22. Ibid., p. 106.
23. Ibid., p. 144.
24. Ibid., pp. 148–149.
25. Ibid., p. 150.
26. Ibid., pp. 152–153.
27. Ibid., pp. 153–154.
28. R. A. Goodman, "On the Operationality of the Maslow Need Hierarchy," *British Journal of Industrial Relations*, 6(1), pp. 51–57.
29. Abraham H. Maslow, *Motivation and Personality* (New York: Harper & Row, 1970), p. 38.
30. Maslow, *Maslow on Management*, p. 3.
31. Letter from Douglas McGregor to Abraham Maslow, November 16, 1956, Archives for the History of American Psychology, University of Akron.
32. Marvin R. Weisbord, *Productive Workplaces* (San Francisco: Jossey-Bass, 1989), pp. 109–110, 114.
33. Ibid., p. 114.
34. Ibid., p. 112; author interview with Richard Beckhard, New York City, 1997.
35. Weisbord, *Productive Workplaces*, pp. 112–113.
36. Ibid., pp. 120–121.
37. Author telephone interview with Carl Frost, 1998; Warren G. Bennis, *An Invented Life: Reflections on Leadership and Change* (Reading, Mass.: Addison-Wesley Publishing Company, 1993), p. 14.
38. Author telephone interview with Edgar Schein, 1997, and interview with Dick Beckhard, New York City, 1997.
39. Author telephone interview with Edgar Schein, 1997.
40. Weisbord, *Productive Workplaces*, pp. 96, 98, 88.
41. Ibid., pp. 96, 88.
42. Author interview with Chris Argyris, 1997.
43. Weisbord, *Productive Workplaces*, pp. 75–76.
44. Ibid., p. 76.
45. Author interviews with Richard Beckhard, New York City, 1997, and Warren Bennis, Los Angeles, 1997.
46. Art Kleiner, *The Age of Heretics* (New York: Doubleday, 1996), pp. 30–31; Weisbord, *Productive Workplaces*, p. 71.
47. Weisbord, ibid., pp. 82–83.
48. Ibid., p. 85.
49. Ibid.
50. Ibid., pp. 88–89.
51. Ibid., p. 89.
52. Ibid., pp. 84, 86, 104; Kleiner, *The Age of Heretics*, p. 32.
53. Weisbord, ibid., pp. 89–90.
54. Hoffman, *The Right to Be Human*, p. 94.
55. Kleiner, *The Age of Heretics*, pp. 33–34.
56. Ibid., pp. 34–35.
57. Ibid.

58. Ibid., pp. 35–36; author interview with Richard Beckhard, New York City, 1997.

59. Kleiner, ibid., p. 36; Hoffman, *The Right to Be Human*, p. 271.

60. Kleiner, ibid.

61. Author interview with Chris Argyris, Cambridge, Mass., 1997.

62. Author telephone interview with Paul Davis, 1997.

63. John Hoerr, *And the Wolf Finally Came* (Pittsburgh: University of Pittsburgh Press, 1988).

64. Ibid., pp. 267–268.

65. Ibid., pp. 272–273.

66. Ibid., p. 274.

67. Author telephone interview with Carl Frost, 1997.

68. Ibid.; Hoerr, *And the Wolf Finally Came*, p. 284.

69. Hoerr, ibid., pp. 285–286.

70. Author telephone interview with Carl Frost, 1997.

71. Ibid.

72. Bennis, *An Invented Life*, p. 10; Weisbord, *Productive Workplaces*, pp. 124–125.

73. Letter from Douglas McGregor to Abraham Maslow, September 26, 1957, University of Akron.

74. Douglas McGregor, *The Human Side of Enterprise* (New York: McGraw-Hill Book Company, 1985), pp. ix, x.

75. Ibid., p. 34.

76. Ibid., p. 40.

77. Ibid.

78. Frederick Herzberg, "One More Time: How Do You Motivate Employees," *Harvard Business Review*, September–October, 1987, reprint of article published in January–February, 1968.

79. Gabor, *The Man Who Discovered Quality*, pp. 250–266.

80. McGregor, *The Human Side of Enterprise*, pp. 49, 56.

81. Ibid., p. 52.

82. Author telephone interview with Jay Forrester, 1997.

83. Ibid.

84. Ibid.

85. Ibid.

86. Ibid.

87. McGregor, *The Human Side of Enterprise*, p. 125.

88. Maslow, *Maslow on Management*, p. 94; Abraham Maslow, "The Human Side of Enterprise," unpublished lecture, May 17, 1965.

89. Maslow, *Maslow on Management*, p. 94; Hoffman, pp. 267–268.

90. Hoffman, *The Right to Be Human*, p. 168.

91. Hoffman, ibid., p. 269; Maslow, ibid., p. 94.

92. Maslow, ibid., p. xxi.

93. Ibid., pp. 22–23, 108–111.

94. Maslow, *Maslow on Management*, galleys, pp. 20, 88; Hoffman, *The Right to Be Human*, pp. 269–270.

95. Maslow, ibid., p. ix.

96. Ibid., pp. 8–9.

97. Ibid., pp. 1–2.

98. Ibid., pp. 25, 44.

99. Ibid., pp. 46.

100. Ibid., p. 69.

101. Ibid., p. 71.

102. Marvin Bower, *The Will to Lead* (Boston: Harvard Business School Press, 1997), p. 57.

7: W. Edwards Deming: The Prophets of the Quality Movement and the
Learning Organization

1. John Byrne, "Jack: A Close-up Look at How America's No. 1 Manager Runs GE,"
   Business Week, June 8, 1998, pp. 92–111.
2. Author telephone interviews with Jeff Kennard and Subir Chowdhury, American
   Supplier Institute, 1998.
3. Author telephone interview with Peter Senge, 1998.
4. Author telephone interview with Fred Simon, 1998.
5. Author e-mail correspondence with Art Kleiner, 1998.
6. Andrea Gabor, *The Man Who Discovered Quality* (New York: Times Books, 1990),
   pp. 45–48.
7. Ibid., p. 48.
8. Ibid.
9. Ibid.
10. Ibid.
11. Author telephone interview with Peter Senge, 1998.
12. Gabor, *The Man Who Discovered Quality*, p. 72.
13. Ibid., p. 4.
14. Ibid., p. 5.
15. Ibid., p. 238.
16. Ibid., p. 139.
17. Ibid., p. 126; author telephone interview with Fred Simon, 1998.
18. Gabor, ibid., p. 128.
19. Ibid., p. 4.
20. Author telephone interview with Fred Simon, 1998.
21. Gabor, *The Man Who Discovered Quality*, p. 129.
22. Ibid., p. 134.
23. Ibid.
24. Ibid., p. 136.
25. Ibid., pp. 136–137.
26. Ibid., p. 144.
27. Ibid.
28. Ibid., pp. 145–146.
29. Author telephone interview with Subir Chowdhury, American Supplier Institute,
    1998.
30. W. Edwards Deming, *The New Economics* (Cambridge, Mass.: Massachusetts
    Institute of Technology, Center for Advanced Engineering Study, 1993), pp.
    104–105, 109.
31. Ibid., pp. 104–105.
32. Gabor, *The Man Who Discovered Quality*, p. 259; Jeffrey Pfeffer, "Six Dangerous
    Myths About Pay," *Harvard Business Review*, May–June 1998, pp. 109–119.
33. Gabor, ibid., p. 253.
34. Andrea Gabor, "Take This Job and Love It," *The New York Times*, January 26,
    1992, sec. 3, p. 1.
35. Ibid.
36. Ibid.
37. Pfeffer, "Six Dangerous Myths About Pay."
38. Ibid., pp. 109–119; Joel Kurtzman, "An Interview with Jeffrey Pfeffer," *Strategy
    and Business*, Third Quarter 1998, pp. 85–94; Charles Fishman, "Sanity Inc.," *Fast
    Company*, January 1999, p. 84.
39. Author phone interview with David F. Russo, 1999.
40. Gabor, *The Man Who Discovered Quality*, pp. 242–243, 254–256.

41. Ibid.
42. Author telephone interview with Bill Tate, 1999; Gabor, "Take This Job and Love It."
43. Gabor, ibid., pp. 38–39.
44. Ibid.
45. Ibid., pp. 39–40.
46. Ibid., p. 40.
47. Ibid., p. 40–41.
48. Ibid.
49. Ibid., p. 74.
50. Ibid., pp. 75–76.
51. Ibid., p. 76.
52. Ibid.
53. Ibid., pp. 80–81.
54. Ibid., pp. 81–82.
55. Ibid., pp. 70, 87–88.
56. Ibid., p. 82.
57. Ibid.
58. Ibid.
59. Ibid., p. 73.
60. Author telephone interview with Fred Simon, 1998.
61. Author telephone interview with Peter Senge, 1998.
62. Ibid.; Gabor, *The Man Who Discovered Quality*, p. 39.
63. Author telephone interview with Peter Senge, 1998.
64. Peter M. Senge, "The Leader's New Work: Building Learning Organizations," *Sloan Management Review*, Fall 1990, 32 (1), pp. 7–23.
65. Fred Kofman and Peter Senge, "Communities of Commitment: The Heart of Learning Organizations," *Organizational Dynamics*, AMA reprint, 1993, p. 19; Peter Senge, "The Leader's New Work."
66. Kofman and Senge, ibid.
67. Peter Senge, *The Fifth Discipline* (New York: Currency/Doubleday, 1990), p. 7.
68. Ibid., p. 9.
69. Ibid., pp. 8–9.
70. Ibid., *The Fifth Discipline*, pp. 236–237.
71. Ibid., pp. 6–7; author telephone interview with Peter Senge, 1998.
72. Ibid., p. 203.
73. Kofman and Senge, "Communities of Commitment," p. 18.
74. Author telephone interview with Fred Simon, 1999.
75. Ibid.
76. Ibid.
77. Author telephone interview with Fred Simon, 1999, and Peter Senge, 1998.
78. Author telephone interview with Fred Simon, 1999.
79. Ibid.
80. Brian Dumaine, "Mr. Learning Organization," *Fortune*, October 17, 1994, p. 147.
81. Ibid.
82. Author telephone interview with Fred Simon, 1999.
83. Ibid.
84. Ibid.; Dumaine, "Mr. Learning Organization," *Fortune*. p. 147.
85. Author telephone interview with Fred Simon, 1999.
86. Ibid.
87. Ibid.
88. Ibid.
89. Ibid.

90. Ibid.
91. Ibid.
92. Author telephone interview with Peter Senge, 1998.
93. Chris Argyris, "Empowerment: The Emperor's New Clothes," *Harvard Business Review,* May–June 1998, pp. 98–105.
94. Ibid.
95. Author telephone interview with Fred Simon, 1999.
96. Peter M. Senge, "Leading Learning Organizations," *The Leader of the Future* (San Francisco: Jossey-Bass, 1996), pp. 41–57.

8: Herbert A. Simon: The Needle and the Haystack

1. E-mail from Oliver Williamson to author, May 27, 1999.
2. Doug Stewart, "Herbert Simon: Artificial Intelligence Pioneer: Interview," *Omni,* June 1994, p. 70.
3. Corinne Kraus, *The Reminiscences of Herbert A. Simon,* Oral History Research Office, Columbia University, 1979, p. 114; Constance Holden, "The Rational Optimist," *Psychology Today,* October 1986, p. 54.
4. Herbert A. Simon, *Models of My Life* (New York: Basic Books, 1991), p. 114; James G. March, "The 1978 Nobel Prize in Economics," *Science,* November 1978, pp. 858–861.
5. Herbert Simon, *Administrative Behavior* (New York: Free Press, 1997), p. 88.
6. Letter from James March to author, September 28, 1998.
7. Letter from Chester Barnard to Herbert Simon, May 11, 1945.
8. Letter from James March to author, September 28, 1998.
9. Ibid.
10. Ibid.; Richard H. Day and Shyam Sunder, "Ideas and Work of Richard M. Cyert," *Journal of Economic Behavior & Organization,* 31 (1996), pp. 139–148; "Herbert Simon's Economics" (no date or author available, photocopy from Carnegie Mellon University archives).
11. Ibid.
12. Author interview with Peter Drucker, Claremont, Calif., 1997.
13. Author telephone interviews with Katherine S. Frank and Barbara Simon, 1997; e-mail from Herbert Simon, June 17, 1999.
14. Author telephone interview with Phil Bromley, 1997.
15. Herbert Simon, "Charles E. Merriam and the 'Chicago School' of Political Science," monograph, Department of Political Science, University of Illinois at Urbana-Champaign, 1985, p. 5.
16. Herbert Simon, *Models of My Life,* p. 8.
17. Ibid., pp. 8–9, 20, 21.
18. Ibid., pp. 3, 8, 20.
19. Ibid., p. 109.
20. Ibid., pp. 25, 8–9.
21. Ibid., pp. 147–148; also author interview with Herbert Simon, Pittsburgh, 1998.
22. Ibid., p. 370; Simon, *Administrative Behavior,* p. 289.
23. Author interview with Herbert Simon, Pittsburgh, 1998; Simon, *Models of My Life,* p. 370.
24. Author interview with Herbert Simon, Pittsburgh, 1998.
25. Simon, *Administrative Behavior,* p. 289.
26. Ibid.
27. Simon, *Models of My Life,* p. 370.
28. Ibid.
29. Ibid.

30. Author interview with Herbert Simon, Pittsburgh, 1998.

31. Simon, *Reminiscences*, p. 72.

32. Herbert Simon, "Charles E. Merriam and the 'Chicago School' of Political Science," pp. 3–4.

33. Louis Brownlow, *A Passion for Politics* (Chicago: University of Chicago Press, 1955), pp. 234, 288–289.

34. Ibid., pp. 288–289.

35. Simon, *Models of My Life*, pp. 119–120.

36. Herbert Simon, "Guest Editorial," *Public Administration Review*, 55(5) (1995), pp. 404–405.

37. Simon, "Charles E. Merriam and the 'Chicago School' of Political Science," pp. 2–3, 5, 6.

38. Simon, *Models of My Life* p. 73.

39. Author interview with Herbert Simon, Pittsburgh, 1998; Simon, *Reminiscences*, p. 123.

40. Letter from William H. Drury to Herbert A. Simon, December 22, 1971. Carnegie Mellon.

41. Simon, *Models of My Life*, p. 118.

42. Herbert Simon, "Birth of an Organization: The Economic Cooperative Administration," *Public Administration Review*, (13) (Autumn 1953), pp. 227–236.

43. Simon, *Models of My Life*, p. 118.

44. Ibid., pp. 101, 107; Kraus, *The Reminiscences of Herbert A. Simon*, pp. 113–114.

45. Kraus, ibid., p. 165; Simon, *Models of My Life*, p. 103.

46. Letter from Chester Barnard to Herbert A. Simon, May 11, 1945; author interview with Herbert A. Simon, Pittsburgh, 1998; and archive notes.

47. Simon, *Models of My Life*, pp. 135–136.

48. Robert E. Gleeson and Steven Schlossman, "George Leland Bach and the Rebirth of Graduate Management Education in the United States, 1945–1975," *Selections*, Spring 1995, p. 9.

49. Ibid., p. 10.

50. Ibid., pp. 14, 20.

51. Steven Schlossman, Robert E. Gleeson, Michael Sedlak, and David Grayson Allen, *The Beginnings of Graduate Management Education in the United States* (Santa Monica, Calif.: GMAC, 1994), pp. 114–115, 118.

52. Simon, *Models of My Life*, p. 141.

53. Schlossman et al., pp. 115–116.

54. Ibid.; Gleeson and Schlossman, "George Leland Bach," pp. 14, 20.

55. Simon, *Models of My Life*, pp. 138–139.

56. Richard Cyert and James March, *The Behavioral Theory of the Firm* (Cambridge, Mass.: Blackwell Publishers, 1992), pp. 20, 50; Herbert A. Simon, "Recent Advances in Organizational Theory," *Research Frontiers in Politics and Government* (Washington, D.C.: Brookings Institution, 1955).

57. Simon, *Administrative Behavior*, p. 100.

58. James G. March, "The 1978 Nobel Prize in Economics," *Science*, November 1978, pp. 858–861.

59. James G. March and Herbert A. Simon, *Organizations* (New York: John Wiley & Sons, 1958), pp. 48, 50.

60. Simon, *Administrative Behavior*, pp. 11, 214, 293, 295.

61. March and Simon, *Organizations*, p. 56.

62. Cyert and March, *The Behavioral Theory of the Firm*, p. 116.

63. Ibid., pp. 55–56.

64. Author interview with James G. March, New York City, 1998.

65. Letter from James G. March to author, September 28, 1998.

66. Ibid.
67. Cyert and March, *The Behavioral Theory of the Firm*, p. 99; author interview with James G. March, New York City, 1998; e-mail from Herbert Simon to author, June 17, 1999; letter from James G. March to author, September 28, 1998.
68. C. K. Prahalad and Gary Hamel, "The Core Competence of the Corporation," *Harvard Business Review*, May–June 1990, pp. 79–93.
69. Author interview with Richard Cyert, Pittsburgh, 1998; David J. Teece, Gary Pisano, and Amy Shuen, "Dynamic Capabilities and Strategic Management," *Strategic Management Journal*, 18(7) (March 1997), pp. 509–533.
70. Author interview with Oliver Williamson, Berkeley, Calif., 1997; Oliver Williamson, "Transaction Cost Economics and the Carnegie Connection," *Journal of Economic Behavior & Organization*, 31 (1996), pp. 149–155; also phone conversation October, 1999.
71. Warren J. Samuels, ed., *American Economists of the Late Twentieth Century* (Cheltenham, U.K.: Edward Elgar, 1996), pp. 194–209.
72. Ibid.
73. Ibid.
74. Williamson, "Transaction Cost Economics and the Carnegie Connection," pp. 149–155.
75. Simon, *Models of My Life*, p. 144.
76. Ibid., p. 146.
77. Off-the-record interviews.
78. Author interview with Lester Lave, Pittsburgh, 1998.
79. Simon, *Models of My Life*, p. 144; off-the-record interview.
80. Simon, ibid., pp. 66, 336.
81. Author telephone interview with Katherine Frank Simon, 1997.
82. Ibid.
83. Pamela McCorduck, notes, Chapter 4: "The Carnegie-Rand Group to 1956," p. 3; Simon, *Models of My Life*, p. 189.
84. Herbert A. Simon, *Allen Newell: 1927–1992, A Biographical Memoir* (Washington, D.C.: National Academy of Sciences, 1997), p. 5.
85. Simon, *Models of My Life*, p. 201.
86. Constance Holden, "The Rational Optimist," *Psychology Today*, October 1986, p. 54.
87. Simon, *Models of My Life*, pp. 250–251.
88. Ibid., p. 323.
89. Ibid., p. 324.
90. Letter from Serena Modigliani to Dorothea Simon, November 3, 1978; letter from Mrs. David Hughes to Herbert Simon, October 17, 1978; Internet communication from Ed Feigenbaum to Herbert Simon, October 18, 1978, University Archives of Carnegie Mellon.
91. Letter from Herbert Simon to Jane Stecher, October 21, 1978; letter from Herbert Simon to Bertha Goes, October 21, 1978, University Archives of Carnegie Mellon.
92. Letter from Robert Solow to Herbert Simon, October 17, 1978; letter from Sidney G. Winter to Herbert Simon, October 18, 1978, University Archives of Carnegie Mellon.
93. Author telephone interview with Phil Bromley, 1997.
94. Simon, *Models of My Life*, p. 325.
95. Ibid., pp. 325–326.
96. Oliver Williamson, *The Mechanisms of Governance* (New York: Oxford University Press, 1996), p. 28; Williamson, "Transaction Cost Economics and the Carnegie Connection"; letter from John A. Dimling to Herbert Simon, October 19, 1978, University Archives of Carnegie Mellon.

9: Alfred Du Pont Chandler and Alfred Sloan: The Historian and the CEO

1. Author telephone interview with Alfred D. Chandler, 1999.
2. Peter F. Drucker, *Adventures of a Bystander* (New York: HarperCollins Publishers, 1978), p. 261.
3. Author interview with Thomas K. McCraw, Boston, 1997.
4. Unpublished manuscript by Thomas K. McCraw; author interview with McCraw, Boston, 1997.
5. Unpublished manuscript by Nina Murray.
6. Ibid.
7. Ibid.
8. Ibid.
9. Ibid.
10. Ibid.; author interview with Alfred D. Chandler, Cambridge, Mass., 1997.
11. Unpublished manuscript by Nina Murray.
12. Ibid.
13. Thomas McCraw, *The Essential Alfred Chandler* (Boston: Harvard Business School Press; 1988), p. 174.
14. Ibid., pp. 174, 465–504.
15. Author interview with Alfred D. Chandler, Cambridge, Mass., 1997.
16. Unpublished manuscript by Nina Murray.
17. Ibid., p. 74; author interview with Alfred D. Chandler, Cambridge, Mass., 1997.
18. Murray, ibid., p. 5.
19. McCraw, *The Essential Alfred Chandler*, p. 5; unpublished manuscript by Nina Murray.
20. McCraw, ibid., pp. 3–4.
21. Ibid., pp. 4–5.
22. Ibid.
23. Ibid.
24. Nancy Jackson, "Living History: Alfred Chandler and the Rise of Big Business," *Harvard Business School* Bulletin, April 1990, pp. 34–42; author telephone conversation with Thomas McCraw, 1998.
25. McCraw, *The Essential Alfred Chandler*, pp. 23, 25–28.
26. Ibid., p. 30.
27. Ibid., pp. 23–25.
28. Ibid., pp. 25–26.
29. Ibid., p. 28.
30. Ibid., p. 32.
31. Alfred D. Chandler, *Strategy and Structure* (Cambridge, Mass.: The MIT Press, 1995), p. 21.
32. McCraw, *The Essential Alfred Chandler*, pp. 34–35.
33. Ibid., p. 35.
34. Ibid., p. 22; Chandler, *Strategy and Structure*, p. 21.
35. McCraw, ibid., pp. 344–345.
36. Author interviews with Alfred D. Chandler, Cambridge, Mass., 1997, and Thomas McCraw, Boston, 1998.
37. McCraw, *The Essential Alfred Chandler*, p. 121.
38. Chandler, *Strategy and Structure*, pp. 41, 44.
39. Delos R. Smith, "Managerial Roots: How the Heirs of Sloan and du Pont Are Faring." *Conference Board*, 70 (May 1986), p. 24; McCraw, *The Essential Alfred Chandler*, p. 126.
40. Ibid., pp. 162–163; Chandler, *Strategy and Structure*, introduction.
41. Chandler, ibid., introduction, p. 301.

42. Ibid., p. 13; McCraw, *The Essential Alfred Chandler*, p. 175.
43. Alfred Sloan, *My Years at General Motors* (Garden City, N.Y.: Doubleday, 1963), p. 50; Chandler, *Strategy and Structure*, pp. 83, 88–89.
44. Chandler, ibid., pp. 91–93.
45. McCraw, *The Essential Alfred Chandler*, p. 176; The American Historical Association Award for Scholarship Distinction, 1997.
46. Sloan, *My Years at General Motors*, pp. 49–50.
47. Author interview with Alfred D. Chandler, Cambridge, Mass., 1997.
48. Ibid.
49. Ibid.
50. McCraw, *The Essential Alfred Chandler*, p. 157; author telephone interview with Richard Scharchburg, 1998.
51. Author interview with Alfred D. Chandler, Cambridge, Mass., 1997.
52. Sloan, *My Years at General Motors*, pp. 4–5.
53. Ibid., pp. 18, 21.
54. Ibid., pp. 22–23.
55. Ibid., p. 24.
56. Ibid., pp. 27–28.
57. Ibid., pp. 28–31.
58. Ibid., pp. 40–41, 47.
59. Ibid., pp. 49–50.
60. Ibid., p. 50.
61. Ibid., pp. 58, 60.
62. Ibid., pp. 51–52, 70–71, 73.
63. Ibid., pp. 59, 339; author telephone interview with Bob Dorn, 1998.
64. Ibid., p. 79.
65. Ibid., p. 80.
66. Author interview with Alfred D. Chandler, Cambridge, Mass., 1997.
67. Sloan, *My Years at General Motors*, pp. 88–89.
68. Ibid., pp. 82–83.
69. Ibid., pp. 84–85.
70. Ibid., p. 103.
71. Ibid., pp. 105–106.
72. Ibid., p. 106.
73. Ibid.
74. Ibid., p. 89.
75. Chandler, *Strategy and Structure*, pp. 310–311.
76. Ibid., pp. 311–312.
77. Oliver Williamson, *The Mechanisms of Governance* (New York: Oxford University Press), p. 139.
78. Author interview with Alfred D. Chandler, Cambridge, Mass., 1997. Also, author telephone interview with Marvin Bower, 1998.
79. Edith T. Penrose, *The Theory of the Growth of the Firm* (White Plains, N.Y.: M. E. Sharpe, 1980), pp. xi, 12–13.
80. McCraw, *The Essential Alfred Chandler*, pp. 392–393.
81. Ibid., pp. 465–504.
82. Ibid., p. 487.
83. Ibid., pp. 465–504.
84. Oliver Williamson, "Transaction Cost Economics and the Evolving Science of Organization," in Arnold Heertje, ed., *Makers of Modern Economics*, vol. 2 (London: Harvester Wheatsheaf, 1993), pp. 114–169.
85. Oliver Williamson, *The Mechanisms of Governance* (New York: Oxford University Press, 1996), pp. 114–116, 138–140.

86. Author interview with Oliver Williamson, Berkeley, Calif., 1997.

87. David J. Teece, Richard P. Rumelt, and Dan E. Schendel, eds., *Fundamental Issues in Strategy*, (Boston: Harvard Business School Press, 1994), p. 27.

88. Alfred D. Chandler, "Paths of Learning: The Evolution of High Technology Industries," unpublished manuscript.

89. Ibid.

90. Alfred D. Chandler, "Computers and Consumer Electronics—an Overview," unpublished manuscript, 1998.

91. Ibid.

92. Ibid.

93. Ibid.

94. Ibid.

95. Ibid.

96. Ibid.

97. Author telephone interview with Pankaj Ghemawat, 1997; off-the-record interview.

98. Author telephone interview with Pankaj Ghemawat, 1997.

99. McCraw, *The Essential Alfred Chandler*, p. 5; unpublished manuscript by Nina Murray, p. 11.

100. McCraw, ibid.

101. Oliver Williamson, "Transaction Cost Economics and the Evolving Science of Organization"; Teece et al., *Fundamental Issues in Strategy*, pp. 39–40.

10: Peter F. Drucker: The Big Idea Man

1. Author interview with Jack Welch, Fairfield, Conn., 1998.

2. Ibid.

3. Ibid.

4. Ibid.; John A. Byrne, "Jack: A Close-up Look at How America's No. 1 Manager Runs GE," *Business Week*, June 8, 1998, pp. 92–111; author telephone conversation with Bruce Bunch.

5. Author interview with Jack Welch, Fairfield, Conn., 1998.

6. Ibid.

7. Peter F. Drucker, *Adventures of a Bystander* (New York: Harper & Row Publishers, 1978), p. 263.

8. Letter from Peter F. Drucker to Elton Mayo, May 10, 1946, Box 1, Baker Library, Harvard Business School.

9. Letter from Peter F. Drucker to Elton Mayo, March 6, 1947, Box 1, Baker Library, Harvard Business School.

10. Ibid.

11. Ibid.

12. Author interviews with Herbert Simon, Pittsburgh, 1998, and Peter F. Drucker, Claremont, Calif., 1997; off-the-record interview; Drucker, *Adventures of a Bystander*, p. 256.

13. Author interview with Peter F. Drucker, Claremont, Calif., 1997.

14. Robert Lenzner and Stephen S. Johnson, "Peter Drucker—Still the Youngest of Minds," *Forbes*, March 10, 1997, pp. 122–128; author interview with Peter F. Drucker, Claremont, Calif., 1997; John J. Tarrant, *Drucker: The Man Who Invented the Corporate Society* (Boston: Cahners Books, 1976), p. 19.

15. Author interview with Peter F. Drucker, Claremont, Calif., 1997.

16. Ibid.; author interviews with Herbert Simon, Pittsburgh, 1997, and Alfred D. Chandler, Cambridge, Mass., 1997.

17. Author interview with Peter F. Drucker, Claremont, Calif., 1997.

18. Ibid.; Drucker, *Bystander*, p. 159.

19. Ibid., pp. 108, 109.

20. Ibid., p. 109.

21. Ibid., p. 105.

22. Ibid., pp. 83, 60.

23. Author interview with Peter F. Drucker, Claremont, Calif., 1997.

24. Ibid.

25. Ibid.

26. Ibid.

27. Ibid.

28. Drucker, *Bystander*, pp. 27, 32.

29. Author interview with Peter F. Drucker, Claremont, Calif., 1997.

30. Drucker, *Bystander*, p. 105.

31. Author interview with Peter F. Drucker, Claremont, Calif., 1997; also Drucker, ibid., pp. 161–162.

32. Tony H. Bonaparte and John E. Flaherty, eds., *Peter Drucker: Contributions to Business Enterprise* (New York: New York University Press, 1970), p. 19.

33. Drucker, *Bystander*, pp. 164–165.

34. Ibid., p. 165.

35. Peter F. Drucker, "How to Be an Employee," *Fortune*, May 1952, p. 126.

36. Drucker, *Bystander*, pp. 105, 170, 179; Jack Beatty, *The World According to Peter Drucker* (New York: Free Press, 1998), p. 17.

37. Ibid., pp. 210–211.

38. Ibid., pp. 211–212.

39. Author interview with Peter F. Drucker, Claremont, Calif., 1997.

40. Ibid.

41. Ibid.

42. Ibid.

43. Drucker, *Bystander*, pp. 224–225.

44. Ibid., pp. 225–227.

45. Author interview with Peter F. Drucker, Claremont, Calif., 1997.

46. Ibid.

47. Ibid.

48. Ibid.; Drucker, *Bystander*, p. 257; letter from Peter F. Drucker to author, March 3, 1999.

49. Drucker, *Bystander*, pp. 256–257.

50. Ibid., pp. 134, 257.

51. Ibid., p. 258.

52. Letter from Peter F. Drucker to author, March 3, 1999.

53. Peter F. Drucker, *The Future of Industrial Man* (New Brunswick, N.J.: Transaction Publishers, 1995), pp. 78, 135, 137; Drucker, *Bystander*, p. 256; Peter F. Drucker, *Concept of the Corporation* (New York: John Day Company, 1946), p. 131; Bonaparte and Flaherty, *Peter Drucker: Contributions to Business Enterprise*, p. 41.

54. Drucker, *The Future of Industrial Man*, p. 137; Drucker, *Bystander*, p. 256.

55. Drucker, *Concept of the Corporation*, pp. 140–141; Tarrant, *Drucker*, p. 35.

56. Drucker, ibid., pp. 14, 15.

57. Drucker, *Bystander*, pp. 258, 263, 264.

58. Tarrant, *Drucker*, p. 14.

59. Drucker, *Concept of the Corporation*, pp. 7–9, 14.

60. Ibid., pp. viii, 5, 11.

61. Ibid., pp. 121, 49–50.

62. Ibid., pp. 65–67, 124.

63. Ibid., pp. 125, 33, 78.
64. Ibid., pp. 125, 127–128.
65. Ibid., pp. 88–89.
66. Ibid., pp. 187, 189.
67. Drucker, *Bystander*, pp. 270–71.
68. Ibid.
69. Ibid.
70. Ibid.
71. Ibid.
72. Ibid.
73. Questionnaire on employment in UAW-CIO plants for three plants—two Cadillac plants, Union Local 174, and one Fleetwood plant, Union Local 15, Walter Reuther Archives, Wayne State University.
74. Drucker, *Concept of the Corporation*, pp. 192–193.
75. Drucker, *Bystander*, pp. 276–277.
76. Ibid., p. 276.
77. Tarrant, *Drucker: The Man Who Invented the Corporate Society* (London: Barrie and Jenkins, 1976), pp. 48–51, 31; Drucker, *Bystander*, p. 140; Drucker, *Concept of the Corporation*, pp. 158–159.
78. Drucker, *Concept of the Corporation*, pp. 144–145, 206, 180–181; author interview with Peter F. Drucker, Claremont, Calif., 1997.
79. Drucker, *Bystander*, pp. 261–262.
80. Ibid.
81. Letter from Peter F. Drucker to author, March 3, 1999.
82. Drucker, *Concept of the Corporation*, pp. 201–203; Peter F. Drucker, "The Mirage of Pensions," *Harper's*, February 1950, p. 31.
83. Drucker, *Bystander*, p. 274; Drucker, *Concept of the Corporation*, pp. 202–203.
84. Tarrant, *Drucker*, p. 32.
85. Drucker, *Bystander*, pp. 262–263.
86. Ibid.
87. Author interview with Peter F. Drucker, Claremont, Calif., 1997; William B. Harris, "The Overhaul of General Electric," *Fortune*, December 1955; Robert Lacey, *Ford: The Men and the Machine* (Boston: Little, Brown & Company, 1986), p. 432.
88. *Professional Management in General Electric*, Book Two: *General Electric's Organization 1955*, p. 23.
89. Author interview with Peter F. Drucker, Claremont, Calif., 1998; Harris, "The Overhaul of General Electric."
90. Author interview with Peter F. Drucker, Claremont, Calif., 1998.
91. Harris, "The Overhaul of General Electric."
92. Author interviews with Hugh Estes and Robert E. Newman, Southport, Conn., 1997; *Manager Development Guidebooks*, GE, 1956, p. 15.
93. *Manager Development Guidebooks*, GE, 1956, pp. v–vi.
94. Peter F. Drucker, *Management: Tasks, Responsibilities, Practices*, p. 573; author interviews with Hugh Estes and Robert E. Newman, Southport, Conn., 1997; Harris, "The Overhaul of General Electric," p. 110.
95. Author interview with Peter F. Drucker, Claremont, Calif., 1997; Harris, "The Overhaul of General Electric."
96. Drucker, *Management*, p. 519.
97. Harris, "The Overhaul of General Electric."
98. *Manager Development Guidebooks*, GE, 1956, pp. v–vi; Harris, "The Overhaul of General Electric."
99. Author interviews with Hugh Estes and Robert E. Newman, Southport, Conn., 1997.

100. *Professional Management in General Electric*, Book Two: *General Electric's Organization 1955*, p. 267.
101. Harris, "The Overhaul of General Electric."
102. Author interview with Robert E. Newman, Southport, Conn., 1997.
103. Gerhard Neumann, *Herman the German* (New York: William Morrow and Company, 1984), p. 5.
104. Author interview with Peter F. Drucker, Claremont, Calif., 1997.
105. Ibid.
106. Ibid.
107. Ibid.
108. Ibid.
109. Ibid.
110. Ibid.
111. Ibid.
112. Ibid.
113. Drucker, *Management*, pp. 434–435.
114. Ibid., p. 575.
115. Ibid.
116. Author interview with Peter F. Drucker, Claremont, Calif., 1997.
117. Ibid.
118. Author interview with Jack Welch, Fairfield, Conn., 1998.
119. Ibid.
120. Ibid.
121. Ken Auletta, "Demolition Man," *The New Yorker*, November 11, 1997, pp. 38–45.
122. Beatty, *The World According to Peter Drucker*, p. 186.
123. Ibid., pp. 170–171.
124. Ibid., p. 169.
125. Ibid., p. 173.

Epilogue

1. Arie De Geus, *The Living Company* (Boston: Harvard Business School Press, 1997), p. 1.
2. Ibid., p. vii.
3. Keith Bradsher, "New Leaders Hope to Help Motor City Come Clean," *The New York Times*, May 19, 1999, p. G1.
4. De Geus, *The Living Company*, pp. 6–7, 111, 115, 121.
5. Michael C. Dorf and Charles F. Sabel, "A Constitution of Democratic Experimentation," *Columbia Law Review*, March 1998, p. 297.
6. Dani Rodrik, "The Global Fix," *The New Republic*, November 2, 1998, p. 17.
7. Harry Pearce, keynote speech for *Automotive News*, World Congress, January 13, 1998.

Selected Bibliography

Books

Argyris, Chris. *Knowledge for Action*. San Francisco: Jossey-Bass Publishers, 1993.
——, and Donald A. Schön. *Organizational Learning II*. Reading, Mass.: Addison-Wesley Publishing, 1993.
Barnard, Chester I. *The Functions of the Executive*. Cambridge, Mass.: Harvard University Press, 1968.
——. *Organization and Management*. Cambridge, Mass.: Harvard University Press, 1948.
Beatty, Jack. *The World According to Peter Drucker*. New York: Free Press, 1998.
Bennis, Warren G. *An Invented Life: Reflections on Leadership and Change*. Reading, Mass.: Addison-Wesley Publishing, 1993.
——, and Edgar H. Schein, eds. *Leadership and Motivation*. Cambridge, Mass.: MIT Press, 1965.
Berle, Adolf A., and Gardiner C. Means. *The Modern Corporation and Private Property*. New Brunswick, N.J.: Transaction Publishers, 1991.
Bonaparte, Tony H., and John E. Flaherty, eds. *Peter Drucker: Contributions to Business Enterprise*. New York: New York University Press, 1970.
Bower, Marvin. *The Will to Lead*, Boston: Harvard Business School Press, 1997.
Brownlow, Louis. *A Passion for Politics*. Chicago: University of Chicago Press, 1955.
Byrne, John A. *The Whiz Kids*. New York: Currency/Doubleday, 1993.
Chandler, Alfred D. *Strategy and Structure*. Cambridge, Mass.: MIT Press, 1995.
——, with Stephen Salsburg. *Pierre S. du Pont and the Making of the Modern Corporation*. New York: Harper & Row, 1971.
Christensen, C. Roland, Kenneth R. Andrews, and Joseph L. Bower. *Business Policy*. Homewood, Ill.: R. D. Irwin, 1978.
Cray, Ed. *Chrome Colossus: General Motors and Its Times*. New York: McGraw-Hill Book Company, 1980.
Cruikshank, Jeffrey L. *A Delicate Experiment: The Harvard Business School 1908–1945*. Boston: Harvard Business School Press, 1987.
Cyert, Richard, and James March. *The Behavioral Theory of the Firm*. Cambridge, Mass.: Blackwell Publishers, 1992.

De Geus, Arie. *The Living Company.* Boston: Harvard Business School Press, 1997.

Deming, W. Edwards. *The New Economics.* Cambridge, Mass.: Massachusetts Institute of Technology, Center for Advanced Engineering Study, 1993.

——. *Out of the Crisis.* Cambridge, Mass.: Massachusetts Institute of Technology, Center for Advanced Engineering Study, 1982.

Doray, Bernard. *From Taylorism to Fordism.* London: Free Association Books, 1988.

Drucker, Peter F. *Adventures of a Bystander.* New York: Harper & Row Publishers, 1978.

——. *Concept of the Corporation.* New York: John Day Company, 1946.

——. *The Future of Industrial Man.* New Brunswick, N.J.: Transaction Publishers, 1995.

——. *Management: Tasks, Responsibilities, Practices.* New York: Harper & Row, 1974.

——. *Managing in Turbulent Times.* New York: HarperCollins, 1993.

——. *The New Realities.* New York: Harper Business, 1990.

Enthoven, Alain C., and K. Wayne Smith. *How Much Is Enough?* New York: Harper & Row, 1971.

Foner, Philip S. *History of the Labor Movement in the United States,* Vol. 2: *From the Founding of the American Federation of Labor to the Emergence of American Imperialism.* New York: International Publishers, 1955.

——. *History of the Labor Movement in the United States,* Vol. 5: *The AFL in the Progressive Era, 1910–1915.* New York: International Publishers, 1980.

Ford, Harold P. *CIA and the Vietnam Policymakers: Three Episodes 1962–1968.* Springfield, Va.: History Staff Center for the Study of Intelligence, Central Intelligence Agency, 1998.

Gabor, Andrea. *The Man Who Discovered Quality.* New York: Times Books, 1990.

General Electric. *Professional Management in General Electric,* Book Two: *General Electric's Organization.* Fairfield, Ct.: General Electric Company, 1955.

General Electric. *Manager Development Guidebooks.* Fairfield, Ct.: General Electric, 1956.

Graham, Pauline, ed. *Mary Parker Follett: The Prophet of Management.* Boston: Harvard Business School Press, 1995.

Halberstam, David. *The Reckoning.* New York: William Morrow and Company, 1986.

Heertje, Arnold, ed., *Makers of Modern Economics,* Vol. 2, 1994. London: Harvester Wheatsheaf, 1993.

Hoerr, John. *And the Wolf Finally Came.* Pittsburgh: University of Pittsburgh Press, 1988.

Hoffman, Edward. *The Right to Be Human.* Comack, N.Y.: Four World Press, 1997.

Homans, George Caspar. *Coming to My Senses: The Autobiography of a Socialist.* New Brunswick, N.J.: Transaction Books, 1984.

Jacoby, Sanford M. *Modern Manors: Welfare Capitalism Since the New Deal.* Princeton, N.J.: Princeton University Press, 1997.

Kakar, Sudhir. *Frederick Taylor: A Study in Personality and Innovation.* Cambridge, Mass.: MIT Press, 1970.

Kanigel, Robert. *The One Best Way.* New York: Viking, 1997.

Kleiner, Art. *The Age of Heretics.* New York: Doubleday, 1996.

Lacey, Robert. *Ford: The Men and the Machine.* Boston: Little, Brown & Company, 1986.

March, James G., and Herbert A. Simon. *Organizations.* New York: John Wiley & Sons, 1958.

Maslow, Abraham H. *Maslow on Management.* New York: John Wiley & Sons, 1998.

——. *Motivation and Personality.* New York: Harper & Row, 1970.

Mayo, Elton. *Human Problems of An Industrial Civilization.* New York: Macmillan Company, 1938.

——. *Social Problems of an Industrial Civilization.* London: Routledge and Kegan Paul, 1975.

McCraw, Thomas K., ed. *The Essential Alfred Chandler.* Boston: Harvard Business School Press, 1988.

——. *Prophets of Regulation.* Cambridge, Mass.: Belknap Press of the Harvard University Press, 1984.

McGregor, Douglas. *The Human Side of Enterprise.* New York: McGraw-Hill Book Company, 1960.

——. *The Professional Manager.* New York: McGraw-Hill, 1967.

McNamara, Robert S. In Retrospect. New York: Times Books, 1995.

——, with James Blight, Robert Brigham, Thomas Biersteker, and Herbert Schandler. *Argument Without End.* New York: Public Affairs, 1999.

Micklethwait, John, and Adrian Wooldridge. *The Witch Doctors.* New York: Times Books, 1996.

Miner, John B., ed. *Administrative and Management Theory.* Aldershot, U.k.: Dartmouth Publishing Company, 1995.

Nelson, Daniel. *Frederick W. Taylor and the Rise of Scientific Management.* Madison: The University of Wisconsin Press, 1980.

Neumann, Gerhard. *Herman the German.* New York: William Morrow and Company, 1984.

Niles, Mary Cushing. *The Essence of Management.* New York: Harper and Brothers, 1958.

——. *Middle Management.* New York: Harper and Brothers, 1949.

Penrose, Edith, T. *The Theory of the Growth of the Firm,* White Plains, N.Y.: M. E. Sharpe.

Pfeffer, Jeffrey. *New Directions for Organization Theory.* New York: Oxford University Press, 1997.

Piore, Michael J., and Charles F. Sabel. *The Second Industrial Divide.* New York: Basic Books, 1984.

Polanyi, Karl. *The Great Transformation.* New York: Farrar and Rinehard, 1944.

Roethlisberger, Fritz J. *The Elusive Phenomenon.* Cambridge, Mass.: Harvard University Press, 1977.

——. *Management and Morale*. Cambridge, Mass.: Harvard University Press, 1955.

——, and William J. Dickson. *Management and the Worker*. Cambridge, Mass.: Harvard University Press, 1946.

Samuels, Warren J., ed. *American Economists of the Late Twentieth Century*. Cheltenham, U.K.: Edward Elgar, 1996.

Schlossman, Steven, Robert E. Gleeson, Michael Sedlak, and David Grayson Allen. *The Beginnings of Graduate Management Education in the United States*. Santa Monica, Calif.: GMAC, 1994.

Scott, William G. *Chester I. Barnard and the Guardians of the Managerial State*. Lawrence, Kan.: University Press of Kansas, 1992.

Senge, Peter. *The Fifth Discipline*. New York: Currency/Doubleday, 1990.

Simon, Herbert A. *Administrative Behavior*. New York: Free Press, 1997.

——. *Allen Newell: 1927–1992, A Biographical Memoir*. Washington, D.C.: National Academy of Sciences, 1997.

——. *Models of Man*. New York: John Wiley & Sons, 1957.

——. *Models of My Life*. New York: Basic Books, 1991.

Sloan, Alfred P., Jr., *My Years at General Motors*. Garden City, N.Y.: Doubleday and Company, 1963.

Smith, Douglas K., and Robert C. Alexander. *Fumbling the Future*. New York: William Morrow and Company, 1988.

Smith, Roy C. *The Money Wars*. New York: Dutton, 1990.

Sobel, Robert. *The Age of Giant Corporations*. Westport, Conn.: Praeger, 1993.

——. *ITT: The Management of Opportunity*. New York: Times Books, 1982.

Tarrant, John J. *Drucker: The Man Who Invented Corporate Society*. London: Barrie and Jenkins, 1976.

Teece, David J., Richard P. Rumelt, and Dan E. Schendel, eds. *Fundamental Issues in Strategy*. Boston: Harvard Business School Press, 1994.

Trahair, Richard C. S. *The Humanist Temper: The Life and Work of Elton Mayo*. New Brunswick, N.J.: Transaction Books, 1984.

Urwick, Lyndall, and E. F. L. Brech. *The Making of Scientific Management*. London: Sir Isaac Pitman and Sons, 1963.

Weisbord, Marvin R. *Productive Workplaces*. San Francisco: Jossey-Bass, 1989.

Wever, Kirsten S. *Negotiating Competitiveness*. Boston: Harvard Business School Press, 1995.

White, D. J. *Operational Research*. New York: John Wiley, 1985.

Whyte, William H., & Sons, Jr. *The Organization Man*. New York: Simon & Schuster, 1956.

Williamson, Oliver. *The Mechanisms of Governance*. New York: Oxford University Press, 1996.

Wilson, Woodrow. *Congressional Government*. New York: Meridian Books, 1956.

Wolf, William B. *Conversations with Chester I. Barnard*. Ithaca, N.Y.: New York State School of Industrial and Labor Relations, Cornell University, January 1973, ILR Paperback No. 12.

Wrege, Charles D., and Ronald G. Greenwood. *Frederick Winslow Taylor: The Father of Scientific Management*. Homewood, Ill.: Business One Irwin, 1991.

Yost, Edna. *Frank and Lillian Gilbreth.* New Brunswick, N.J.: Rutgers University Press, 1949.

Articles

Argyris, Chris. "Empowerment: The Emperor's New Clothes," *Harvard Business Review,* May–June 1998, pp. 98–105.
——. "Good Communication That Blocks Learning." *Harvard Business Review,* July–August 1994, pp. 77–85.
——. "Skilled Incompetence." *Harvard Business Review,* September–October 1986, pp. 74–79.
Auletta, Ken. "Demolition Man." *The New Yorker,* November 11, 1997, pp. 38–45.
Baker, Ray Stannard. "Fred. W. Taylor—Scientist in Business Management." *The American Magazine,* March 1911, pp. 565–792.
Bradsher, Keith. "Can Motor City Come Up with a Clean Machine?" *The New York Times,* May 19, 1999, p. G1.
Byrne, John. "Jack: A Close-up Look at How America's No. 1 Manager Runs GE" *Business Week,* June 8, 1998, pp. 92–111.
Cooper, W. W. "Some Implications of the Newer Analytic Approaches to Management." *California Management Review,* November 1961, pp. 51–64.
Day, Richard H., and Shyam Sunder. "Ideas and Work of Richard M. Cyert." *Journal of Economic Behavior & Organization,* 31, 1996, pp. 139–148.
Dorf, Michael C., and Charles F. Sabel. "A Constitution of Democratic Experimentalism." *Columbia Law Review,* March 1998, pp. 267–473.
Dowling, William F. "Conversation with Fritz J. Roethlisberger." *Organizational Dynamics,* Autumn 1972, pp. 31–45.
Dumaine, Brian. "Mr. Learning Organization." *Fortune,* October 17, 1994, p. 147.
Drucker, Peter F. "How Big Is Too Big?" *Harper's,* July 1950, pp. 23–28.
——. "How to Be an Employee." *Fortune,* May 1952, pp. 126–174.
——. "The Mirage of Pensions." *Harper's,* February 1950, pp. 31–38.
Fishman, Charles. "Sanity Inc." *Fast Company,* January 1999, p. 84.
Follett, Mary Parker. "The Illusion of Final Authority." *Bulletin of the Taylor Society,* 11(5), December 1926, pp. 243–255.
Gabor, Andrea. "Take This Job and Love It," *The New York Times,* January 26, 1992, sec. 3, p. 1.
Gantt, H. L. "A Practical Application of Scientific Management," *The Engineering Magazine,* April 1911, p. 1.
Gleeson, Robert E., and Steven Schlossman. "George Leland Bach and the Rebirth of Graduate Management Education in the United States." *Selections,* Spring 1995, pp. 8–44.
Goodman, R. A. "On the Operationality of the Maslow Need Hierarchy." *British Journal of Industrial Relations,* 6(1), pp. 51–57.
Harris, William B. "The Overhaul of General Electric." *Fortune,* December 1955, pp. 110–240.

Herzberg, Frederick. "One More Time: How Do You Motivate Employees." *Harvard Business Review*, January–February, 1968.

Holden, Constance. "The Rational Optimist." *Psychology Today*, October 1986, p. 54.

Jackson, Nancy. "Living History: Alfred Chandler and the Rise of Big Business." *Harvard Business School Bulletin*, April 1990, pp. 34–42.

Kleiner, Art. "The Battle for the Soul of Corporate America." *Wired* 3.08, on-line article.

Kofman, Fred, and Peter Senge. "Communities of Commitment: The Heart of Learning Organizations." *Organizational Dynamics*, AMA reprint, 1993.

Krause, Corinne. "The Reminiscences of Herbert A. Simon." Oral History Research Office, Columbia University, 1979.

Kurtzman, Joel. "An Interview with Jeffrey Pfeffer." *Strategy and Business*, Third Quarter 1998, pp. 85–94.

——. "An Interview with Warren Bennis." *Strategy and Business*, Reprint No. 97308.

Lessing, Lawrence. "Barnard's Behaviorism." *Fortune*, June 1948, pp. 188–194.

Lenzner, Robert and Stephen S. Johnson, "Peter Drucker—Still the Youngest of Minds," *Forbes*, March 10, 1997.

Lewis, Henry Harrison. "The Taylor Way: How the Plan and Instruction Sheet Are Doing Away with Guess Work in Shop Management," *Business and the Book-Keeper.*

Lindeman, Eduard. "Mary Parker Follett." *The Survey*, February 1934.

March, James G. "The 1978 Nobel Prize in Economics." *Science*, November 1978, pp. 858–861.

McGregor, Douglas. "An Uneasy Look at Performance Appraisal." *Harvard Business Review*, May–June 1957, pp. 89–94.

McNair, Malcolm P. "Thinking Ahead: What Price Human Relations?" *Harvard Business Review*, March–April 1957, pp. 15–39.

Myers, Steven Lee. "Pentagon 'Maverick' Sounds Alarm." *The New York Times*, January 18, 1999, p. A15.

Nicholson, Nigel. "How Hardwired Is Human Behavior?" *Harvard Business Review*, July–August 1998.

North, Douglass C. "The Adam Smith Address: Economic Theory in a Dynamic Economic World." *Business Economics*, January 1995, p. 7.

Prahalad, C. K., and Gary Hamel. "The Core Competence of the Corporation." *Harvard Business Review*, May–June 1990, pp. 79–93.

Rodrik, Dani, "The Global Fix," *The New Republic*, November 2, 1998.

Roethlisberger, Fritz J. "Roethlisberger on Roethlisberger." *Harvard Business School Bulletin*, January–February 1978, pp. 10–13.

Schoen, Donald R. "Human Relations: Boon or Bogle?" *Harvard Business Review*, November–December 1957, p. 41.

Senge, Peter. "Leading Learning Organizations," in *The Leader of the Future*. San Francisco: Jossey-Bass, 1996, pp. 41–57.

——. "The Leader's New Work: Building Learning Organizations." *Sloan Management Review*, 32(1), (Fall 1990), (reprint; no page numbers given).

Simon, Herbert A. "Birth of an Organization: The Economic Cooperative Administration." *Public Administration Review,* Autumn 1953, pp. 227–236.

——. "Charles E. Merriam and the 'Chicago School' of Political Science." Monograph, Department of Political Science, University of Illinois at Urbana-Champaign, 1985.

——. "Guest Editorial." *Public Administration Review,* September–October, 1995, pp. 404–405.

——. "The Incidence of a Tax on Urban Real Property." *Quarterly Journal of Economics,* 57(3) (May 1943), pp. 416–435.

——. "Recent Advances in Organizational Theory." In *Research Frontiers in Politics and Government.* Washington, D.C.: Brookings Institution, 1955.

Sinclair, Upton. "The Principles of Scientific Management: A Criticism by Upton Sinclair and an Answer by Frederick W. Taylor." *The American Magazine,* June 1911.

Smith, Richard Austin. "The Incredible Electrical Conspiracy, Part I." *Fortune,* April 1961, pp. 132–180.

——. "The Incredible Electrical Conspiracy, Part II." *Fortune,* May 1961, pp. 161–224.

Smith, Delos R. "Managerial Roots: How the Heirs of Sloan and du Pont Are Faring." *Conference Board,* 70 (May 1986), pp. 24–35.

Smith, J. H. "The Three Faces of Elton Mayo, 'a Marginal Man.' " *The Times Higher Education Supplement,* December 26, 1980, p. 9.

Sonnenfeld, Jeffrey A. "Shedding Light on the Hawthorne Experiments." *Journal of Occupational Behavior,* 1985.

Stewart, Doug. "Herbert Simon: Artificial Intelligence Pioneer: Interview." *Omni,* June 1994, p. 70.

Stever, James A. "Mary Parker Follett and the Quest for Pragmatic Administration." *Administration & Society,* August 1986.

Tarbell, Ida. "The Golden Rule in Business," Part 1. *The American Magazine,* November 1914, pp. 11–17.

——. "The Golden Rule in Business." *The American Magazine,* December 1914, pp. 24–29.

——. "The Golden Rule in Business." *The American Magazine,* January 1915, pp. 29–83.

Taylor, F. W. "The Principles of Scientific Management." *The American Magazine,* March 1911, pp. 101–245.

Teece, David J., Gary Pisano, and Amy Shuen. "Dynamic Capabilities and Strategic Management." *Strategic Management Journal,* 18(7) (March 1997), pp. 509–533.

"Testimony of Frederick W. Taylor at Hearings Before Special Committee of the House of Representatives, January 1912." *Bulletin of the Taylor Society,* June–August 1926, 11(3, 4).

Towne, Henry R. "The Evolution of Industrial Management." *Industrial Management,* April 1, 1921, pp. 231–233.

Wharton, John F. "The Anatomy of Cooperation." *The Saturday Review of Literature,* October 26, 1946.

Whitman, Howard. "United in War, Divorced in Peace." *Daily News,* June 12, 1943.

Williamson, Oliver. "Transaction Cost Economics and the Carnegie Connection." *Journal of Economic Behavior & Organization*, Vol. 31, 1996, pp. 149–155.

Wolf, William B. "Precepts for Managers—Interviews with Chester I. Barnard." *California Management Review*, Fall 1963.

Unpublished Manuscripts, Speeches, Etc.

Committee on Extended Use of School Buildings, 1911–1912. "Report of the East Boston Centre." *The Women's Municipal League of Boston Bulletin*, May 1912.

Barnard, Chester I. "Riot of the Unemployed at Trenton, N.J. 1935," Lecture at Harvard University, 1938–1941.

Davis, Albie M. "An Interview with Mary Parker Follett," draft of article to appear in July 1989 edition of the *Negotiation Journal*, June 1989.

Helper, Susan, John Paul MacDuffie, and Charles Sabel. "Pragmatic Collaborations: Advancing Knowledge While Controlling Opportunism," Prepared for "Make versus Buy: The New Boundaries of the Firm" conference, Columbia Law School, May 1998. Revised March 1999.

Jardini, David. "Thinking Through the Cold War: Rand, National Security and Domestic Policy," unpublished Ph.D. dissertation.

Maslow, Abraham, unpublished lecture on "The Human Side of Enterprise," May 17, 1965.

Merkle, Judith. "Managing Democracy: The Political Theory of Mary Parker Follett." Paper given at the 43rd Annual Meeting of the Academy of Management, Dallas, Texas, August 14–17, 1983.

Murray, Nina Chandler. "A Year Out of Time: The Pedagogic Schooner." Unpublished manuscript, n.d.

Pearce, Harry. Keynote speech for *Automotive News*, World Congress, January 13, 1998.

Taylor, Frederick Winslow. Transcript of talk, December 5, 1901, p. 95.

Typed review of Roxbury. *The Women's Municipal League of Boston Bulletin*.

Urwick, Lyndall F. "Mary Parker Follett, 1858–1933." Unpublished manuscript, May 20, 1969.

——. "Some Americans." Speech before the annual dinner of the Fellows Group, Academy of Management, Boston, August 21, 1973.

——. "The Truth About Schmidt." Unpublished manuscript, March 23, 1972.

White, Eva Whiting. "Tribute to the Memory of Mary Parker Follett." Paper given at the 25th Anniversary Banquet of the Boston School Centers, October 16, 1937.

"Work Loads for Professional Staff in a Public Welfare Agency." Summary Report. Chicago, Ill.: American Public Welfare Association.

Index